BEST BOOKS
for
YOUNG ADULTS

Second Edition

BETTY CARTER
WITH SALLY ESTES
AND LINDA WADDLE

**Young Adult
Library Services
Association**

Project editor: Linda S. Cohen

Text design by Dianne Rooney

While extensive effort has gone into ensuring the reliability of information appearing in this book, the publisher makes no warranty, express or implied, on the accuracy or reliability of the information, and does not assume and hereby disclaims any liability to any person for any loss or damage caused by errors or omissions in this publication.

The paper used in this publication meets the minimum requirements of American National Standard for Information Sciences—Permanence of Paper for Printed Library Materials, ANSI Z39.48-1992. ∞

Composed by the dotted i in Melior and Optima using QuarkXpress 4.04.

Printed on 50-pound white offset, a pH-neutral stock, and bound in 10-point cover stock by Data Reproductions.

Library of Congress Cataloging-in-Publication Data

Carter, Betty, 1944–
    Best books for young adults / Betty Carter, with Sally Estes and Linda Waddle ;
  Young Adult Library Services Association.—2nd ed.
      p.   cm.
    Includes bibliographical references and index.
    ISBN 0-8389-3501-X
    1. Teenagers—United States—Books and reading—Bibliography. 2. Young adult literature, English—Bibliography. 3. Best books for young adults. I. Estes, Sally. II. Waddle, Linda. III. Young Adult Library Services Association. IV. Title.
Z1037.C34 2000
[PN1009.A1]
028.1′62—dc21
                                      00-035583

Printed in the United States of America

04 03 02 01   5 4 3 2

CONTENTS

PART 2: THE BOOK LISTS, 1966–1999

PREFACE

In the preface to the second edition of *Literature for Today's Young Adults,* Alleen Nilsen and Ken Donelson discuss the process of revising their groundbreaking textbook on young adult literature. One night they brought up the topic with Robert Cormier who "sounded almost envious that our kind of writer gets a second chance at a book while with novelists—notwithstanding the 5,000 corrections made on James Joyce's *Ulysses*—once a book is published it belongs to the ages" (1985, i).

When Linda Waddle, Deputy Executive Director of the Young Adult Library Services Association (YALSA), first suggested an update of *Best Books for Young Adults: The History, the Selections, the Romance* (Carter 1994), I was honestly content to have the original belong "to the ages," or, as might be more appropriate, the decade. Five years ago I'd covered the history of the Best Books for Young Adults (BBYA) Committee, the perennial issues surrounding that body, and an outline of three of the "Best of the Best" preconferences. Little had changed since the first book and I was reluctant to revisit what was essentially old news. Linda bluntly began our conversation: "We don't want any more of that. What readers liked was the books; we want more about books." So, books it is.

And books it should be. The purpose of the BBYA Committee is to identify what fifteen young adult librarians consider the best books for young adults in a particular year. These individuals evaluate hundreds of books and make suggestions that will, in turn, reach teenagers through either their own inquisitiveness or through adult intermediaries, such as librarians, teachers, and parents. A parallel purpose logically extends to any discussion of all the books, that those books anointed "the best" for over thirty-five years should be showcased to help contemporary reader's advisors. Consequently, this book highlights such titles through various topical lists that also give a sense of the diversity and strength of the over 1,800 selections.

In no way are these lists intended to supersede the work of those who participated in four previous preconferences identifying the "Best of the Best" or the work of librarians compiling their choices for the Best of the Best Revisited: Bo Jo Jones and Beyond preconference held during the 2000 ALA Annual Conference. For organizational purposes, past preconference leaders directed participants to select a set number of books published within a specific time frame or from among a list of particular authors. Here the lists are free from those kinds of constraints that balance years of publication or individual author output. In addition, that illusive element of popularity, which often took precedence during several "Best of the Best" discussions, did not govern these choices, although each showcased book should find many satisfied readers. The lists contained in this book cover the entire body of best books since 1966, reflect topics that repeated themselves over the years, and include particular books for the ways in which they filled gaps in those topics.

The history of BBYA is available in the first publication (Carter 1994). This book, which in splitting nomenclature hairs is more a sequel than a second edition, slightly updates that history. (Note to weeders: Keep both on your shelves.) But the emphasis here is on books: books for facile readers and books for less-able readers, books for sophisticated tastes and books for less-mature ones, books for avid readers and books for reluctant readers, and books originally published for adults and books aimed directly at a young adult audience. For some of you, individual titles will bring a trip down memory lane. For others, the books may introduce older releases that deserve a new, or perhaps a first, look. And for many others, the lists will prompt questions, disbelief, and even outrage: How could they leave out this title or that one? The aim in producing these lists mirrors as closely as possible the purpose of creating the yearly ones: to help you, through practical suggestions and by triggering thoughts of other titles, better serve contemporary teen readers. That's who each BBYA list addresses and what best books are all about.

These lists are formatted so that they may be easily reproduced for handouts or flyers. No bibliography is longer than three pages. Permission to copy these lists for nonprofit educational purposes is granted. There's a place at the end of each for you to add the name of your library. It is my hope that the lists will be shared with many individuals concerned with teens and their reading.

I've selected an idiosyncratic method of documentation for the text of the book. Articles and professional books mentioned in the beginning sections are documented within the text and listed at the end of each chapter. Individual books that have appeared on a yearly BBYA list are not documented in the text; the author and title indexes allow adequate referencing of these titles within the bibliographic portion of the book. BBYA books are referenced solely by the text edition used by the original committee selecting them. Consequently, some of these editions may be out of print. Don't despair; the books may well be available in other editions and imprints that are not indicated in the bibliographic information.

There are invariably many individuals who contribute to a book such as this, individuals whose work may well be behind the scenes but nonetheless invaluable to the content of the finished product. First of all, there's Linda Waddle, Deputy Executive Director of the Young Adult Library Services Association, and Sally Estes, former Books for Youth Editor at *Booklist* and fifteen-year consultant for the BBYA Committee. The three of us compiled the lists in the following pages with each drawing on long histories with BBYA; strong reading backgrounds in young adult literature; and special, distinct interests in different genres. Sally also wrote a portion of the section on trends in young adult publishing. Esther Murphy, YALSA's administrative assistant par excellence, took the individual recommended titles and transcribed them into the master database of BBYA books. Three graduate library students at Texas Woman's University, Sherry Stauffer, Tanya Tullos, and Christine Tyner, collected data and conducted research that repeatedly shows up in these pages. And Neta Siegel prepared part of the manuscript despite vague instructions, incompatible computer systems, and strong limits on her time. Others who influence the final product cannot be named here: the hundreds, even thousands, of librarians who participated in BBYA committees; the even greater number of librarians who shared the recommended books with teenagers; and the publishers who year after year support the work of the committee. The work in the following pages is yours much more so than mine.

Works Cited

Carter, Betty. 1994. *Best Books for Young Adults: The History, the Selections, the Romance.* Chicago: American Library Association.

Nilsen, Alleen Pace, and Kenneth L. Donelson. 1985. *Literature for Today's Young Adults.* Glenview, Ill.: Scott, Foresman.

PART ONE

Background

Selecting the Best

In 1930, Americans were humming "I Got Rhythm" and "Georgia on My Mind"; reading *As I Lay Dying, Laughing Boy,* and *The Maltese Falcon;* and watching *Blue Angel* and *All Quiet on the Western Front.* They were eating the first frozen foods brought to consumers by William Birdseye; undertaking the construction of Boulder Dam; and hearing scientific reports of a ninth planet, later named Pluto (*Chronicle of the Twentieth Century* 1995). And, also in 1930, members of the School Libraries Section of the American Library Association were creating a list of recommended books emphasizing recreational reading for teenage readers. That list, "Books for Young People, 1930," is the precursor of today's Best Books for Young Adults (BBYA) lists.

Since then our country has inaugurated eleven new presidents; microwaved its dinners; discovered Velcro; read *Superman* and *Beloved;* sung songs about the visionary Age of Aquarius and the more pedestrian YMCA; watched *It Happened One Night, Gone with the Wind,* and three episodes of *The Godfather,* four of *Star Wars,* and thirteen of *Halloween;* and sent men and women into space. During that time librarians have gathered from across these United States to produce almost seventy lists of recommended books for young adults.

Over the years, the BBYA list has been the product of ten separate committees and has appeared under seven names. Over time, the committee's charge and constituency have changed. Both will continue to evolve. Currently, the Best Books for Young Adults Committee is composed of fifteen members of the Young Adult Library Services Association (YALSA) directed "to select from the year's publications, significant adult and young adult books" and "to annotate the selected titles" (*Best Books for Young Adults Policies and Procedures* 1994). Those selected books, which comprise the annual Best Books for Young Adults List, should contain "proven or potential appeal to the personal reading tastes of the young adult . . . [and] acceptable literary quality" (*Best Books for Young Adults Policies and Procedures* 1994).

CHALLENGES

No committee ever created a perfect list. There are always books others think should be included that weren't; books that were included that individuals think should not have been; and books that committee members regret voting for or against, or just not having had the time to read. Nonetheless, every year the committee produces a fine list, a list that deserves respect and attention from librarians and teenagers alike.

That said, there remain areas of controversy about the books and the composition of the lists. Beyond discussions of individual book titles, disagreement centers around length of the list and youth participation in the voting procedures.

Length of the List

The 1993 list weighed in at ninety-seven titles, the longest in the history of BBYA. Size mattered. The list's length provoked strong discussion, with some members of YALSA calling for a ceiling on the number of books allowed each year and others praising the committee for truly addressing the reading needs and tastes of so many different young adults. As with so many controversial topics within YALSA, this one faded with no resolution. Still, subsequent lists have been shorter than the behemoth of 1993. The 1994 list contained seventy-six books, 1995 fell to seventy-three, 1996 inched up with eighty titles, 1997 reduced that number by ten, 1998 jumped to eighty-four, and 1999 dropped to seventy-one recommended books. These figures show the length of the lists declined after 1993 but give no reasons. Unless the YALSA membership decides to cap the number of books eligible each year, the length will fluctuate according to many variables: the number of books published each year, the availability of those books, the standards of the committee, and the amount of reading from committee members.

A nominated book appears on a BBYA list if nine committee members vote to include it. Some books receive the minimum number of nine positive votes, some books receive the maximum of fifteen, and most books receive endorsements falling somewhere in the middle. As a way of highlighting the most favored books of a particular year, the YALSA board approved the addition of a "Top Ten" list for BBYA selections. The first such super-list appeared in 1997 and continues as a feature of BBYA. Some, but not all, of the top ten books have unanimous committee votes. Other titles require some give and take as the committee creates this additional list. Sally Estes, *Booklist* consultant who has been with the committee over these years, says: "It's usually the ninth and tenth books that cause the most debate" (Estes 1999), reminding us that when lists have a number cap they really become selective. For those who want to think small in terms of numbers, the "Top Ten" should fill the bill.

Youth Participation

A second perennial issue that plagues BBYA committees is that of youth participation. Plenty of evidence exists to support the fact that, when given the chance, teenagers and adults do not always select or even like the same books. So, the question arises: How do adults effectively select a list for teenagers without their opinions? The quick answer is "year after year"; the real answer is "they seldom do." Although not given voting privileges on the committee, young adults have noticeable voices in the procedure by posting opinions to YALSA-BK, by interacting with librarians on the committee, and by attending annual conferences and speaking of their favorites. Committee members listen to these comments but are not ruled by them. After all, as it stands, the list remains one created and validated by adults.

Still, evidence exists that selected books do speak to young adults. The Teens' Top Ten Best Books Task Force from YALSA is in the process of discovering how to gauge popularity of BBYA selections. Task force members began by evaluating two methodologies designed to identify the most popular books from among the 1999 BBYA selections. Two groups of youngsters, one from Pittsburgh, Pennsylvania, and one from Mesa, Arizona, read at least twenty books from the 1999 list and then voted on their top ten favorites. The population of books differed between the two groups. Young adults from Pittsburgh read from the twenty-seven books most favored by the committee while the teens from Mesa read from the entire BBYA list.

It is significant that these young adults identified favorites. Although there is no allowance in the balloting for teens to indicate their dislike for all titles, one can suppose that some amount of reading pleasure kept these participants going as they completed twenty books. There's no surprise that Harry Potter (*Harry Potter and the Sorcerer's Stone*) topped this list, since the series has dominated juvenile publishing over the past two years. Other favorites, however, include books critically acclaimed by the literary community, such as the 1999 Newbery Medal recipient, *Holes,* and the 1999 Newbery Honor recipient, *A Long Way from Chicago.* Mysteries (*The Killer's Cousin*), historical fiction (*Soldier's Heart*), realistic fiction (*A Door near Here*), and social science fiction (*Armageddon Summer*) round out the favorites from these two groups of teen readers ("Testing" 1999).

Still, the teenagers participating in the preceding balloting had restricted choices: The books they considered were all chosen by the 1999 BBYA committee. No such restrictions govern books selected by teens in the International Reading Association's (IRA) annual Young Adults' Choices (YAC) poll. Here, ten thousand teenagers across the United States read and evaluate publications from the previous year. They vote on each book they read, the final votes are tabulated by the IRA, and the top thirty vote-getters appear in the November issue of the *Journal of Adolescent and Adult Literacy* as that year's Young Adults' Choices. According to the guidelines of this project, adults may not interfere in any way with the teenagers' reading—they may not assign books, campaign for books, or favor one book over another. The young adults involved in YAC do not read every book submitted for the project but rather read and vote on those individual books they freely select. Publishers submit books for the pool published in the previous year that received at least two positive reviews from a respected reviewing source.

Since 1994, at least one-fifth of the Young Adults' Choices have appeared on previous BBYA lists, again showing these books have some degree of popularity among teen readers. Table 1 shows the favorites; the discrepancy in dates occurs because books typically are published one year before they are eligible for YAC.

TABLE 1   Master List of Consensus Titles

Title	Author	Year on YAC	Year on BBYA
100 Questions and Answers about AIDS: A Guide for Young People	Ford, Michael Thomas	1994	1993
Bearing Witness: Stories of the Holocaust	Rochman, Hazel, selected by, and Darlene Z. McCampbell	1997	1996
Beyond the Western Sea: Book One, the Escape from Home	Avi	1998	1997
Blood and Chocolate	Klause, Annette Curtis	1999	1998
Bomb, The	Taylor, Theodore	1997	1996
Chasing Redbird	Creech, Sharon	1999	1998
Come In from the Cold	Qualey, Marsha	1996	1995
Crazy Lady!	Conly, Jane Leslie	1995	1994
Danger Zone	Klass, David	1998	1997
Don't You Dare Read This, Mrs. Dunphrey	Haddix, Margaret Peterson	1998	1997
Driver's Ed	Cooney, Caroline B.	1996	1995
Ella Enchanted	Levine, Gail Carson	1999	1998
Family of Strangers	Pfeffer, Susan Beth	1994	1993
Far North	Hobbs, Will	1998	1997
Flight of the Dragon Kyn	Fletcher, Susan	1995	1995
Freak the Mighty	Philbrick, Rodman	1995	1994
From the Notebooks of Melanin Sun	Woodson, Jacqueline	1997	1996
Hannah In Between	Rodowsky, Colby	1996	1995
Heartbreak and Roses: Real Life Stories of Troubled Love	Bode, Janet, and Stan Mack	1996	1995
In My Father's House	Rinaldi, Ann	1995	1994
It's Nothing to a Mountain	Hite, Sid	1996	1995
Johnny Voodoo	Lane, Dakota	1998	1997
Jumper	Gould, Steven	1994	1993
Kids at Work: Lewis Hine and the Crusade against Child Labor	Freedman, Russell. Ill. with photos. Lewis Hine	1996	1995
Little Bit Dead, A	Reaver, Chap	1994	1993
Malcolm X: By Any Means Necessary	Myers, Walter Dean	1995	1994
Middle Passage, The	Feelings, Tom	1997	1996
Missing the Piano	Rapp, Adam	1996	1995
Much Ado about Prom Night	McCants, William D.	1997	1996

Continued

TABLE 1 *Continued*

Title	Author	Year on YAC	Year on BBYA
Painting the Black	Deuker, Carl	1999	1998
Phoenix Rising	Hesse, Karen	1996	1995
Rosa Parks: My Story	Parks, Rosa, with Jim Haskins	1994	1993
Rosie the Riveter: Women Working on the Home Front	Colman, Penny	1997	1996
Slam!	Myers, Walter Dean	1998	1997
Slot Machine	Lynch, Chris	1997	1996
Someone to Love	Lantz, Francess	1999	1998
Stranded in Harmony	Shoup, Barbara	1999	1998
Tangerine	Bloor, Edward	1999	1998
Teenage Fathers	Gravelle, Karen, and Leslie Peterson	1994	1993
Tell Them We Remember: The Story of the Holocaust	Bachrach, Susan D.	1996	1995
Time for Dancing, A	Hurwin, Davida Wills	1997	1996
Unconditional Surrender: U.S. Grant and the Civil War	Marrin, Albert	1996	1995
Virginia's General: Robert E. Lee and the Civil War	Marrin, Albert	1996	1996
Voice on the Radio, The	Cooney, Caroline B.	1998	1997
Voices of AIDS, The	Ford, Michael Thomas	1997	1996
Watsons Go to Birmingham —1963, The	Curtis, Christopher Paul	1997	1996
Weeping Willow	White, Ruth	1994	1993
Whatever Happened to Janie?	Cooney, Caroline B.	1995	1994
White Lilacs	Meyer, Carolyn	1995	1994
Window, The	Ingold, Jeanette	1998	1997
Woman in the Wall, The	Kindl, Patrice	1999	1998
Zoo Book: The Evolution of Wildlife Conservation Centers	Koebner, Linda	1996	1995

From Christine Tyner, "A Critical Analysis of the *Booklist* Reviews for the Titles Appearing on Both Best Books for Young Adults and Young Adults' Choices from 1993 to 1999" (Texas Woman's University, Denton, Texas, 1999, paper).

AUTHORS

Young adults have favorites and so do librarians. Over the past five years, several authors have had multiple appearances on BBYA lists, indicating these writers repeatedly produce fine books. Those who have appeared at least three times in the past five years are listed in table 2:

TABLE 2   Repeat Performances

Author	Title	Year on BBYA
Cooney, Caroline B.	Driver's Ed	1995
	Whatever Happened to Janie?	1995
	Voice on the Radio, The	1997
	What Child Is This?	1998
Cormier, Robert	In the Middle of the Night	1996
	Tenderness	1998
	Heroes	1999
Fleischman, Paul	Bull Run	1994
	Dateline: Troy	1997
	Seedfolks	1998
	Whirligig	1999
Freedman, Russell	Eleanor Roosevelt	1994
	Kids at Work	1995
	Life and Death of Crazy Horse	1997
	Martha Graham: A Dancer's Life	1999
Glenn, Mel	Who Killed Mr. Chippendale?	1997
	Jump Ball	1998
	Taking of Room 114	1998
Haddix, Margaret P.	Don't You Dare Read This, Mrs. Dunphrey	1997
	Running Out of Time	1997
	Leaving Fishers	1998
	Among the Hidden	1999
Hesse, Karen	Phoenix Rising	1995
	Music of Dolphins	1997
	Out of the Dust	1998
Hobbs, Will	Beardance	1994
	Far North	1997
	Maze	1999
Janeczko, Paul	Stardust otel	1994
Janeczko, Paul, editor	Looking for Your Name	1994
Janeczko, Paul with Naomi Shihab Nye	I Feel a Little Jumpy around You	1997
Lynch, Chris	Shadow Boxer	1994
	Gypsy Davey	1995
	Iceman	1995
	Slot Machine	1996
Marrin, Albert	Unconditional Surrender	1995
	Virginia's General	1996
	Commander-in-Chief	1999
McKissack, Patricia, and Fred McKissack	Red-Tail Angels	1996
	Rebels against Slavery	1997
	Young, Black, and Determined	1999
Meyer, Carolyn	White Lilacs	1994
	Drummers of Jerico	1996
	Gideon's People	1997
	Jubilee Journey	1998

Continued

TABLE 2   *Continued*

Author	Title	Year on BBYA
Myers, Walter Dean	*Malcolm X: By Any Means Necessary*	1994
	Glory Field	1995
	One More River to Cross	1997
	Harlem	1998
Napoli, Donna Jo	*Magic Circle*	1994
	Song of the Magdalene	1997
	Stones in Water	1998
	Sirena	1999
Nye, Naomi Shihab	*The Tree Is Older Than You Are*	1996
Nye, Naomi Shihab with Paul Janeczko	*I Feel a Little Jumpy around You*	1997
Nye, Naomi Shihab	*Habibi*	1998
	The Space between My Footsteps	1999
Paulsen, Gary	*Nightjohn*	1994
	Winterdance	1995
	Puppies, Dogs, and Blue Northers	1997
	Shernoff Discovery	1998
	Soldier's Heart	1999
Peck, Richard	*Last Safe Place on Earth*	1996
	Strays Like Us	1999
	Long Way from Chicago	1999
Rinaldi, Ann	*In My Father's House*	1998
	Hang a Thousand Ribbons	1997
	Acquaintance with Darkness	1998
Sweeney, Joyce	*Tiger Orchard*	1994
	Shadow	1995
	Spirit Window	1999
Weaver, Will	*Striking Out*	1994
	Farm Team	1996
	Hard Ball	1999
Woodson, Jacqueline	*I Hadn't Meant to Tell You This*	1995
	From the Notebooks of Melanin Sun	1996
	If You Come Softly	1999

From Tanya Tullos, "An Examination of the Authors, Titles, and Readers of Best Books for Young Adults" (Texas Woman's University, Denton, Texas, 1999, paper).

Works Cited

Best Books for Young Adults Policies and Procedures. 1994. Chicago: American Library Association. <http://www.ala.org/yalsa.info/bbyapolproc.html> Last accessed 15 September 1999.

Chronicle of the Twentieth Century: The Ultimate Record of Our Times. 1995. New York: DK Inc.

Estes, Sally. 1999. Conversation with Betty Carter, 26 September.

"Testing . . . The Teens' Top Ten Best Books 1999." 1999. <http://www.ala.org/yalsa/booklists/teentopwinners.html> Last accessed 1 December 1999.

Trends in
Young Adult Publishing

Over the years, young adult (YA) literature has both changed and, in some cases, come full circle. We've come through the squeaky-clean tales of the 1950s that dealt with adolescent feelings and values in a narrow range of teenage experience. Then taboos crumbled in the turbulent 1960s and the "realistic" YA novel was born in such books as *Run Softly, Go Fast; His Own Where;* and *Man without a Face.* The 1970s mark the period when the realistic teenage novel came into its own and just about every possible personal, social, and political problem was introduced, unfortunately too often with a heavy didacticism, usually in what became known as "problem novels." The best of this lot include *Slake's Limbo, The Friends,* and *Deathwatch.* In the 1980s, the problem novel diversified, moving away from single issues and toward more depth and dimension and more fully developed plots, characters, settings, and themes in such books as *The Runner* or *Gentlehands.* This trend continued in the 1990s, with novels establishing a more reasonable relationship between young people and their parents and grandparents. In short, in their literature young adults are escaping the shadowy world of stereotypes, being portrayed with some dimension, having their own problems, sometimes succeeding, sometimes not, sometimes facing their responsibilities, sometimes not, sometimes relating well to one another, sometimes not.

New on the YA scene during the past year or so is what has been referred to widely as "bleak" books, novels that are uncomfortable to deal with because they center on such unsettling topics as madness, mental torture, serial killing, rape, and murder. These books, such as *When She Was Good,* come from some of today's top YA authors, who are writing sophisticated, edgy books about issues that reflect today's more complex society and culture. These books explore the same concerns, the same solutions (or nonsolutions) as do their counterparts for adults. YA authors are experimenting with language *(Make Lemonade)*, characterization *(Letters from the Inside)*, structure *(Nothing but the Truth: A Documentary Novel)*, and nonlinear plots *(Holes)* with varying degrees of success. And many of these titles are being packaged to appeal to more sophisticated, even adult, audiences. It is apparent that the YA novel has matured over the past twenty or so years, gaining in substance, diversity, and literary excellence.

What has come full circle are books in series. Following the pattern established by Horatio Alger and cemented forever in juvenile publishing by Edward Stratemeyer, books conceptualized by one person but produced by another are still viable components of young adult publishing. Fiction and nonfiction series are widely published, bought, and read, but few of these books appear on BBYA lists. That they are popular is a given; that they are one of a number of best books of the year is not.

Nonfiction does not exist solely as series entries, and single titles reflect major changes over the years. Scholarly underpinnings and genuine interest on the author's part ensure authenticity and reflect enthusiasm for a subject, encouraging a sense of wonder and exploration on the part of the reader. Subjects today are often approached seriously and without condescension; perceptive, in-depth writing has placed many informational books solidly in the category of quality literature. Also, there is a new emphasis on documentation: Most nonfiction books contain bibliographies of sources, and more and more are providing footnotes, either at the end of chapters or appended to the text. Books on diverse subjects, ranging from social issues *(Hearing Us Out: Voices from the Gay and Lesbian Community)*, to science *(When Plague Strikes: The Black Death, Smallpox, and AIDS)*, to biography *(Eleanor Roosevelt; the Abracadabra Kid;* and *Young, Black, and Determined)* to self-help *(Heartbreak and Roses)* and more, are available in plenitude. Controversial topics are generally given a balanced presentation with the authors' biases clearly stated. Curriculum-related materials have also improved, with clearer treatments of subjects, better and more pertinent illustrative material, and documentation.

YOUNG ADULT LITERATURE AS A PUBLISHING CATEGORY

A point of discussion about BBYA is the numbers of books published specifically for young adults as compared to the numbers of books that appeal to young adults but are published primarily for adult readers. Before 1973, committee members considered adult books only. Consequently, touchstone titles in young adult literature, such as S. E. Hinton's *The Outsiders* (1967) and Paul Zindel's *The Pigman* (1968), do not appear on best books lists for their respective years. But eleven years after these groundbreaking books surfaced, young adult publishers produced so many fine books read and respected by teenagers that the committee relaxed its adult-only policy and began considering books originally published for young adults. Today, the lists are composed primarily of titles specifically aimed at teenagers (Stauffer 1999).

In years past, the gauge for measuring the age-appropriateness of a list frequently became a simple determination of the ratio of adult books to young adult books, with YA books primarily addressing younger teenagers and adult books appealing to older readers. A panel of five editors who spoke at the 1994 Best of the Best YALSA preconference confirmed that publishers saw the YA market as one composed of young adolescents. "Young adult now ends at 14," stated respected editor Richard Jackson, who voiced the publishing policy of the industry as a whole (Cart 1994). In such a climate, the adult/young adult division made sense as a rough way of trying to ensure representation of the wide age levels addressed by this list.

But the times they were a'changing. Young adult publishing does not now restrict itself to books primarily for the eleven-to-fourteen age range, but instead prides itself on many publications aimed at senior high readers. There's a possibility that editors and publishers recognized the lack of books aimed at older teenagers and began to address this void. There's a possibility that publishers saw the large body of teenagers who were fourteen years old in 1994 growing older and thus creating a new market for young adult books. There's also the possibility that authors, acting independently, began writing for older teenagers. Whatever the reason, books aimed directly at older teenagers (think of such books as *Blood and Chocolate* or *The Killer's Cousin*) currently appear on publishers' annual lists as well as on BBYA lists.

On looking back at the phenomenon, David Gale, now executive editor at Simon and Schuster Books for Young Readers, remembers the first such book that came across his desk. It was Annette Curtis Klause's *The Silver Kiss,* also incidentally the first manuscript he acquired. Gale knew Klause through his previous experience as an editor for *School Library Journal* where Klause's day job as a YA librarian led her to become an SLJ reviewer. David recalls: "When I saw this book I knew it was something different. I liked it. So did George [Nicholson] and Craig [Virden] and we decided to publish it. We wanted to be honest about the book, so on the flap we put the age designation as age 14 and up, and excerpted part of the book on the back jacket so readers would know exactly what they were getting" (Gale 1999). The book received strong reviews, sold well to its audience, became a Best Book for Young Adults in 1991, and was selected as one of a hundred "Best of the Best" books in 1994..

Marc Aronson, senior editor at Henry Holt, cites *Smack* by Melvin Burgess as that publisher's watershed book for this age group. *Smack* clearly spoke to older teens. It also sold well, indicating that older teenagers constitute a sizable market for young adult books written especially for them. As Aronson adds, "Once authors who dealt with sophisticated subjects realized we would support them, then these kinds of books could be a corner of our publishing output." Aronson continues, "With this new audience we're able to experiment with all kinds of formats and subjects which should really open up young adult publishing" (Aronson 1999).

In an appropriate twist, these books that appeal to older teens are also being marketed to adult readers. An adult house picked up the paperback rights for Michael Cart's *My Father's Scar* while Rob Thomas's *Rats Saw God* sold in airports right next to John Grisham and Alice Hoffman (Gale 1999). *Booklist* published two columns concerning crossover books or titles originally written for young adults but of interest to adult readers (Crossovers 1998; Zvirin 1999). BBYA titles, such as *The Golden Compass, The Killer's Cousin,* and *Leaving Home,* appear prominently in these lists.

ADULT BOOKS

Even with this mini-renaissance in young adult publishing, BBYA committees cannot ignore adult books. As young adults are trying to become more adultlike, they naturally turn to the books read by an older audience. Often their forays into adult books begin with best-sellers, such as *The Hot Zone, Rule of the Bone,* and *The Relic,* all recognized by the 1996 committee. But there's also an issue for genre readers, especially those drawn to science fiction and fantasy. Certainly books published in juvenile houses and recognized by BBYA committees, such as *The Golden Compass* and *Harry Potter and the Sorcerer's Stone,* have found legions of young adult readers, but avid fans usually move to adult fiction early in the junior high years. Fantasy is represented more frequently than science fiction with such books as Robin McKinley's *Deerskin,* Charles Lint's *Trader,* and Connie Willis's *To Say Nothing of the Dog* marking the kind of adult books that BBYA must continue to recognize.

Notice, though, that the books discussed thus far are fiction. And therein lies another problem. Young adults read nonfiction. They read nonfiction for pleasure and diversion, often as underground readers not recognized by their librarians and teachers. About one-half the total reading of younger teenagers is nonfiction and that figure jumps to about 80 percent of the reading matter of older teens. Still, nonfiction fails to appear in representative numbers on BBYA lists. Part of that failure may be because of the reading tastes of the committee, but part is also because of publishing output.

Consider these figures. In 1998, I tallied starred reviews for juvenile books in *Booklist, School Library Journal, Bulletin of the Center for Children's Books,* and *Horn Book.* Three hundred six books received stars in 1998; 74 books received more than one star. Of those, 181 or 59 percent, are fiction; 125, or 41 percent, are nonfiction. Although these figures may look evenly distributed, they include in nonfiction folklore and poetry and other nonfiction books by form. I further divided the reviews into young adult and children's books and discovered that 41 percent of the starred reviews were for young adult books. Of that number, 53 books, or 43 percent, are nonfiction. But, once I removed the stories, the folklore, the poetry, and the biographies, only 25 books were nonnarrative nonfiction, frequently the kinds of books teenagers are reading. So, according to the reviewers, 20 percent of the young adult starred reviews, or 8 percent of the total juvenile starred reviews, are the kinds of books that young adults circulate between 50 and 80 percent of the time.

When talking about the publishing movement toward more books for older young adults, Marc Aronson (1999) added: "While we publish many books for older teens, nonfiction books for the same audience are pushed way in the back." Until young adult publishing catches up with these interests, adult books remain the last best bet to target some teens' non-fiction reading. Before 1973, when the list was primarily an adult one, nonfiction reigned. Today, the decline is noticeable. Committees recognizing books like *The Encyclopedia of the Cat, Into the Wild,* and *A Midshipman's Hope* are to be commended for trying to pick up this neglected area of YA interest.

Works Cited

Aronson Marc. 1999. Telephone interview with Betty Carter, 18 October.

Cart, Michael. "Young Adult Literature—Past and Future." *Booklist* 91 (October 15): 411.

"Crossovers: Juvenile Books for Adult Readers." 1998. *Booklist* 94 (June): 1716–1719.

Gale, David. 1999. Telephone interview with Betty Carter, 18 October.

Stauffer, Sherry. 1999. "Age Designations for BBYA Books." Texas Woman's University, Denton, Texas. Paper.

Zvirin, Stephanie. 1999. "Crossovers." *Booklist* 96 (April 1): 1382–1383.

Topical Lists

In 1983, Sally Estes, Linda Waddle, and I met one another. We were all serving on the Best Books for Young Adults (BBYA) Committee that year. Linda, then a high school librarian in Cedar Falls, Iowa, had been on the committee for one year. She was all expertise and experience, the "old hand" in this triumvirate. Sally and I came on as members of the "B" team, both filling in terms for others. Sally, then young adult book reviewer at *Booklist,* took over Barbara Duree's consultant position to the committee—Barbara was unable to attend the meetings because of her recently broken arm. I was called in at midyear to replace a member who was ill. We met over books, and we became friends through heated discussions of books.

Over the years, we changed: All of us grew a lot more gray hair and even grew a lot more. We shared our children's growing up years, traded pictures of our grandchildren, moved to different jobs, and read more books. The latter activity held us together more than our shared personal passages, for as we read books we talked about books, and in talking about books, we revealed much about ourselves. Books, in these cases, were the platforms upon which we sorted out, and tried to discard, our personal biases as we examined the literary ones before us. Book discussions gave us the opportunities to move beyond the hunch recommendations we'd had as librarians and examine the specific features within particular pages that defined each work's value. And individual books became the springboards to offer other reading suggestions, to widen our knowledge of genres, forms, and subjects.

When Linda and I discussed how to update the previous edition of this book, we wrestled with several options, finally deciding that a compilation of bibliographies would serve readers well. We further discussed the idea with Sally, who agreed, and to us it was part of the natural order of things that the three of us would create those bibliographies. We began with ideas quite different from the final product. For example, we thought we would be inventive and create lists that drew from various genres using atypical subjects, such as nonlinear fiction narratives, as the topics for our bibliographies. We even considered examining trends through hot topics, such as the "bleak books" that are receiving much national press, thinking that our bibliographies would show the history of such books, from Cormier's *The Chocolate War* to Mazer's *When She Was Good.* We abandoned that cleverness by concluding that our ingenuity would not serve readers well, that readers working with young adults would be searching for "funny books" or "good love stories" or "exciting books." In other words, we suspected adults serving teenagers, who are, after all, the audience for this book, would find more value in lists of books that answered the kinds of everyday requests they heard from young adults.

To create these lists we used the following procedure. Each of us took the compiled lists of the best books and read over them. Individually we reread titles we remembered as having great appeal at the time of publication but wondered if they would last. We thought about the books we considered the most outstanding and began creating categories to hold them. Then we met for a three-day marathon in which we went over every book on the list, highlighting the titles we considered the best (such as *Motel of the Mysteries* and *I Am the Cheese* and *Weetzie Bat*) and leaving those that had not, in our collective opinion, stood the test of time (such as *Daddy Was a Numbers Runner* or *Cold Feet* or *Missile Crisis*). We noted those books with particular subjects that might well cycle around to a new generation of readers. Bill Bradley's *Life on the Run,* for example, merited a second look because of his contemporary run for the presidency, although we finally eliminated that book, deeming it locked in the full court press of the seventies rather than providing insight into Bradley's current political aspirations and platform. Similarly, John Powers's *Diana: The Making of a Terrorist* deals with the all-too-common contemporary problem of terrorism. Yet, the political climate of Weatherwoman Diana Oughton differs greatly from that of today where terrorism is as likely to come from classmates or to be sanctioned by governments as it is to represent a small group's idealism. When measured against such titles as *Deathwatch* or *Maus* or *This Boy's Life* or *The People Therein* or *Cold Sassy Tree,* books like *Life on the Run* and *Diana,* though both interesting and readable, stuck out as lesser entries.

Before compiling the lists, we debated various subjects for the bibliographies. Unable to agree, we let them emerge from the books. Just the mention of one title would lead us to companion pieces. For example, Chris Crutcher's *Stotan!* reminded us of Richard Peck's *Remembering the Good Times,* a book about friendship, more than it reminded us of Tessa Duder's *In Lane Three, Alex Archer,* an Australian title concerning competitive swimming. We wrote down a category for friendship, and from these initial two links, began building a tentative bibliography on that subject. Sometimes subjects, such as science fiction, appeared obvious in terms of teen reading interests, but lacked numbers of books on the yearly lists to create them. In those cases, the outstanding books originally in that category, such as *Eva* by Peter Dickinson and *Fantastic Voyage* by Isaac Asimov, appear on other lists.

Admittedly, there are some favorites we couldn't classify. How does one, for example, categorize Olive Ann Burns's *Cold Sassy Tree*? Is it a family story, a humorous story, or historical fiction? Each of these categories shortchanged the overall power of the book. Other books defied clean categories: *If Beale Street Could Talk, Go and Come Back, Stories I Ain't Told Nobody Yet,* and *War of Jenkins' Ear.* So we created a slush pile of greats and called that list "Too Good to Miss." In it, such books as *Corpses, Coffins, and Crypts,* which had been in an original category of nonfiction, an idiosyncratic bibliography that lacked any semblance of practicality, found a comfortable slot. Some books, such as *I Will Call It Georgie's Blues* and *Rats Saw God,* were originally featured in a crowded list on the family. Unwilling to abandon either title because each is so powerful, we moved them to their new spot, thus further building the category. This bibliography also includes more books from the 1990s than any other single list. Perhaps they haven't had time to find an identifiable segment of readers or perhaps we need more distance from them to identify overriding topics. In any case, they're "too good to miss."

TOO GOOD TO MISS

Abelove, Joan. *Go and Come Back.* Young Alicia wonders why the two white women have come to her Peruvian village because they hoard their liquor, value work over partying, and don't have a clue about marriage or sex.

Anderson, Rachel. *Bus People.* Six heart-wrenching, interconnected stories tell about the disabled children who ride Bertram's bus to their special school.

Baldwin, James. *If Beale Street Could Talk.* A young black couple, separated by his unjust imprisonment, are bolstered by their love for each other and the determination of her loyal family.

Burns, Olive Ann. *Cold Sassy Tree.* As his tiny rural Georgia hometown undergoes many changes in the year 1906, Will Tweedy survives family scandal, his first kiss, and being run over by a train.

Carson, Jo. *Stories I Ain't Told Nobody Yet: Selections from the People Pieces.* Haunting, funny and full of folk wisdom and honesty, these powerful poems bring to life the colorful personalities and the lifestyle of the Appalachian region.

Colman, Penny. *Corpses, Coffins, and Crypts: A History of Burial.* Colman's well-researched account of death and burial answers questions for the curious and satisfies a taste for the morbid.

Crew, Linda. *Children of the River.* Sundara struggles with the conflict between her Cambodian heritage and her growing love for Jonathan.

Feelings, Tom. *The Middle Passage: White Ships/Black Cargo.* Feelings's heartrending illustrations document the horrific journey of slaves from Africa to America.

Greenberg, Joanne. *Of Such Small Differences.* Immersed in the world of twenty-five-year-old blind and deaf John Moon, the reader experiences not only John's attempts to survive alone, but also the turmoil, passion, and love brought into his life by Leda, a sighted, hearing actress.

Morpurgo, Michael. *War of Jenkins' Ear.* Convinced that Christopher is the Son of God, Toby watches as miracles unfold at his English boarding school.

Newton, Suzanne. *I Will Call It Georgie's Blues.* In music, Neil has a secret escape from the dark tensions beneath his family's smooth public facade—but the strain pushes his little brother Georgie over the edge of sanity.

Thomas, Rob. *Rats Saw God.* "Troubled teen" Steve York reflects on his life and his relationship with his famous father.

Compliments of: [_____]
NAME OF LIBRARY

From *Best Books for Young Adults,* 2d ed., ALA 2000
Young Adult Library Services Association, a division of the American Library Association

For more book lists go to <www.ala.org/yalsa/booklists>

ADVENTURE

Teenagers may well think that their lives lack adventure. Consider how often a teenager has said, "There's nothing to do around here" or "It's just a boring day." For the individuals in these books, life is just the opposite, perhaps giving young adult readers some amount of wish fulfillment as they endure, enjoy, or even inspect their own situations. Some individuals, such as Jon Krakauer and Robin Graham, chose their adventures. Others, such as Jesse in *Downriver,* set their adventure in motion by a single act. And still others, like Ben, the protagonist in *Deathwatch,* have their adventures imposed on them. Imposition can come from unusual circumstances *(The Hitchhiker's Guide to the Galaxy)* or unusual times *(Paladin)* or even everyday pressures *(Jumper).* Whatever the case, these stories offer exciting alternatives to a trip to the mall or an hour of algebra.

Adams, Douglas. *The Hitchhiker's Guide to the Galaxy.* The hilarious journey of Arthur Dent and his friend Ford Prefect, a space hitchhiker, who escape from earth seconds before it is demolished and travel to a variety of galactic civilizations while gathering information for a hitchhiker's guidebook.

Campbell, Eric. *Place of Lions.* After surviving a plane crash on the African Serengeti Plain, fourteen-year-old Chris sets off to find help for his father and the pilot, who are injured, and forges a magical relationship with an aging lion.

Garfield, Brian. *Paladin.* A fifteen-year-old boy, recruited by Winston Churchill to be his personal secret agent, is involved in murder, assassination, and sabotage on both sides of the front lines in this World War II novel.

Gould, Steven. *Jumper.* Davy jumps for the first time when he escapes a beating by teleporting to the library. Now he's on the run from his alcoholic father, the police, and a secret government agency—but who can catch a jumper?

Graham, Robin Lee, and Derek L. T. Gill. *Dove.* Setting out in his sloop *Dove* to encircle the globe, a sixteen-year-old boy finds adventure and romance.

Hobbs, Will. *Downriver.* Fifteen-year-old Jesse and other rebellious teenage members of a wilderness survival team abandon their adult leader, steal his van and rafts, and run the dangerous whitewaters of the Grand Canyon.

Ives, John. *Fear in a Handful of Dust.* Four kidnapped psychiatrists, one a woman, manage to survive the rigors and horrors of the desert after being left to die by a psychotic killer.

(Continued)

Krakauer, Jon. *Into Thin Air: A Personal Account of the Mt. Everest Disaster.* Courage, cowardice, foolishness, and great adventure marked the 1996 rival expeditions' efforts to reach the summit of Everest when everything went terribly wrong.

Lawrence, Iain. *The Wreckers.* Eighteenth-century Cornwall provides an eerie backdrop for this heart-pounding mystery full of nautical adventure and with a fourteen-year-old hero.

Peterson, P. J. *Nobody Else Can Walk It for You.* Eighteen-year-old Laura desperately tries to lead a group of young backpackers to safety as they are pursued by three threatening motorcyclists through isolated mountain country.

Sherman, D. R. *Lion's Paw.* An obsessed white hunter, a young bushman, and a crippled lion confront one another in the conflict for survival.

White, Robb. *Deathwatch.* Ben's hunting expedition for bighorn sheep becomes a deathwatch in the desert—with hope of survival forty-five miles away!

Books about animals allow readers either to view the world in nonego-centric ways or to look at their own lives from another point of view. Two of the books *(Ratha's Creature* and *Arrows of the Queen)* appearing on this list concern a single animal, and both of those are fantasies featuring animal helpmates that use unusual powers to serve the protagonists. *Watership Down* and *Jurassic Park* also venture into the fantastic with the former anthropomorphizing rabbits within a quest for survival and the latter creating dinosaurs to serve civilization's basest needs. Personal accounts of life with animals *(Woodsong),* a passion to understand them *(Walking with the Great Apes),* concern for them *(Time Is Short and the Water Rises),* an attempt to live with them *(Night of the Grizzlies),* and a fascination with them *(Daywatchers)* round out the list.

Adams, Richard. *Watership Down.* Follow the epic Tolkienesque adventures of Fiver, Hazel, and a ragtag lapin band. Rabbits will never seem the same again.

Bell, Clare. *Ratha's Creature.* Ratha, born into a society of intelligent prehistoric felines, is banished from the Clan, is rescued by an unnamed male cat, and helps the Clan when she learns to tame fire.

Brandenburg, Jim. *To the Top of the World: Adventures with Arctic Wolves.* In a wildlife photo-documentary, Brandenburg enters the world of a wolf pack on Ellesmen Island and captures the animals' behaviors, personalities, and intelligence.

Crichton, Michael. *Jurassic Park.* Dinosaurs created from fossilized DNA for a fabulous theme park are not supposed to be capable of breeding, but they do—and they're hungry.

Derby, Pat, and Peter Beagle. *Lady and Her Tiger.* You can train wild animals by love rather than force, and Pat Derby proves it. One of her favorites is Chauncey, the Lincoln-Mercury cougar.

Lackey, Mercedes. *Arrows of the Queen.* Discovered by a telepathic steed, Talia, a misfit in her society, is taken to be educated as herald to the queen.

Montgomery, Sy. *Walking with the Great Apes: Jane Goodall, Dian Fossey, Birute Galdikas.* These are the fascinating stories of three intrepid women who leave civilization to study and share the lives of primates.

Olsen, Jack. *Night of the Grizzlies.* On the night of August 12, 1967, grizzlies attack a campground in Glacier National Park—a violent and inevitable clash between a vanishing species and the humans invading its territory.

Parnall, Peter. *Daywatchers.* This is a beautifully illustrated, nontechnical narrative of Parnall's observations of and experiences with various birds of prey.

(Continued)

Paulsen, Gary. *Woodsong.* Through his dogsledding adventures in the Minnesota wilderness where there are wolves, deep snow, and minus-30-degree temperatures, the author comes to understand nature's ways and harrowing surprises.

Psihoyos, Louie, and John Knoebber. *Hunting Dinosaurs.* With beautiful photographs and a zany sense of humor, Psihoyos and Knoebber impart the adventure of digging for fossils the world over.

Walsh, John, and Robert Gannon. *Time Is Short and the Water Rises.* "Operation Gwamba: The story of the rescue of 10,000 animals from certain death in a South American rain forest" is the subtitle.

Compliments of: [_____]
NAME OF LIBRARY

From *Best Books for Young Adults,* 2d ed., ALA 2000
Young Adult Library Services Association, a division of the American Library Association

For more book lists go to <www.ala.org/yalsa/booklists>

One of the pieces of collective wisdom about young adult literature is that it should be about teenagers.[1] Other characters, particularly parents, need to move off center stage or exit the books altogether. After all, the thinking goes, what teenager wants to read about a main character who depends on his or her parents or siblings? We hope many of them do, for, surprisingly, this category became the largest of those we identified. We listed page after page of outstanding books dealing with families, so many books that we divided them into three additional categories: Leaving Home, Fathers and Sons, and Mothers and Daughters. Here are books where teens try to find themselves within a family *(Mermaids)*, create their own family structures *(Weetzie Bat)*, cope with family horror *(Solitary Secret)*, and discover family secrets *(Dixie Storms)*. Teenagers in these books also leave home, some to escape *(I Know Why the Caged Bird Sings)*, some to seek security *(Home before Dark)*, and others for adventure *(Rule of the Bone)*. And they work through family problems and unique relationships with both their mothers *(The Joy Luck Club)* and their fathers *(Iceman)*.

Ansa, Tina McElroy. *Baby of the Family.* Lena is special, not only because she is the baby of her middle-class African-American family but also because of the supernatural gifts she received at birth.

Block, Francesca Lia. *Weetzie Bat.* Lanky lizards! Punk teens Weetzie and Dirk search for love in a modern fairy tale that is funny, moving, and unlike any book you've read before.

Bradford, Richard. *Red Sky at Morning.* Joshua Arnold, a wise, wry man-child, must cope with an absent father and a sherry-tippling mother, and learn to live in a new town, make friends, and finish growing up.

Dann, Patty. *Mermaids.* In this quietly bizarre story, fourteen-year-old Charlotte wants to become a saint—if only she can stop lusting after the gardener at the nearby convent.

Gaan, Margaret. *Little Sister.* Little Sister, a third-generation Chinese American, visits Shanghai at the beginning of a revolution and learns about her family from family members.

Hall, Barbara. *Dixie Storms.* Spending all her fourteen years in a small Virginia farming town, Dutch Peyton has found life to be pretty good until the drought-plagued summer when her sophisticated cousin Norma arrives and family secrets bring trouble.

Hermes, Patricia. *Solitary Secret.* Abandoned by her mother, a lonely and frightened fourteen-year-old girl becomes the victim of her father's sexual abuse.

(Continued)

---

1. Nancy Werlin. "YA Talk: Get Rid of the Parents," *Booklist* 95 (July 1999). <http://www.ala.org/booklist/v95/youth/jul/55yatalk.html> Last accessed 1 December 1999.

Mazer, Norma Fox. *When She Was Good.* Seventeen-year-old Em remembers what it was like living with her emotionally disturbed, abusive sister, Pamela.

Pfeffer, Susan Beth. *Year without Michael.* The unexplained disappearance of a high school student throws his family into a state of uncertainty and agony.

Staples, Suzanne Fisher. *Shabanu: Daughter of the Wind.* Torn between allegiance to her family and her growing independence and strength, Shabanu tells the story of her life as a member of a nomadic tribe in the Pakistani desert.

Leaving Home

Angelou, Maya. *I Know Why the Caged Bird Sings.* This remarkable, poetic, and frank autobiography of a black girl who grew up in Arkansas, St. Louis, and San Francisco is for mature readers.

Banks, Russell. *Rule of the Bone.* Fourteen-year-old runaway Chappie becomes known as "Bone" during an adventurous year full of pot, travel, danger, and new friends.

Bridgers, Sue Ellen. *Home before Dark.* When her father takes his migrant family back to his childhood home in Florida, fourteen-year-old Stella Willis is determined to put down roots and never leave again.

Conway, Jill Ker. *Road from Coorain.* Jill Ker Conway survives the physically harsh life of Australia's outback in the 1930s and becomes the first woman president of Smith College.

Rochman, Hazel, ed. *Leaving Home.* Leaving whatever one considers "home" can cause many emotions, as experienced in this collection of short stories, poems, and essays.

Fathers and Sons

Lynch, Chris. *Iceman.* Eric plays hockey with a savage intensity, hoping that this only link to his father will improve their troubled relationship.

Naylor, Phyllis Reynolds. *Keeper.* His father's mental illness paralyzes the entire family, forcing Nick to make an agonizing decision.

Peck, Richard. *Father Figure: A Novel.* The security that Jim Atwater finds in his role as surrogate father to his eight-year-old brother is threatened when, after their mother's suicide, the boys are packed off to spend the summer with their father, who had long ago abandoned them.

Pringle, Terry. *Preacher's Boy.* The community keeps an eagle eye on Michael's blossoming romance with Amy as her career and his first college year complicate his struggles for a better relationship with his father.

(Continued)

Shannon, George. *Unlived Affections.* Discovering a box of old letters, Willie learns the truth about his parents' relationship.

Mothers and Daughters

Cook, Karin. *What Girls Learn.* When two sisters go with their divorced mother from their southern home to live with their mother's boyfriend in the North, he becomes their caretaker after their mother's death.

Gingher, Marianne. *Bobby Rex's Greatest Hit.* A suggestive hit song by a small North Carolina town's heartthrob catapults its namesake, Pally Thompson, into the national limelight and passionate disavowal.

Matsubara, Hisako. *Cranes at Dusk.* Like her defeated country of Japan, ten-year-old Saya faces painful readjustments after World War II, as her mother, who can neither abandon tradition nor accept changes, attempts to turn Saya against her wise and progressive father.

Sanders, Dori. *Clover.* When her father is killed in an automobile accident in rural South Carolina, ten-year-old Clover is left to be reared by her white stepmother within the black community.

Tan, Amy. *The Joy Luck Club.* Chinese-American daughters find conflict, love, and connection with their mothers, who are haunted by their early lives in China.

Fantasy allows readers to use their imaginations, to consider characters, plots, and themes in places and situations that cannot exist in our world as we know it. That world may be rooted in the present *(War for the Oaks)* or in the past *(Seventh Son)*. It can build on legend *(I Am Mordred* or *The Magic Circle)* or it can exist in a setting created entirely by the author *(Sabriel)*. But even though fantasy is imaginary, good fantasy is never fluff literature. Here are the stories that tackle big issues, such as the struggle between good and evil. By asking readers to consider the unimaginable, fantasy poses questions, and seeks answers to those questions, that readers may never have known they had.

Bull, Emma. *War for the Oaks.* A mad phouka, the queen of the Faeries, and band leader Eddi McCandry battle the Dark Court's evil power, in a tale of rock music in Minneapolis.

Card, Orson Scott. *Seventh Son.* Alvin, born seventh son of a seventh son, is destined for greatness, but something evil is trying to keep him from growing up.

Jones, Diana Wynne. *Sudden Wild Magic.* The good witches of Earth band together to stop the magicians of Arth from stealing Earth's technology and creating disasters.

Jordan, Robert. *Eye of the World.* Three teenagers take on a classic fantasy quest in this epic struggle between good and evil.

McKillip, Patricia A. *Fool's Run.* Masked musician The Queen of Hearts and her band entertain in an orbiting prison and create an intergalactic emergency.

McKinley, Robin. *Blue Sword.* Harry Crewe, bored with her dull and sheltered life, finds new magic, love, and her destiny as a woman warrior when kidnapped by a handsome king who has mysterious powers.

Napoli, Donna Jo. *The Magic Circle.* When the Ugly One succumbs to the demons' trickery and is changed from good sorceress to evil witch, she flees to a remote forest, but her destiny lies in the arrival of two children, Hansel and Gretel.

Nix, Garth. *Sabriel.* Sabriel makes a desperate quest through the Gates of Death to free her necromancer father from the strengthening powers of the spirits of the dead.

Pullman, Philip. *The Golden Compass.* With the aid of friends, witches, and armored polar bears, twelve-year-old Lyra fights the evil that is stealing children and conducting horrible experiments on them.

Springer, Nancy. *I Am Mordred: A Tale from Camelot.* Mordred struggles to escape a fate that will lead him to kill his own father.

(Continued)

Stewart, Mary. *The Crystal Cave.* Merlin, the base-born son of royalty in fifth-century Britain, uses magic to outwit his enemies until he sets the stage for the birth of Arthur, the future king.

Wrede, Patricia C. *Dealing with Dragons.* Unconventional Cimorene, fed up with her dull life as a princess, runs away to join the dragons in this fun book that turns fairy tales upside down.

During the teen years, friends become increasingly important in youngsters' lives. Young adults seek friends, rely on friends, stand up for friends, love friends, follow friends, fight with friends, and pit friends against family, but they have few opportunities to read about friendship. Friends certainly populate young adult literature, but books dealing with the nature of friendship appear less regularly. The following books address friendships that grow into substitute families *(Stotan!)*, friendships that show compassion *(Fighting Back)*, friendships that weather problems *(Sex Education)*, friendships that disappoint *(Whistle Me Home)*, and friendships that rescue *(Bruises)*.

Bennett, James. *I Can Hear the Mourning Dove.* Struggling to recover from her father's death and her own suicide attempt, Grace meets rebellious Luke, a fellow patient and her first real friend.

Crutcher, Chris. *Stotan!* A high school coach invites four members of his swim team to a week of rigorous training that tests their moral fiber as well as their physical stamina.

Davis, Jenny. *Sex Education.* The semester project for freshman biology appears to be a snap: Find someone you never thought much about and care about them. Yet good intentions are sabotaged, with fatal consequences, when David and Livvie adopt a reclusive neighbor.

De Vries, Anke. *Bruises.* Although her teacher suspects the truth about Judith's frequent absences from school, Michael believes her tale of being attacked, and offers his help, protection, and friendship.

Deaver, Julie Reece. *Say Goodnight, Gracie.* Sharing a zany sense of humor and anxieties about their futures, Jimmy and Morgan are best friends on the brink of love when Jimmy is killed by a drunk driver, leaving Morgan to cope with the reality of death.

Kimble, Bo. *For You, Hank: The Story of Hank Gathers and Bo Kimble.* Bo and Hank are inseparable friends and teammates who know that basketball is the road up, but Hank is in trouble, then dead, and all of Bo's memories lead to the same question—why?

Kuklin, Susan. *Fighting Back: What Some People Are Doing about AIDS.* A moving look—in words and inspired photographs—at a team of volunteers fighting the war against AIDS by offering practical and emotional support to patients.

Peck, Richard. *Remembering the Good Times.* Meeting at a time of change in their lives, Kate, Buck, and Trav develop a special friendship— but even their mutual caring can't keep the gap from widening or avert the tragedy of Trav's suicide.

Potok, Chaim. *The Chosen.* Two Jewish boys growing to manhood in Brooklyn discover that differences can strengthen friendship and understanding.

(Continued)

Uhlman, Fred. *Reunion.* Thirty years later, the Jewish narrator recalls his doomed friendship with the son of a nobleman in Nazi Germany. A poignant and provocative novella.

Wersba, Barbara. *Whistle Me Home.* Tomboy Noli and TJ are friends and almost a couple, and Noli is totally shocked when she discovers that TJ is gay.

Wharton, William. *Birdy.* In a VA hospital, Birdy is prompted by his friend Al to review his bird-obsessed youth, and discovers freedom without flight.

Much young adult fiction deals with the here and now. And, in a sense, so does outstanding historical fiction. Although the settings in the books listed here are far removed from the everyday realities of contemporary teenagers, the characters and themes still offer readers much to contemplate about living in today's world. In *Clan of the Cave Bear,* the protagonist tries to carve out her own identity in a society that questions her worth. Blue Roan *(Tracks)* deals with prejudice and racism as does Miss Jane Pittman *(The Autobiography of Miss Jane Pittman).* Lyddie *(Lyddie)* and Tomi *(Under the Blood-Red Sun)* must take on family responsibilities far before their time. Hatshepsut *(Child of the Morning)* and Joe and Mary Alice *(A Long Way from Chicago)* learn about their individual families. And Elenor and Thomas *(The Ramsay Scallop)* wrestle with the meaning of love. For many teenagers the settings of these novels may not be as accessible as the Internet, but the stories nonetheless address timeless concerns.

Auel, Jean. *Clan of the Cave Bear.* A Cro-Magnon girl-child, adopted by a tribe of Neanderthals, struggles to subdue her strong feminine creativity while growing up in their mystical and instinctive male-dominated society.

Bess, Clayton. *Tracks.* Eleven-year-old Blue Roan persuades his older brother to take him on the rails in Depression-era Oklahoma, where their adventures range from vicious attacks by a hobo to an almost fatal encounter with the Ku Klux Klan.

Clapp, Patricia. *Witches' Children: A Story of Salem.* A frightening tale of the Salem witchcraft trials, based on historical fact and told from the perspective of one of the ten "afflicted girls."

Cushman, Karen. *Catherine, Called Birdy.* Fighting fleas, unsuitable suitors, and her mother's attempts to make a lady of her, Catherine writes in her diary about her frustrations with her life as a young noblewoman in medieval times.

Gaines, Ernest J. *The Autobiography of Miss Jane Pittman.* Born a slave in Louisiana before the Civil War, Jane Pittman lives to witness the struggle in the 1960s for civil rights in this fictional autobiography that reflects the courage and fortitude of African Americans.

Gedge, Pauline. *Child of the Morning.* Reared by her Pharaoh father to assume his throne upon his death, Hatshepsut—a real historical figure—has to contend with her weak half-brother before she can realize her dream.

Paterson, Katherine. *Lyddie.* Unable to pay off the debt on the family farm, feisty, single-minded Lyddie survives the dangers of the textile mills in 1840s Massachusetts, determined not to forfeit her dreams.

(Continued)

Paton Walsh, Jill. *Parcel of Patterns.* Vividly and dramatically, Mall Percival writes in her journal of the tragic events that befell her and the other villagers of Eyam during the disastrous plague of the 1660s in England.

Peck, Richard. *A Long Way from Chicago.* Grandma Dowdel creates more fun and surprises for Joe and Mary Alice during their summer visits to her small Illinois town.

Salisbury, Graham. *Under the Blood-Red Sun.* Tomi, a Japanese American teen living in Hawaii, must become the man of his family when his father and grandfather are interned after the bombing of Pearl Harbor.

Temple, Frances. *The Ramsay Scallop.* Betrothed, though they barely know each other, fourteen-year-old Elenor and eighteen-year-old Thomas are sent by their castle priest on a pilgrimage from their English village through France to Spain in 1299.

Although the following books cover the same period, each does so differently. *The Diary of a Young Girl* is often the first glimpse readers see of the Holocaust. It should not be the only one. Such books as *Tell Them We Remember* demand that readers interact with the horror while *The Final Journey* asks them to travel to a concentration camp with the author. *Auschwitz Album* puts them in one camp and *The Man from the Other Side* shows a single man's own brand of heroism in keeping individuals out of the camps. *Maus* explores the effects of the Holocaust on a survivor and *Gentlehands* carries the residue to another generation. The variety in viewpoints allows for a number of questions. Individual readers may ask if they would be brave or cowardly or leaders or followers. They may also be moved to ask the central question: How can I prevent this from ever happening again?

Bachrach, Susan D. *Tell Them We Remember.* The story of the Holocaust is told clearly and dramatically.

Frank, Anne. *The Diary of a Young Girl: The Definitive Edition.* This new edition contains the complete diary, some of which was not published in the original work.

Gies, Miep, and Alison Leslie Gold. *Anne Frank Remembered: The Story of Miep Gies, Who Helped to Hide the Frank Family.* The story of quiet personal courage by the woman who hid the Frank family and retrieved Anne's diary so that the world would never forget is itself unforgettable—and inspiring.

Hellman, Peter, and Lili Meier. *Auschwitz Album: A Book Based upon an Album Discovered by Concentration Camp Survivor, Lili Meier.* A powerful visual presentation of the extermination process at Auschwitz is viewed through candid photographs of its victims.

Kerr, M. E. *Gentlehands.* Buddy's world is turned upside down when he falls in love and then, catastrophically, when he discovers that his refined and cultured grandfather is a notorious Nazi war criminal.

Lobel, Anita. *No Pretty Pictures: A Child of War.* A moving account of the award-winning illustrator's childhood in Nazi-occupied Poland, her imprisonment in a series of concentration camps, and her life after the war as a displaced person in Sweden.

Meltzer, Milton. *Rescue: The Story of How Gentiles Saved Jews in the Holocaust.* In an account of individuals who risked their own lives to save thousands of others during the Holocaust, Meltzer shows the quiet but impressive courage of those who chose to stand firm in the face of monstrous evil.

Orlev, Uri. *The Man from the Other Side.* Knowing the way through the sewers, Marek leads a Polish Jew, who wants to die among Jews, back to the doomed Warsaw Ghetto.

(Continued)

Pausewang, Gudrun. *The Final Journey.* Horrid images emerge in this story of the two days a young girl spends on a railway car on her way to a concentration camp.

Ramati, Alexander. *And the Violins Stopped Playing: A Story of the Gypsy Holocaust.* Based on a young survivor's account, this gripping story tells of the Nazi massacre of the Gypsies during World War II.

Spiegelman, Art. *Maus: A Survivor's Tale.* In a comic book of revolutionary graphic design, a cartoonist juxtaposes his frustration with his father's insensitivity today and his father's desperate struggle to stay alive forty years earlier during the Holocaust.

Volavkova, Hana, ed. *I Never Saw Another Butterfly: Children's Drawings and Poems from Terezin Concentration Camp, 1942–1944.* Through the agony and hope expressed in the poems and drawings of the children of Terezin, the reader sees the sheer hell experienced by the 15,000 children under age fifteen who passed through the Terezin Concentration Camp between 1942 and 1945.

Humor crosses all genres, including fantasy *(Enter Three Witches)*, biography and autobiography *(Lost in Place)*, realistic fiction *(The Heroic Life of Al Capsella)*, and natural science *(Last Chance to See)*. Humor also appears in many forms, including slapstick *(Harris and Me)*, satire *(Simple Gifts)*, and parody *(Motel of the Mysteries)*. Situations *(Getting Lincoln's Goat)*, characters *(One Fat Summer)*, and plots all deliver a few belly laughs if matched with the right teenager. It takes fewer facial muscles to smile than to frown, so consider the following the literary equivalent of energy conservation.

Adams, Douglas, and Mark Carwardine. *Last Chance to See.* Adams, author of the Hitchhiker trilogy, and zoologist Carwardine embark on a personal journey filled with humor, irony, and frustrations as they attempt to observe some of the earth's exotic endangered species.

Clarke, J. *The Heroic Life of Al Capsella.* Fourteen-year-old Al wants to be "like everyone else"—but with weird parents like his, he hasn't got a chance.

Durrell, Gerald. *Rosy Is My Relative.* Adrian Rookwhistle inherits Rosy, a lovable beer-drinking elephant, and on their journey through the English countryside to find a circus home for Rosy, their progress is marked by many disquieting events.

Gilmore, Kate. *Enter Three Witches.* Sixteen-year-old Bren finds living with witches hard enough, but how can he prevent his girlfriend from discovering their existence?

Goldman, E. M. *Getting Lincoln's Goat.* When Lincoln High's beloved mascot—an old goat— disappears before the big football game, Elliot has the perfect opportunity to excel in a class assignment to learn about the world of private detectives.

Greenberg, Joanne. *Simple Gifts.* A simple, poor family of engaging misfits turns their ranch into a place where visitors pay to sample "authentic" 1880s homestead life.

Koertge, Ron. *Arizona Kid.* Working one summer at a racetrack, living with his gay uncle, and falling madly in love make wimpy, short, tenth-grader Billy Kennedy more self-confident and wiser in the ways of the world.

Lipsyte, Robert. *One Fat Summer.* Overweight Bobby Marks confronts the ridicule of friends and sheds his excess pounds in a comical story of his last fat summer.

Macaulay, David. *Motel of the Mysteries.* "Plastic is forever" illustrates the wonderful things discovered by archaeologists in the year 4022, when they excavate the ruins of the Toot 'n' C'mon Motel.

(Continued)

Paulsen, Gary. *Harris and Me: A Summer Remembered.* The narrator and his cousin share adventures—often with both painful and hilarious results—in this short, action-packed story of one summer spent on a farm.

Robinson, Spider. *Callahan's Crosstime Saloon.* The misfits of earth and elsewhere who belly up to Callahan's bar have lived some of the wildest and funniest stories in the galaxies.

Salzman, Mark. *Lost in Place: Growing Up Absurd in Suburbia.* Growing up in the Connecticut suburbs is not easy for a wanna-be kung fu expert and wandering Zen monk.

Who or what "done" it is the question that lies at the heart of all mysteries. Still, when teenagers ask "Can you recommend a good mystery?" librarians see the soul of the genre. More than any other kind of fiction, mysteries cross age levels and reading abilities, appealing to a great number of teenagers. Here we find mysteries set in ancient Rome *(Silver Pigs),* Victorian England *(Mary Reilly),* and contemporary America *(Wolf Rider).* Some mysteries blend genres, such as romance and historical fiction in *Ruby in the Smoke* or sports and realistic fiction in *When No One Was Looking. The Secret House* addresses mysteries of the natural world; *Father's Arcane Daughter,* the mysteries of morality; and *The Beekeeper's Apprentice,* the essence of detective fiction.

Avi. *Wolf Rider.* When fifteen-year-old Andy gets a crank call from a man claiming to have murdered a woman, his life turns into a psychological nightmare.

Bodanis, David. *The Secret House: Twenty-Four Hours in the Strange and Unexpected World in Which We Spend Our Nights and Days.* The microbiological drama found within a house is explored from early morning to late evening.

Davis, Lindsey. *Silver Pigs.* The murder of a senator's daughter forces Marcus Didius Falco (Bogey in a toga) to investigate a possible attempt to overthrow the emperor of ancient Rome.

Freeman, Suzanne. *Cuckoo's Child.* In Beirut, Mia longed for a normal American life, but after her parents are lost at sea, she finds life in Tennessee a real challenge.

Henry, Sue. *Murder on the Iditarod Trail.* Money, dogs, and reputation are at stake during the intense competition of the Iditarod. As mushers are murdered, state trooper Jensen looks at the race with new eyes.

Hillerman, Tony. *Dance Hall of the Dead.* When Navajo police lieutenant Joe Leaphorn is called upon to investigate the murder of the young fire god, he becomes involved in the world of Zuni religious beliefs.

King, Laurie R. *The Beekeeper's Apprentice; or, On the Segregation of the Queen.* Sherlock Holmes meets an intellectual equal, fifteen-year-old Mary Russell, who challenges him to investigate yet another case.

Konigsburg, E. L. *Father's Arcane Daughter.* Overprotected children of wealthy parents get a chance to grow up normally because of the efforts of their mysterious half sister.

Martin, Valerie. *Mary Reilly.* Intrigued by the mysterious Dr. Jekyll, housemaid Mary Reilly finds life taking a different twist as she learns more about his late-night prowling in Victorian England.

(Continued)

Namioka, Lensey. *Village of the Vampire Cat.* Two young masterless samurai solve the mystery of the vampire cat that has been terrorizing the villagers.

Pullman, Philip. *Ruby in the Smoke.* Sally, sixteen and an orphan, must find her way through a maze of nineteenth-century villains to claim her inheritance and her independence.

Wells, Rosemary. *When No One Was Looking.* Fourteen-year-old Kathy thrives on pressure to become a tennis star until the death, possibly murder, of a competitor forces her to question her ambition and her future.

In creating this category we rounded up the usual suspects: ghosts *(Ammie, Come Home)*, vampires *(Those Who Hunt by Night)*, werewolves *(Blood and Chocolate)*, and shapechangers *(Owl in Love)*. But expect a few surprises. For example, there's Willow from *Magic Kingdom for Sale—Sold!* Ben finds himself attracted to her, until he discovers she likes to put down roots each night. There's also sixteen-year-old Olwen *(Keeper of the Isis Light)*, who discovers that even though her parents were both from Earth, she, with her green and scaly skin, doesn't resemble the colonists who land on her planet. Dragons aren't human, but are they real? Peter Dickinson and Wayne Anderson serve up a pretty convincing argument in *Flight of Dragons.*

Brooks, Terry. *Magic Kingdom for Sale—Sold!* In a funny fantasy adventure, disillusioned sorrowing widower Ben buys a magic kingdom for $1 million only to find a run-down castle operated by a motley group of inept courtiers.

Dickinson, Peter, and Wayne Anderson. *Flight of Dragons.* Dragons aren't real . . . or are they? This carefully constructed and beautifully illustrated case for the existence of dragons will convince even the skeptics.

Hambly, Barbara. *Those Who Hunt the Night.* The silent tombs of London's Highgate Cemetery and the gaiety of 1906 Paris are the settings when James Asher is forced to investigate the mystery of who is killing the vampires of London.

Hughes, Monica. *Keeper of the Isis Light.* Never having seen another human, Olwen does not know how different she is until Earth settlers come to Isis and she falls in love.

Kerner, Elizabeth. *Song in the Silence.* Vibrant young Lanen Kaelar is compelled to leave the farm on which she was raised to seek out the awe-inspiring dragons that she's dreamed of since childhood.

Kindl, Patrice. *Owl in Love.* Girl by day, owl by night, fourteen-year-old Owl Tycho finds life is complicated—not only by a crush on her science teacher, but also by the presence of a deranged boy in the woods.

Klause, Annette Curtis. *Blood and Chocolate.* Beautiful teenage werewolf Vivian falls in love with Aiden, a human—a meat-boy—and longs to share her secret with him.

McKinley, Robin. *Beauty: A Retelling of the Story of Beauty and the Beast.* Fantasy and romance are beautifully blended in an evocative, much-expanded version of the classic fairy tale.

Michaels, Barbara. *Ammie, Come Home.* A ghost that never quite materializes and the spirit of "Ammie" Campbell haunt an old Georgetown house, threatening the lives of its occupants.

(Continued)

Pierce, Meredith Ann. *Darkangel.* Although both fascinated and repelled by the vampyre, Aeriel tries to save her mistress and the other vampyre brides.

Vande Velde, Vivian. *Companions of the Night.* Is Ethan really just an innocent college student kidnapped by vampire-hunting crazies? Sixteen-year-old Kerry, who saves him and loves him, finds that the allure of the vampire is alive and well.

Wilson, David Henry. *Coachman Rat.* When the clock tolls midnight, the rat, accidentally turned into a coachman by the fairy godmother, remains human in all but physical form; will he be as inhumane as the people he encounters?

As teenagers try to make sense out of their own lives, they often turn to the real lives of others for inspiration. Sometimes they're looking for role models, and they can certainly find positive ones in *The Right Stuff* or *Days of Grace*. Sometimes they look for the individuals who met adversity face on *(Ditchdigger's Daughters)* or the person who created her own hell *(Buried Alive)*. There's also room for an ordinary individual caught up in extraordinary circumstances *(Red Scarf Girl)* or existing in a seemingly bleak childhood *(This Boy's Life)*. Yet, none of these features is worth the time to catalog a book unless there's a strong story underlying the immediate subject. And story is what Alexis De Veaux delivers as she sings a literary song to Billie Holiday. Add to that the near love story Russell Freedman writes about Eleanor Roosevelt and the unflinching one Barry Denenberg tells about Charles Lindbergh and readers will find that other lives may be more compelling than their own.

Ashe, Arthur. *Days of Grace.* Ashe's memoir reveals why he was considered a champion—both on and off the tennis court.

De Veaux, Alexis. *Don't Explain: A Song of Billie Holiday.* The life of the incredibly gifted yet tragically insecure American jazz singer Billie Holiday, nicknamed "Lady Day," is told in this free verse "song."

Denenberg, Barry. *An American Hero: The True Story of Charles A. Lindbergh.* This is an honest look at the man whose solo transatlantic flight in 1927 captured the heart of the nation.

Freedman, Russell. *Eleanor Roosevelt: A Life of Discovery.* A compelling photo-biography of Eleanor Roosevelt relates the remarkable story of a shy, lonely girl who grows up to be a powerful force in the fight for world peace and equality and an inspiration to millions of people.

Friedman, Myra. *Buried Alive: The Biography of Janis Joplin.* Janis Joplin, the great legendary rock singer of the 1960s, has a passion for life but is also a tortured and driven woman.

Jiang, Ji-Li. *Red Scarf Girl: A Memoir of the Cultural Revolution.* Ji Li Jiang's quiet, prosperous way of life is destroyed during the turmoil and tragedy of the Chinese Cultural Revolution.

Krentz, Harold. *To Race the Wind: An Autobiography.* He is totally blind, but Harold and his parents determine that he will not be limited by his blindness.

Littlefield, Bill. *Champions: Stories of Ten Remarkable Athletes.* The accomplishments and contributions of ten extraordinary athletes, from both genders and many cultural backgrounds, are explored through moving essays and evocative full-color paintings.

(Continued)

Thornton, Yvonne S., and Jo Coudert. *Ditchdigger's Daughters: A Black Family's Astonishing Success Story.* Dr. Yvonne Thornton tells the story of her 1950s upbringing by her father, a poor African American man who raises five daughters to succeed in a world that prefers them invisible.

Wolfe, Tom. *The Right Stuff.* Wolfe provides a fascinating and often irreverent history of manned space flight from the late-1940s exploits of Chuck Yeager to the NASA missions of John Glenn, Alan Shepard, and Gus Grissom—who all had the "right stuff."

Wolff, Tobias. *This Boy's Life: A Memoir.* A witty, wrenching autobiography of Wolff's coming-of-age with a loving mother and a cruel stepfather.

Teenagers are often searching for good books about searching. As they try to define themselves and their futures, they frequently turn to books written around a quest that appear to mirror those very real developmental tasks. Quest stories are often associated with fantasy, and the list offers a fine representative in that genre, *Sword of Shannara*. But there are quests for honor *(Rules of the Road)*, quests for a better life *(Journey of the Sparrows)*, quests for self *(Yellow Raft in Blue Water)*, and quests for atonement *(Whirligig)*. Like many of the lists, this one crosses genres and includes historical fiction *(In Country)*, fantasy *(To Say Nothing of the Dog)*, science fiction *(Emergence)*, realistic fiction *(Queen's Gambit)*, and sports fiction *(Vision Quest)*.

Bauer, Joan. *Rules of the Road.* Seventeen-year-old Jenna's job at crusty Mrs. Gladstone's shoe store leads to her driving Mrs. Gladstone across the country to Texas to prevent a company takeover.

Beake, Lesley. *Song of Be.* In newly independent Namibia, teenager Be despairs of finding her place in the new political culture, which seems to be destroying the traditional way of life of her San people.

Brooks, Terry. *Sword of Shannara.* A small band of humans, elves, and dwarfs must face the armies of an evil sorcerer in order to reach the sword that can destroy him.

Buss, Fran Leeper. *Journey of the Sparrows.* Maria makes the dangerous trip across the border to the United States, where jobs are scarce and she must evade immigration officers.

Davis, Terry. *Vision Quest.* As he prepares himself for adulthood, eighteen-year-old Louden finds a special joy in competitive wrestling, in the uniqueness of the Columbia River, and in his live-in girlfriend, Carla.

Dorris, Michael. *Yellow Raft in Blue Water.* Half-Native American, half-African American Rayona's agonizing search for her true self is told from the perspective of three generations—Rayona's, her mother's, and her grandmother's.

Fleischman, Paul. *Whirligig.* After killing a girl when driving drunk, Brent Bishop learns a lot about himself and life when he's forced to pay for his crime by traveling to the four corners of the United States to build whirligigs in her memory.

Garland, Sherry. *Song of the Buffalo Boy.* Running away to Ho Chi Minh City with the boy she loves after being promised in marriage to a menacing old man, seventeen-year-old Loi tries to find out about her American soldier father.

Mason, Bobbie Ann. *In Country.* On a pilgrimage to the Vietnam War Memorial in Washington, D.C., Sam, a recent high school graduate, tries to understand the strange behavior of her uncle Emmett and the death of the father she never knew, both victims of the Vietnam War.

(Continued)

Palmer, David R. *Emergence.* Heroic deeds become the daily routine for eleven-year-old Candy Smith-Foster who, as a member of a new human species, begins a trek with her pet macaw, Terry D., across an American landscape scarred by bionuclear war.

Tevis, Walter. *Queen's Gambit.* In the orphanage where she lives, Beth learns the game of chess, beginning an obsession that takes her all the way to the top.

Willis, Connie. *To Say Nothing of the Dog; or, How We Found the Bishop's Bird Stump at Last.* When time-traveling historian Ned Henry rescues a cat in Victorian England, the twenty-first century begins to unravel.

Love stories are for the moment but romance is for the ages. Here are stories that go beyond dating and transcend sex. The novelists and poets represented here deal with deep feelings, great sacrifice, and a mystical knowledge about the nature of love. Their stories and poems are the literary equivalents of *Casablanca, An Affair to Remember,* and *Sleepless in Seattle*—delicious books that beg to be read while curled up in a corner with a robe and fuzzy slippers.

Berry, Liz. *The China Garden.* Seventeen-year-old Londoner Clare spends a summer in Ravensmere, where she and handsome biker Mark find themselves enmeshed in a labyrinth of magic.

Boissard, Janice. *Matter of Feeling.* From the safety of her suburban Paris family home, seventeen-year-old French schoolgirl Pauline Moreau reaches out in a brief and tender love affair in a Parisian garret with forty-year-old artist Pierre.

Garden, Nancy. *Annie on My Mind.* Lisa and Annie meet at New York's Metropolitan Museum of Art, fall in love, and then find that a public declaration is too threatening to their friends and relatives.

Gordon, Ruth, ed. *Under All Silences: Shades of Love: An Anthology of Poems.* From e. e. cummings and Sappho to Emily Dickinson and Yosan Akiko, this collection of poems celebrates the universal experience of love and passion.

Hahn, Mary Downing. *The Wind Blows Backward.* High school seniors Lauren and Spencer try to return to their innocent days of reading fantasies together, but fantasy worlds and Lauren's love cannot save Spencer from the insistent, disturbing memories of his father.

Hambly, Barbara. *Dragonsbane.* John, the Dragonsbane, fights the dreaded Black Dragon, but Jenny, a half-taught sorceress and mother of John's two sons, pays the price of the dragon's surrender.

Jordan, June. *His Own Where.* Refusing to be trapped by the hopelessness of life in a black ghetto, sixteen-year-old Buddy Rivers escapes with his girl, Angela, to a deserted cemetery shed in this short, honest, and poignant inner-city love story for mature readers.

Lee, Mildred. *People Therein.* A turn-of-the-century love story set in southern Appalachia joins Lanthy, resigned to life without marriage because she is crippled, and Drew, a botanist who comes to the Great Smoky Mountains from Boston to cure his fondness for alcohol.

Lockley, Ronald. *Seal Woman.* Truth and fantasy blend in this haunting story of an Irish girl who becomes a princess of the seals and of the man she chooses as her prince.

Mahy, Margaret. *Changeover: A Supernatural Romance.* With the help of an older boy who loves her, Laura "changes over" into a witch to fight the evil forces that are attacking her little brother.

(Continued)

Sherman, Josepha. *Child of Faerie, Child of Earth.* Percinet, the son of the queen of Faerie, is in love with a mortal girl, but can she accept his love and the presence of magic in her life?

Tepper, Sheri S. *Beauty.* In this modern retelling of the fairy tale, Beauty avoids the sleeping spell and trips through time into different worlds, searching for beauty and love.

According to Constance Mellon, short stories and magazine articles offer the most appealing formats for teenagers choosing their leisure reading materials.[2] Most of the selections below are outstanding short-story collections that vary in tone and topic, but not in quality. Two books, however, offer brief, but compelling, material in formats other than prose short stories. First is *Dear America: Letters Home from Vietnam,* a compilation of letters written by service personnel and civilians during the Vietnam War, and second is *Trail of Stones,* a collection of narrative poetry drawing on the thematic elements of potent folktales. Both stand as reminders that teenagers with limited leisure reading time can still explore a wealth of literature beyond story.

Bauer, Marion Dane, ed. *Am I Blue? Coming Out from the Silence.* Sixteen short stories, told from gay and lesbian perspectives by popular young adult authors, explore pride, individuality, and struggle.

Bradbury, Ray. *I Sing the Body Electric!* In this collection of eighteen stories, the author writes of mechanical grandmothers and fourth-dimensional babies as well as the Irish Republican Army and Texas chicken farmers.

Cofer, Judith Ortiz. *An Island Like You.* Twelve beautifully written stories capture the pain and joy of teens growing up Puerto Rican in a New Jersey barrio.

Crutcher, Chris. *Athletic Shorts: Six Short Stories.* These tales of love, death, bigotry, and heroism tell of real people with the courage to stand up to a world that often puts them down.

Edelman, Bernard. *Dear America: Letters Home from Vietnam.* In their personal letters, soldiers and civilians reveal the pain, frustration, confusion, and anger that were part of their daily lives in Vietnam.

Fink, Ida. *Scrap of Time: And Other Stories.* Unforgettable stories evoke the horrific time when Polish Jews waited and suffered while the Nazis destroyed their lives.

King, Stephen. *Night Shift.* The author of *Carrie* serves up a horrifying collection of short stories packed with vampires, bogeymen, a cellar full of rats, and a fatal can of beer.

Lee, Tanith. *Red as Blood; or, Tales from the Sisters Grimmer.* These bizarre and chilling new twists to old fairy tales are told by a master fantasy writer.

Lester, Julius. *This Strange New Feeling.* Three black slave couples reach freedom by different paths, but all experience an emancipation made richer by their dangerous struggle.

(Continued)

---

2. Constance Mellon. "Leisure Reading Choices of Rural Teens," *School Library Media Quarterly* 18 (summer 1990): 223–228.

Sieruta, Peter D. *Heartbeats and Other Stories.* Depicting joy and pain, love and sorrow, family conflicts and relationships, these nine short stories feature teenagers dealing with life's problems and issues.

Strauss, Gwen. *Trail of Stones.* These dark and dramatic retellings of fairy tales in poetic monologues are accompanied by equally stark drawings.

Zolotow, Charlotte, ed. *Early Sorrow: Ten Stories of Youth.* Themes range from the end of a special relationship to the loss of a special possession, from the death of a loved one to a loss of self, in these stories about the first sorrows of youth.

Compliments of: [_____]
NAME OF LIBRARY

From *Best Books for Young Adults,* 2d ed., ALA 2000
Young Adult Library Services Association, a division of the American Library Association

For more book lists go to <www.ala.org/yalsa/booklists>

There's no question that sports play an important role in the lives of many teenagers. Some want to read about the struggles of real athletes, and for these readers we offer such books as *Little Girls in Pretty Boxes* and *Winning Ways*. Others may choose to read fictional stories where sports serve as a metaphor for life, and for them entries include such works as *Moves Make the Man* and *Runner*. Still others may ask for books about a particular sport, such as hockey *(Bad Boy)*, basketball *(The Last Shot)*, or football *(Winning)*. But sports aren't the exclusive domain of novelists and chroniclers; they are also the raw material of many fine poets, showcased here in *American Sports Poems*.

Blais, Madeleine. *In These Girls, Hope Is a Muscle.* The Amherst Lady Hurricanes have always been good but never quite good enough to go to the girl's basketball championship. One season, though, things are different.

Brancato, Robin F. *Winning.* After sustaining a paralyzing injury in a high school football game, Gary Madden is forced to face the fact that he may never walk again.

Brooks, Bruce. *Moves Make the Man.* As Jerome, a black athlete, shares his skills and interest in basketball with Bix, a white baseball player, their friendship grows and the game becomes a reflection of both their lives.

Deuker, Carl. *On the Devil's Court.* Seventeen-year-old Joe Faust must decide if it's worth selling his soul to the devil for one perfect season of basketball.

Frey, Darcy. *The Last Shot: City Streets, Basketball Dreams.* Journalist Frey follows the lives of four hoop stars of Abraham Lincoln High School as they pursue their dreams of athletic scholarships.

Knudson, R. R., and May Swenson, eds. *American Sports Poems.* Representing a wide variety of sports, from skateboarding to baseball, this treasury of nearly two hundred poems conveys the vigor of American sports and their heroes and heroines.

Macy, Sue. *Winning Ways: A Photohistory of American Women in Sports.* Macy's social and photographic history treats women's sports in the United States—from the 1800s, when even bicycle riding was unacceptable, to the present.

Ritter, John H. *Choosing Up Sides.* Luke's preacher father believes that left-handedness is a sign of the devil, and Luke's love of baseball, especially his left-handed pitching, leads to a family tragedy.

Ryan, Joan. *Little Girls in Pretty Boxes: The Making and Breaking of Elite Gymnasts and Figure Skaters.* You'll never look at Olympic champion gymnasts and figure skaters in the same way after reading this startling exposé of how young female athletes suffer physically and psychologically for their gold.

(Continued)

Voigt, Cynthia. *Runner.* Bullet, a seventeen-year-old cross country runner, finds that compromise is sometimes necessary if an athlete is going to be the best.

Wallace, Rich. *Wrestling Sturbridge.* Living in Sturbridge, Pennsylvania, where wrestling is king, high school senior Benny must compete against his best friend for a spot on the team.

Wieler, Diana. *Bad Boy.* AJ and Tulley have been best friends both on and off the ice for years, but AJ's discovery of Tulley's secret threatens their friendship and AJ's control over his own violence.

Adolescence is a time of possibilities, and one possibility is starting over. Some of these beginnings are forced because of a nuclear holocaust *(Children of the Dust),* while others *(Unicorns in the Rain)* reflect a choice on the part of gutsy protagonists. Heroines must make the best of their situations *(Eva)* and heroes discover that they can make themselves fit into the role rather than being born to it *(The Postman).* There's real-life drama here *(The Great Fire)* and situations readers can only begin to imagine *(Z for Zachariah).* But whether set in ancient Egypt or contemporary California, these books all offer the possibilities of remaking lives—the readers' as well as the protagonists'.

Brin, David. *The Postman.* Wearing the uniform of a long-dead postman, Gordon Krantz travels among scattered communities in the western United States, struggling against survivalists and uniting people in a post–nuclear-holocaust America.

Cohen, Barbara. *Unicorns in the Rain.* Violence, pollution, and overcrowding have reached the point of no return. One family has built a large ship, an ark, and filled it with animals, and now it's starting to rain. . . .

Dickinson, Peter. *Eva.* After a violent auto accident, thirteen-year-old Eva wakes up in a hospital to find she must learn how to live as a chimpanzee.

Kovic, Ron. *Born on the Fourth of July.* Beginning with the battle that leaves him paralyzed from the chest down, Kovic tells of his struggle to reenter American society—a struggle that leads him to become a leading antiwar activist.

Lawrence, Louise. *Children of the Dust.* Three generations of the same family represent the two human factions—those who mutated because of exposure to the nuclear holocaust and those who were sheltered.

Le Guin, Ursula K. *Beginning Place.* Irena and Hugh each follow a hidden path to Tembreabrezi, a fantasy place, where they struggle to save their friends and make peace with the real world.

Levitin, Sonia. *Escape from Egypt.* Miracles, plagues, and love are only part of what two teens—Jesse, a Hebrew slave, and Jennat, a half-Egyptian, half-Syrian girl—confront in this retelling of the biblical story of the Exodus.

Marsden, John. *Tomorrow, When the War Began.* When they return from a wilderness camping trip, Ellie and her friends are shocked to discover Australia has been invaded and soon find fighting and surviving have become their way of life.

McIntyre, Vonda N. *Dreamsnake.* Snake, a young healer in a dangerous post-holocaust world, undertakes an arduous search for a replacement for Grass, the slain dreamsnake vital to her profession.

(Continued)

Murphy, Jim. *The Great Fire.* The terrible Chicago Fire of 1871 is seen from the viewpoints of eyewitnesses and illustrated with period drawings in Murphy's vivid look at the famous disaster.

Murphy, Pat. *City, Not Long After.* Following a devastating plague, a teenage girl leads the surviving residents of San Francisco, all artists and dreamers, against an invasion by a cruel despot.

O'Brien, Robert C. *Z for Zachariah.* In a peaceful valley, two survivors of an atomic holocaust are brought together—one a self-sufficient young girl, the other a killer bent on killing again.

One might think that because young adults live their own survival stories they would show little interest in those of others fighting for their lives. Not so. Tales of survival, ranging from surviving the elements of nature *(Adrift)* to surviving the treachery of humankind *(I Am the Cheese),* repeatedly rank high on teen interest polls. There's a mix here of the real *(Alive)* and the fictional *(Between a Rock and a Hard Place),* of the triumphant *(Tulku)* and the tragic *(Where the Broken Heart Still Beats),* reminding readers that surviving isn't always a given.

Callahan, Steven. *Adrift: Seventy-Six Days Lost at Sea.* When his small sailboat sinks in the Atlantic, Steve Callahan spends seventy-six days in a five-foot inflatable raft, drifting 1,800 miles before rescue.

Carter, Alden R. *Between a Rock and a Hard Place.* Stranded in the Minnesota wilderness, Mark and Randy have only each other to rely on.

Cormier, Robert. *I Am the Cheese.* A victim of amnesia, and under the influence of drugs administered by mysterious and unidentified questioners, teenager Adam searches through haunting memories that must not be recalled or revealed if he is to survive.

Courlander, Harold. *African, a Novel.* Captured by slavers in a village raid, Wes Hunu survives the ocean crossing from Dahomey and life on a Georgia plantation, eventually escaping with the hope that somewhere in America there is a future for him.

Dickinson, Peter. *Tulku.* Surviving a Boxer massacre at a Christian mission in China, thirteen-year-old Theodore accompanies an eccentric British plant collector and her guide lover through danger-laden territory to Tibet and a Buddhist monastery.

Elder, Lauren, and Shirley Streshinsky. *And I Alone Survived.* The true story of a courageous young woman, who, as sole survivor of a plane crash in the High Sierras, spends a grueling ordeal in the mountains.

Gibbons, Sheila. *Ellen Foster.* After her mother's untimely death, young Ellen must survive despite her abusive father and other relatives who want no part of her.

Holman, Felice. *Slake's Limbo.* A loser and loner picked on by everyone, Slake finds refuge in a subway that becomes his home for 121 days.

Kazimiroff, Theodore L. *Last Algonquin.* Joe Two Trees, an Algonquin Native American orphaned at age thirteen, first tries to make his way in the hostile white man's world, but finally returns to a traditional lifestyle.

Meyer, Carolyn. *Where the Broken Heart Still Beats: The Story of Cynthia Ann Parker.* Discovered and forced to return to her own family in 1836, twenty-four years after her capture by Commanche Indians, Cynthia Ann Parker is tragically unable to adjust to life away from the tribe she now claims as her own.

(Continued)

Read, Piers Paul. *Alive: The Story of the Andes Survivors.* A compassionate account of sixteen young rugby players who survive a plane crash in the Andes and live for ten weeks on faith, finally choosing to use the bodies of their dead comrades for sustenance.

Renvoize, Jean. *Wild Thing.* Morag, a foster child, runs away to the isolated wilderness of the Scottish mountains, where she is happy for a time but soon realizes that no one can survive alone.

Books of suspense are designed to keep readers on the edges of their seats, whether reading about miniaturized scientists engaged in a race against time *(Fantastic Voyage)* or terrorists holding a youngster hostage *(On the Edge).* In many books there's a chilling element—the ambiguity concluding *The Killer's Cousin,* the delicious ghost story in *Woman in Black,* and the all-too-real threat to family farms in *The Auctioneer.* Occasionally, as in *Killing Mr. Griffin,* suspense comes from unexpected quarters. After all, readers know on the first page who killed the English teacher, but the suspense plays out as one member of the guilty group stalks the others. And, in Avi's *The Fighting Ground,* suspense comes through situation and language, as the reader, like the protagonist, Jonathon, must struggle with the mostly unfamiliar German language of the Hessian captors.

Asimov, Isaac. *Fantastic Voyage.* How a miniaturized submarine carrying a team of doctors travels through the bloodstream of a brilliant scientist in order to save his life.

Avi. *The Fighting Ground.* Jonathon sees his dream of heroic battle turn to a nightmare when he is captured by Hessian soldiers during the American Revolution.

Childress, Mark. *V for Victor.* Victor stumbles on a plot to land spies on the Alabama coast when his motorboat collides with a German U-boat sneaking into the harbor.

Cross, Gillian. *On the Edge.* Tug, the son of a well-known British newswoman, is captured by terrorists in a story of relentless suspense.

Duncan, Lois. *Killing Mr. Griffin.* A group of high school students kidnaps a strict English teacher in order to get even with him—and what begins as a prank becomes a horror.

Griffin, Adele. *The Other Shepards.* Geneva and Holland Shepard must travel far from their Greenwich Village townhouse to dispel the ghosts of their older brothers and sister, who died nearly twenty years earlier.

Hill, Susan. *Woman in Black.* An old-fashioned ghost story of quiet horror is set on the desolate English moors.

Samson, Joan. *The Auctioneer.* What begins as a harmless Saturday pastime turns sinister when the auctioneering stranger in town becomes its most influential and evil citizen.

Shusterman, Neal. *The Dark Side of Nowhere.* Feeling trapped and bored in his normal, peaceful hometown, Jason slowly learns that he and most of the townspeople are aliens.

Sleator, William. *House of Stairs.* Five sixteen-year-old orphans find themselves alone in an experimental nightmare where stairs and landings stretch as far as the eye can see and a weird red light trains them to dance for their food.

(Continued)

Werlin, Nancy. *The Killer's Cousin.* After David is acquitted of murder and moves in with his aunt and uncle, he finds his new home to be less safe and secure than he'd hoped.

Yolen, Jane, and Bruce Coville. *Armageddon Summer.* In alternating chapters, Marina and Jed tell how they witnessed a cult's preparation for the end of the world.

Like tales of survival, fine accounts of war often strip events and characters to their most basic elements and thus offer readers opportunities to contemplate what it means to be human in this most inhuman of all activities. The following accounts cover many armed conflicts by examining the historical figures *(Unconditional Surrender)*, archetypal soldiers *(Fallen Angels)*, civilians *(Manzanar)*, resistors *(Bright Candles)*, survivors *(The Girl with the White Flag)*, and military institutions *(Ender's Game)*.

Armor, John, and Peter Wright. *Manzanar.* The tragic internment of Japanese Americans during World War II at one California relocation center is documented through Armor's evocative words and Ansel Adams's photos.

Benchley, Nathaniel. *Bright Candles: A Novel of the Danish Resistance.* Two teenagers turn from pranks to sabotage in this tense story of a people pushed to their limits by the tyranny of the Nazi regime in Denmark.

Card, Orson Scott. *Ender's Game.* Andrew "Ender" Wiggin, a young genius in Battle School, where he is training to fight the alien Buggers, has to put his skills to the ultimate test much sooner than he expected.

Dijk, Lutz Van. *Damned Strong Love: A True Story of Willi G. and Stefan K.* Based on a true event, this moving narrative tells the tragic story of a gay Polish teenager who falls in love with an occupying German soldier in 1941 and is tortured and imprisoned for the relationship.

Fast, Howard. *Hessian.* War is the awful villain and two boys are among the victims in this quiet, powerful novel of the American Revolution.

Fleischman, Paul. *Dateline: Troy.* History comes full circle in a retelling of the Trojan War accompanied by newspaper clippings of current events that show how history does indeed repeat itself.

Higa, Tomiko. *The Girl with the White Flag: An Inspiring Tale of Love and Courage in War Time.* Inspired by a World War II photograph, Higa recounts her harrowing childhood ordeal wandering Okinawa alone at the end of the war.

Leffland, Ella. *Rumors of Peace.* Growing up in California, a young girl finds the anxieties of childhood and adolescence complicated by the turmoil of World War II.

Marrin, Albert. *Unconditional Surrender: U. S. Grant and the Civil War.* In addition to pointing out the many ironies in Grant's life and his pivotal role in the Civil War, Marrin portrays a soldier's life, early medical services, and battle tactics.

(Continued)

Mason, Robert C. *Chickenhawk.* The account of an American helicopter pilot in Vietnam who recalls his military training, the horror of Vietnam combat, and the pain of coming home.

Myers, Walter Dean. *Fallen Angels.* Seventeen-year-old Richie Perry's stint in Vietnam brings home to him the agony and futility of war as he learns to kill and watches his comrades die.

Wharton, William. *Midnight Clear.* A group of unseasoned teenage soldiers standing guard in an old chalet in the Ardennes Forest in December 1944 experience firsthand the irony and tragedy of war when they desperately try to set up peaceful communications with a similar group of Germans.

This category created itself. Book after book appeared on our lists that dealt with the West, in both historical and contemporary times. There's a humorous horse opera *(Sunshine Rider),* a tragic love story *(The Man Who Loved Cat Dancing),* a lighthearted romp *(Righteous Revenge of Artemis Bonner),* an exploration of early settlers escaping their own lives "back East" *(Beyond the Divide),* and a gripping coming-of-age story *(Sweetgrass).* Although the selections vary, they retain a common element: The geographic West houses individuals who face life on their own merits and succeed or fail through their own efforts.

Bonner, Cindy. *Lily.* When hardworking farm girl Lily DeLony falls in love with Marion, the youngest member of the outlaw Beatty gang, the town of McDade, Texas, is set on its ear.

Capps, Benjamin. *Woman of the People.* Captured by the Comanches as a child, Helen fights tribal customs until she falls in love with a young warrior.

Durham, Marilyn. *The Man Who Loved Cat Dancing.* A Western, a relentless character study, a violent tragedy, but, most of all, this is a love story.

Hardman, Ric Lynden. *Sunshine Rider: The First Vegetarian Western.* On his first cattle drive, Wylie encounters a cast of colorful characters, adventures galore, and Roselle, a "cattalo" (a cross between a cow and a buffalo) that becomes his best friend.

Heidish, Marcy. *Secret Annie Oakley.* Told in flashback, this is a novelization of Annie Oakley's cruel and abused childhood.

Hudson, Jan. *Sweetgrass.* A fifteen-year-old Blackfoot girl of the 1830s must prove herself a capable woman before she can marry Eagle Sun.

Lasky, Kathryn. *Beyond the Divide.* Meribah runs away to join her father on a trek to California—and ends up surviving alone in the Sierra Nevada Mountains.

Matcheck, Diane. *The Sacrifice.* A fifteen-year-old Apsaalooka girl overcomes the objections of her family and her tribe as she tries to become a warrior, a hunter, and the "Great One" prophesied at her and her twin brother's birth.

Myers, Walter Dean. *Righteous Revenge of Artemis Bonner.* Wanting to recover his Uncle Ugly Ned's lost fortune for his widowed aunt, Artemis tracks evil Catfish Grimes through the Old West in a chase that turns into a wild, hilarious romp.

Power, Susan. *Grass Dancer.* A multigenerational story about a Sioux family begins with the love of Ghost Horse and Red Dress and ends in the 1980s with Charlene Thunder, who falls in love with Harley Wind Soldier, a grass dancer.

(Continued)

Wagoner, David. *Road to Many a Wonder.* Setting out with his wheelbarrow to seek his fortune in western gold fields, Ike Bender marries a high-spirited young woman, and together they travel roads that do indeed lead to many a wonder.

Watson, Larry. *Montana 1948.* The summer he is twelve, David watches as his family and small town are shattered by scandal and tragedy.

Compliments of: [_____]
NAME OF LIBRARY

From *Best Books for Young Adults,* 2d ed., ALA 2000
Young Adult Library Services Association, a division of the American Library Association

For more book lists go to <www.ala.org/yalsa/booklists>

Young adults may wonder about the authors who produce the literature they read. Some may even want to become writers one day. Others may read engaging literature just because librarians recommend it. Whatever the case, the books included in this list nicely satisfy these needs as each explores various components of writing. Rita Mae Brown puts her sassy imprint on advice for aspiring writers *(Starting from Scratch),* Paul Janeczko *(Poetspeak)* gives poets an opportunity to discuss the background of individual works, and Gary Blackwood *(The Shakespeare Stealer)* delivers an entertaining tale that puts Shakespeare on center stage. By far the largest number of these selections are individual author autobiographies, including Lee Bennett Hopkins's narrative verse *(Been to Yesterdays),* Sid Fleischman's and M. E. Kerr's humorous recollections (*The Abracadabra Kid* and *Me Me Me Me Me: Not a Novel,* respectively), and Lois Duncan's focused account of her literary beginnings *(Chapters: My Growth as a Writer).*

Banks, Lynne Reid. *Dark Quartet: The Story of the Brontës.* The brilliant but tortured lives of the Brontës are presented in a biographical novel that is as dramatic as *Wuthering Heights* or *Jane Eyre.*

Blackwood, Gary L. *The Shakespeare Stealer.* Widge, an orphan in Elizabethan England, is forced to use his talent for transcribing shorthand to steal Mr. Shakespeare's *Hamlet* for a rival theater company.

Brown, Rita Mae. *Starting from Scratch: A Different Kind of Writers' Manual.* Unorthodox, funny, but very practical advice on how to write—plus the author's irreverent comments on life in general.

Dahl, Roald. *Boy: Tales of Childhood.* A famous author recalls his struggle from school days to maturity in a humorous autobiography.

Duncan, Lois. *Chapters: My Growth as a Writer.* A popular author tells about her need and desire to be a writer from the time she was ten years old; examples of her early writing are used to demonstrate how life becomes fiction and to show how her career develops.

Fleischman, Sid. *The Abracadabra Kid: A Writer's Life.* From budding vaudevillian-type magician to popular writer of children's books— Fleischman describes his journey with humor and warmth.

Gallo, Donald R., ed. *Speaking for Ourselves: Autobiographical Sketches by Notable Authors of Books for Young Adults.* Popular young adult authors, from Lloyd Alexander to Paul Zindel, write brief sketches about their lives and work.

Hopkins, Lee Bennett. *Been to Yesterdays: Poems of Life.* Hopkins's autobiographical poems capture his teenage feelings, experiences, and aspirations as he deals with his parents' divorce, his grandmother's death, and his hopes to become a writer.

(Continued)

Janeczko, Paul B., ed. *Poetspeak: In Their Work, about Their Work.* Sixty-two living North American poets select and comment on their works for a teenage audience.

Kerr, M. E. *Me Me Me Me Me: Not a Novel.* A series of autobiographical anecdotes from Kerr's youth relate to their use in her novels.

McKissack, Patricia C., and Fredrick L. McKissack. *Young, Black, and Determined: A Biography of Lorraine Hansberry.* A lively biography of the young black playwright who achieved success and recognition for her contribution to the arts and her hard work as a civil rights activist.

Zindel, Paul. *Pigman and Me.* Zindel recounts his bizarre adventures growing up on Staten Island, when his neighbor's father becomes his personal "pigman" and teaches him to cope with his rootless family.

Dramatic accounts require conflict and the following books offer conflict aplenty. And it's that very conflict that is a given in the lives of young adults. Most teenagers face some kind of peer pressure. Some succumb to it *(Up Country)* while others do not *(The Chocolate War)*. Many young adults find conflict in their families *(Don't You Dare Read This, Mrs. Dunphrey)* and with social institutions *(Way Past Cool)*, but most conflict takes place within themselves *(Tears of a Tiger)*. Although the type of conflict differs, in each of the following books the protagonists deal with it themselves, sometimes with satisfactory conclusions *(Holes)* and sometimes without such happy endings *(Riding in Cars with Boys)*.

Avi. *Nothing but the Truth: A Documentary Novel.* It's against regulations to hum the national anthem in school. Philip decides to disobey the rule, and the whole nation watches what happens.

Carter, Alden R. *Up Country.* Sent to live with relatives in the country while his alcoholic mother receives treatment, city kid Carl faces a serious problem from the past.

Cole, Brock. *Goats.* Stripped naked by fellow campers and left on a deserted island, social misfits Laura and Howie survive humiliation, natural dangers, and each other.

Cormier, Robert. *The Chocolate War: A Novel.* "Sweets" abound at Trinity High while a schoolmaster feasts on his students' fear—a bitter story of one student's resistance and the high price he pays.

Cross, Gillian. *Chartbreaker.* Love and rage permeate the story of Janis Mary "Finch," a British rock star who sings "like concentrated danger."

Donofrio, Beverly. *Riding in Cars with Boys.* Denied college, Beverly loses interest in everything but riding around, drinking, smoking, and rebelling against authority. After a divorce, she arrives in New York City with a young son and turns her life around.

Draper, Sharon M. *Tears of a Tiger.* High school senior Andy Jackson is overcome by guilt after his best friend dies in an automobile accident that happened when Andy was driving drunk.

Haddix, Margaret Peterson. *Don't You Dare Read This, Mrs. Dunphrey.* Hoping that her teacher will keep her promise not to read her English journal, Tish reveals her growing anxiety, which begins with the return of her abusive father.

Mowry, Jess. *Way Past Cool.* Struggling to survive the streets of Oakland, California, thirteen-year-old Gordon and his gang of "friends" join forces with a neighboring gang to run the local drug dealer off their turf, but are hindered rather than helped by the police.

(Continued)

Sachar, Louis. *Holes.* Stanley Yelnats is sentenced to Camp Green Lake, where he finds a treasure and puts an end to a long-running curse on his family.

Swarthout, Glendon. *Bless the Beasts and Children.* Five misfits in an Arizona boys' camp sneak out on a daring escapade to save a herd of buffalo from bloodthirsty gun-toting tourists.

Turner, Megan Whalen. *The Thief.* Gen prides himself on being a master thief and is delighted to be rescued from prison under the condition that he steal a precious item from a long-lost temple.

Compliments of: [_____]

NAME OF LIBRARY

From *Best Books for Young Adults,* 2d ed., ALA 2000

Young Adult Library Services Association, a division of the American Library Association

For more book lists go to <www.ala.org/yalsa/booklists>

PART TWO

The Book Lists, 1966–1999

The Books by Author

Throughout the following complete listing of the Best Books for Young Adults, 1966 to 1999, some of the titles are noted with icons. These icons represent titles selected in three preconferences sponsored by the Young Adult Library Services Association and its predecessor, the Young Adult Services Division. The titles selected at the three preconferences were subsequently published in pamphlet form as "best of the best" lists. Not all titles selected for the best of the best lists are included in this section. A ■ indicates selection in "Still Alive: Selections from 1960 to 1974." A ▲ indicates selection in "The Best of the Best Books: Selections from 1970 to 1983." A ◆ indicates selection in "Nothin' but the Best: Selections from 1966 to 1986." A ● indicates selection in "Here We Go Again . . . 25 Years of Best Books: Selections from 1967 to 1992." Some titles were selected in more than one of the three preconferences and are so indicated. A complete roster of the titles and their authors appears in the section "The Best of the Best by Preconference."

Rolling Stone Illustrated History of Rock and Roll, 1950-1980, Rolling Stone Press, 1977. ◆
In-depth portraits illustrate the most important movers of rock and roll, from the 1950s to the present. (Nonfiction)

Aaron, Henry, and Wheeler, Lonnie. *I Had a Hammer,* HarperCollins, 1992.
Henry Aaron, the man who broke Babe Ruth's home-run record, found that his accomplishments brought cheers from some but unleashed ugly racial hatred in others. (Nonfiction)

Abdul-Jabbar, Kareem, and McCarthy, Mignon. *Kareem,* Random, 1991.
Action and day-to-day routine are combined in Abdul-Jabbar's quiet reflections in a behind-the-scenes look at his last year in professional basketball. (Nonfiction)

Abel, Elie. *Missile Crisis,* Lippincott, 1966.
President Kennedy's decisive action during the 1962 nuclear confrontation between Russia and the U.S. over missile sites in Cuba is chronicled. (Nonfiction)

Abelove, Joan. *Go and Come Back,* DK Inc./Richard Jackson, 1999.
Young Alicia wonders why the two white women have come to her Peruvian village since they hoard their liquor, value work over partying, and don't have a clue about marriage or sex. (Fiction)

■ Selected for "Still Alive: The Best of the Best, 1960–1974"

▲ Selected for "The Best of the Best Books: 1970–1983"

◆ Selected for "Nothin' but the Best: Best of the Best Books for Young Adults, 1966–1986"

● Selected for "Here We Go Again: 25 Years of Best Books: Selections from 1967 to 1992"

Abercrombie, Barbara. *Run for Your Life,* Morrow, 1984.
Writing a mystery that climaxes with a marathon while training for a similar contest, Sarah finds herself in a race with death as her fiction becomes reality. (Fiction)

Adams, Douglas. *The Hitchhiker's Guide to the Galaxy,* Harmony, 1980. ◆ ●
The hilarious journey of Arthur Dent and his friend Ford Prefect, a space hitchhiker, who escape from earth seconds before it is demolished and travel to a variety of galactic civilizations while gathering information for a hitchhiker's guidebook. (Fiction)

————, **and Carwardine, Mark.** *Last Chance to See,* Crown/Harmony, 1992.
Adams, author of the Hitchhiker's trilogy, and zoologist Carwardine embark on a personal journey filled with humor, irony, and frustations as they attempt to observe some of the earth's exotic endangered species. (Nonfiction)

Adams, Richard. *Watership Down,* Macmillan, 1974. ■ ▲
Follow the epic Tolkienesque adventures of Fiver, Hazel, and a ragtag lapin band. Rabbits will never seem the same again. (Fiction)

Adler, C. S. *Shell Lady's Daughter,* Coward, 1983.
Kelly, living in Florida with her disapproving grandmother and senile grandfather because of her mother's nervous breakdown, must decide whether her mother's needs or her own struggle for independence comes first. (Fiction)

Adoff, Arnold. *Slow Dance Heart Break Blues,* Lothrop, 1996.
Sparkling explosions of soul, this collection of contemporary poems captures the essence of teen experience. (Nonfiction)

————, **ed.** *Celebrations: A New Anthology of Black American Poetry,* Follett, 1978.
This outstanding compilation of poems by eighty-five black poets, familiar and new, is a celebration of black life as reflected in diverse themes, including "The Idea of Ancestry," "The Southern Road," "Young Soul," and "Make Music with Your Life." (Nonfiction)

Agard, John, comp. *Life Doesn't Frighten Me at All,* Holt, 1991.
A stimulating collection of poetry by writers from all over the world, from unknowns to Bob Marley and Maya Angelou. (Nonfiction)

Alabisco, Vincent, et al., eds. *Flash! The Associated Press Covers the World,* Abrams, 1999.
This tribute to the fearless men and women who have put their lives on the line for 150 years to bring us information and photographs of worldwide events is both moving and exciting. (Nonfiction)

Alcock, Vivien. *Singer to the Sea God,* Delacorte, 1994.
Marooned on a mysterious island, Phaidon must confront the ancient gods and monsters that he and his uncle have always scorned. (Fiction)

Alder, Elizabeth. *King's Shadow,* Farrar, 1996.
Despite having had his tongue cut out while watching his father's murder, Evyn rises from serfdom to become the king's foster son. (Fiction)

Aldridge, James. *Sporting Proposition,* Little, 1973.
A poor teenage boy and the town's richest girl are pitted against each other for the ownership of a pony. (Fiction)

Alexander, Lloyd. *Beggar Queen,* Dutton, 1984.
As the kingdom of Westmark is torn by brutal civil strife, Theo must balance his personal and political responsibilities and face the monster in himself. (Fiction)

————. *Kestrel,* Dutton, 1982.
In this sequel to *Westmark,* Theo, along with his revolutionary friends, helps Mickie, now the queen, to victory when Westmark is invaded by the neighboring country. (Fiction)

————. *The Iron Ring,* Dutton, 1998.
There's high adventure in this quest for honor, as young King Tamar loses everything in a dice game and enters a battle between good and evil while trying to resolve his debt. (Fiction)

————. *Westmark,* Dutton, 1981. ▲
Forced to leave town because of a murder he thinks he committed, Theo becomes involved with a medicine showman, a dwarf, and a beautiful girl—and with Cabbarus, who is influencing the king against him. (Fiction)

Ali, Muhammad, and Durham, Richard. *Greatest: My Own Story,* Random, 1975. ▲
Heavyweight boxing champ and outrageous poet, Muhammad Ali reveals the man behind the gloves. (Nonfiction)

Allen, Maury. *Jackie Robinson: A Life Remembered,* Watts, 1987.
A compassionate biography/oral history of the first black pro baseball player, who demonstrated competitiveness and courage. (Nonfiction)

Allen, Terry, ed. *Whispering Wind; Poetry by Young American Indians,* Doubleday, 1972.
The wind whispers and the heart soars with the eagle in these brief, moving poems on loneliness, love, and the search for self. (Nonfiction)

Alvarez, Julia. *In the Time of the Butterflies,* Algonquin, 1995.
Dede and her three sisters, "Las Mariposas," turn from being interested in hair ribbons to gun-

running and acts of political sabotage against the despotic Dominican Republic dictator, Trujillo. (Fiction)

Amos, James. *Memorial: A Novel of the Vietnam War,* Crown, 1990.
Standing in front of the Vietnam War Memorial, Marine Lt. Jakes vividly recalls the horrors leading to its creation. (Fiction)

Amosov, Nikolai. *Open Heart,* Simon & Schuster, 1967.
Life and death drama fills this absorbing personal diary of two days and nights in the life of a compassionate Russian heart surgeon. (Nonfiction)

Anastos, Phillip. *Illegal: Seeking the American Dream,* Rizzoli, 1992.
Expressions of bleak desperation and tentative hope are captured in photographs of "illegal aliens" crossing the Rio Grande and searching for a better life in America. (Nonfiction)

Anderson, Joan. *American Family Farm,* Harcourt Brace Jovanovich, 1990.
Focusing on three separate families from Massachusetts, Georgia, and Iowa, this photo essay examines the typical joys and struggles of running the small family farm. (Nonfiction)

Anderson, Rachel. *Bus People,* Holt, 1994.
Six heart-wrenching, interconnected stories tell about the disabled children who ride Bertram's bus to their special school. (Fiction)

Anderson, Scott. *Distant Fires,* Pfeifer-Hamilton, 1991.
Risking both life and sense of humor, two young men recreate Eric Severeid's 1930 portage and canoe trip over 1,700 miles from the tip of Lake Superior to the shores of Hudson Bay. (Nonfiction)

Andronik, Catherine M. *Quest for a King: Searching for the Real King Arthur,* Atheneum, 1990.
Andronik unravels the mysteries of King Arthur's life and places the legends in historical and geographical perspective. (Nonfiction)

Angell, Judie. *One-way to Ansonia,* Bradbury, 1985.
At the turn of the century, Rose and her siblings emigrate from Russia to New York, where—with great determination—they fight to succeed in their new environment. (Fiction)

Angelou, Maya. *All God's Children Need Traveling Shoes,* Random, 1986.
The experience of finding a "home" where she has never lived before becomes the catalyst for insights about African and American blackness for this astute and celebrated author. (Nonfiction)

————. *Gather Together in My Name,* Random, 1974. ■
This sequel to *I Know Why the Caged Bird Sings* continues the moving autobiography of a dauntless young woman forced to undertake a variety of jobs to support herself and her infant son. (Nonfiction)

————. *I Know Why the Caged Bird Sings,* Random, 1970. ■ ▲ ◆ ●
This remarkable, poetic and frank autobiography of a black girl who grew up in Arkansas, St. Louis, and San Francisco is for mature readers. (Nonfiction)

————. *Swingin' & Singin' & Gettin' Merry Like Christmas,* Random, 1976.
Angelou continues her autobiography, telling of her brief marriage, her efforts to raise her young son, and her beginning successes in show business. (Nonfiction)

Anonymous. *Go Ask Alice,* Prentice-Hall, 1971. ■ ▲ ●
The painful diary of a young girl when she accidentally falls into the contemporary drug scene. (Fiction)

Ansa, Tina McElroy. *Baby of the Family,* Harcourt Brace Jovanovich, 1991.
Lena is special, not only because she is the baby of her middle-class African American family but also because of the supernatural gifts she received at birth. (Fiction)

Anson, Jay. *Amityville Horror,* Prentice-Hall, 1977.
Bone-chilling cold, poltergeist activity, nauseating stench, unnatural noise, and green slime are only a few of the manifestations that terrify a family in their new home. Is this story a hoax or not? (Nonfiction)

Anson, Robert Sam. *Best Intentions: The Education and Killing of Edmund Perry,* Random, 1987.
This is the gripping story of events surrounding the death of black prep school student Edmund Perry at the hands of an undercover cop. (Nonfiction)

■ Selected for "Still Alive: The Best of the Best, 1960–1974"

▲ Selected for "The Best of the Best Books: 1970–1983"

◆ Selected for "Nothin' but the Best: Best of the Best Books for Young Adults, 1966–1986"

● Selected for "Here We Go Again: 25 Years of Best Books: Selections from 1967 to 1992"

Anthony, Piers. *On a Pale Horse,* Ballantine/ Del Rey, 1984. ●
During his attempted suicide, Zane kills Death and thereafter must do Death's job of collecting souls. (Fiction)

Appel, Allen. *Till the End of Time,* Doubleday, 1991.
Transported back to the time of the bombing of Pearl Harbor, Alex Balfour uses his knowledge of contemporary history to try to stop the bombing of Hiroshima and Nagasaki. (Fiction)

————. *Time after Time,* Carroll & Graf, 1986.
After traveling through time to 1917 Russia, Alex wonders if he should change history or simply escape. (Fiction)

Appelt, Kathi. *Just People and Other Poems for Young Readers & Paper/Pen/Poem: A Young Writer's Way to Begin,* Absey, 1998.
Want to write your own original poetry? These poems and commentaries on them can help you get started. (Nonfiction)

Archer, Jeffrey. *Not a Penny More, Not a Penny Less,* Doubleday, 1976.
Discovering they have been conned by a fast-talking promoter, four strangers get together to recover their million dollars. (Fiction)

Archer, Jules. *Incredible Sixties: The Stormy Years That Changed America,* Harcourt Brace Jovanovich, 1986.
Archer's thematic overview of the 1960s presents the important historical, political, and social events and personalities of the period. (Nonfiction)

Armor, John, and Wright, Peter. *Manzanar,* Times Books, 1990.
The tragic internment of Japanese Americans during World War II at one California relocation center is documented through Armor's evocative words and Ansel Adams's photos. (Nonfiction)

Armstrong, Charlotte. *Gift Shop,* Coward-McCann, 1967.
An exciting mystery in which Jean Cunliffe helps Harry Fairchild find and save a kidnapped child threatened with death. (Fiction)

Armstrong, Jennifer. *Steal Away,* Orchard/Richard Jackson, 1993.
During a dangerous escape to the north, orphaned Susannah and her unwanted gift slave, Bethlehem, form a lifelong friendship. (Fiction)

Arnoldi, Katherine. *The Amazing True Story of a Teenage Single Mom,* Hyperion; dist. by Little, Brown, 1999.
The remarkable story of a teen mom's struggle to support and educate herself comes across well in this true-to-life graphic work. (Nonfiction)

Arnosky, Jim. *Flies in the Water, Fish in the Air: A Personal Introduction to Fly Fishing,* Lothrop, 1986.
Author, illustrator, and trout fisherman, Arnosky shares his knowledge of fly-fishing, his intimate acquaintance with water, and his love of nature. (Nonfiction)

Arrick, Fran. *God's Radar,* Bradbury, 1983.
Roxie and her family, newcomers in a small town in Georgia, are seduced by religious neighbors into joining a fundamentalist church, and Roxie must make decisions, some of them against the tide. (Fiction)

————. *Steffie Can't Come Out to Play,* Dutton, 1978.
When naive fourteen-year-old Steffie runs away to New York to be a model, she meets Favor and becomes one of his prostitutes before a concerned cop intervenes. (Fiction)

————. *What You Don't Know Can Kill You,* Bantam/Starfire, 1993.
Ellen's agenda is exciting—graduation, college, lots of romance, and marriage. If it weren't for this "bug," everything would be perfect, but Ellen is HIV-positive. (Fiction)

Arter, Jim. *Gruel and Unusual Punishment,* Delacorte, 1992.
Always in trouble, Arnold jokes his way through school to hide the pain of repeating seventh grade, being friendless and fatherless and protecting a mother others consider crazy. (Fiction)

Ash, Brian, ed. *Visual Encyclopedia of Science Fiction,* Crown/Harmony, 1978.
A visually appealing compendium of SF info contains views on major themes by notable writers, a history of the genre, notes on fandom, science fiction art, movie tie-ins, and much more. (Nonfiction)

Ashabranner, Brent. *Always to Remember: The Vietnam Veterans Memorial,* Dodd, 1988.
The story of Vietnam veteran Jan C. Scruggs's struggle to build a national monument honoring Americans who died or are missing in the Vietnam War. (Nonfiction)

————. *To Live in Two Worlds: American Indian Youth Today,* Dodd, 1984.
Through words and photographs, young Native American men and women talk about their lives, on and off the reservation, and their hopes for the future. (Nonfiction)

Ashe, Arthur. *Days of Grace,* Knopf, 1994.
Ashe's memoir reveals why he was considered a champion—both on and off the tennis court. (Nonfiction)

Asimov, Isaac. *Fantastic Voyage*, Houghton-Mifflin, 1966. ■
How a miniaturized submarine carrying a team of doctors travels through the blood stream of a brilliant scientist in order to save his life. (Fiction)

———, **et al., eds.** *Creations: The Quest for Origins in Story and Science*, Crown, 1983.
Speculations on the creation of the universe and its parts in fiction, scientific observation, and religious belief are described clearly. (Nonfiction)

Atkin, S. Beth. *Voices from the Fields: Children of Migrant Farmworkers Tell Their Stories*, Little, Brown/Joy Street, 1994.
Photos and poetry accompany personal stories of the everyday problems, hopes, and dreams of Latino migrant young people, ages nine to eighteen. (Nonfiction)

———. *Voices from the Streets: Young Former Gang Members Tell Their Stories*, Little, Brown, 1997.
This is a collection of raw, unedited interviews with former gang members. (Nonfiction)

Atwood, Ann. *Haiku-Vision: In Poetry and Photography*, Scribner, 1977.
The fusion of seeing and feeling is an experience of the spirit in an exquisitely illustrated book of haiku poetry and photography. (Nonfiction)

Atwood, Margaret. *Handmaid's Tale*, Houghton, 1986.
Offred, a handmaid living in a near-future time, endures life in a society in which women able to bear children are used for procreation. (Fiction)

Auel, Jean. *Clan of the Cave Bear*, Crown, 1980. ▲
A Cro-Magnon girl-child, adopted by a tribe of Neanderthals, struggles to subdue her strong feminine creativity while growing up in their mystical and instinctive male-dominated society. (Fiction)

Avi. *Beyond the Western Sea, Book One: The Escape from Home*, Orchard Books/Richard Jackson, 1997.
Driven from their Irish home and struggling to get to America, Maura and Patrick become trapped in the slimy slums of Liverpool. (Fiction)

———. *Blue Heron*, Bradbury, 1993.
A solitary blue heron becomes a symbol of strength and peace for thirteen-year-old Maggie when she discovers a troubling change has come over her father and his new family. (Fiction)

———. *The Fighting Ground*, Lippincott, 1984.
Jonathon sees his dream of heroic battle turn to a nightmare when he is captured by Hessian soldiers during the American Revolution. (Fiction)

———. *Nothing but the Truth*, Orchard/Richard Jackson, 1992. ●
It's against regulations to hum the national anthem in school. Philip decides to disobey the rule, and the whole nation watches what happens. (Fiction)

———. *True Confessions of Charlotte Doyle*, Watts/Orchard, 1991.
The only passenger on a ship sailing from England to America in 1832, Charlotte finds herself accused of murder as she becomes involved in a plot to overthrow the villainous captain. (Fiction)

———. *Wolf Rider*, Bradbury, 1986.
When fifteen-year-old Andy gets a crank call from a man claiming to have murdered a woman, his life turns into a psychological nightmare. (Fiction)

Ayer, Eleanor, et al. *Parallel Journeys*, Simon & Schuster/Atheneum, 1996.
Looking back at their teen years, Helen Waterford, a concentration camp survivor, and Alfons Heck, who was an enthusiastic member of the Hitler Youth Group, tell about their experiences during the Third Reich. (Nonfiction)

Bach, Alice. *Waiting for Johnny Miracle*, Harper, 1980.
Twins Becky and Theo Maitland do everything together, but when cancer strikes Becky, they know that life will never be the same again in this sensitive portrait of a family in crisis. (Fiction)

Bach, Richard. *Biplane*, Harper, 1966.
Trading in his modern plane for a 1929 open cockpit biplane, the writer makes a hazardous cross country flight from North Carolina to California. (Nonfiction)

Bachman, Richard. *Long Walk*, Signet, 1979.
Of the one hundred boys who begin a grueling marathon walk, ninety-nine will die—and one

---

- ■ Selected for "Still Alive: The Best of the Best, 1960–1974"
- ▲ Selected for "The Best of the Best Books: 1970–1983"
- ◆ Selected for "Nothin' but the Best: Best of the Best Books for Young Adults, 1966–1986"
- ● Selected for "Here We Go Again: 25 Years of Best Books: Selections from 1967 to 1992"

will have his every wish granted. Or will he? (Fiction)

Bachrach, Susan D. *Tell Them We Remember: The Story of the Holocaust,* Little, Brown, 1995.
The story of the Holocaust is told clearly and dramatically. (Nonfiction)

Bacon, Katherine Jay. *Shadow and Light,* Macmillan/Margaret K. McElderry, 1987.
During a summer at her beloved grandmother's farm in Vermont, fifteen-year-old Emma learns to cope with her grandmother's dying. (Fiction)

Bagley, Desmond. *Landslide,* Doubleday, 1967.
Amnesiac Bob Boyd struggles to find out who he really is in this adventure and suspense novel. (Fiction)

————. *Vivero Letter,* Doubleday, 1968.
The discovery of a sixteenth-century golden plate leads to murder and an ancient Mayan city in Quintana Roo. (Fiction)

Balducci, Caroyln. *Is There a Life after Graduation, Henry Birnbaum?* Houghton, 1971.
Henry Birnbaum and David Schoen, best friends in Queens, enroll in separate colleges and find life away from home almost overwhelmingly complicated by women and activists. (Fiction)

Baldwin, J., ed. *Whole Earth Ecolog: The Best of Environmental Tools and Ideas,* Crown, 1991.
A browser's delight, this catalog of the best ecological books, information, processes, tools, and ideas allows individuals to make an enviromental difference. (Nonfiction)

Baldwin, James. *If Beale Street Could Talk,* Dial, 1974. ■ ▲ ●
A young black couple, separated by his unjust imprisonment, are bolstered by their love for each other and the determination of her loyal family. (Fiction)

Ball, John Dudley. *Cool Cottontail,* Harper, 1967.
Virgil Tibbs, the African American detective of *In the Heat of the Night,* is assigned to a case involving a murder committed in a nudist colony. (Fiction)

————. *Johnny Get Your Gun,* Little, 1969.
Detective Virgil Tibbs is called into a case involving nine-year-old Johnny McGuire, who sets out to murder a schoolmate for breaking his transistor radio, but shoots a popular teenager instead. (Fiction)

Ballard, J. G. *Empire of the Sun,* Simon & Schuster, 1985.
Eleven-year-old Jim's orderly life in 1939 Shanghai turns into a nightmare when the Japanese attack, separate him from his family, and imprison him for three years. (Fiction)

Banfield, Susan. *Rights of Man, The Reign of Terror: The Story of the French Revolution,* Lippincott, 1990.
Do the ends justify the means? The French Revolution in all its glory and terror is chronicled in fascinating detail. (Nonfiction)

Banks, Lynne Reid. *Dark Quartet: The Story of the Brontës,* Delacorte, 1977.
The brilliant but tortured lives of the Brontës are presented in a biographical novel that is as dramatic as *Wuthering Heights* or *Jane Eyre.* (Fiction)

————. *Writing on the Wall,* Harper/Charlotte Zolotow, 1982.
Tracy is bicycling through Holland with her "punk" boyfriend when she innocently becomes involved in drug smuggling. (Fiction)

Banks, Russell. *Rule of the Bone,* HarperCollins, 1996.
Fourteen-year-old runaway Chappie becomes known as "Bone" during an adventurous year full of pot, travel, danger, and new friends. (Fiction)

Barjavel, Rene. *Ice People,* Morrow, 1971.
In a cryogenic vault under the polar ice cap an international team of scientists discovers a man and a woman who are 900,000 years old. (Fiction)

Barker, S. Omar. *Little World Apart,* Doubleday, 1966.
Two brothers find excitement and adventure while growing up on a small cattle ranch in New Mexico. (Fiction)

Barlow, Wayne Douglas, and Summers, Ian. *Barlow's Guide to Extraterrestrials,* Workman, 1980. ●
Have you ever wondered what a Puppeteer or a Vegan Mother Thing looks like? How Pegulas move or Polarians reproduce? This fascinating and meticulously detailed, illustrated guide to great science fiction aliens can tell you all that and more. (Nonfiction)

Barron, T. A. *The Lost Years of Merlin,* Putnam/Philomel, 1997.
Emrys, a young boy who washes ashore with no memory, travels to the mythical land of Fincayra to discover his true parentage and destiny. (Fiction)

Bartoletti, Susan Campbell. *Growing Up in Coal Country,* Houghton, 1998.
The harsh life of immigrant workers in the Pennsylvania coal mines is vividly brought to life in this haunting photo-essay. (Nonfiction)

Bauer, Joan. *Rules of the Road,* Putnam, 1999.
Seventeen-year-old Jenna's job at crusty Mrs. Gladstone's shoe store leads to her driving Mrs. Gladstone across country to Texas to prevent a company takeover. (Fiction)

————. *Thwonk*, Delacorte, 1996.
Teen photographer A. J. is the lucky—or is it unlucky?—recipient of a visitation from Jonathan, a wily Cupid who pierces the heart of the high-school hunk, bringing him to A. J. on his knees. (Fiction)

Bauer, Marion Dane, ed. *Am I Blue? Coming Out from the Silence*, HarperCollins, 1995.
Sixteen short stories, told from gay and lesbian perspectives by popular young adult authors, explore pride, individuality, and struggle. (Fiction)

Bauer, Steven. *Satyrday: A Fable*, Putman, 1981.
Evil Owl's attempt to rule the world requires that Matthew, a satyr, and Dairn, a boy, try to save the moon and all creatures. (Fiction)

Beake, Lesley. *Song of Be*, Holt/Edge, 1995.
In newly independent Namibia, teenager Be despairs of finding her place in the new political culture, which seems to be destroying the traditional way of life of her San people. (Fiction)

Beattie, Owen, and Geiger, John. *Buried in Ice: The Mystery of a Lost Arctic Expedition*, Scholastic, 1993.
The story of Owen Beattie's discovery of the remains of Sir John Franklin's doomed 1845 expedition through the Northwest Passage is dramatic and exciting. (Nonfiction)

Beck, Calvin. *Heroes of the Horrors*, Macmillan, 1975.
All those movie monster favorites—Karloff, Lugosi, Chaney, and Price—are here in a splendid brew of photos and text. (Nonfiction)

Begay, Shonto. *Navajo: Voices and Visions across the Mesa*, Scholastic, 1996.
Begay portrays both the traditional and the contemporary worlds of the Navajo people through his beautiful poetry, stories, and paintings. (Nonfiction)

Begley, Kathleen. *Deadline*, Putnam, 1977.
The experiences of a young newspaper reporter, whose personal and professional lives become intertwined when, for example, she celebrates her birthday in a police station, and when she writes her own mother's obituary. (Nonfiction)

Bell, Clare. *Ratha and Thistle-chaser*, Macmillan/Margaret K. McElderry, 1991.
Ratha's encounter with outsider Thistle-chaser reunites her with her forgotten past as her tribe of intelligent cats fights for survival during a severe drought. (Fiction)

————. *Ratha's Creature*, Atheneum, 1983.
Ratha, born into a society of intelligent prehistoric felines, is banished from the Clan, rescued by an unnamed male cat, and helps the Clan when she learns to tame fire. (Fiction)

Bell, David, M.D. *Time to Be Born*, Morrow, 1975.
A two-pound "preemie" and a newborn addict are only two of the many babies that Dr. Bell, a young pediatrician, cares for and also deeply cares about. (Nonfiction)

Bell, Ruth. *Changing Bodies, Changing Lives: A Book for Teens on Sex and Relationships*, Random, 1981. ▲ ◆
Here's everything you want to know about teenage sexuality, presented in an honest, explicit manner, inspired by *Our Bodies, Ourselves* and written by some of the same people. (Nonfiction)

Benchley, Nathaniel. *Bright Candles: A Novel of the Danish Resistance*, Harper, 1974.
Two teenagers turn from pranks to sabotage in this tense story of a people pushed to their limits by the tyranny of the Nazi regime in Denmark. (Fiction)

Benedict, Helen. *Safe, Strong, and Streetwise*, Little, Brown/Joy Street Books, 1987.
Both men and women can learn how to protect themselves from sexual assault. (Nonfiction)

Bennett, Cherie. *Life in the Fat Lane*, Delacorte, 1999.
Shallow, self-centered, thin homecoming queen Laura's life is turned upside down when she inexplicably starts to pile on pound after pound after pound. (Fiction)

Bennett, James. *Dakota Dream*, Scholastic, 1995.
Floyd (or Charly Black Crow, as he prefers to be called) runs away from his group home to seek his destiny as a member of the Dakota tribe. (Fiction)

————. *I Can Hear the Mourning Dove*, Houghton, 1991.
Struggling to recover from her father's death and her own suicide attempt, Grace meets rebellious Luke, a fellow patient and her first real friend. (Fiction)

- ■ Selected for "Still Alive: The Best of the Best, 1960–1974"
- ▲ Selected for "The Best of the Best Books: 1970–1983"
- ◆ Selected for "Nothin' but the Best: Best of the Best Books for Young Adults, 1966–1986"
- ● Selected for "Here We Go Again: 25 Years of Best Books: Selections from 1967 to 1992"

————. *Squared Circle,* Scholastic, 1996.
Sonny lives for basketball until his college program becomes the subject of an NCAA investigation and he begins to question his family, his coaches, and his life. (Fiction)

Berg, Elizabeth. *Durable Goods,* Random, 1994.
After their mother's death, Katie and her older sister struggle to establish a workable relationship with their harsh father on a Texas military base. (Fiction)

————. *Joy School,* Random, 1998.
Teenage Katie deals with the complexities of an unstable home when she falls in love with a young married man. (Fiction)

Bernstein, Sara Tuvel. *The Seamstress,* Putnam, 1998.
A powerful and engrossing story of twelve-year-old Seren Tuvel's lifesaving decision to walk out of her classroom in war-torn Romania and into a new life. (Nonfiction)

Berry, James. *Ajeemah and His Son,* HarperCollins/Willa Perlman, 1993.
Snatched by African slave traders, Ajeemah and his soon-to-be-married son, Atu, are shipped to Jamaica, where, though separated, they never accept their status as slaves or give up their desire for freedom. (Fiction)

Berry, Liz. *The China Garden,* Farrar, 1997.
Seventeen-year-old Londoner Clare spends a summer in Ravensmere, where she and handsome biker Mark find themselves enmeshed in a labyrinth of magic. (Fiction)

Bess, Clayton. *Tracks,* Houghton, 1986.
Eleven-year-old Blue Roan persuades his older brother to take him on the rails in Depression-era Oklahoma, where their adventures range from vicious attacks by a hobo to an almost fatal encounter with the KKK. (Fiction)

Bickham, Jack M. *Katie, Kelly and Heck,* Doubleday, 1973.
A lady, a tough guy, and a kid clash in this funny, fast-moving tale set in a rough, raw frontier town of the 1880s. (Fiction)

Bing, Leon. *Do or Die,* HarperCollins, 1992.
A bone-chilling account of gang-banging in which Bing lets Crips and Bloods, infamous rival Los Angeles gangs, speak for themselves. (Nonfiction)

Birmingham, John. *Our Time Is Now: Notes from the High School Underground,* Praeger, 1970.
In this stinging anthology uncensored high school students speak out about the injustices in the schools and in America, the home of the not-so-brave, and of changes needed now. (Nonfiction)

Bitton-Jackson, Livia. *I Have Lived a Thousand Years,* Simon & Schuster, 1998.
Thirteen when she and her family were sent to Auschwitz, Bitton-Jackson vividly describes the horrors they faced. (Nonfiction)

Blackwood, Gary L. *The Shakespeare Stealer,* Dutton, 1999.
Widge, an orphan in Elizabethan England, is forced to use his talent for transcribing shorthand to steal Mr. Shakespeare's *Hamlet* for a rival theater company. (Fiction)

Blais, Madeleine. *In These Girls, Hope Is a Muscle,* Atlantic Monthly; dist. by Publishers Group West, 1996.
The Amherst Lady Hurricanes have always been good but never quite good enough to go to the girl's basketball championship—one season, though, things are different. (Nonfiction)

Blake, Jeanne. *Risky Times: How to Be AIDS-Smart and Stay Healthy,* Workman, 1991.
The author and six teens bring you a book of facts on AIDS: how you get it, how you don't, and the decisions you must make for a healthy life. (Nonfiction)

Blankfort, Michael. *Take the A Train,* Dutton, 1978.
After he becomes the protege of black pimp and numbers man Mr. Gilboa, "Doc" Henshel, a seventeen-year-old white boy, learns some hard facts about life, love, and friendship on the electric streets of Harlem. (Fiction)

Bleier, Rocky, and O'Neill, Terry. *Fighting Back,* Stein & Day, 1975. ▲
Rocky Blair tells how he overcame the battle wounds of Vietnam through rigid self-discipline to play in the Super Bowl. (Nonfiction)

Block, Francesca Lia. *Baby Be-Bop,* HarperCollins, 1996.
Sixteen-year-old Dirk struggles to come to terms with being gay, fearful that family and friends will no longer love or accept him. (Fiction)

————. *Cherokee Bat and the Goat Guys,* HarperCollins/C. Zolotow, 1993.
Cherokee and the Goat Guys rock band descend into the wild excess of the drug-rock-punk scene and need to be rescued by Native American Coyote's wise spiritual friendship. (Fiction)

————. *Missing Angel Juan,* HarperCollins, 1994.
Witch Baby gets help from ghostly Grandpa Charlie Bat in her search for Angel Juan in New York City. (Fiction)

————. *Weetzie Bat,* Harper/C. Zolotow, 1990. ●
Lanky lizards! Punk teens Weetzie and Dirk search for love in a modern fairy tale that is

funny, moving, and unlike any book you've read before. (Fiction)

Bloor, Edward. *Tangerine*, Harcourt, 1998.
Is Tangerine, Florida, like the Bermuda Triangle? A sinkhole swallows the middle school, lightning strikes repeatedly, underground fires burn endlessly—and all newcomer Paul Fisher wants to do is play soccer, despite his thick glasses, his parents' indifference, and his evil brother. (Fiction)

Blue, Vida, and Libby, Bill. *Vida: His Own Story*, Prentice-Hall, 1972.
Baseball pitcher Vida Blue tells what it feels like to achieve instant stardom and then be expected to produce miracles on the field every day. (Nonfiction)

Blum, Joshua, and Pellington, Mark, eds., et al. *The United States of Poetry*, Abrams, 1997.
Contemporary poems are enhanced by outstanding photographs highlighting poets from Nobel laureates to rappers. (Nonfiction)

Blum, Ralph. *Old Glory and the Real-Time Freaks*, Delacorte, 1972.
Quintus Ells is encouraged by his grandfather to write, while stoned, a "map" of his seventeenth summer, describing his close relationships with family and friends for his future grandson. (Fiction)

————. *Simultaneous Man*, Little, Brown, 1970.
American scientists replace a man's mind with the memory and personality of another in this chilling tale of U.S. and Russian intrigue. (Fiction)

————, **and Blum, Judy.** *Beyond Earth: Man's Contact with UFO's*, Bantam, 1974.
A rational account documents the UFO sightings of 1973—the objects, the terrified people who saw and/or were taken aboard them, and the stories they told afterward. (Nonfiction)

Blume, Judy. *Here's to You Rachel Robinson*, Orchard/Richard Jackson, 1994.
While dealing with her own adolescent angst, Rachel Robinson, a thirteen-year-old prodigy, must endure the return home of her rebellious brother, Charles, who has been expelled from boarding school. (Fiction)

————. *Letters to Judy: What Your Kids Wish They Could Tell You*, Putnam, 1986.
A popular author responds to a large variety of letters from many young fans who have confided in her. (Nonfiction)

————. *Tiger Eyes*, Bradbury, 1981.
After her father's murder, Davey moves to Los Alamos, where she meets Wolf, a college boy whose father is dying of cancer. (Fiction)

Boas, Jacob. *We Are Witnesses: The Diaries of Five Teenagers Who Died in the Holocaust*, Holt, 1996.
The compelling and poignant diaries of five teenagers who died during the Holocaust tell their tragic, courageous stories. (Nonfiction)

Bober, Natalie. *Abigail Adams: Witness to a Revolution*, Simon & Schuster/Atheneum, 1996.
Romance, fame, and hard work are all facets of Abigail Adams' life in this vivid narrative of the American Revolution. (Nonfiction)

Bodanis, David. *Secret House: Twenty-Four Hours in the Strange and Unexpected World in Which We Spend Our Nights and Days*, Simon & Schuster, 1986.
The microbiological drama found within a house is explored from early morning to late evening. (Nonfiction)

Bode, Janet. *Beating the Odds: Stories of Unexpected Achievers*, Watts, 1992.
Racial discrimination, abuse, poverty, depression: teens and adults talk about dealing with the problems of life and making it in spite of them. (Nonfiction)

————. *Kids Having Kids: The Unwed Teenage Parent*, Watts, 1980.
Sexual conduct, the health risks associated with teenage pregnancy, birth control, and the options open to unwed mothers are covered in this guide for pregnant teenagers as well as those in danger of becoming pregnant because of lack of information. (Fiction)

————. *New Kids on the Block: Oral Histories of Immigrant Teens*, Watts, 1990.
Eleven teenage immigrants reveal the trials, frustrations and joys of making a new life in the United States after escaping poverty, repression, and even war in their native countries. (Nonfiction)

■ Selected for "Still Alive: The Best of the Best, 1960–1974"
▲ Selected for "The Best of the Best Books: 1970–1983"
◆ Selected for "Nothin' but the Best: Best of the Best Books for Young Adults, 1966–1986"
● Selected for "Here We Go Again: 25 Years of Best Books: Selections from 1967 to 1992"

————. *Voices of Rape,* Watts, 1991.
Date and stranger rape are explored through interviews with victims, perpetrators, and those involved in the medical and justice systems. (Nonfiction)

————, **and Mack, Stan.** *Hard Time: A Real Life Look at Juvenile Crime and Violence,* Delacorte, 1997.
Hard-hitting stories from young people whose lives have been dramatically affected by crime and violence—as both victims and perpetrators. (Nonfiction)

————, ————. *Heartbreak and Roses: Real-life Stories of Troubled Love,* Delacorte, 1995.
In this eye-opening collection of narratives, teens talk about their troubled love relationships. (Nonfiction)

Bogle, Donald. *Brown Sugar: Eighty Years of America's Black Female Superstars,* Harmony, 1980.
In a dazzling and informative portrait, selected black female performers are presented as individuals and as important social symbols. (Nonfiction)

Boissard, Janice. *Matter of Feeling,* Little, Brown, 1980.
From the safety of her suburban Paris family home, seventeen-year-old French schoolgirl Pauline Moreau reaches out in a brief and tender love affair in a Parisian garret with forty-year-old artist Pierre. (Fiction)

Bolden, Tonya. *Thirty-three Things Every Girl Should Know: Stories, Songs, Poems, and Smart Talk by Thirty-three Extraordinary Women,* Crown, 1999.
In poems, short stories, letters, essays, and a comic strip, thirty-three prominent and successful women share words of wisdom for young women. (Nonfiction)

Bond, Nancy. *Place to Come Back To,* Atheneum/Margaret K. McElderry, 1984.
As Charlotte finds herself strongly attracted to one of her childhood friends, she discovers how difficult it is to give and receive love. (Fiction)

Bonner, Cindy. *Lily,* Algonquin, 1993.
When hard-working farm girl Lily DeLony falls in love with Marion, the youngest member of the outlaw Beatty gang, the town of McDade, Texas, is set on its ear. (Fiction)

————. *Looking after Lily,* Algonquin, 1995.
It is 1884, and Lily is very young and very pregnant, and her outlaw husband is in a Texas jail. (Fiction)

Booher, Dianna Daniels. *Rape: What Would You Do If . . . ?* Messner, 1981.
These clear guidelines on how to judge a potential rape situation spell out specifics about what to do if a rape should occur. (Nonfiction)

Bosse, Malcolm. *Captives of Time,* Delacorte, 1987.
To escape not only plague but also the barbaric hordes that killed their parents, Anne and her mute brother make their way to their eccentric uncle in the city. (Fiction)

————. *The Examination,* Farrar, 1995.
Hong sacrifices everything to travel with his impractical, intelligent older brother Chen, protecting him from danger as they journey to the government examinations, with their promise of wealth and position. (Fiction)

Boston Women's Health Book Collective. *Our Bodies, Ourselves: A Book by and for Women,* Simon & Schuster, 1976. ■ ▲ ●
New medical findings and rethought feminist attitudes are incorporated into a completely revised edition of the now classic handbook on the female body. (Nonfiction)

Boulle, Pierre. *Whale of the Victoria Cross,* Vanguard, 1983.
A blue whale, saved from killer orcas by a British destroyer bound for the Falkland Islands, becomes a friend to the entire fleet. (Nonfiction)

Bouton, Jim. *Ball Four: My Life and Hard Times Throwing the Knuckleball in the Big Leagues,* World, 1970.
Definitely not for hero worshippers, this is a lively, often funny but devastating account of the antics of baseball players, managers, and coaches by former big leaguer Bouton. (Nonfiction)

Bova, Ben. *Multiple Man: A Novel of Suspense,* Bobbs-Merrill, 1976.
President James J. Halliday has a top-level security secret—several exact duplicates of himself have been mysteriously and secretly killed. Press secretary Meric Albano wants to know why. (Fiction)

————. *Welcome to Moonbase,* Ballantine, 1988.
From lunar cuisine to low gravity football, this handbook introduces new employees to Moonbase, Inc. (Fiction)

Boyd, Malcolm. *Are You Running with Me, Jesus?* Holt, 1966.
These are the provocative prayers of a former campus chaplain who is concerned with all facets of modern life. (Nonfiction)

Bradbury, Ray. *I Sing the Body Electric!* Knopf, 1969.
In this collection of eighteen stories the author writes of mechanical grandmothers and fourth-dimensional babies as well as the Irish Republican Army and Texas chicken farmers. (Fiction)

Bradford, Richard. *Red Sky at Morning,* Lippincott, 1968.
Joshua Arnold, a wise, wry man-child, must cope with an absent father and a sherry-tippling

mother, and learn to live in a new town, make friends, and finish growing up. (Fiction)

Bradley, Marion Zimmer. *Hawkmistress!* NAL/DAW, 1982.
Forbidden to use her gift for communicating with animals and pushed by her father to marry a man she hates, Romilly MacAran flees to the hills of Darkover. (Fiction)

Bradley, William Warren. *Life on the Run,* Quadrangle, 1976.
Knicks veteran Bradley talks about the sport he loves, his teammates, and the pressures of professional basketball. (Nonfiction)

Bradshaw, Gillian. *Beacon at Alexandria,* Houghton, 1987.
Charis flees ancient Ephesus disguised as a man to avoid an arranged marriage and makes her way to Alexandria to study medicine. (Fiction)

————. *Hawk of May,* Simon & Schuster, 1980.
The war between good and evil is portrayed in this fantasy in which King Arthur's nephew, Gwalchmai, a reluctant warrior, first turns to his mother, an evil sorceress, for knowledge and power, then sets out to join King Arthur. (Fiction)

Braithwaite, Edward. *Paid Servant,* McGraw-Hill, 1968.
Too white for an African American family, too black for a white family, four-year-old Roddy poses a problem for welfare officer Braithwaite, who tries desperately to find him a home. (Nonfiction)

Brancato, Robin F. *Come Alive at 505,* Knopf, 1980.
Danny Fetzer copes with senior-year anxiety through his imaginary radio station WHUP, 505 on the dial, and through it becomes involved and obsessed with classmate Mimi. (Fiction)

————. *Sweet Bells Jangled out of Tune,* Knopf, 1982.
Everybody in Windsor laughs at Eva Dohrmann, the town eccentric—everybody but Ellen, her fifteen-year-old granddaughter. (Fiction)

————. *Winning,* Knopf, 1977. ▲ ◆
After sustaining a paralyzing injury in a high school football game, Gary Madden is forced to face the fact that he may never walk again. (Fiction)

Brand, Stewart. *Last Whole Earth Catalog,* Random, 1971.
This supercatalog, a kind of counterculture *Consumer Reports,* lists everything from papoose-packs to Moog synthesizers and all items are "useful as tools, relevant to independent education, high quality or low cost, and easily available by mail." (Nonfiction)

Brandenburg, Jim. *An American Safari: Adventures on the North American Prairie,* Walker, 1996.
Prairie dogs, bison, and rattlesnakes are only a part of the endangered ecological treasures captured in Brandenburg's exquisite color photographs and memorable personal experiences. (Nonfiction)

————. *To the Top of the World: Adventures with Arctic Wolves,* Walker, 1994.
In a wildlife photo-documentary, Brandenburg enters the world of a wolf pack on Ellesmen Island and captures the animal's behaviors, personalities, and intelligence. (Nonfiction)

Branscum, Robbie. *Girl,* Harper, 1986.
Though left in the exploitive care of their grandmother, a girl and her siblings find strength in each other as well as hope in the dream of their mother's return. (Fiction)

Bredes, Don. *Hard Feelings,* Atheneum, 1977.
Explicit in language and incident, this is sixteen-year-old Bernie Hergruter's story of growing up—confronting a class bully intent on hurting him, getting along with his family, and understanding his sexuality. (Fiction)

Brenner, Joseph H., and Coles, Robert M.D., et al. *Drugs and Youth: Medical, Psychiatric and Legal Facts,* Liveright, 1970.
The authors give clinical studies and young drug users equal time in an objective, informative report. (Nonfiction)

Bridgers, Sue Ellen. *All Together Now,* Knopf, 1979. ◆
Twelve-year-old Casey befriends thirty-three-year-old retarded Dwayne and saves him from being sent to a home. (Fiction)

————. *Home before Dark,* Knopf, 1976.
When her father takes his migrant family back to his childhood home in Florida, fourteen-year-old Stella Willis is determined to put down roots and never leave again. (Fiction)

■ Selected for "Still Alive: The Best of the Best, 1960–1974"

▲ Selected for "The Best of the Best Books: 1970–1983"

◆ Selected for "Nothin' but the Best: Best of the Best Books for Young Adults, 1966–1986"

● Selected for "Here We Go Again: 25 Years of Best Books: Selections from 1967 to 1992"

———. *Notes for Another Life,* Knopf, 1981. ▲
Caught between their father's recurrent bouts with mental illness and their mother's career ambitions, teenagers Kevin and Wren attempt to preserve their fragile identities and relationships. (Fiction)

———. *Permanent Connections,* Harper, 1987. ●
While caring for an ill relative, Rob finds that spending his junior year in a rural town is living hell, until he meets equally unhappy Ellery. (Fiction)

———. *Sara Will,* Harper, 1985.
In a story of acceptance and coming of age, Sara Will's life is disrupted forever by the arrival of her brother-in-law, his unwed teenage niece, and her baby. (Fiction)

Briggs, Raymond. *When the Wind Blows,* Schocken, 1983. ◆
In this grim, cartoon-style satire an elderly British couple innocently—and futilely—try to prepare for nuclear attack by following government directives. (Fiction)

Brin, David. *The Postman,* Bantam, 1985.
Wearing the uniform of a long dead postman, Gordon Krantz travels among scattered communities in the western United States, struggling against survivalists and uniting people in a post–nuclear-holocaust America. (Fiction)

Brooks, Bruce. *Midnight Hour Encores,* Harper, 1986.
Arrogant and musically gifted Sib and her father travel across country so that she can audition for a musical genius and meet the "hippie" mother who deserted her at birth. (Fiction)

———. *The Moves Make the Man,* Harper, 1985. ●
As Jerome, a black athlete, shares his skills and interest in basketball with Bix, a white baseball player, their friendship grows and the game becomes a reflection of both their lives. (Fiction)

———. *No Kidding,* Harper, 1990.
In a not-too-distant future where alcoholism is rampant, fourteen-year-old Sam must decide the fate of his alcoholic mother and younger brother. (Fiction)

———. *On the Wing,* Scribner, 1990.
A companion to the PBS-TV series *Nature,* this beautifully written and illustrated book explores the life of birds—from feathers to flight. (Nonfiction)

———. *Predator!* Farrar, Straus & Giroux, 1992.
Stunning color photographs and a fascinating text illuminate the never-ending quest for food that faces all animals in the wild. (Nonfiction)

———. *What Hearts,* HarperCollins/Laura Geringer, 1993.
Follow Asa from age seven to age twelve as he learns how to appreciate his family. (Fiction)

Brooks, Earle, and Brooks, Rhoda. *Barrios of Manta,* New American Library, 1966.
A young sales engineer and his schoolteacher wife describe their Peace Corps activities among the poverty-stricken people of Manta, Ecuador. (Nonfiction)

Brooks, Martha. *Bone Dance,* Orchard, 1998.
When Alexandra inherits a log cabin in the wilderness from a father she never met, she goes there to make sense of their relationship—and meets Lonny. (Fiction)

———. *Traveling on into the Light and Other Stories,* Orchard/Melanie Kroupa, 1995.
In eleven short stories, readers meet teens, ranging from Laker, a throwaway dealing with his mother's rejection, to Sidonie and Kieran in their journey toward adulthood. (Fiction)

———. *Two Moons in August,* Little, Brown, 1993.
Surrounded by a family unable to come to terms with the death of her mother, Sidonie conquers her self-doubts and faces the fact that survival means accepting life with all its tragedies and triumphs. (Fiction)

Brooks, Polly Schoyer. *Beyond the Myth: The Story of Joan of Arc,* HarperCollins/Lippincott, 1991.
Condemned as a witch but later canonized as a saint, young Joan, inspired by her love of France, leads her countrymen in their battle against the English. (Nonfiction)

Brooks, Terry. *Magic Kingdom for Sale—Sold!* Ballantine/Del Ray, 1986.
In a funny fantasy adventure, disillusioned sorrowing widower Ben buys a magic kingdom for one million dollars only to find a run-down castle operated by a motley group of inept courtiers. (Fiction)

———. *Sword of Shannara,* Random, 1977.
A small band of humans, elves, and dwarfs must face the armies of an evil sorcerer in order to reach the sword that can destroy him. (Fiction)

Brown, Dee. *Bury My Heart at Wounded Knee: An Indian History of the American West,* Holt, 1971. ▲
Battle by battle, massacre by massacre, broken treaty by broken treaty, this is a documented, gripping chronicle of the Native American struggle from 1860 to 1890 against the white man. (Nonfiction)

———. *Creek Mary's Blood,* Holt, 1980.
They call her Creek Mary, a proud and beautiful daughter of a Muskogee chief and a leader among

her people. The story of Creek Mary and her descendants, four generations of Native Americans, begins with Revolutionary War Georgia and ends with the 1905 White House. (Fiction)

Brown, Mary. *Pigs Don't Fly*, Baen; dist. by St. Martin's, 1995.
With the help of her magic unicorn-horn ring, Somerdai acquires a horse, a dog, a bird, a turtle, a handsome knight, and a flying pig on her quest to find home and happiness. (Fiction)

Brown, Michael. *Laying Waste: The Poisoning of America by Toxic Chemicals*, Pantheon, 1980.
The dumping of industrial chemical waste creates a disaster at Love Canal, and the reporter who breaks the story warns that it can happen again. (Nonfiction)

Brown, Rita Mae. *Starting from Scratch: A Different Kind of Writers' Manual*, Bantam, 1988.
Unorthodox, funny, but very practical advice on how to write—plus the author's irreverent comments on life in general. (Nonfiction)

Brown, Turner, Jr. *Black Is*, Grove, 1969.
"Black is when somebody brings you home to lunch during Brotherhood Week—after dark" and other definitions of black not in the dictionary. (Nonfiction)

Bruchac, Joseph. *Dawn Land*, Fulcrum, 1994.
Young Hunter and his three faithful dog companions travel far to the West to save the Only People and his newly adopted family from the vicious Stone People. (Fiction)

Buck, Rinker. *Flight of Passage*, Hyperion; dist. by Little, Brown, 1998.
In this true coming-of-age adventure, two teenage brothers pilot a Piper Cub from New York to San Diego. (Nonfiction)

Bull, Emma. *Finder: A Novel of the Borderlands*, Tor; dist. by St. Martin's, 1995.
A human living in the Borderlands fantasy world, Orient (known as the Finder) is asked by the police to use his talent for locating missing things and people in a murder investigation. (Fiction)

————. *War for the Oaks*, Berkley/Ace, 1987.
A mad phouka, the queen of the Faerie, and band leader Eddi McCandry battle the Dark Court's evil power, in a tale of rock music in Minneapolis. (Fiction)

Bunting, Eve. *If I Asked You, Would You Stay?* Lippincott, 1984.
Crow and Valentine step tentatively out of their private worlds of hurt and loneliness toward one another. (Fiction)

————. *Jumping the Nail*, Harcourt, 1993.
Some teens see jumping off the Nail, a ninety-foot cliff above the bottomless sea, as a way to prove their love for another, but Elisa jumps for a more sinister reason. (Fiction)

Burch, Jennings Michael. *They Cage the Animals at Night*, NAL, 1984.
The author recalls the sometimes kind but often brutal treatment he received between ages eight and eleven when he was placed in a series of institutions and foster homes by his mother, who was ill and could no longer care for him or his brothers. (Nonfiction)

Burchard, Sue. *Statue of Liberty: Birth to Rebirth*, Harcourt Brace Jovanovich, 1985.
Packed full of facts and anecdotes about Miss Liberty, this book chronicles the statue's conception to its centennial reconstruction and plans for the future. (Nonfiction)

Burgess, Melvin. *Smack*, Holt, 1999.
English teens Tar and Gemma run away from home and into heroin's fearsome grip. (Fiction)

Burnford, Sheila. *Bel Ria*, Atlantic/Little, 1978.
How an abandoned but spunky circus dog, who lives through the Nazi takeover of France, shipboard life, and the bombing of England, affects the lives of those he encounters. (Fiction)

Burns, Olive Ann. *Cold Sassy Tree*, Ticknor & Fields, 1985.
As his tiny rural Georgia hometown undergoes many changes in the year 1906, Will Tweedy survives family scandal, his first kiss, and being run over by a train. (Fiction)

Buss, Fran Leeper, and Cubias, Daisy. *Journey of the Sparrows*, Dutton/Lodestar, 1992.
Maria makes the dangerous trip across the border to the United States, where jobs are scarce and she must evade immigration officers. (Fiction)

Busselle, Rebecca. *Bathing Ugly*, Watts/Orchard, 1990.
When thirteen-year-old Betsy represents her cabin in their camp's beauty and ugly contests, her absurd behavior causes peers and adults to

---

■ Selected for "Still Alive: The Best of the Best, 1960–1974"

▲ Selected for "The Best of the Best Books: 1970–1983"

◆ Selected for "Nothin' but the Best: Best of the Best Books for Young Adults, 1966–1986"

● Selected for "Here We Go Again: 25 Years of Best Books: Selections from 1967 to 1992"

reevaluate their attitudes toward outward appearance. (Fiction)

Butler, Octavia E. *Parable of the Sower,* Four Walls Eight Windows, 1995.
Armed with hope for the future and her unusual ability to feel the pain of others, eighteen-year-old Lauren leads a band of survivors north from the ruins of 2025 Los Angeles. (Fiction)

Butterworth, Emma Macalik. *As the Waltz Was Ending,* Scholastic/Four Winds, 1982.
The German occupation of Vienna interrupts a promising ballet career for Emma, and life becomes a desperate struggle to stay alive. (Nonfiction)

Butterworth, W. E. *Leroy and the Old Man,* Four Winds, 1980.
After witnessing a gang mugging, LeRoy leaves his home in Chicago to live with his grandfather in Mississippi. When the victim dies, LeRoy must decide if he wants to continue to hide or if he should testify against the gang members. (Fiction)

Bykov, Vasil. *Pack of Wolves,* Crowell, 1981.
Paralyzed with fear and betrayed by comrades, a wounded Russian partisan leads his small band through swamps in a terrifying escape from German soldiers. (Fiction)

Cable, Mary. *Blizzard of '88,* Atheneum, 1988.
Shocked Easterners rally to survive the blizzard of 1888, considered one of the most serious natural disasters in American history. (Nonfiction)

Cagin, Seth. *We Are Not Afraid: The Story of Goodman, Schwerner, and Chaney and the Civil Rights Campaign for Mississippi,* Macmillan, 1988.
Cagin describes the battle for civil rights in Mississippi—and the murders of three young activists, tragic casualities of that 1964 summer. (Nonfiction)

Callahan, Steven. *Adrift: Seventy-Six Days Lost at Sea,* Houghton, 1986. ◆
When his small sailboat sinks in the Atlantic, Steve Callahan spends seventy-six days in a five-foot inflatable raft, drifting 1,800 miles before rescue. (Nonfiction)

Calvert, Patricia. *Snow Bird,* Scribner, 1980.
Orphaned fourteen-year-old Willie Bannerman and her brother, T. J., come to the Dakota Territory in 1883 to live with an aunt and uncle. With the help of Snow Bird, a white mare, Willie begins to repair her life and discover her true strength. (Fiction)

———. *Yesterday's Daughter,* Scribner, 1986.
Hurt and resentful, sixteen-year-old Leenie vows to shut her returning mother out of her life—until a brief romantic interlude opens her mind and heart. (Fiction)

Campbell, Eric. *Place of Lions,* Harcourt, 1993.
After surviving a plane crash on the African Serengeti Plain, fourteen-year-old Chris sets off to find help for his father and the pilot, who are injured, and forges a magical relationship with an aging lion. (Fiction)

Campbell, Hope. *No More Trains to Tottenville,* McCall, 1971.
When her mother "splits the scene" to India, Jane suddenly finds herself woman of the house and involved with a strange young man named Scorpio. (Fiction)

Campbell, Wright R. *Where Pigeons Go to Die,* Atheneum, 1978.
While waiting for the overdue return of his racing pigeon Dickens, entered in a 600-mile competition, ten-year-old Hugh is forced to cope with the death of his beloved grandfather. (Fiction)

Cannon, A. E. *Amazing Gracie,* Delacorte, 1992. ●
When her mother remarries, Gracie's life changes: she moves away from her best friend, gets a weird six-year-old stepbrother, and watches her mother sink into total depression. (Fiction)

———. *Shadow Brothers,* Delacorte, 1991.
Marcus discovers that change is the only constant in his life when his Navajo foster brother Henry begins a search for his Native American identity and the girl next door becomes more than a friend. (Fiction)

Capps, Benjamin. *Woman of the People,* Duell, 1966.
Captured by the Comanches as a child, Helen fights tribal customs until she falls in love with a young warrior. (Fiction)

Caras, Roger. *Mara Simba: The African Lion,* Holt, 1986.
The birth, maturation, and death of an African lion are fictionalized against the larger landscape of Africa, its people, and their interdependency. (Fiction)

Card, Orson Scott. *Ender's Game,* Tor, 1985. ◆ ●
Andrew "Ender" Wiggin, a young genius in Battle School, where he is training to fight the alien Buggers, has to put his skills to the ultimate test much sooner than he expected. (Fiction)

———. *Pastwatch: The Redemption of Christopher Columbus,* Tor; dist. by St. Martin's, 1997.
To rid the world of slavery, three twenty-third-century scientists travel back in time to change history—even though it means the extinction of themselves and their culture. (Fiction)

———. *Seventh Son,* Tor, 1987.
Alvin, born seventh son of a seventh son, is destined for greatness, but something evil is trying to keep him from growing up. (Fiction)

————. *Speaker for the Dead,* Tor, 1986.
"Ender" Wiggin seeks a chance to redeem himself when Portuguese colonists on the planet Lusitania discover an intelligent species whose brutal customs threaten to start another war. (Fiction)

Carlson, Dale. *Girls Are Equal Too: The Women's Movement for Teenagers,* Atheneum, 1973.
How girls grow up, what is expected (and not expected) of them, how girls got where they are, and what they can do about it are all covered in this book for younger readers. (Nonfiction)

————. *Mountain of Truth,* Atheneum, 1972.
In a remote Tibetan lamasery Michael finds his mystic destiny, but his brother Peter finds only questions that haunt him the rest of his life. (Fiction)

Carlson, Lori M., ed. *American Eyes: New Asian-American Short Stories for Young Adults,* Holt, 1996.
These ten memorable stories evoke the voices and visions of Asian American teens as they merge ancient traditions and American culture. (Fiction)

————. *Cool Salsa: Bilingual Poems on Growing Up Latino in the United States,* Holt/Edge, 1995.
Party times, hard times, memories, and dreams come to life in these English, Spanish, and Spanglish poems by twenty-nine Latino writers. (Nonfiction)

Carrighar, Sally. *Home to the Wilderness,* Houghton, 1973.
An intimate, moving self-portrait of a famous naturalist who at the age of six learns to adjust to her mother's hatred and cruelty and eventually finds a home in the wilderness. (Nonfiction)

Carroll, Joyce Armstrong, and Wilson, Edward E. *Poetry after Lunch: Poems to Read Aloud,* Absey, 1998.
This collection of poems offers attractive entries, some appealing to the eye, others to the ear, for pleasure reading aloud after lunch, or anytime. (Nonfiction)

Carson, Jo. *Stories I Ain't Told Nobody Yet: Selections from the People Pieces,* Watts/Orchard, 1990.
Haunting, funny, and full of folk wisdom and honesty, these powerful poems bring to life the colorful personalities and the lifestyle of the Appalachian region. (Nonfiction)

Cart, Michael. *My Father's Scar,* Simon & Schuster, 1997.
In a series of flashbacks, Andy, now a college freshman entering a relationship with another man, recalls his lonely childhood in a homophobic community. (Fiction)

Carter, Alden R. *Between a Rock and a Hard Place,* Scholastic, 1996.
Stranded in the Minnesota wilderness, Mark and Randy have only each other to rely on. (Fiction)

————. *Bull Catcher,* Scholastic, 1998.
"Bull" Larsen hopes to cap his high-school baseball career with a college scholarship and then a move to the pros, but, like his love life, Bull's baseball dreams don't turn out as expected. (Fiction)

————. *Growing Season,* Putnam/Coward-McCann, 1984.
During his senior year in high school, Rick Simon moves to the country to help his family realize their lifelong dream of owning a farm. (Fiction)

————. *Sheila's Dying,* Putman, 1987.
Basketball jock Jerry is planning to break up with his steady girl Sheila until he learns she is dying of cancer. (Fiction)

————. *Up Country,* Putnam, 1990. •
Sent to live with relatives in the country while his alcoholic mother receives treatment, city kid Carl faces a serious problem from the past. (Fiction)

————. *Wart, Son of Toad,* Putman/Pacer, 1985.
Nicknamed "Wart" by the school jocks, Steve, son of the most disliked teacher in his school, is constantly in conflict with his father about his grades, his friends, and his love of auto mechanics. (Fiction)

Carter, Peter. *Borderlands,* Farrar, Straus & Giroux, 1991.
Heroes, villains, cowboys, and common settlers populate a tale of the 1870s as thirteen-year-old Ben Curtis struggles to find his place in the vast frontier. (Fiction)

————. *Bury the Dead,* Farrar, Straus & Giroux, 1987.
The lives of promising high jumper Erika and her family in East Berlin are tragically changed

---

■   Selected for "Still Alive: The Best of the Best, 1960–1974"
▲   Selected for "The Best of the Best Books: 1970–1983"
◆   Selected for "Nothin' but the Best: Best of the Best Books for Young Adults, 1966–1986"
●   Selected for "Here We Go Again: 25 Years of Best Books: Selections from 1967 to 1992"

when her grandmother's long-gone brother suddenly appears from West Germany. (Fiction)

Cary, Lorene. *Black Ice,* Knopf, 1992.
As a black scholarship student in a formerly all-white private school, the author struggles with racism, her family's expectations, peer pressure, and her own idealism. (Nonfiction)

Caseley, Judith. *Kisses,* Knopf/Borzoi, 1991.
Hannah is looking for answers: Why is her chest so flat? Why does everyone think she's a snob? Will anything ever turn out the way she wants? (Fiction)

————. *My Father, the Nutcase,* Knopf/Borzoi, 1993.
Just when fifteen-year-old Zoe needs him the most, her father quits his job and leaves his family because he is clinically depressed. (Fiction)

Castaneda, Carlos. *Journey to Ixtlan: The Lessons of Don Juan,* Simon & Schuster, 1973. ■
The story of how the author became a "man of knowledge" through a long and arduous apprenticeship to the Yaqui Indian sorcerer, Don Juan Matus. (Nonfiction)

Cavagnaro, David, and Cavagnaro, Maggie. *Almost Home: A Life-style,* American West, 1975.
Through an appealing combination of photographs and narrative, the author describes his down-to-earth harmony with nature. (Nonfiction)

Chadwick, Douglas, and Sartore, Joel. *The Company We Keep: America's Endangered Species,* National Geographic Society, 1998.
The world's endangered and threatened plants and animals are featured in stunning photographs and fascinating text. (Nonfiction)

Chambers, Aidan. *Dance on My Grave,* Harper/Zolotow, 1983.
Hal, the romantic, and Barry, the cad, are lovers. When Barry is killed in a motorcycle accident, Hal cannot come to grips with his loss. (Fiction)

Chambers, Veronica. *Mama's Girl,* Putman/Riverhead, 1997.
This is an autobiography of a woman who learned to make peace with her mother on her journey from a troubled Brooklyn childhood to *Glamour* magazine editor. (Nonfiction)

Chang, Pang-Mei Natasha. *Bound Feet & Western Dress,* Doubleday, 1998.
This engrossing memoir, based on the life of the author's Chinese aunt, as told to the author during her own search for identity, is a tale of survival and struggle amid a sea of tradition. (Nonfiction)

Cherry, Mike. *On High Steel: The Education of an Ironworker,* Quadrangle, 1974.
An articulate ironworker discusses his lifestyle in an absorbing book about his trade and his co-workers. (Nonfiction)

Chester, Deborah. *Sign of the Owl,* Scholastic/Four Winds, 1981.
Wint must recapture his father's land from an evil uncle in this medieval tale. (Fiction)

Chestnut, J. L. *Black in Selma: The Uncommon Life of J. L. Chestnut, Jr.,* Farrar, Straus & Giroux, 1991.
The life of J. L. Chestnut is detailed against the dramatic backdrop of the civil rights movement in his native Selma, Alabama. (Nonfiction)

Chetwin, Grace. *Collidescope,* Bradbury, 1991.
When his space ship crashes on Earth, a highly advanced alien interferes in the lives of two teenagers living on the island of Manhattan during different centuries. (Fiction)

Childers, Thomas. *Wings of Morning: The Story of the Last American Bomber Shot Down over Germany in World War II,* Addison-Wesley, 1996.
Howard Goodner was barely out of his teens when he flew on the last doomed bombing raid in the "Black Cat." This riveting account describes the fears and bravery of young U.S. airmen in World War II. (Nonfiction)

Childress, Alice. *Hero Ain't Nothin but a Sandwich,* Coward, 1973. ■ ▲ ◆
Benjie, a thirteen-year-old in Harlem, cannot face the reality of his drug addiction or the realization that someone cares for him. (Fiction)

————. *Rainbow Jordan,* Coward, 1981. ◆ ●
Frequently abandoned and neglected by her young and carefree mother, fourteen-year-old Rainbow suffers—until she learns to accept love and compassion from others. (Fiction)

Childress, Mark. *V for Victor,* Knopf, 1990.
Victor stumbles on a plot to land spies on the Alabama coast when his motorboat collides with a German U-boat sneaking into the harbor. (Fiction)

Chisholm, Shirley. *Unbought and Unbossed,* Houghton, 1970.
The first black woman to be elected to the U.S. Congress, Shirley Chisholm wins this unique distinction against the odds of her race and sex, and by being "unbought and unbossed." (Fiction)

Choi, Sook Nyul. *Year of Impossible Goodbyes,* Houghton, 1992.
A North Korean family barely survives the Japanese occupation during World War II only to find that after the war they must flee Russian Communists. (Fiction)

Christiansen, C. B. *I See the Moon,* Simon & Schuster/Atheneum, 1996.
Bitte, overjoyed to be an aunt, learns what true love is when her fifteen-year-old sister puts her baby up for adoption. (Fiction)

Claire, Keith. *Otherwise Girl,* Holt, 1976.
What can fifteen-year-old Matt do when he discovers that the beautiful redhead he befriends is really the ghost of a girl who drowned eight years before? (Fiction)

Clapp, Patricia. *Witches' Children: A Story of Salem,* Lothrop, 1982.
A frightening tale of the Salem witchcraft trials, based on historical fact and told from the perspective of one of the ten "afflicted girls." (Fiction)

Clarke, Arthur C. *Imperial Earth,* Harcourt, 1976.
Find out what happens to Duncan Makenzie when he is sent from Titan, a moon of Saturn, to Earth's quincentennial celebration. (Fiction)

———. *Rendezvous with Rama,* Harcourt, 1973.
A brief encounter with an alien world, Rama, proves perilous and baffling to the humans who explore its mysteries. (Fiction)

Clarke, J. *The Heroic Life of Al Capsella,* Holt, 1991.
Fourteen-year-old Al wants to be "like everyone else"—but with weird parents like his, he hasn't got a chance. (Fiction)

Cleary, Beverly. *Girl from Yamhill: A Memoir,* Morrow, 1988.
An honest and humorous account of the Depression-era childhood and adolescence of Beverly Cleary in Oregon, where she encountered many of the same situations that teens do today. (Nonfiction)

Cleaver, Eldridge. *Soul on Ice,* McGraw-Hill, 1968. ■
In a collection of essays and open letters written while in prison, Eldridge Cleaver talks about the inner feelings and drives of the outraged black man in the United States today. (Nonfiction)

Clements, Bruce. *Tom Loves Anna Loves Tom,* Farrar, Straus & Giroux, 1991.
Tom and Anna find love at first sight and together face Anna's deepest secret. (Fiction)

Clifford, Francis. *Naked Runner,* Coward-McCann, 1966.
A former British intelligence agent has his Frankfurt vacation turned into a cold war nightmare. (Fiction)

Clinton, Catherine, ed. *I, Too, Sing America: Three Centuries of African American Poetry,* Houghton, 1999.
With informative narration and stunning art, this collection of African American poetry appeals to both the mind and the heart. (Nonfiction)

Clute, John. *Science Fiction: The Illustrated Encyclopedia,* DK Inc., 1996.
This beautifully illustrated exploration of science fiction is complete with themes, author profiles, television shows, and videos. (Nonfiction)

Cofer, Judith Ortiz. *An Island Like You,* Orchard/Melanie Kroupa, 1996.
Twelve beautifully written stories capture the pain and joy of teens growing up Puerto Rican in a New Jersey barrio. (Fiction)

Cohen, Barbara. *Unicorns in the Rain,* Atheneum/Argo, 1980.
Violence, pollution, and overcrowding have reached the point of no return. One family has built a large ship, an ark, and filled it with animals, and now it's starting to rain. (Fiction)

———, and Lovejoy, Bahija. *Seven Daughters and Seven Sons,* Atheneum, 1982.
In this retelling of a traditional Arabic tale, a poor merchant's daughter, disguised as a boy, makes a fortune and takes satisfying revenge on seven insulting male cousins. (Fiction)

Cohen, Susan, and Cohen, Daniel. *Six-pack and a Fake I.D.,* Evans, 1986.
Here's an objective discussion of alcohol and its role in today's society of adults and young adults. (Nonfiction)

———, ———. *When Someone You Know Is Gay,* Little, Brown, 1990.
The authors describe what it's really like and what it means to be gay and include a list of books and videos for more information. (Nonfiction)

Cohn, Nik. *Rock from the Beginning,* Stein & Day, 1969.
If you dig rock, Nik Cohn gives it to you straight—the lowdown and feel of the now sounds from folk to protest to psychedelic, from

---

Elvis to Dylan to the Jefferson Airplane and be-yond. (Nonfiction)

Cole, Brock. *Celine,* Farrar, Straus & Giroux, 1990.
Casualities of divorce, independent teenager Celine and her seven-year-old neighbor, Jake, share an interest in television and Jake's father. (Fiction)

———. *The Goats,* Farrar, Straus & Giroux, 1987. •
Stripped naked by fellow campers and left on a deserted island, social misfits Laura and Howie survive humiliation, natural dangers, and each other. (Fiction)

Cole, Ernest, and Flaherty, Thomas. *House of Bondage,* Random House, 1967.
The oppression suffered by blacks in South Africa is compellingly reported in text and photographs. (Nonfiction)

Coleman, Lonnie. *Orphan Jim,* Doubleday, 1975.
As if life in the Depression isn't hard enough, Trudy and her young brother choose to be "orphans" but avoid being sent to an orphans' home. (Fiction)

Coles, William E. *Another Kind of Monday,* Simon & Schuster/Atheneum, 1997.
Mark Bettors finds money and a note hidden between the pages of a Dickens novel inviting him to pick a female partner for a secret quest. (Fiction)

Collier, James Lincoln. *When the Stars Begin to Fall,* Delacorte, 1986.
Angry that he's treated as "thieving trash," Harry decides to prove himself by exposing a local carpet factory's illegal polluting. (Fiction)

Collins, Larry, and Lapierre, Dominique. *Or I'll Dress You in Mourning,* Simon & Schuster, 1968.
Manuel Benitez, an impoverished juvenile de-linquent, fights tragedy and hunger to become the highest paid matador in the world and a symbol of the new Spain. (Nonfiction)

Collins, Max Allan. *Dark City,* Bantam, 1987.
After leaving Chicago, legendary gangbuster Eliot Ness goes to Cleveland to clean up a corrupt police force. (Fiction)

Colman, Penny. *Corpses, Coffins, and Crypts: A History of Burial,* Holt, 1999.
Colman's well-researched account of death and burial answers questions for the curious and satisfies a taste for the morbid. (Nonfiction)

———. *Rosie the Riveter,* Crown, 1996.
More than sixty posters and photographs at-tractively depict working women during World War II. (Nonfiction)

Coman, Carolyn. *Body and Soul: Ten American Women,* Hill & Company, 1988.
These personal narratives and photo essays about unusual women, including Susan Butcher, two-time Iditarod winner, and "S & M business-woman" Belle de Jour, portray lives of courage and perseverance. (Nonfiction)

Comfort, Alex, and Comfort, Jane. *Facts of Love: Living, Loving and Growing Up,* Crown, 1979.
Birth control and respect for one's partner are stressed in a warm and readable guide to re-sponsible sex for younger teens. (Nonfiction)

Conford, Ellen. *Alfred G. Graebner Memorial High School Handbook of Rules and Regulations: A Novel,* Little, Brown, 1976.
These humorous episodes of a girl's first year in high school as she copes with every fresh-man's nightmare—the school's unbelievable of-ficial handbook of regulations. (Fiction)

Conly, Jane Leslie. *Crazy Lady!* HarperCollins/ Laura Geringer, 1994.
The neighborhood's "crazy lady" and her de-velopmentally disabled son, Ronald, teach Ver-non the true meaning of love. (Fiction)

———. *Trout Summer,* Holt, 1997.
While spending the summer mostly on their own along a Maryland river, siblings Shana and Cody meet a grouchy old man who teaches them about boating and life and death. (Fiction)

Conot, Robert. *Rivers of Blood, Years of Darkness,* Bantam, 1967.
The violent events before, during, and after the 1965 Watts riots in Los Angeles are told in vivid on-the-scene detail. (Nonfiction)

Conover, Ted. *Rolling Nowhere,* Viking, 1984.
Ivy League Denverite Ted Conover drops out of his safe existence and experiences life as a rail-road hobo, scavenging for food, hopping trains, and making friends with other hobos who help him realize what people have in common. (Nonfiction)

Conrad, Pamela. *My Daniel,* Harper, 1990.
Years after treacherous and unscrupulous di-nosaur hunters try to steal Daniel's discovery, Grandmother Julia reveals the exciting secrets of the now-famous bones. (Fiction)

———. *Prairie Songs,* Harper, 1985.
Louisa idealizes Emmeline, the local doctor's beautiful, cultured wife, who, unable to adjust to the harsh and lonely pioneer life on the bleak Nebraska prairie, goes mad. (Fiction)

———. *What I Did for Roman,* Harper, 1987.
Vulnerable Darcie becomes involved with a handsome, disturbed young man while work-ing at the zoo. (Fiction)

Conrat, Maisie, and Conrat, Richard. *Executive Order 9066: The Internment of 110,000 Japanese Americans,* California Historical Society, 1972.
A nation's paranoia is strikingly revealed in this photographic view of World War II concentration camps, American style. (Nonfiction)

Conway, Jill Ker. *Road from Coorain,* Knopf, 1990.
Jill Ker Conway survives the physically harsh life of Australia's outback in the 1930s and becomes the first woman president of Smith College. (Nonfiction)

Cook, Karin. *What Girls Learn,* Pantheon, 1998.
When two sisters go with their divorced mother from their southern home to live with their mother's boyfriend in the North, he becomes their caretaker after their mother's death. (Fiction)

Cook, Robin. *Coma,* Little, Brown, 1977.
A young woman medical student discovers the horrifying truth—a black market in spare parts—about the rash of mysterious death of patients who have undergone surgery in a Boston hospital. (Fiction)

Cooney, Caroline B. *Don't Blame the Music,* Putnam/Pacer, 1986.
Susan's plans for an uneventful senior year are dashed when her older sister, Ashley, an embittered, failed rock musician, returns to cause her family anguish. (Fiction)

———. *Driver's Ed,* Delacorte, 1995.
Guilt and fear permeate Remy and Morgan's new romance when a street-sign-stealing caper planned in driving class takes a deadly turn. (Fiction)

———. *Flight #116 Is Down,* Scholastic, 1993.
A 747 crashes on the grounds of her family's estate, and sixteen-year-old Heidi, alone and terrified, pulls herself together to help rescue the survivors. (Fiction)

———. *The Voice on the Radio,* Delacorte, 1997.
Janie is humiliated when her former loving boyfriend reopens old wounds by splashing her story on the airwaves while hosting a radio show. (Fiction)

———. *What Child Is This? A Christmas Story,* Delacorte, 1998.
Several teens discover the true meaning of Christmas. (Fiction)

———. *Whatever Happened to Janie?* Delacorte, 1994.
In this sequel to *The Face on the Milk Carton,* Janie's heartfelt decision leads her to leave her former parents and boyfriend to begin a new life with her "real" family. (Fiction)

Cooper, Henry S. F., Jr. *Thirteen: The Flight That Failed,* Dial, 1973.
This is a riveting minute-by-minute account of the intense efforts to save the ill-fated Apollo 13 and its precious three-man crew. (Nonfiction)

Cooper, J. California. *Family,* Doubleday, 1992.
From beyond the grave, Clora narrates the story of her family as she watches her children emerge from slavery during the Civil War. (Fiction)

Cooper, Louise. *Sleep of Stone,* Atheneum, 1993.
Shapechanger Ghysla is jealous of Prince Anyr's fiancee and tries to take her place, with tragic results. (Fiction)

Corbett, Sara. *Venus to the Hoop,* Doubleday, 1998.
This exciting account tells of the extraordinary young American athletes who won basketball gold at the Atlanta Olympics. (Nonfiction)

Corman, Avery. *Prized Possessions,* Simon & Schuster, 1992. ●
Months after being raped during her first week in college, Elizabeth presses charges, precipitating a campus protest and her own healing. (Fiction)

Cormier, Robert. *After the First Death,* Pantheon, 1979. ▲ ◆
Ben tries unsuccessfully to balance his father's betrayal and his own failure after a busload of children is hijacked by a group of ruthless terrorists. (Fiction)

———. *Bumblebee Flies Anyway,* Pantheon, 1983.
In an experimental hospital for the terminally ill, his memory shattered by mind-altering drugs, sixteen-year-old Barney is told that he is the "control" and should not get involved with the dying; but he cannot stop himself from reaching out to others as he slowly discovers the truth about himself. (Fiction)

———. *The Chocolate War: A Novel,* Pantheon, 1974. ■ ▲ ◆
"Sweets" abound at Trinity High while a schoolmaster feasts on his students' fear—a bitter story

---

■ Selected for "Still Alive: The Best of the Best, 1960–1974"

▲ Selected for "The Best of the Best Books: 1970–1983"

◆ Selected for "Nothin' but the Best: Best of the Best Books for Young Adults, 1966–1986"

● Selected for "Here We Go Again: 25 Years of Best Books: Selections from 1967 to 1992"

of one student's resistance and the high price he pays. (Fiction)

———. *Fade*, Doubleday/Delacorte, 1988.
One boy in each generation of the Moreaux family inherits the power—and the curse—of invisibility. (Fiction)

———. *Heroes*, Delacorte, 1999.
Eighteen-year-old Francis returns home from World War II with his face blown off and a mission to murder the childhood hero he feels betrayed him. (Fiction)

———. *I Am the Cheese*, Pantheon, 1977. ▲
A victim of amnesia, and under the influence of drugs administered by mysterious and unidentified questioners, teenager Adam searches through haunting memories that must not be recalled or revealed if he is to survive. (Fiction)

———. *In the Middle of the Night*, Delacorte, 1996.
Sixteen-year-old Danny answers the phone and finds that a tragic accident twenty-five years earlier has set a dangerous chain of events in motion. (Fiction)

———. *Tenderness*, Delacorte, 1998.
Fifteen-year-old Lori loves eighteen-year-old serial killer Eric Poole. (Fiction)

———. *Tunes for Bears to Dance To*, Delacorte, 1993.
Henry discovers evil when his bigoted boss manipulates him into betraying his friend, an elderly Holocaust survivor. (Fiction)

———. *We All Fall Down*, Delacorte, 1992. •
All is not peaceful in small-town Burnside—drunk teenagers trash a house, a young girl is flung down the stairs, a murderer is quietly planning revenge, and Jane Jerome falls in love with a lost soul. (Fiction)

Counter, S. Allen. *North Pole Legacy: Black, White, and Eskimo*, Univ. of Massachusettes, 1992.
Counter's interest in black explorer Matthew Henson, who accompanied Robert E. Peary to the North Pole, triggers his search beyond the Arctic Circle for still living Eskimo descendants of both men. (Nonfiction)

Couper, Heather, and Pelham, David. *Universe*, Random, 1985.
Through pop-ups and pull tabs, paper mechanics provide three-dimensional illustrations of the Big Bang, star birth, and star death. (Nonfiction)

Courlander, Harold. *African, a Novel*, Crown, 1968.
Captured by slavers in a village raid, Wes Hunu survives the ocean crossing from Dahomey and life on a Georgia plantation, eventually escaping with the hope that somewhere in America there is a future for him. (Fiction)

Cousteau, Jacques-Yves, and Cousteau, Philippe. *Shark: Splendid Savage of the Sea*, Doubleday, 1970.
The Cousteaus present a world of beauty and danger as they study the shark and carry out research face to face with the most savage animal in the sea. (Nonfiction)

———, **and Diole, Philippe.** *Life and Death in a Coral Sea*, Doubleday, 1971.
The authors guide the reader through the beautiful coral jungles of the Red Sea and Indian Ocean, introducing their inhabitants along the way. (Nonfiction)

Coville, Bruce. *Oddly Enough*, Harcourt/Jane Yolen, 1995.
An angel, a unicorn, a vampire, and a werewolf are among the featured creatures in these nine funny, poignant, and riveting short stories. (Fiction)

Craig, John. *Chappie and Me: An Autobiographical Novel*, Dodd, 1979.
Wearing blackface in order to play with Chappie Johnson and His Colored All Stars in the summer of 1939, a young white Canadian boy gains understanding of what being black means. (Fiction)

Craig, Kit. *Gone*, Little, Brown, 1993.
Mrs. Hale's children are sure she'll have breakfast ready, but where is she? She's been kidnapped by a pyromaniac who is about to reunite the family in a modern-day chamber of horrors. Someone will soon die. (Fiction)

Craven, Margaret. *I Heard the Owl Call My Name*, Doubleday, 1974. ■
Native American beliefs and nature lore enhance the poignant story of a dying young minister who wins their respect and friendship while coming to terms with death. (Fiction)

Creech, Sharon. *Chasing Redbird*, HarperCollins, 1998.
Zinny, at odds with her siblings, escapes the chaos by restoring a historic trail and unearths fascinating information about her family. (Fiction)

Crew, Linda. *Children of the River*, Delacorte, 1990. •
Sundara struggles with the conflict between her Cambodian heritage and her growing love for Jonathan. (Fiction)

Crichton, Michael. *Andromeda Strain*, Knopf, 1969. ■
Four scientists race against the clock to isolate a deadly microorganism from outer space which has killed all but two people in a small Arizona town. (Fiction)

———. *Electronic Life: How to Think about Computers,* Knopf, 1984.
In this informal introduction to computers and the information society, a best-selling author explains computer terminology and considers what computers can and cannot do. (Nonfiction)

———. *Jurassic Park,* Knopf, 1992.
Dinosaurs created from fossilized DNA for a fabulous theme park are not supposed to be capable of breeding, but they do—and they're hungry. (Fiction)

———. *Terminal Man,* Knopf, 1972.
Terror spreads as a man wearing bandages, a bathrobe, and wires in his brain disappears from his hospital room. (Fiction)

Crispin, A. C. *Starbridge,* Berkley, 1991.
Mahree Burroughs discovers her talent for languages and diplomacy when, on a routine flight to Earth, Spaceship Desiree encounters intelligent beings from other planets. (Fiction)

Cross, Gillian. *Chartbreaker,* Holiday, 1987.
Love and rage permeate the story of Janis Mary "Finch," a British rock star who sings "like concentrated danger." (Fiction)

———. *On the Edge,* Holiday, 1985.
Tug, the son of a well-known British newswoman, is captured by terrorists in a story of relentless suspense. (Fiction)

Crutcher, Chris. *Athletic Shorts: Six Short Stories,* Greenwillow, 1992. ●
Tales of love, death, bigotry, and heroism are of real people with the courage to stand up to a world that often puts them down. (Fiction)

———. *Chinese Handcuffs,* Greenwillow, 1990.
A winning triathlete's need to understand his older brother's suicide is complicated by memories and daring challenges. (Fiction)

———. *Crazy Horse Electric Game,* Greenwillow, 1987.
Star athlete Willie Weaver's crippling accident forces him to leave his family and friends to rebuild his shattered life. (Fiction)

———. *Ironman,* Greenwillow, 1996.
When he calls his teacher an asshole in class, Bo is forced to attend an anger management program, where he learns to deal with his real problem—his cruel father. (Fiction)

———. *Running Loose,* Greenwillow, 1983. ◆
Louie takes a stand against his coach and playing dirty football, falls in love, and loses his girlfriend in a fatal accident—all in his senior year. (Fiction)

———. *Staying Fat for Sarah Byrnes,* Greenwillow, 1994.
When the horrific truth about Sarah's past is revealed, only her true friend Eric ("Moby") Calhoun can help her come to terms with her family and plan for her future. (Fiction)

———. *Stotan!* Greenwillow, 1986. ◆ ●
A high school coach invites four members of his swim team to a week of rigorous training that tests their moral fiber as well as their physical stamina. (Fiction)

Culin, Charlotte. *Cages of Glass, Flowers of Time,* Bradbury, 1979.
Abused by her mother (who in turn is still being beaten by her mother), fourteen-year-old Claire is afraid to trust anyone—until she meets kindness from some special friends. (Fiction)

Cullen, Brian. *What Niall Saw,* St. Martin's, 1987.
The misspelled fragments in a seven-year-old Irish boy's diary after the Bomb offer a chilling testament to the end of the world. (Fiction)

Currie, Elliott. *Dope and Trouble: Portraits of Delinquent Youth,* Pantheon, 1993.
This appeal to the social consciousness of America gives graphic and disturbing insight into the hopes and dreams of troubled teens. (Nonfiction)

Curtis, Christopher Paul. *The Watsons Go to Birmingham—1963,* Delacorte, 1996.
Because Kenny Watson's older brother, Byron, is fast becoming a juvenile delinquent, the family drives from Detroit to Birmingham so Grandma can straighten him out. (Fiction)

Curtis, Edward S. *Girl Who Married a Ghost, and Other Tales from the North American Indian,* Scholastic/Four Winds, 1978.
Ghost stories, trickster tales, and other pieces of authentic Native American folklore are combined with Edward Curtis's haunting photographs. (Nonfiction)

Curtis, Patricia. *Animal Rights: The Stories of People Who Defend the Rights of Animals,* Four Winds, 1980.
The stories of seven imaginary people provide a thoughtful look at the rights of animals, ways

---

■ Selected for "Still Alive: The Best of the Best, 1960–1974"
▲ Selected for "The Best of the Best Books: 1970–1983"
◆ Selected for "Nothin' but the Best: Best of the Best Books for Young Adults, 1966–1986"
● Selected for "Here We Go Again: 25 Years of Best Books: Selections from 1967 to 1992"

in which they are abused, and what can be done to correct the abuse. (Nonfiction)

Cushman, Karen. *Catherine, Called Birdy,* Clarion, 1995.
Fighting fleas, unsuitable suitors, and her mother's attempts to make a lady of her, Catherine writes in her diary about her frustrations with her life as a young noblewoman in medieval times. (Fiction)

————. *The Midwife's Apprentice,* Clarion, 1996.
Beetle, a homeless girl, is found in a dung heap and apprenticed to the village midwife in this sensitive fourteenth-century tale set in England. (Fiction)

Cushman, Kathleen, and Miller, Montana. *Circus Dreams,* Little, Brown, 1991.
Follow Montana Miller through her first year at a circus school in France as she realizes her dream of becoming a trapeze artist. (Nonfiction)

D'Aguiar, Fred. *The Longest Memory,* Pantheon, 1996.
A young slave's father misguidedly betrays his son's attempted escape in this painfully intimate view of "peculiar institution" of slavery. (Fiction)

Dahl, Roald. *Boy: Tales of Childhood,* Farrar, Straus & Giroux, 1985. •
A famous author recalls his struggle from school days to maturity in a humorous autobiography. (Nonfiction)

————. *Going Solo,* Farrar, Straus & Giroux, 1986.
Dahl's recollections become a collage of events from time spent in Africa to exciting flying experiences in Greece during World War II. (Nonfiction)

Dana, Barbara. *Necessary Parties,* Harper/C. Zolotow, 1986.
With the help of an offbeat lawyer/auto mechanic, fifteen-year-old Chris goes to court to fight his parents' divorce. (Fiction)

Dann, Patty. *Mermaids,* Ticknor & Fields, 1986.
In this quietly bizarre story, fourteen-year-old Charlotte wants to become a saint—if only she can stop lusting after the gardener at the nearby convent. (Fiction)

Dash, Joan. *We Shall Not Be Moved: The Woman's Factory Strike of 1909,* Scholastic, 1997.
A lively picture of women in the New York garment industry rebelling against unfair conditions and organizing the first women's labor strike in the early twentieth century is inspiring. (Nonfiction)

David, Jay, ed. *Growing Up Black,* Morrow, 1968.
Violence, hatred, and degradation have marked the childhood of nineteen black Americans from the days of slavery to today's ghettos. (Nonfiction)

Davies, Hunter. *Beatles: The Authorized Biography,* McGraw-Hill, 1968.
John, Paul, George, and Ringo are seen as interesting, fallible human beings, each quite different from the others, each with his own history, hang-ups, and hopes. (Nonfiction)

Davis, Daniel S. *Behind Barbed Wire: Imprisonment of Japanese Americans during World War II,* Dutton, 1982.
An absorbing chronicle of an episode in American history when Japanese Americans were forcibly interned in "relocation" camps. (Nonfiction)

Davis, Jenny. *Checking on the Moon,* Orchard/Richard Jackson, 1992.
Thirteen-year-old Cab spends the summer with her grandmother in a decaying neighborhood helping the area's despairing residents, and learning to rely on her own resourcefulness. (Fiction)

————. *Good-bye and Keep Cold,* Watts/Orchard/Richard Jackson, 1987.
The death of Edda's father in a strip-mining accident unleashes inexplicable currents of love and hate that threaten the family's fragile survival. (Fiction)

Davis, Lindsey. *Silver Pigs,* Crown, 1990.
The murder of a senator's daughter forces Marcus Didius Falco (Bogey in a toga) to investigate a possible attempt to overthrow the emperor of ancient Rome. (Fiction)

Davis, Mildred. *Tell Them What's Her Name Called,* Random, 1975.
Three murders are all preceded by the same mysterious message—is it just coincidence? (Fiction)

Davis, Terry. *If Rock and Roll Were a Machine,* Delacorte, 1993.
After a teacher humiliates Bert, motorcycles, writing, racquetball, and a few caring adults help him regain his devastated self-confidence. (Fiction)

————. *Vision Quest,* Viking, 1979. •
As he prepares himself for adulthood, eighteen-year-old Louden finds a special joy in competitive wrestling, in the uniqueness of the Columbia River, and in his live-in girlfriend, Carla. (Fiction)

De Larrabeiti, Michael. *Borribles,* Macmillan, 1978.
The savage epic battle between the Borribles—strange children with pointed ears—and the Rumbles—intelligent ratlike creatures—is the focal point of an unusual, disconcerting fantasy set in London. (Fiction)

De Lint, Charles. *Trader,* Tor; dist. by St. Martin's, 1998.
Max, a guitar maker, discovers he has lost his identity to another man and, determined to get it back, is drawn into a dream world where spirits are not what they seem. (Fiction)

De Veaux, Alexis. *Don't Explain: A Song of Billie Holiday,* Harper & Row, 1980.
The life of the incredibly gifted yet tragically insecure American jazz singer Billie Holiday, nicknamed "Lady Day," is told in this free verse "song." (Nonfiction)

De Vries, Anke. *Bruises,* Front Street, 1997.
Although her teacher suspects the truth about Judith's frequent absences from school, Michael believes her tale of being attacked, and offers his help, protection, and friendship. (Fiction)

Dear, William. *Dungeon Master: The Disappearance of James Dallas Egbert III,* Houghton, 1984.
When computer genius James Dallas Egbert III disappears from Michigan State University in 1979, private investigator William Dear suspects that the fantasy world of "Dungeons & Dragons" has become too real for this sixteen-year-old. (Nonfiction)

Deaver, Julie Reece. *Say Goodnight, Gracie,* Harper/C. Zolotow, 1988.
Sharing a zany sense of humor and anxieties about their futures, Jimmy and Morgan are best friends on the brink of love when Jimmy is killed by a drunk driver, leaving Morgan to cope with reality of death. (Fiction)

Decker, Sunny. *Empty Spoon,* Harper, 1969.
At a high school in Philadelphia's black ghetto, the school with the highest crime and drop-out rates in the city, Sunny Decker, a young white college graduate, attempts to overcome the hostility and belligerence of her students. (Nonfiction)

Del Calzo, Nick, et al. *The Triumphant Spirit: Portraits & Stories of Holocaust Survivors . . . Their Messages of Hope & Compassion,* Triumphant Spirit, 1998.
Current photographs of Holocaust survivors, who have not only survived but have also thrived, accompany brief sketches of their lives from Hitler's ghettos and camps to today. (Nonfiction)

Del Rey, Lester. *Pstalemate,* Putnam, 1972.
When engineer Harry Bronson discovers he has psi powers, he vows that he will not become insane like other telepaths. (Fiction)

Delany, Sarah, and Delany, A. Elizabeth. *Having Our Say: The Delany Sisters' First 100 Years,* Kodansha, 1994.
The colorful, thoughtful reminiscences of African American sisters Sadie and Bessie Delany (both more than 100 years old), recount their battles against racism and sexism in this remarkable oral history. (Nonfiction)

Demas, Vida. *First Person, Singular,* Putnam, 1974.
In a rambling diary-like letter to her psychiatrist Pam recounts her struggles to find herself despite an unstable family and her own feelings of inadequacy. (Fiction)

Denenberg, Barry. *An American Hero: The True Story of Charles A. Lindbergh,* Scholastic, 1997.
This is an honest look at the man whose solo transatlantic flight in 1927 captured the heart of the nation. (Nonfiction)

————. *Voices from Vietnam,* Scholastic, 1996.
Gripping descriptions by American men and women, Vietnamese citizens and North Vietnamese soldiers convey what it was like to be in Vietnam during the war. (Nonfiction)

Derby, Pat. *Visiting Miss Pierce,* Farrar, Straus & Giroux, 1986.
For a school social concerns class project, Barry Wilson, a shy, awkward ninth grader, regularly visits Miss Pierce, an eighty-three-year-old convalescent-hospital resident, and becomes intrigued by her tales of her older brother. (Fiction)

————, **and Beagle, Peter.** *Lady and Her Tiger,* Dutton, 1976.
You can train wild animals by love rather than force, and Pat Derby proves it. One of her favorites is Chauncey, the Lincoln-Mercury cougar. (Fiction)

Dessen, Sarah. *Someone Like You,* Viking, 1999.
Halley's friendship with Scarlett changes during their junior year, after Scarlett's boyfriend dies, her pregnancy is revealed, and Halley experiences her own first serious relationship. (Fiction)

————. *That Summer,* Orchard/Melanie Kroupa, 1997.
Fifteen-year-old Haven struggles through a summer in which her sister gets married, her father remarries, and her mother plans big changes in their lives. (Fiction)

■ Selected for "Still Alive: The Best of the Best, 1960–1974"

▲ Selected for "The Best of the Best Books: 1970–1983"

◆ Selected for "Nothin' but the Best: Best of the Best Books for Young Adults, 1966–1986"

● Selected for "Here We Go Again: 25 Years of Best Books: Selections from 1967 to 1992"

Deuker, Carl. *Heart of a Champion,* Little, Brown/Joy Street, 1994.
Seth Barham tells the story of his friendship with Jimmy Winter, a gifted but troubled high school baseball star. (Fiction)

————. *On the Devil's Court,* Joy Street/Little, Brown, 1990. ●
Seventeen-year-old Joe Faust must decide if it's worth selling his soul to the devil for one perfect season of basketball. (Fiction)

————. *Painting the Black,* Houghton, 1998.
While catching for Josh during pitching practice, Ryan decides to try out for the team but finds himself in an ethical dilemma when he discovers his friend has a serious flaw. (Fiction)

Dickinson, Peter. *AK,* Delacorte, 1993.
Paul, an orphaned twelve-year-old warrior in the 5th Commando Unit of the NLA, fights for freedom in his African homeland, both with and without his AK-47 assault rifle. (Fiction)

————. *Bone from a Dry Sea,* Delacorte, 1994.
The bone Vinny finds on an archaeological dig in Africa is the same bone that Li, a thinker among her prehistoric sea ape people, wore as a sign of magical abilities. (Fiction)

————. *Eva,* Delacorte, 1990. ●
After a violent auto accident, thirteen-year-old Eva wakes up in a hospital to find she must learn how to live as a chimpanzee. (Fiction)

————. *Tulku,* Dutton, 1979.
Surviving a Boxer massacre of a Christian mission in China, thirteen-year-old Theodore accompanies an eccentric British plant collector and her guide-lover through danger-laden territory to Tibet and a Buddhist monastery. (Fiction)

————, **and Anderson, Wayne.** *Flight of Dragons,* Harper, 1979.
Dragons aren't real . . . or are they? This carefully constructed and beautifully illustrated case for the existence of dragons will convince even the skeptics. (Nonfiction)

Dickson, Margaret. *Maddy's Song,* Houghton, 1985.
Sixteen and musically gifted, Maddy Dow is abused by a brutal father who is seemingly a model citizen in their community. (Fiction)

Dijk, Lutz Van. *Damned Strong Love: A True Story of Willi G. and Stefan K.,* Holt, 1996.
Based on a true event, this moving narrative tells the tragic story of a gay Polish teenager who falls in love with an occupying German soldier in 1941 and is tortured and imprisoned for the relationship. (Fiction)

Dixon, Paige. *May I Cross Your Golden River?* Atheneum, 1975.
The rare, terminal disease which killed Lou Gehrig is also killing eighteen-year-old Jordan, but with his family's support he tries to lead a normal life. (Fiction)

Doherty, Berlie. *Dear Nobody,* Orchard, 1993.
High school seniors Chris and Helen are ready for love, but not for its responsibilities, which include a baby. (Fiction)

————. *White Peak Farm,* Watts/Orchard, 1991.
As a teenager on her family's isolated Derbyshire farm, Jeannie Tanner faces secrets, change, and growing up. (Fiction)

Dolan, Edward F. *Adolf Hitler: A Portrait in Tyranny,* Dodd, 1981.
An examination of the man, what he stood for, and how he came to assume power. (Nonfiction)

————. *How to Leave Home—and Make Everybody Like It,* Dodd, 1977.
This is a guidebook for the young person longing to get away from home—how to tell the family, find a job, manage money, and locate a place to live. (Nonfiction)

Dolmetsch, Paul, and Mauricette, Gail, eds. *Teens Talk about Alcohol and Alcoholism,* Dolphin/Doubleday, 1987.
Young people talk about how alcoholism affects their lives, families, and friends. (Nonfiction)

Donofrio, Beverly. *Riding in Cars with Boys,* Morrow, 1991.
Denied college, Beverly loses interest in everything but riding around, drinking, smoking, and rebelling against authority. After a divorce, she arrives in New York City with a young son and turns her life around. (Nonfiction)

Dorman, Michael. *Under Twenty-one: A Young People's Guide to Legal Rights,* Delacorte, 1970.
Legal advice for those under twenty-one is presented in a clear, straightforward manner on such subjects as dress, hairstyle, free speech, employment, driving, contracts, voting, criminal law, drug use, and parental problems. (Nonfiction)

Dorris, Michael. *The Window,* Hyperion; dist. by Little, Brown, 1998.
After being moved from one foster home to another, eleven-year-old Rayona Taylor learns the importance of family when she's finally sent to live with relatives she doesn't know in Kentucky. (Fiction)

————. *Yellow Raft in Blue Water,* Holt, 1987.
Half-Native American, half-African American Rayona's agonizing search for her true self is told from a three-generation perspective—Rayona's, her mother's, and her grandmother's. (Fiction)

Dowdey, Landon, comp. *Journey to Freedom: A Casebook with Music,* Swallow, 1970.
From the Bible to the Beatles, material gathered from poetry, plays, folk songs, and spiri-

tuals is combined in a joyous statement on the brotherhood of man and the celebration of life. (Nonfiction)

Dragonwagon, Crescent, and Zindel, Paul. *To Take a Dare,* Harper, 1982.
Thirteen-year-old Chrysta is already into drugs and sex when she runs away from home. After a couple of years on the road learning life the hard way, she meets several people who teach her about love, happiness, and giving. (Fiction)

Draper, Sharon M. *Forged by Fire,* Simon & Schuster/Atheneum, 1998.
Gerald, who has struggled his entire life to survive in spite of his drug-addicted mother, now must protect his sister from an abusive stepfather. (Fiction)

————. *Tears of a Tiger,* Simon & Schuster/Atheneum, 1996.
High-school senior Andy Jackson is overcome by guilt after his best friend dies in an automobile accident that happened when Andy was driving drunk. (Fiction)

Dribben, Judith. *Girl Called Judith Strick,* Cowles, 1970.
Seventeen-year-old Judith Strick lures Germans into partisan traps, spies for the Polish underground, bamboozles and charms her German captors, and survives three prisons, including Auschwitz. (Nonfiction)

Drucker, Olga Levy. *Kindertransport,* Holt, 1994.
Drucker relates her six years as a child evacuee from Nazi Germany and her encounters with anti-semitism while in foster care in England. (Nonfiction)

Duder, Tessa. *In Lane Three, Alex Archer,* Houghton, 1990.
Overcoming injuries, Alex competes with her rival for a spot on the New Zealand Olympic swim team. (Fiction)

Due, Linnea A. *High and Outside,* Harper, 1980. ▲
Niki, the star pitcher on the girls softball team, has a drinking problem. Her catcher knows, her coach knows, but Niki won't admit it. (Fiction)

Dufresne, Frank. *My Way Was North,* Holt, 1966.
As a field agent for the U.S. Biological Survey, Dufresne spends twenty years in Alaska enjoying the frozen wastes, unusual animals, and individualistic people. (Nonfiction)

Duncan, Lois. *Chapters: My Growth as a Writer,* Little, 1982.
A popular author tells about her need and desire to be a writer from the time she was ten years old; examples of her early writing are used to demonstrate how life becomes fiction and to show how her career develops. (Nonfiction)

————. *Don't Look behind You,* Delacorte, 1990.
April's life changes forever when her family must disappear into the federal witness protection program after her father testifies against members of a drug ring. (Fiction)

————. *Killing Mr. Griffin,* Little, 1978. ▲ ◆ ●
A group of high school students kidnaps a strict English teacher in order to get even with him—and what starts as a prank becomes a horror. (Fiction)

————. *Stranger with My Face,* Little, 1981. ▲
Will Laurie's evil twin sister, Lia, already experienced in astral projection, succeed in taking over Laurie's body and comfortable life? (Fiction)

————. *Who Killed My Daughter? The True Story of a Mother's Search for Her Daughter's Murderer,* Delacorte, 1993.
Determined to find her daughter's murderer, author Lois Duncan seeks the aid of psychics and uncovers startling parallels to her YA novels. (Nonfiction)

Durham, Marilyn. *The Man Who Loved Cat Dancing,* Harcourt, 1972.
A western, a relentless character study, a violent tragedy, but, most of all, this is a love story. (Fiction)

Durham, Michael S. *Powerful Days: The Civil Rights Photography of Charles Moore,* Stewart, Tabori & Chang, 1992.
Graphic black-and-white photographs by a noted photojournalist vividly document events of the civil rights movement. (Nonfiction)

Durkin, Barbara Wernecke. *Oh, You Dundalk Girls, Can't You Dance the Polka?* Morrow, 1984.
Fat but smart and gutsy Beatrice (Bebe) Schmidt becomes one of the crowd in her 1950s suburb of Baltimore. (Fiction)

■ Selected for "Still Alive: The Best of the Best, 1960–1974"

▲ Selected for "The Best of the Best Books: 1970–1983"

◆ Selected for "Nothin' but the Best: Best of the Best Books for Young Adults, 1966–1986"

● Selected for "Here We Go Again: 25 Years of Best Books: Selections from 1967 to 1992"

Durrell, Gerald. *Birds, Beasts, and Relatives,*
Viking, 1969.
An owl in the attic, a bear in the parlor, an overweight sister with acne, and a brother who col-
lects eccentric humans are part of the Durrell
"menagerie" which invades Corfu for a season
and occupies it for five years. (Nonfiction)

————. *Rosy Is My Relative,* Viking, 1968.
Adrian Rookwhistle inherits Rosy, a lovable
beer-drinking elephant, and on their journey
through the English countryside to find a circus home for Rosy, their progress is marked by
many disquieting occasions. (Fiction)

————. *Two in the Bush,* Viking, 1966.
A noted animal collector humorously relates
his travels through New Zealand, Australia, and
Malaysia to observe and photograph flying lizards, lyre birds, and other species close to extinction. (Nonfiction)

————, **and Durrell Lee.** *Amateur Naturalist,*
Knopf, 1984.
In seventeen "nature walks" the authors guide
both amateur and seasoned naturalists from the
beaches to the woodlands, suggesting observations and experiments that do not intrude on
the natural world. (Nonfiction)

Dyer, Daniel. *Jack London: A Biography,*
Scholastic, 1998.
This exciting portrait of the author of *The Call
of the Wild* focuses on London's true-life adven-
tures riding the rails, dogsledding during the
Yukon gold rush, and sailing the South Seas.
(Nonfiction)

Eagan, Andrea Boroff. *Why Am I So
Miserable If These Are the Best Years of My
Life? A Survival Guide for the Young
Woman,* Lippincott, 1976.
This is straight talk on women's anatomy, sex,
and legal rights. (Nonfiction)

Eckert, Allan. *Song of the Wild,* Little, 1981.
The unusual gift of being able to project his
mind inside other living creatures separates
Caleb Erikson from other fourteen-year-olds and
causes tension between his parents and himself. (Fiction)

Edelman, Bernard. *Dear America: Letters
Home from Vietnam,* Norton, 1985. ◆
In their personal letters, soldiers and civilians
reveal the pain, frustration, confusion, and
anger that were part of their daily lives in Vietnam. (Nonfiction)

Edelman, Marian Wright. *Measure of Our
Success: A Letter to My Children and
Yours,* Beacon, 1993.
A powerful mix of personal anecdote and moral
conviction, Edelman's twenty-five lessons for life
are an inspiration for everyone. (Nonfiction)

Edgerton, Clyde. *Floatplane Notebooks,*
Algonquin, 1988.
The love and strength of the Copelands are portrayed generationally as they chronicle their
adventures from a locked shed in rural Georgia. (Fiction)

Edmonds, Walter D. *South African Quirt,*
Little, Brown, 1985.
Natty Dunston, a young boy on a New York
farm, is unwilling to give up his own standards
to adjust to his father's tyrannical demands.
(Fiction)

Einstein, Charles, ed. *Fireside Book of
Baseball,* 4th ed., Simon & Schuster, 1987.
This collection of pictures, cartoons, history,
and poetry in praise of "America's favorite pastime," is a treasury of works by many of America's most talented baseball writers and fans.
(Nonfiction)

Eisen, Jonathan, ed. *Altamont: Death of
Innocence in the Woodstock Nation,* Avon,
1970.
The Altamont Rock Festival, intended to be a
West Coast Woodstock but instead became a
disaster, is clearly examined in relation to its
meaning for the future of the counter-culture.
(Nonfiction)

Elder, Lauren, and Streshinsky, Shirley. *And I
Alone Survived,* Dutton, 1978. ▲
The true story of a courageous young woman,
who, as sole survivor of a plane crash in the
High Sierras, spends a grueling ordeal in the
mountains. (Nonfiction)

Elders, Joycelyn, and Chanoff, David.
*Joycelyn Elders, M.D.: From Sharecropper's
Daughter to Surgeon General of the United
States of America,* Morrow, 1998.
Overcoming poverty and prejudice in a small
farm town in Arkansas, Elders succeeds in becoming a dedicated doctor, advocating for the
poor, and serving as a controversial U.S. Surgeon General. (Nonfiction)

Elfman, Blossom. *Girls of Huntington House,*
Houghton, 1972. ■ ▲
"What can you teach pregnant girls that they
do not already know," ask Blossom Elfman's
friends when they learn she has accepted a
teaching assignment in a school for unwed
mothers. (Fiction)

————. *House for Jonnie O.,* Houghton, 1977.
Jonnie and her three friends—students at a
school for pregnant unmarried teenagers—
search for a "dream house" where they can be
independent and support one another and their
babies. (Fiction)

Ellison, Harlan. *Deathbird Stories: A Pantheon of Modern Gods,* Harper, 1975.
In these tales set in some future time, the objects and rites of man's worship are stretched to the limits of believability and horror. (Fiction)

Embury, Barbara. *Dream Is Alive: A Flight of Discovery Aboard the Space Shuttle,* HarperCollins, 1991.
Based on three shuttle flights, with photographs taken on a 1984 mission, this photoessay describes what takes place on a typical space flight. (Nonfiction)

Epstein, Sam, and Epstein, Beryl. *Kids in Court: The ACLU Defends Their Rights,* Scholastic/Four Winds, 1982.
Eleven case histories that involve the rights of young people who were defended by the American Civil Liberties Union during the 1950s and 1960s become precedents for many of today's court cases. (Nonfiction)

Esquivel, Laura. *Like Water for Chocolate,* Doubleday, 1994.
Tita's life and the food she cooks take a strange twist when her true love Pedro is forbidden her in this tale of magic, comedy, romance, and tragedy. (Fiction)

Faber, Doris. *Love and Rivalry: Three Exceptional Pairs of Sisters,* Viking, 1983.
This narrative examines the relationships between Emily Dickinson, Charlotte Cushman, and Harriet Beecher Stowe and their respective sisters. (Nonfiction)

Fair, Ronald. *We Can't Breathe,* Harper, 1972.
For Ernie Johnson, life in Chicago's black ghetto in the 1930s means roaches and rats, wine and grass, street games and violence, and even the "wow" of discovering a book. (Nonfiction)

Fall, Thomas. *Ordeal of Running Standing,* McCall, 1970.
Running Standing, a Kiowa, and his girl-wife, Crosses-the-River, marry for love but part—she to help her people, he to search for success in the white man's world, a choice which inevitably leads to his betrayal and death. (Fiction)

Fante, John. *1933 Was a Bad Year,* Black Sparrow, 1986.
High school senior Dominic Molise dreams of making it in the major leagues as a pitcher and of making out with his best friend's sister, in this witty and poignant story set in the Depression. (Fiction)

Farmer, Nancy. *The Ear, the Eye, and the Arm,* Orchard/Richard Jackson, 1995.
When General Matsika's three children are kidnapped after they leave the safety of their armed compound, their mother hires the best detective team available in 2194 Zimbabwe—the appropriately named mutant partners—the Ear, the Eye, and the Arm. (Fiction)

———. *A Girl Named Disaster,* Orchard/Richard Jackson, 1997.
When her family arranges her marriage to a cruel man with three wives, Nhamo escapes by canoe to seek a better future. (Fiction)

Farrell, Jeanette. *Invisible Enemies: Stories of Infectious Disease,* Farrar, 1999.
This is a fascinating account of the behaviors, treatments, and control of seven deadly diseases and the scientists who tamed them. (Nonfiction)

Fast, Howard. *Hessian,* Morrow, 1972.
War is the awful villain and two boys are among the victims in this quiet, powerful novel of the American Revolution. (Fiction)

Feelings, Tom. *The Middle Passage: White Ships/Black Cargo,* Dial, 1996.
Feelings' heartrending illustrations document the horrific journey of slaves from Africa to America. (Nonfiction)

———. *Soul Looks Back in Wonder,* Dial, 1994.
The poetry of thirteen African Americans, including Maya Angelou and Langston Hughes, complement Feelings' beautiful illustrations. (Nonfiction)

Feinstein, John. *Season on the Brink: A Year with Bob Knight and the Indiana Hoosiers,* Macmillan, 1987.
The 1985–86 season of controversial coach Bob Knight and the Indiana Hoosiers is chronicled in detail. (Nonfiction)

Feintuch, David. *Midshipman's Hope,* Warner/Aspect, 1996.
Through a series of freak accidents and tragic illnesses, sixteen-year-old Midshipman Nicholas Seafort finds himself in charge of the space vessel U.N.S. Hibernia. (Fiction)

Feldbaum, Carl B., and Bee, Ronald J. *Looking the Tiger in the Eye: Confronting the Nuclear Threat,* Harper, 1988.

■ Selected for "Still Alive: The Best of the Best, 1960–1974"

▲ Selected for "The Best of the Best Books: 1970–1983"

◆ Selected for "Nothin' but the Best: Best of the Best Books for Young Adults, 1966–1986"

● Selected for "Here We Go Again: 25 Years of Best Books: Selections from 1967 to 1992"

This passionate and clear look at the atom bomb examines the way it has changed civilization—and, perhaps, will end it. (Fiction)

Ferazani, Larry. *Rescue Squad,* Morrow, 1975. Being a member of a fire department rescue squad with all the joys and tragedies can lead to enormous emotional and physical costs. (Nonfiction)

Ferris, Jean. *Across the Grain,* Farrar, Straus & Giroux, 1991. Will is dragged from his beloved beach to live in the desert with his irresponsible older sister, where he adjusts with the help of new friends. (Fiction)

————. *Invincible Summer,* Farrar, Straus & Giroux, 1987. While hospitalized with leukemia, Robin and Rick fall in love. (Fiction)

————. *Love among the Walnuts,* Harcourt, 1999. A chicken in a coma? Alexander Huntington-Ackerman can barely cope with the serious stuff, like his diabolical uncles who try to bump off his parents and steal the family fortune. (Fiction)

Ferris, Louanne. *I'm Done Crying,* Evans, 1969. For Louanne Ferris it takes a strong determination to raise a family in a hopeless ghetto neighborhood; but it takes more than determination to survive as a nurse in the inhuman world of a ghetto hospital. (Nonfiction)

Ferris, Timothy. *Spaceshots: The Beauty of Nature beyond Earth,* Pantheon, 1985. Spectacular photographs (with textual explanation) taken from space picture earth, the moon, and a variety of planets, stars, and galaxies. (Nonfiction)

Ferry, Charles. *Binge,* DaisyHill Press, 1993. When his drunken joy ride kills several teenagers, eighteen-year-old Weldon must face the consequences. (Fiction)

————. *Raspberry One,* Houghton, 1983. Two young men, both of whom fall in love before shipping out to the Pacific to fight the Japanese, return home changed and scarred by their war experiences. (Fiction)

Fields, Jeff. *Cry of Angels,* Atheneum, 1974. The antics, adventures, and friendships of an assorted bunch of misfits are woven into a compelling story of a man's capacity for cruelty and love. (Fiction)

Fine, Judylaine. *Afraid to Ask: A Book for Families to Share about Cancer,* Lothrop, 1986. The terrifying subject of cancer is dispassionately explained in Fine's description of the causes, treatment, types, and emotional impact on victims and their families. (Nonfiction)

Fink, Ida. *Scrap of Time: And Other Stories,* Pantheon, 1987. Unforgettable stories evoke the horrific time when Polish Jews wait and suffer while the Nazis destroy their lives. (Fiction)

Finnegan, William. *Crossing the Line: A Year in the Land of Apartheid,* Harper, 1986. While teaching in a "colored" high school in South Africa, Finnegan, a white Californian, witnessed extreme racial segregation and educational repression. (Nonfiction)

Finney, Jack. *Time and Again,* Simon & Schuster, 1970. As part of a top-secret government project, Simon Morley steps out of the twentieth century to take up residence in the New York of 1882, where he becomes involved in blackmail and romance. (Fiction)

Flake, Sharon G. *The Skin I'm In,* Hyperion; dist. by Little, Brown, 1999. Her extremely dark complexion makes thirteen-year-old Malleka the butt of jokes and an outcast—until her teacher shows her that she can accept herself. (Fiction)

Flanigan, Sara. *Alice,* St. Martin's, 1988. A nearly deaf, epileptic teen who has been abused by her family, Alice blossoms after two young neighbors rescue her from a locked shed in rural Georgia. (Fiction)

Fleischman, Paul. *Borning Room,* HarperCollins/C. Zolotow, 1992. Life and death, triumph and tragedy, occur throughout generations of an Ohio farm family in their "borning room." (Fiction)

————. *Bull Run,* HarperCollins/Laura Geringer, 1994. Sixteen individuals voice their hopes and fears in this interwoven collage of "snapshots" set during the first battle of the Civil War. (Fiction)

————. *Dateline: Troy,* Candlewick, 1997. History comes full circle in a retelling of the Trojan War accompanied by newspaper clippings of current events that show how history does indeed repeat itself. (Nonfiction)

————. *Joyful Noise: Poems for Two Voices,* Harper/C. Zolotow, 1988. "Book Lice" and the other delightful two-voice poems in this collection are direct, rhythmic, and great for reading aloud. (Nonfiction)

————. *Seedfolks,* HarperCollins/Joanna Cotler, 1998. Urban neighbors splintered by race, economy, ethnicity, and age join hands in an empty lot to make a garden. (Fiction)

————. *Whirligig,* Holt, 1999. After killing a girl when driving drunk, Brent Bishop learns a lot about himself and life when he's forced to pay for his crime by traveling to the four corners of the U.S. to build whirligigs in her memory. (Fiction)

Fleischman, Sid. *The Abracadabra Kid: A Writer's Life,* Greenwillow, 1997.
From budding vaudevillian-type magician to popular writer of children's books—Fleischman describes his journey with humor and warmth. (Nonfiction)

Fletcher, Susan. *Flight of the Dragon Kyn,* Atheneum/Jean Karl, 1995.
In a story set in the same fantasy world as *Dragon's Milk,* fifteen-year-old Kara is being forced by the king to use her gift of calling birds to help him destroy the dragons who once saved her life. (Fiction)

———. *Shadow Spinner,* Simon & Schuster/Atheneum, 1999.
Crippled Marjan is brought in secret to the sultan's harem to replenish Scheherazade's supply of the tales she tells the sultan so that he won't have her killed. (Fiction)

Fluek, Toby Knobel. *Memories of My Life in a Polish Village, 1930–1949,* Knopf, 1992.
Intimate drawings and paintings portray Jewish life in Poland in the years before, during, and after the Russian and German WWII occupations. (Nonfiction)

Fogle, Bruce. *Encyclopedia of the Cat,* DK Inc., 1998.
This complete and colorful guide to the history, lore, and literature of cats includes many photos as well as tips on cat care. (Nonfiction)

Ford, Michael Thomas. *100 Questions and Answers about AIDS: A Guide for Young People,* Macmillan/New Discovery, 1993.
With reliable and up-to-date research, Ford presents candid and comprehensive answers to questions about AIDS. (Nonfiction)

———. *Voices of AIDS,* Morrow, 1996.
Men and women tell what it is like to be HIV-positive, to have AIDS, or to love someone confronting the disease. (Nonfiction)

Ford, Richard. *Quest for the Faradawn,* Delacorte/Eleanor Friede, 1982.
Nab, raised by forest animals from birth, begins a quest with Beth and several animal companions to save the world from destruction by mankind. (Fiction)

Forman, James D. *Ballad for Hogskin Hill,* Farrar, Straus & Giroux, 1979.
Deciding that big city life is not for him, David Kincaid returns to Kentucky, where he helps his father and grandfather do battle against a powerful coal company. (Fiction)

———. *Becca's Story,* Scribner, 1993.
Becca can't decide which of her two beaus to choose—serious, secure Alex or exciting, unpredictable Charlie—but the Civil War takes away her choice. (Fiction)

Foster, Rory C. *Dr. Wildlife: A Northwoods Veterinarian,* Watts, 1985.
Founder of a hospital for orphaned or injured wild animals, Dr. Foster shows not only his reverence for animal life but also his struggles with the government to establish his practice. (Nonfiction)

Fox, Paula. *Monkey Island,* Orchard/Richard Jackson, 1992.
Awakening in a welfare hotel to find his mother gone, eleven-year-old Clay takes to the streets of New York City and finds shelter with two homeless men who help him survive. (Fiction)

———. *One-Eyed Cat,* Bradbury, 1984. ♦ ●
Sneaking out one night, young Ned Wallace shoots the air rifle his father has forbidden him to use and shortly thereafter becomes guilt-ridden at the appearance of a one-eyed cat. (Fiction)

Fradin, Dennis B. *Planet Hunters,* Simon & Schuster/Margaret K. McElderry, 1998.
Are we alone in space? Explore the universe with those who have sought answers and contact since A.D. 100. (Nonfiction)

Francke, Linda Bird. *Ambivalence of Abortion,* Random, 1978.
Adults and teenagers, women and men, convey their honest feelings about the abortion experience and its effect on their lives. (Nonfiction)

Frank, Anne. *Diary of a Young Girl: The Definitive Edition,* Doubleday, 1996.
This new edition contains the complete diary—some of which was not published in the original work. (Nonfiction)

Fraustino, Lisa R. *Ash,* Orchard, 1996.
When Ash leaves for college, his younger brother, Wes, assumes that Ash will succeed brilliantly—but Ash suddenly becomes an odd stranger. (Fiction)

■ Selected for "Still Alive: The Best of the Best, 1960–1974"

▲ Selected for "The Best of the Best Books: 1970–1983"

♦ Selected for "Nothin' but the Best: Best of the Best Books for Young Adults, 1966–1986"

● Selected for "Here We Go Again: 25 Years of Best Books: Selections from 1967 to 1992"

Frazier, Walt, and Berkow, Ira. *Rockin'
Steady: A Guide to Basketball and Cool,*
Prentice, 1974. ■
"Clyde" explains how to get it all together and be
cool on and off the basketball court. (Nonfiction)

Freedman, Russell. *Eleanor Roosevelt: A Life
of Discovery,* Clarion, 1994.
A compelling photo-biography of Eleanor Roosevelt relates the remarkable story of a shy,
lonely girl who grows up to be a powerful force
in the fight for world peace and equality and an
inspiration to millions of people. (Nonfiction)

————. *Franklin Delano Roosevelt,* Clarion,
1991.
The complex and controversial life and times
of FDR are revealed in Freedman's powerful
photobiography. (Nonfiction)

————. *Indian Chiefs,* Holiday, 1987.
Words and pictures tell the stories of six legendary Native American chiefs who are forced
off their lands by westward expansion and the
United States government. (Nonfiction)

————. *Indian Winter,* Holiday, 1993.
Paintings by Karl Bodmer and journal entries
by German prince Maximilian immerse you in
their 1833–34 winter stay-over in Missouri River
Indian country. (Nonfiction)

————. *Kids at Work: Lewis Hine and the
Crusade against Child Labor,* Clarion, 1995.
Through the impressive photography of reformer-
photographer Hine and direct writing, Freedman
chronicles the state of child labor in early-
twentieth century America. (Nonfiction)

————. *The Life and Death of Crazy Horse,*
Holiday, 1997.
This vivid portrait of Crazy Horse and his times
traces his development from a shy, sensitive
young warrior to the brave Sioux leader at the
Battle of Little Big Horn. (Nonfiction)

————. *Lincoln: A Photobiography,* Clarion,
1988.
This skillfully written, appealing overview of
Lincoln's life from boyhood to death is accompanied by carefully chosen photographs and
prints. (Nonfiction)

————. *Martha Graham: A Dancer's Life,*
Clarion, 1999.
An eloquent photo-biography of a woman who,
after being told she was too old, too short, too
heavy, and too plain to become a professional
dancer, goes on to revolutionize the world of
modern dance through determination and talent. (Nonfiction)

————. *Wright Brothers: How They Invented
the Airplane,* Holiday, 1992.
Freedman tells the fascinating story of how two
self-taught bicycle mechanics solve the prob-

lems that had baffled generations of scientists
and engineers. (Nonfiction)

Freedman, Samuel G. *Small Victories: The
Real World of a Teacher, Her Students, and
Their High School,* HarperCollins, 1991.
The neglected students at Stewart Park High
School in Manhattan and their caring teacher,
Jessica Siegel, find a way to beat the odds and
make a future. (Nonfiction)

Freeman, Suzanne. *The Cuckoo's Child,*
Greenwillow, 1997.
In Beirut, Mia longed for a normal American
life, but after her parents are lost at sea, she
finds life in Tennessee a real challenge. (Fiction)

Freemantle, Brian. *Good-bye to an Old
Friend,* Putnam, 1973.
A Russian space scientist appears to defect to
England, but a British investigator, a scruffy and
intelligent civil servant, has his doubts. (Fiction)

Fremon, Celeste. *Father Greg & the
Homeboys,* Hyperion, 1996.
Through his work with L.A. gang members, Father Greg proves that one person can make a
difference. (Nonfiction)

French, Albert. *Billy,* Viking, 1995.
In 1930 Mississippi, it is punishable by death
for a black to kill a white, even if it is an accident—and even if the "killer" is only ten years
old. (Fiction)

Fretz, Sada. *Going Vegetarian: A Guide for
Teen-agers,* Morrow, 1983.
This complete guide includes the reasons why
people become vegetarians and how to plan a
healthy, meatless diet, along with wonderful
recipes. (Nonfiction)

Frey, Darcy. *The Last Shot: City Streets,
Basketball Dreams,* Houghton, 1996.
Journalist Frey follows the lives of four hoop
stars of Abraham Lincoln High School as they
pursue their dreams of athletic scholarships.
(Nonfiction)

Friedman, Ina R. *Other Victims: First-Person
Stories of Non-Jews Persecuted by the
Nazis,* Houghton, 1991.
Would you be considered "unworthy of life"?
Hitler's persecution extended beyond Jews; those
often forgotten victims are remembered in these
compelling first-person narratives. (Nonfiction)

Friedman, Myra. *Buried Alive: The Biography
of Janis Joplin,* Morrow, 1973. ■
Janis Joplin, the great legendary rock singer of
the '60s, has a passion for life but is also a tortured and driven woman. (Nonfiction)

Friedman, Philip. *Rage,* Atheneum, 1972.
Dying, as is his son, from exposure to experimental nerve gas, Dan Logan uses the last reserves of his strength to take revenge. (Fiction)

Friel, Brian. *Philadelphia, Here I Come!*
Farrar, Straus & Giroux, 1966.
Gar's last night at home, as dramatized in this contemporary play, exposes the lack of communication between generations. (Nonfiction)

Fuer, Elizabeth. *Paper Doll,* Farrar, Straus & Giroux, 1991.
An amputee, Leslie has centered on becoming a concert violinist, but now her developing relationship with Jeff is forcing her to reevaluate her choices. (Fiction)

Fuller, John G. *Ghost of Flight 401,* Berkley, 1976.
Ghosts of crew members killed in the 1972 Eastern Airlines Everglades disaster haunt the crews and passengers of other flights. (Nonfiction)

———. *Incident at Exeter,* Putnam, 1966.
A journalist investigaties unexplained UFO phenomena. (Nonfiction)

———. *Poison That Fell from the Sky,* Random, 1978.
Fuller dramatically reports the 1976 accident at a chemical factory that left a small Italian town permanently poisoned and its evacuated inhabitants physically and emotionally scarred. (Nonfiction)

Fussell, Samuel Wilson. *Muscle: Confessions of an Unlikely Bodybuilder,* Poseidon, 1992.
His muscles are like iron and ripple under the stage lights; steroids have made him perfect. But something is wrong! (Fiction)

Gaan, Margaret. *Little Sister,* Dodd, 1983.
Little Sister, a third-generation Chinese American, visits Shanghai at the beginning of a revolution and learns about her family from family members. (Fiction)

Gaiman, Neil, and Pratchett, Terry. *Good Omens: The Nice and Accurate Prophecies of Agnes Nutter, Witch,* Workman, 1992.
In this zany romp, living on Earth is so much fun that Crowley, the demon, and Aziraphale, the angel, disobey orders and team up to prevent the Apocalypse. (Fiction)

Gaines, Ernest J. *The Autobiography of Miss Jane Pittman,* Dial, 1971. ■ ●
Born a slave in Louisiana before the Civil War, Jane Pittman lives to witness the struggle in the 1960s for civil rights in this fictional autobiography that reflects the courage and fortitude of America's blacks. (Fiction)

———. *Gathering of Old Men,* Knopf, 1983.
When a white man is killed by an African American in Louisiana, more than a dozen aging black men and one young white woman each confess to the sheriff, each with a different long-standing motive. (Fiction)

———. *A Lesson before Dying,* Knopf, 1994.
Jefferson, a black youth likened to a hog and sentenced to death for a crime he did not commit, must learn to regain his self-esteem and face death with dignity. (Fiction)

Gaines, William, and Feldstein, Albert, eds. *Ridiculously Expensive MAD,* World, 1969. ■
MAD is seventeen years old and this is a collection of the best of the worst from the magazine which takes on the Establishment with vigor and revels in its inanities. (Nonfiction)

Gale, Jay. *Young Man's Guide to Sex,* Holt, 1984.
A comprehensive and explicit guide to sex and sexuality, written specifically for young men. (Nonfiction)

Gallagher, Hugh Gregory. *FDR's Splendid Deception,* Dodd, 1985.
New insights into Roosevelt's life are provided as Gallagher reveals the way in which FDR refused to admit or expose his physical handicap—paralysis resulting from polio. (Nonfiction)

Gallery, Daniel. *Stand By-y-y to Start Engines,* Norton, 1966.
Ensign Willie Wigglesworth is the ringleader of above-deck monkey business in a series of salty anecdotes about life aboard the atomic carrier *Guadalcanal.* (Fiction)

Gallo, Donald R., ed. *No Easy Answers: Short Stories about Teenagers Making Tough Choices,* Delacorte, 1998.
Teens face tough ethical and moral choices in this collection of sixteen stories. (Fiction)

———. *Sixteen: Short Stories by Outstanding Writers for Young Adults,* Delacorte, 1984. ◆ ●
School, friendship, family, and love are all found within this unusual collection of humorous and serious short stories. (Fiction)

■ Selected for "Still Alive: The Best of the Best, 1960–1974"
▲ Selected for "The Best of the Best Books: 1970–1983"
◆ Selected for "Nothin' but the Best: Best of the Best Books for Young Adults, 1966–1986"
● Selected for "Here We Go Again: 25 Years of Best Books: Selections from 1967 to 1992"

———. *Speaking for Ourselves: Autobiographical Sketches by Notable Authors of Books for Young Adults,* NCTE, 1991.
Popular young adult authors, from Lloyd Alexander to Paul Zindel, write brief sketches about their lives and work. (Nonfiction)

———. *Visions: Nineteen Short Stories by Outstanding Writers for Young Adults,* Delacorte, 1987.
Stories of youthful discoveries, among them, Richard Peck's "Shadows," in which an orphan learns about love, and Todd Strasser's "On the Bridge," in which Seth learns about betrayal from a friend. (Fiction)

Galloway, Priscilla. *Truly Grim Tales,* Delacorte, 1996.
Not for the faint of heart! Eight familiar fairy tales are twisted into sinister, macabre stories. (Fiction)

Garani, Gary, and Schulman, Paul. *Fantastic Television,* Harmony, 1977.
This pictorial history of the best of fifties and sixties television serials and science fiction includes *Star Trek, Batman, Twilight Zone,* and *Superman.* (Nonfiction)

Garden, Nancy. *Annie on My Mind,* Farrar, Straus & Giroux, 1982. ▲ ◆ ●
Lisa and Annie meet at New York's Metropolitan Museum of Art, fall in love, and then find that a public declaration is too threatening to their friends and relatives. (Fiction)

Garfield, Brian. *Paladin,* Simon & Schuster, 1980. ◆
A fifteen-year-old boy, recruited by Winston Churchill to be his personal secret agent, is involved in murder, assassination, and sabotage on both sides of the front lines in this World War II novel. (Fiction)

———. *Recoil,* Morrow, 1977.
With his government-manufactured cover blown and syndicate men closing in, a former star government witness decides to turn the tables on his pursuers. (Fiction)

Garland, Sherry. *Indio,* Harcourt, 1996.
Ipa-tah-chi survives an Apache raid on her pueblo. Later, on her wedding day, strange white-skinned men riding horses capture her. Can she escape? (Fiction)

———. *Shadow of the Dragon,* Harcourt, 1994.
Sixteen-year-old Danny Vo must resolve the conflict between his recently immigrated Vietnamese cousin, a Vietnamese gang, Danny's girlfriend, and her skinhead brother's gang. (Fiction)

———. *Song of the Buffalo Boy,* Harcourt, 1993.
Running away to Ho Chi Minh City with the boy she loves after being promised in marriage to a menacing old man, seventeen-year-old Loi tries to find out about her American soldier father. (Fiction)

Gaylin, Willard, M.D. *In the Service of Their Country: War Resistors in Prison,* Viking, 1970.
Six imprisoned war resistors tell their stories in compelling case histories as recorded by Dr. Gaylin, a psychiatrist. (Nonfiction)

Gedge, Pauline. *Child of the Morning,* Dial, 1977.
Reared by her Pharaoh father to assume his throne upon his death, Hatshepsut—a real historical figure—has to contend with her weak half-brother before she can realize her dream. (Fiction)

Gee, Maurice. *The Champion,* Simon & Schuster, 1994.
The arrival of an African American soldier in a small New Zealand community during World War II changes the lives of twelve-year-old Rex and his friends forever. (Fiction)

Gelman, Rita Golden. *Inside Nicaragua: Young People's Dreams and Fears,* Watts, 1988.
The fear and danger surrounding the war between the Sandinistas and the Contras are recorded through the lives of Nicaragua's youth. (Fiction)

Geras, Adele. *Voyage,* Atheneum, 1983.
A group of young Jewish immigrants share love, friendship, hope, and fears during their two-week voyage in steerage to America, the land of freedom. (Fiction)

Gibbons, Kaye. *Charms for an Easy Life,* Putnam, 1994.
In the years before and during World War II, Margaret comes of age with the help of a self-educated and highly successful doctor/grandmother and a mother in search of the perfect man. (Fiction)

———. *Ellen Foster,* Algonquin, 1987.
After her mother's untimely death, young Ellen must survive despite her abusive father and other relatives who want no part of her. (Fiction)

Giblin, James Cross. *Charles A. Lindbergh: A Human Hero,* Clarion, 1998.
"Lucky Lindy" becomes an American hero when he makes the first nonstop transatlantic flight, but he falls into disgrace after being accused of sympathizing with the Nazis. (Nonfiction)

———. *When Plague Strikes: The Black Death, Smallpox, AIDS,* Harper Collins, 1996.
This eye-opening account of three of humankind's most serious epidemics is told with compassion and depth. (Nonfiction)

Giddings, Robert. *War Poets,* Orion, 1988.
The work of a variety of World War I poets, many of whom died in that conflict, is reinforced with illustrations, biographical notes, and a brief history of "the war to end all wars." (Nonfiction)

Gies, Miep, and Gold, Alison Leslie. *Anne Frank Remembered: The Story of Miep Gies, Who Helped to Hide the Frank Family,* Simon & Schuster, 1987. ●
The story of quiet personal courage by the woman who hid the Frank family and retrieved Anne's diary so that the world would never forget is itself unforgettable—and inspiring. (Nonfiction)

Gilman, Dorothy. *Clairvoyant Countess,* Doubleday, 1975.
Exotic Madame Karitska and her psychic powers help the police handle some of their more distressing dilemmas: robbery, murder, voodoo possession, and a missing person. (Fiction)

———. *Unexpected Mrs. Pollifax,* Doubleday, 1966.
Volunteering her services to the CIA the irrepressible Mrs. Pollifax accepts a job as courier to Mexico where her safe assignment suddenly becomes sinister. (Fiction)

Gilmore, Kate. *Enter Three Witches,* Houghton, 1991.
Sixteen-year-old Bren finds living with witches hard enough, but how can he prevent his girlfriend from discovering their existence? (Fiction)

Gilstrap, John. *Nathan's Run,* HarperCollins, 1997.
Having escaped from a juvenile detention center after killing a guard, twelve-year-old Nathan is running for his life, searching for someone who will believe he really is a victim of circumstance. (Fiction)

Gingher, Marianne. *Bobby Rex's Greatest Hit,* Atheneum, 1986.
A suggestive hit song by a small North Carolina town's heartthrob catapults its namesake, Pally Thompson, into the national limelight and passionate disavowal. (Fiction)

Giovanni, Nikki. *Gemini,* Bobbs, 1972.
A dynamic young African American writer explores her life and times with the fierce intensity of a poet. (Nonfiction)

———. *My House: Poems,* Morrow, 1973.
A well-known African American author celebrates love in all its many facets with gentle, compelling immediacy. (Nonfiction)

———. *Women and the Men,* Morrow, 1975.
Poems, from the heart and soul of a spirited young woman, that speak directly to the lives of young and old, women and men. (Nonfiction)

Girion, Barbara. *Handful of Stars,* Scribner, 1982.
Julie Meyers, fifteen, must learn to cope with epilepsy as her resentment mounts against the thoughtless cruelties of her family and friends. (Fiction)

———. *Tangle of Roots,* Scribner, 1979.
When her mother's unexpected death forces sixteen-year-old Beth Frankle to cope with grief and sorrow, her relationships with family and friends are affected. (Fiction)

Glass, Frankcina. *Marvin & Tige,* St. Martin's, 1978.
Tige, an orphaned eleven-year-old streetwise African American youth, and Marvin, a white alcoholic executive dropout, establish a friendship based on caring for and needing each other. (Fiction)

Glasser, Ronald J. *Ward 402,* Braziller, 1973.
While treating a child dying of leukemia, a young intern is forced to reexamine his attitudes and those of his colleagues toward their daily dealings with life and death. (Nonfiction)

Glenn, Mel. *Class Dismissed! High School Poems,* Clarion, 1982. ▲
Glenn's poems, accompanied by photographs, mirror the agony and the ecstasy of high school as experienced by young people. (Nonfiction)

———. *Jump Ball: A Basketball Season in Poems,* Dutton/Lodestar, 1998.
The rhythm of basketball permeates a series of poems that tell the story of the Tower High School team's winning season. (Nonfiction)

———. *My Friend's Got This Problem, Mr. Candler,* Clarion, 1992.
Poems, both serious and funny, express the thoughts and emotions of students and their families as they speak to a high school guidance counselor. (Nonfiction)

■ Selected for "Still Alive: The Best of the Best, 1960–1974"

▲ Selected for "The Best of the Best Books: 1970–1983"

◆ Selected for "Nothin' but the Best: Best of the Best Books for Young Adults, 1966–1986"

● Selected for "Here We Go Again: 25 Years of Best Books: Selections from 1967 to 1992"

———. *The Taking of Room 114,* Dutton/ Lodestar, 1998.
First-person narrative poems focus on the last day of high school, when a distraught history teacher holds his seniors hostage. (Nonfiction)

———. *Who Killed Mr. Chippendale? A Mystery in Poems,* Dutton/Lodestar, 1997.
A high-school English teacher's murder is witnessed, investigated, and solved in a series of clever poems. (Nonfiction)

Godden, Rumer. *Thursday's Children,* Viking, 1984.
Neglected Doone Penny and his pampered older sister, Crystal, both strive to be the best in the competitive world of ballet. (Fiction)

Golden, Frederic. *Trembling Earth: Probing and Predicting Quakes,* Scribner, 1983.
This a clear and concise statement of present knowledge concerning earthquakes is brief enough to be exciting but complete enough to cover the facts. (Nonfiction)

Goldman, E. M. *Getting Lincoln's Goat,* Delacorte, 1996.
When Lincoln High's beloved mascot—an old goat—disappears before the big football game, Elliot has the perfect opportunity to excel in a class assignment to learn about the world of private detectives. (Fiction)

Goldman, Peter, and Fuller, Tony. *Charlie Company: What Vietnam Did to Us,* Morrow, 1983. •
Men who served in Vietnam talk with poignancy, pain, and bitterness about their experiences. (Nonfiction)

Goldston, Robert. *Sinister Touches: The Secret War against Hitler,* Dial, 1982.
Dramatic accounts of covert activities and espionage during World War II read like a spy novel. (Nonfiction)

Gordon, Jacquie. *Give Me One Wish,* Norton, 1988.
A mother tells the bittersweet story of the short life of her daughter Chris, who, despite being stricken with cystic fibrosis, eagerly participates in high school activities and in everything from slam dancing and trying pot to Christian fellowship. (Fiction)

Gordon, Ruth, ed. *Pierced by a Ray of Sun,* HarperCollins, 1996.
In this unusually attractive anthology, world-famous poets reflect on the experience of feeling alone. (Nonfiction)

———. *Under All Silences: Shades of Love: An Anthology of Poems,* Harper/C. Zolotow, 1987.
From e. e. cummings and Sappho to Emily Dickinson and Yosan Akiko, this collection of poems celebrates the universal experience of love and passion. (Nonfiction)

Gordon, Sheila. *Waiting for the Rain,* Watts/ Orchard/ Richard Jackson, 1987.
On a South African farm, Tengo, black, and Frikkie, white, forge a friendship that is later challenged by the injustices of apartheid. (Fiction)

Gordon, Sol, and Conant, Roger. *You! The Teenage Survival Book,* Quadrangle, 1976.
A positive, practical, lively approach to learning about "you." Comic book sections include "Ten Heavy Facts about Sex" and "Juice Use." (Nonfiction)

Gordon, Suzanne. *Off Balance: The Real World of Ballet,* Pantheon, 1983.
Behind the glittering facade of ballet lies a darker world of pain, rivalry, and exploitation. (Nonfiction)

Goro, Herb. *Block,* Random, 1970.
The struggle for survival by young blacks in a decaying Bronx neighborhood is told in pictures and text to show the underlying pride and hope of people trapped in a hopeless situation. (Nonfiction)

Goulart, Ron. *What's Become of Screwloose? and Other Inquiries,* Scribner, 1971.
A computer turned author, a homicidal dishwasher, an evil pet dog who is also a cyborg, and a totally automated house are just four of the malign machines which populate these stories. (Nonfiction)

Gould, Steven. *Jumper,* Tor, 1993.
Davy jumps for the first time when he escapes a beating by teleporting to the library. Now he's on the run from his alcoholic father, the police, and a secret government agency—but who can catch a jumper? (Fiction)

———. *Wildside,* Tor; dist. by Little, Brown, 1997.
Eighteen-year-old Charlie faces challenges and danger when he explores a pristine world he found on the other side of his barn door. (Fiction)

Grace, Fran. *Branigan's Dog,* Bradbury, 1981.
After the loss of his beloved dog, Casey Branigan is forced out of his self-imposed isolation and must confront the reason for his impulse to set fires. (Fiction)

Graham, Robin Lee, and Gill, Derek L. T. *Dove,* Harper, 1972. ■
Setting out in his sloop Dove to encircle the globe, a sixteen-year-old boy finds adventure and romance. (Nonfiction)

Granatelli, Anthony. *They Call Me Mister 500,* Regnery, 1969.
Andy Granatelli, daring automobile racer and builder, tells how he made it through poverty

and crashes to become a millionaire at age thirty. (Nonfiction)

Grant, Cynthia D. *Mary Wolf,* Simon & Schuster/Atheneum, 1996.
Sixteen-year-old Mary longs for a normal life as her family travels the country aimlessly in their RV after her father loses his job. (Fiction)

———. *Phoenix Rising; or, How to Survive Your Life,* Atheneum, 1990. ●
Reading her sister Helen's diary of her yearlong bout with cancer helps Jenny cope with her feelings of pain and anger about Helen's death. (Fiction)

———. *Shadow Man,* Atheneum, 1994.
Dead at eighteen, having wrapped his pickup around a tree while drunk, Gabriel McCloud is brought to "life" again through the first-person narratives of those who knew and loved him, including his pregnant girlfriend. (Fiction)

———. *Uncle Vampire,* Atheneum, 1994.
Twins Carolyn and Honey have a family secret— there's a "vampire" in their midst. (Fiction)

Gravelle, Karen, and Peterson, Leslie. *Teenage Fathers,* Messner, 1993.
Thirteen teenage fathers talk about their parenthood with feelings that range from total alienation and irresponsibility to complete devotion to the children they have fathered. (Nonfiction)

Gray, Martin, and Gallo, Max. *For Those I Loved,* Little, 1973.
A Polish Jew survives the horrors of wartime Warsaw and a Nazi death camp only to be deprived of his well-earned peace and happiness by a cruel twist of fate. (Nonfiction)

Green, Connie Jordan. *War at Home,* Macmillan/McElderry Books, 1990.
Chauvinistic Virgil infuriates cousin Mattie when he comes to live with her family in Oak Ridge, Tennessee, during the secretive and security-ridden days of World War II. (Fiction)

Greenbaum, Dorothy, and Laiken, Deidre S. *Lovestrong,* Times Books, 1985.
Dorothy Greenbaum, wife and mother, struggles to get through medical school and become a doctor. (Nonfiction)

Greenberg, Jan. *No Dragons to Slay,* Farrar, Straus & Giroux, 1984.
A high school soccer star afflicted with cancer finds the courage to fight back while working at an exciting archaeological dig. (Fiction)

———, **and Jordan, Sandra.** *American Eye: Eleven Artists of the Twentieth Century,* Delacorte, 1996.
Innovative and energetic images of twentieth-century art are interwoven with biographies of artists and discussions of individual artworks. (Nonfiction)

Greenberg, Joanne. *Far Side of Victory,* Holt, 1983.
Paroled after being sentenced for "driving under the influence," Eric Gordon meets Helen, the woman whose husband and children his car had killed. (Fiction)

———. *In This Sign,* Holt, 1970. ▲ ◆
The isolation and the often frenzied rage of the deaf in trying to cope in a hearing world are vividly portrayed in this story of Abel and Janice Ryder and their hearing daughter, Margaret. (Fiction)

———. *Of Such Small Differences,* Holt, 1988. ●
Immersed in the world of twenty-five-year-old blind and deaf John Moon, the reader experiences not only John's attempts to survive alone, but also the turmoil, passion, and love brought into his life by Leda, a sighted, hearing actress. (Fiction)

———. *Simple Gifts,* Holt, 1986.
A simple poor family of engaging misfits turns their ranch into a place where visitors pay to sample "authentic" 1880s homestead life. (Fiction)

Greenburger, Ingrid. *Private Treason: A German Memoir,* Little, 1973.
Rejecting Nazism completely, this gentile girl leaves her country and family and flees to France where she falls in love with a young French Resistance worker. (Nonfiction)

Greene, Constance C. *Love Letters of J. Timothy Owen,* Harper, 1986.
Tim thinks he will finally have a successful romance when he sends anonymous love letters, but the results are unexpected and discouraging. (Fiction)

Greene, Marilyn, and Provost, Gary. *Finder: The Story of a Private Investigator,* Crown, 1988.
The story of Marilyn Green, no hard-boiled detective but a housewife who finds a career through years of search and rescue training, hard work, and caring. (Nonfiction)

- ■   Selected for "Still Alive: The Best of the Best, 1960–1974"
- ▲   Selected for "The Best of the Best Books: 1970–1983"
- ◆   Selected for "Nothin' but the Best: Best of the Best Books for Young Adults, 1966–1986"
- ●   Selected for "Here We Go Again: 25 Years of Best Books: Selections from 1967 to 1992"

Greenfield, Josh, and Mazursky, Paul. *Harry & Tonto,* Saturday Review Press, 1974.
Forcibly evicted from his condemned apartment house, seventy-two-year-old Harry and his marmalade cat, Tonto, set off on an hilarious cross-country jaunt to a new life in California. (Fiction)

Greenfield, Susan, ed. *The Human Mind Explained: An Owner's Guide to the Mysteries of the Mind,* Holt, 1998.
The ultimate handbook of the brain—full-color graphics and clear explanations bring within reach an understanding of the most complex human system. (Nonfiction)

Gregory, Kristiana. *Earthquake at Dawn,* Harcourt/Gulliver, 1993.
Experience being a survivor of one of the worst earthquakes in American history. (Nonfiction)

Gregory, Susan. *Hey, White Girl!* Norton, 1970.
Susan Gregory attends a black ghetto high school in her senior year and becomes more than another "whitey" in this rare and honest book. (Nonfiction)

Griffin, Adele. *The Other Shepards,* Hyperion; dist. by Little, Brown, 1999.
Geneva and Holland Shepard must travel far from their Greenwich Village townhouse to dispel the ghosts of their older brothers and sister, who died nearly twenty years earlier. (Fiction)

————. *Sons of Liberty,* Hyperion; dist. by Little, Brown, 1998.
Thirteen-year-old Rock is torn about running away from his controlling father, but older brother Cliff sees flight as the only way to deal with those kooky, bizarre midnights working on the roof. (Fiction)

Grisham, John. *Pelican Brief,* Doubleday, 1993.
When the wrong people find Darby Shaw's legal brief outlining her theory about who killed two Supreme Court justices, she must use all her wits to outrun them and save her own life. (Fiction)

Grunwald, Lisa. *Summer,* Knopf, 1986.
Intimate summers with her artistic family on a Massachusetts island have always been perfect, but now Jennifer must bear her dying mother's last summer. (Fiction)

Guest, Judith. *Ordinary People,* Viking, 1976. ▲ ◆ ●
Seventeen-year-old Conrad returns home from a mental institution, where he was sent after his brother's accidental death and his own ensuing suicide attempt. To begin a new life he must learn to accept himself and those close to him. (Fiction)

Guffy, Ossie, and Ledner, Caryl. *Ossie: The Autobiography of a Black Woman,* Norton, 1971.
An African American woman, who is not famous, smart, or rich but just loves her children and wants the best she can get for them, tells a moving story. (Nonfiction)

Gurney, James. *Dinotopia: A Land Apart from Time,* Turner Publishing, 1993.
A newly discovered, illustrated journal reveals life on the lost island of Dinotopia, where shipwrecked human survivors work and play in harmony with dinosaurs. (Fiction)

Guy, David. *Football Dreams,* Seaview, 1981.
Dan Keith desperately wants to succeed as a high school football player—mostly to please and prove himself to his dying father. (Fiction)

————. *Second Brother,* NAL, 1986.
High school freshman Henry underestimates his own special talents in the shadows of his superachieving older brother and his daredevil "Renaissance man" best friend. (Fiction)

Guy, Rosa. *Disappearance,* Delacorte, 1979. ◆
Released from jail in the custody of the Aimsley Family, Imamu Jones immediately becomes a prime suspect when Perk, their youngest daughter, disappears. (Fiction)

————. *Edith Jackson,* Viking, 1978. ▲
Though Edith fails in her struggle to hold her orphaned family of three younger sisters together and has an unhappy love affair, she eventually begins to discover her own identity. (Fiction)

————. *The Friends,* Holt, 1973. ■ ▲ ◆ ●
Rejected by her classmates because she "talks funny," Phyllisia Cathy, a young West Indian girl, is forced to become friends with poor, frazzled Edith, the only one who will accept her. (Fiction)

————. *Music of Summer,* Delacorte, 1993.
Spending the summer on Cape Cod, talented pianist Sara, who is ostracized by Cathy and her "light skinned" friends, overcomes racism with courage and the help of a new love. (Fiction)

————. *Ruby,* Viking, 1976.
Ruby, daughter of a West Indian restaurant owner in Harlem, fights her loneliness by forming a relationship with the beautiful Daphne. (Fiction)

Habenstreit, Barbara. *To My Brother Who Did a Crime . . . : Former Prisoners Tell Their Stories in Their Own Words,* Doubleday, 1973.
Taped interviews with prisoners who are allowed to enroll and live at Long Island University in a rehabilitation experiment reveal that some can make it and some cannot. (Nonfiction)

Haddix, Margaret Peterson. *Among the Hidden*, Simon & Schuster, 1999.
After remaining hidden for twelve years because the population police want to eliminate all third children, Luke finally has hope for a future when he learns there are others like him. (Fiction)

————. *Don't You Dare Read This, Mrs. Dunphrey*, Simon & Schuster, 1997.
Hoping that her teacher will keep her promise not to read her English journal, Tish reveals her growing anxiety, which begins with the return of her abusive father. (Fiction)

————. *Leaving Fishers*, Simon & Schuster, 1998.
Dorry has just moved to Indianapolis and has no friends—until she joins a church group called "Fishers of Men." Soon she is no longer making her own decisions. (Fiction)

————. *Running Out of Time*, Simon & Schuster, 1997.
Thirteen-year-old Jessie learns that she is not living in 1840 but in a historical demonstration village in 1995. (Fiction)

Hahn, Mary Downing. *The Wind Blows Backward*, Clarion, 1994.
High-school seniors Lauren and Spencer try to return to their innocent days of reading fantasies together, but fantasy worlds and Lauren's love cannot save Spencer from the insistent, disturbing memories of his father. (Fiction)

Hailey, Kendall. *Day I Became an Autodidact: And the Advice, Adventures, and Acrimonies That Befell Me Thereafter*, Doubleday, 1988.
This journal records the joys and pitfalls of Kendall Hailey's life after she decided at fifteen to graduate early and stay home to educate herself. (Nonfiction)

Haing, Ngor, and Warner, Roger. *Cambodian Odyssey*, Macmillan, 1988.
Cambodian doctor Haing Ngor chronicles the destruction of his homeland and family under the brutal rule of the Khmer Rouge. (Nonfiction)

Halberstam, David. *Amateurs*, Morrow, 1985.
By providing an in-depth look at the Olympic rowing team, Halberstam truly defines what is involved in "going for the gold." (Nonfiction)

Haley, Alex. *Roots*, Doubleday, 1976.
This poignant and powerful narrative tells the dramatic story of Kunta Kinte, snatched from freedom in Africa and brought by ship to America and slavery, and his descendants. (Nonfiction)

Hall, Barbara. *Dixie Storms*, Harcourt Brace Jovanovich, 1991.
Spending all her fourteen years in a small Virginia farming town, Dutch Peyton has found life to be pretty good until the drought-plagued summer when her sophisticated cousin Norma arrives and family secrets bring trouble. (Fiction)

————. *Fool's Hill*, Bantam, 1993.
Summer is usually long, hot, and boring in Libby's small town, but when two new girls with a convertible move into the area, Libby discovers that excitement also brings frightening choices. (Fiction)

Hall, Elizabeth. *Possible Impossibilities: A Look at Parapsychology*, Houghton, 1977.
This is a sensible look at what's possible and what's impossible about telepathy, clairvoyance, precognition, psychokinesis, and other psychic phenomena. (Nonfiction)

Hall, Lynn. *Flying Changes*, Harcourt Brace Jovanovich, 1992.
The Kansas prairie sizzles as seventeen-year-old Denny faces the aftermath of her first love affair, her rodeo-rider father's crippling injury, and her mother's sudden reentry into her life. (Fiction)

————. *Just One Friend*, Scribner, 1985.
Unattractive and slightly retarded, Dory is desperate for just one friend when she is mainstreamed—with tragic results—into a regular high school. (Fiction)

————. *Leaving*, Scribner, 1980.
After graduation from high school, Roxanne believes it is time to leave her familiar home and family farm. A job in the big city may be her ticket to happiness—or is it? (Fiction)

————. *Solitary*, Scribner, 1986.
Unwilling to accept the support of others, Jane returns to her backwoods childhood home to become independent and self-reliant. (Fiction)

————. *Sticks and Stones*, Follett, 1972. ■
Sixteen and a newcomer to tiny Buck Creek, Iowa, Tom Naylor suddenly realizes that the hostility of his fellow students and teachers is

---

■ Selected for "Still Alive: The Best of the Best, 1960–1974"
▲ Selected for "The Best of the Best Books: 1970–1983"
◆ Selected for "Nothin' but the Best: Best of the Best Books for Young Adults, 1966–1986"
● Selected for "Here We Go Again: 25 Years of Best Books: Selections from 1967 to 1992"

due to his friendship with Ward Alexander. (Fiction)

———. *Uphill All the Way,* Scribner, 1984. Callie, seventeen, learns that being a horse-shoer is easier than helping a troubled delinquent friend. (Fiction)

Hallet, Jean-Pierre. *Congo Kitabu,* Random, 1966. Astounding adventures of a Belgian civil servant arise while working with the people and animals in the jungles of the Congo. (Nonfiction)

Hamanaka, Sheila. *Journey,* Watts, 1991. Hamanaka's mural presents a capsule history of Japanese-American oppression before and during World War II, and the slow healing after the war. (Nonfiction)

Hambly, Barbara. *Dragonsbane,* Ballantine/Del Rey, 1986. John, the Dragonsbane, fights the dreaded Black Dragon, but Jenny, a half-taught sorceress and mother of John's two sons, pays the price of the dragon's surrender. (Fiction)

———. *Stranger at the Wedding,* Ballantine/Del Rey, 1995. Journeyman wizard Kyra returns home to save her sister, Alix, from a sinister wizard's death spell and falls in love with her sister's betrothed. (Fiction)

———. *Those Who Hunt the Night,* Ballantine/Del Rey, 1988. The silent tombs of London's Highgate Cemetery and the gaiety of 1906 Paris are the settings when James Asher is forced to investigate the mystery of who is killing the vampires of London. (Fiction)

Hamilton, Eleanor. *Sex with Love: A Guide for Young People,* Beacon, 1978. Candid and liberal, though advising some restraints, this sex handbook takes a positive approach to human sexuality. (Nonfiction)

Hamilton, Virginia. *Anthony Burns: The Defeat and Triumph of a Fugitive Slave,* Knopf, 1988. Anthony Burns escapes from slavery only to be returned to it under the Fugitive Slave Law—until he regains his freedom through the efforts of the antislavery movement. (Nonfiction)

———. *Cousins,* Putnam/Philomel, 1991. In trying to cope with her grandmother's aging and death, Cammy overlooks the terrifying knowledge that younger people die as well—in deaths that seem to have no reason. (Fiction)

———. *Her Stories: African American Folktales, Fairy Tales, and True Tales,* Scholastic/Blue Sky, 1996. This feast of folktales and fairy tales about and by women is strikingly illustrated. (Nonfiction)

———. *In the Beginning: Creation Stories from Around the World,* Harcourt Brace Jovanovich, 1988. A visually stunning treatment of creation myths, told by people from around the world, reminds us of the spirit and the vivid imagination of the human race. (Nonfiction)

———. *Little Love,* Putnam/Philomel, 1984. Sustained by the love of her boyfriend and her grandparents, Sheema searchs for her father and discovers that, although she feels fat, insecure, and slow, she is strong and beautiful. (Fiction)

———. *M. C. Higgins, the Great,* Macmillan, 1974. M.C.'s illusions and fantasies of escaping the dreary hill country and its threats are shattered, but he gains new insights into his own future and that of his warm but tough family. (Fiction)

———. *Magical Adventures of Pretty Pearl,* Harper/C. Zolotow, 1983. The god-child Pretty Pearl meets the doomed hero John Henry when she joins a hidden community of African Americans who are closely in touch with a Cherokee band deep in the forests of Georgia during Reconstruction times. (Fiction)

———. *Sweet Whispers, Brother Rush,* Philomel, 1982. ▲ Fourteen-year-old Tree learns a lot about her family and the interconnections between their past and present tragedies from Brother Rush, her uncle's ghost. (Fiction)

Hamlin, Liz. *I Remember Valentine,* Dutton, 1987. A seriocomic view of the Depression through the eyes of an eleven-year-old girl who learns about four-letter words and sex when she moves next door to an infamous family. (Fiction)

Hammer, Richard. *One Morning in the War: The Tragedy at Son My,* Coward-McCann, 1970. Without attempting to condemn or excuse, the author presents carefully researched documentation of the 1968 Son My massacre and tries to understand why Americans, sent to protect the Vietnamese, should end up slaughtering them. (Nonfiction)

Hanauer, Cathi. *My Sister's Bones,* Delacorte, 1997. When her beautiful, smart, and "practically perfect" sister returns from college refusing to eat or sleep, Billie knows that something is seriously wrong. (Fiction)

Hanckel, Frances, and Cunningham, John. *Way of Love, A Way of Life: A Young Person's Introduction to What It Means to Be Gay,* Lothrop, 1979. This positive guide to what being homosexual means—physically, emotionally, and socially—

includes profiles of twelve diverse gay lives. (Nonfiction)

Hardman, Ric Lynden. *Sunshine Rider: The First Vegetarian Western,* Delacorte, 1999.
On his first cattle drive, Wylie encounters a cast of colorful characters, adventures galore, and Roselle, a "cattalo" (a cross between a cow and a buffalo) that becomes his best friend. (Fiction)

Hardy, William Marion. *U.S.S. Mudskipper: The Submarine That Wrecked a Train,* Dodd, 1967.
A psychopathic World War II submarine captain takes his crew on shore and blows up a tiny Japanese train to add one more trophy to his collection. (Fiction)

Harris, Marilyn. *Hatter Fox,* Random, 1973. ■ ▲
Seventeen-year-old Hatter Fox, a spirited Navajo loner, is befriended by a young white doctor, Teague Summer, who never stops questioning his involvement with her. (Fiction)

Harris, Rosemary. *Zed,* Faber & Faber, 1984.
Held hostage by a group of terrorists, Zed finds courage, cowardice, kindness, and cruelty in unexpected places and discovers his own strength. (Fiction)

Harrison, Sue. *Mother Earth Father Sky,* Doubleday, 1991.
Chagak, the only survivor of a brutal massacre, endures starvation, cold, and forced marriage as she struggles to find her father's family in prehistoric America. (Fiction)

Hartman, David, and Asbell, Bernard. *White Coat, White Cane,* Playboy, 1979.
The true story of David Hartman, M.D., blind since the age of eight, whose only ambition was to become a doctor, is one of courage, ambition, and fortitude. (Nonfiction)

Hartog, Jan De. *Captain,* Atheneum, 1967.
This is a gripping story of a Dutch tug boat captain facing personal conflict and awesome danger in the North Atlantic during World War II. (Fiction)

Haskins, James. *Black Dance in America,* Harper/Crowell, 1991.
Haskins explores the development of African American dance from the forced dancing on slave ships through the era of music video. (Nonfiction)

——. *Black Music in America: A History through Its People,* Harper, 1987.
Haskins demonstrates the unique place of Afro-American music in American culture. (Nonfiction)

——. *One More River to Cross: The Stories of Twelve Black Americans,* Scholastic, 1993.
Haskins presents the lives of twelve black Americans and their impact on American society. (Nonfiction)

——, **and Benson, Kathleen.** *60's Reader,* Viking Kestrel, 1988.
The authors describe in depth the major movements of the 1960s and how they changed the direction of American history. (Nonfiction)

Hathorn, Libby. *Thunderwith,* Little, Brown, 1992.
Rejected after her mother's death by her father's new wife in the Australian outback, Laura seeks solace in a strange dog she discovers during a storm. (Fiction)

Haugaard, Erik Christian. *Chase Me, Catch Nobody!* Houghton Mifflin, 1980.
Hitler's prewar Germany is the destination for a group of Danish schoolboys on holiday, among them fourteen-year-old Erik who, through the anti-Nazi underground, becomes involved in an adventure filled with intrigue and danger. (Fiction)

Hautman, Pete. *Mr. Was,* Simon & Schuster, 1997.
After witnessing his mother's brutal murder by his father, Jack Lund escapes through a mysterious attic door and finds himself fifty years in the past. (Fiction)

Hautzig, Deborah. *Hey, Dollface,* Greenwillow, 1978.
As Val and Chloe share their home and school experiences during one eventful year, Val becomes concerned that the relationship between the two girls is becoming something more than friendship. (Fiction)

Hay, Jacob, and Keshishian, John M. *Autopsy for a Cosmonaut,* Little, 1969.
Sam Stonebreaker, M.D., is chosen by computer to be the first doctor in space and his assignment is to find out what killed the Russian cosmonauts in a marooned space vehicle. (Fiction)

■ Selected for "Still Alive: The Best of the Best, 1960–1974"

▲ Selected for "The Best of the Best Books: 1970–1983"

◆ Selected for "Nothin' but the Best: Best of the Best Books for Young Adults, 1966–1986"

● Selected for "Here We Go Again: 25 Years of Best Books: Selections from 1967 to 1992"

Hayden, Torey L. *Ghost Girl: The True Story of a Child Who Refused to Talk,* Little, Brown, 1992. ●
Torey Hayden finds that eight-year-old Jadie's bizarre behavior is a result of sexual abuse and a satanic cult. (Nonfiction)

————. *Murphy's Boy,* Putnam, 1983.
Will therapist Torey Hayden be able to help fifteen-year-old Kevin, who is autistic and whose life has been filled with abuse and violence? (Nonfiction)

————. *One Child,* Putman, 1980. ▲
It's not easy to work with emotionally disturbed children when your youth and jeans mean more to the administration than your rapport with your class—but Torey Hayden manages it. (Nonfiction)

Hayes, Billy, and Hoffer, William. *Midnight Express,* Dutton, 1977.
This is a graphic account of a young man's hellish captivity in a Turkish prison after his conviction on a drug charge, and his adventurous escape to freedom. (Nonfiction)

Hayes, Daniel. *Flyers,* Simon & Schuster, 1998.
While shooting a horror film for a school project, Gabe and his friends see unusual sightings in their neighborhood that lead to more than a ghost. (Fiction)

————. *No Effect,* Godine, 1995.
Tyler's adventures escalate in the eighth grade when he falls in love with his science teacher and becomes a fanatical member of the wrestling team. (Fiction)

————. *Trouble with Lemons,* Godine, 1992.
When Tyler and Lymie discover a body floating in the quarry where they are taking a forbidden midnight swim, they fear for their lives. (Fiction)

Hayes, Kent, and Lazzarino, Alex. *Broken Promise,* Putnam, 1978.
Abandoned by their parents en route to California, five children (the oldest eleven years old, the youngest eighteen months old) learn to subsist on their own and to defy a juvenile court system that threatens to separate them. (Fiction)

Haynes, David. *Right by My Side,* New Rivers, 1994.
Marshall's humor helps him through the difficult year in which his mother leaves and he finds he is attracting attention by being one of the only African Americans in his redneck high school. (Fiction)

Hayslip, Le Ly, and Wurts, Jay. *When Heaven and Earth Changed Places: A Vietnamese Woman's Journal from War to Peace,* Doubleday, 1990.
The haunting memoir of a young Vietnamese girl is an account of the brutal Vietnam War and learning to forgive. (Nonfiction)

Head, Ann. *Mr. and Mrs. Bo Jo Jones,* Putnam, 1967. ■ ◆
When July, sixteen and pregnant, rushes into marriage with her high school steady, the two must cope with parental interference and personal problems. (Fiction)

Hearne, Betsy. *Love Lines: Poetry in Person,* Macmillan/Margaret K. McElderry, 1987.
Here are passionate, wryly humorous, and gently regretful lines about love in all its guises. (Nonfiction)

Hedgepeth, William, and Stock, Dennis. *Alternative: Communal Life in New America,* Macmillan, 1970.
Communes as a way of life for "quiet revolutionaries" who feel alienated from the established world and seek the humanness of man, are pictured almost poetically in photographs and text. (Nonfiction)

Heidish, Marcy. *Secret Annie Oakley,* NAL, 1983.
Told in flashback, this is a novelization of Annie Oakley's cruel and abused childhood. (Fiction)

Helfer, Ralph. *Modoc: The Story of the Greatest Elephant That Ever Lived,* HarperCollins, 1999.
The fascinating story of the bond between a circus elephant and the boy who grew up with her is told with love, affection, and admiration. (Nonfiction)

Hellman, Peter, and Meier, Lili. *Auschwitz Album: A Book Based upon an Album Discovered by Concentration Camp Survivor, Lili Meier,* Random, 1982.
A powerful visual presentation of the extermination process at Auschwitz is viewed through candid photographs of its victims. (Nonfiction)

Helms, Tom. *Against All Odds,* Crowell, 1979.
Twice paralyzed by accidents, Tom Helms fought back—not only against his body but against the attitudes of the physically whole. (Nonfiction)

Helprin, Mark. *Swan Lake,* Houghton, 1990.
A totally new and surprising version of a famous ballet, this is a timeless and awesomely beautiful book. (Fiction)

Henderson, Zenna. *Holding Wonder,* Doubleday, 1971.
Some of these twenty science fiction tales deal with "The People," but others treat more mundane subjects such as murder and almost all take place in the author's favorite arena—the classroom. (Fiction)

Hendry, Frances Mary. *Quest for a Maid,* Farrar, Straus & Giroux, 1991.
Young Meg is pitted against political forces and her sister's powerful sorcery when she is chosen to be companion to the Maid of Norway on

her journey to Scotland to ascend to the throne. (Fiction)

Henry, Sue. *Murder on the Iditarod Trail*, Atlantic Monthly Press, 1992.
Money, dogs, and reputation are at stake during the intense competition of the Iditarod. As mushers are murdered, state trooper Jensen looks at the race with new eyes. (Fiction)

Hentoff, Nat. *American Heroes: In and out of School*, Delacorte, 1987. ●
First Amendment rights become part of everyday lives when students and other ordinary people resist infringements on basic freedoms. (Nonfiction)

————. *Does This School Have Capital Punishment?* Delacorte, 1981.
While fighting false charges for possessing dope, Sam makes friends with a famous black jazz trumpeter. (Fiction)

Herbert, Frank. *Soul Catcher*, Putnam, 1972.
Transformed into a mystical spirit named Katsuk, a young Native American sets out to avenge the injustices suffered by his people by performing a ritual murder. (Fiction)

Hermes, Patricia. *Solitary Secret*, Harcourt Brace Jovanovich, 1985.
Abandoned by her mother, a lonely and frightened fourteen-year-old girl becomes the victim of her father's sexual abuse. (Fiction)

Herring, Robert. *Hub*, Viking, 1981.
In this story reminiscent of *Huckleberry Finn*, flood waters trap Hub and Hitesy on an island with a man they saw commit a murder. (Fiction)

Herriot, James. *All Things Bright and Beautiful*, St. Martin's, 1974.
This completely captivating continuation of *All Creatures Great and Small* relates episodes in the life of a veterinarian and the human and animal characters he encounters. (Nonfiction)

Herzog, Arthur. *Swarm*, Simon & Schuster, 1974. ■
Killer bees, moving up from South America, terrorize citizens and baffle scientists who are trying to prevent a national disaster. (Fiction)

Hesse, Karen. *Letters from Rifka*, Holt, 1993.
In letters to her cousin, twelve-year-old Rifka describes what happens when she flees to the United States with her family to escape religious persecution in Russia. (Fiction)

————. *The Music of Dolphins*, Scholastic, 1997.
Lost at sea at age four, Mila was fostered by dolphins. Now, thirteen years later, she is found and returned to "civilization." (Fiction)

————. *Out of the Dust*, Scholastic, 1998.
In a story told through simple, elegant poetry, fifteen-year-old Billie Jo fights to hold on to her dreams in the face of family tragedy and the crushing hardships of the dust-bowl years in Oklahoma. (Fiction)

————. *Phoenix Rising*, Holt, 1995.
After losing almost everyone who matters to her, Nyle does not want to get to know fifteen-year-old Ezra, who has taken refuge in the back bedroom after a nuclear accident. (Fiction)

Hesser, Terry Spencer. *Kissing Doorknobs*, Delacorte, 1999.
Tara struggles to live with her obsessive-compulsive behavior, but before her condition is diagnosed, her relationships with family and friends begin to crumble. (Fiction)

Heyerdahl, Thor. *Ra Expeditions*, Doubleday, 1971.
The spirit of *Kon-Tiki* lives on in the author's dramatic tale of crossing the Atlantic by papyrus reed boat to prove that the ancient Egyptians beat Columbus. (Nonfiction)

Heyman, Anita. *Exit from Home*, Crown, 1977.
Opposing the demands of a dictatorial father, the oldest son of a Jewish family in czarist Russia follows his own commitment to social revolution. (Fiction)

Higa, Tomiko. *Girl with the White Flag: An Inspiring Tale of Love and Courage in War Time*, Kodansha, 1992.
Inspired by a World War II photograph, Higa recounts her harrowing childhood ordeal wandering Okinawa alone at the end of the war. (Nonfiction)

Higgins, Jack. *Eagle Has Landed*, Holt, 1975.
In a small English town, a reporter uncovers the hidden grave of German soldiers and a suspenseful story of a Nazi plot to kidnap Churchill. (Fiction)

Highwater, Jamake. *Anpao: An American Indian Odyssey*, Lippincott, 1977.
Native American legends are combined in the story of Anpao's love for a girl promised to the

---

■   Selected for "Still Alive: The Best of the Best, 1960–1974"

▲   Selected for "The Best of the Best Books: 1970–1983"

◆   Selected for "Nothin' but the Best: Best of the Best Books for Young Adults, 1966–1986"

●   Selected for "Here We Go Again: 25 Years of Best Books: Selections from 1967 to 1992"

Sun and of his search to find proof of the Sun's agreement to let him marry her. (Nonfiction)

———. *Ceremony of Innocence,* Harper/C. Zolotow, 1985.
In the early nineteenth-century Northwest, Amana, a Blackfoot Indian, strives to survive in a white world that refuses to accept her friendship with a French-Cree prostitute and causes Amana's daughter to lose her pride in the culture of her people. (Fiction)

———. *Legend Days,* Harper/Charlotte Zolotow, 1984.
Amana struggles to maintain her heritage even as she witnesses the disintegration of her Native American civilization as a result of famine, disease, and the encroaching presence of white settlers. (Fiction)

Hill, Ernest. *A Life for a Life,* Simon & Schuster, 1999.
In a desperate attempt to save his little brother's life, fifteen-year-old D'Ray kills a young man, but is ultimately given a second chance by the victim's father. (Fiction)

Hill, Susan. *Woman in Black,* Godine, 1986.
An old-fashioned ghost story of quiet horror is set on the desolate English moors. (Fiction)

Hillerman, Tony. *Blessing Way,* Harper, 1970.
Navajo detective Joe Leaphorn must solve the riddle of a mysterious death and an Indian spirit, part wolf, part man, who is frightening the people on a lonely reservation. (Fiction)

———. *Dance Hall of the Dead,* Harper, 1973.
When Navajo policeman Lt. Joe Leaphorn is called upon to investigate the murder of the young fire god he becomes involved in the world of Zuni religious beliefs. (Fiction)

———. *Thief of Time,* Harper, 1988.
The disappearance of an anthropologist propels Navajo tribal policemen Jim Chee and Joe Leaphorn into mysteries of ancient cultures and modern murders. (Fiction)

Hinton, S. E. *Rumblefish,* Delacorte, 1975.
Brothers, caught in an environment of violence, are as incapable of changing their behavior as are the fighting fish who battle to their death. (Fiction)

———. *Taming the Star Runner,* Doubleday/ Delacorte, 1988.
Travis attacks his stepfather and is sent to live with his uncle Ken on a ranch, where he learns how to make friends and how to deal with his inner conflicts. (Fiction)

———. *Tex,* Delacorte, 1979. ▲ ◆
The life of easygoing Tex is complicated by his older brother's serious outlook and the frequent absences of his father. Simply surviving becomes a real challenge. (Fiction)

———. *That Was Then, This Is Now,* Viking, 1971. ■ ◆
In this sequel to *The Outsiders,* Bryon and Mark at sixteen are still inseparable, but Bryon is beginning to care about people while Mark continues to hot-wire cars, steal, and do things for kicks. (Fiction)

Hirshey, Gerri. *Nowhere to Run: The Story of Soul Music,* Random/Times Books, 1984.
Interviews with the artists who produced the music that exploded in the 1960s are interwoven with research results and personal recollections to capture the beat of soul, from Motown to James Brown. (Nonfiction)

Hite, Sid. *It's Nothing to a Mountain,* Holt, 1995.
Stunned by their parents' deaths in a fiery car crash, Lisette and Riley find both healing and a very special guardian angel at their grandparents' home in the Blue Ridge Mountains. (Fiction)

Ho, Minfong. *Rice without Rain,* Farrar, Straus & Giroux, 1991.
From changes in her rural village to the student protests in Bangkok, events propel seventeen-year-old Jinda toward choices that she must make about her own life. (Fiction)

Hobbs, Anne, and Specht, Robert. *Tisha: The Story of a Young Teacher in the Alaskan Wilderness,* St. Martin's, 1976.
True account of a young girl who goes to Chicken, Alaska, in 1927 and is beset by all the problems of frontier living and prejudice. (Nonfiction)

Hobbs, Valerie. *How Far Would You Have Gotten If I Hadn't Called You Back?* Orchard, 1996.
After moving to California in the 1950s, Bron is lonely—until she discovers danger, drag racing, and two boys, J. C. and Will, one of whom she truly loves. (Fiction)

Hobbs, Will. *Beardance,* Atheneum, 1994.
Cloyd, a Ute teen, spends the winter helping two orphaned grizzly cubs survive, in this sequel to *Bearstone* (Fiction)

———. *Bearstone,* Atheneum, 1990.
Coming to terms with his Native American heritage, Cloyd learns to accept himself in a battle for survival in the mountains of Colorado. (Fiction)

———. *Big Wander,* Atheneum, 1993.
In this compelling adventure story, Clay goes on his "big wander" through Arizona's canyon country in search of his missing uncle. (Fiction)

———. *Downriver,* Atheneum, 1992. ●
Fifteen-year-old Jesse and other rebellious teenage members of a wilderness survival team aban-

don their adult leader, steal his van and rafts, and run the dangerous whitewaters of the Grand Canyon. (Fiction)

———. *Far North*, Morrow, 1997.
Stranded in the Canadian wilderness, two boys endure a brutal subarctic winter of bear, wolf, and moose attacks while they repeatedly struggle to escape. (Fiction)

———. *The Maze*, Morrow, 1999.
Fourteen-year-old detention-center escapee Rick finds refuge in Utah's canyon country, where he meets condor preservationist Lon, who becomes both mentor and father figure to him. (Fiction)

Hockenberry, John. *Moving Violations*, Hyperion, 1996.
This fearless journalist takes you along to experience war, chaos, and romance, as he covers the world from his wheelchair. (Nonfiction)

Hodge, Merle. *For the Life of Laetitia*, Farrar, 1994.
Twelve-year-old Laetitia's life changes drastically when she has to leave her loving extended family in a Caribbean village and move in with her abusive father while she attends high school on a government scholarship. (Fiction)

Hodges, Margaret. *Making a Difference: The Story of an American Family*, Scribner, 1990.
Hodges tells the extraordinary story of the Sherwoods, a family whose belief in social responsibility effected changes in women's rights, politics, medicine and conservation. (Nonfiction)

Hoffman, Alice. *At Risk*, Putman, 1988.
When eleven-year-old Amanda Farrell is diagnosed as having AIDS, her family, friends, and neighbors react in unexpected ways, in spite of their best intentions. (Fiction)

———. *Turtle Moon*, Putnam, 1993.
Keith Rosen, the meanest boy in Verity, Florda, runs away, steals a baby, and does other peculiar things, none of which are very strange—considering that it is May and the time of the Turtle Moon. (Fiction)

Hogan, James P. *Bug Park*, Baen; dist. by Simon & Schuster, 1998.
Teenagers Kevin and Taki, who have created the interactive computer game Bug Park, must use the game and their impressive computer skills to save Kevin's father from a murder plot. (Fiction)

Hogan, William. *Quartzsite Trip*, Atheneum, 1980. ▲ ◆
P. J. Cooper takes thirty-six Los Angeles high school seniors into the Arizona desert to discover who and why and how, and to learn that the Great Equalizer cannot always be ignored. (Fiction)

Holland, Isabelle. *Man without a Face*, Lippincott, 1972. ▲ ◆
Not much affection has come Charles' way until the summer he is fourteen, meets McLeod, and learns that love has many facets. (Fiction)

———. *Of Love and Death and Other Journeys*, Lippincott, 1975.
The death of her lovable, easy-going mother forces fifteen-year-old Meg to adjust to a new life with the father she had resented but never known. (Fiction)

Holliday, Laurel, ed. *Heart Songs: The Intimate Diaries of Young Girls*, Bluestocking Books, 1978.
Spanning several centuries and different countries, the writings of these ten young girls reflect the same joys and fears of approaching womanhood as those experienced by young women today. (Nonfiction)

Hollinger, Carol. *Mai Pen Rai Means Never Mind*, Houghton, 1966.
A foreign-service wife becomes a university teacher in Bangkok, crashes head-on with the unfamiliar customs of the Thai people but soon succumbs completely to their charm. (Nonfiction)

Holman, Felice. *Slake's Limbo*, Scribners, 1974. ▲ ◆ ●
A loser and loner picked on by everyone, Slake finds refuge in a subway which becomes his home for 121 days. (Fiction)

———. *Wild Children*, Scribner, 1983.
Overlooked in the arrest of his family, Eric runs with the outlawed and homeless children trying to survive in the bleak aftermath of the Bolshevik Revolution. (Fiction)

Holt, Kimberly Willis. *My Louisiana Sky*, Holt, 1999.
In rural 1950s Louisiana, Tiger Ann must balance her shame at having mentally slow parents against the changes brought on by complicated family secrets and responsibility. (Fiction)

■   Selected for "Still Alive: The Best of the Best, 1960–1974"

▲   Selected for "The Best of the Best Books: 1970–1983"

◆   Selected for "Nothin' but the Best: Best of the Best Books for Young Adults, 1966–1986"

●   Selected for "Here We Go Again: 25 Years of Best Books: Selections from 1967 to 1992"

Homes, A. M. *Jack,* Macmillan, 1990.
Still dealing with his parents' divorce and a wacko friend, fifteen-year-old Jack is hit with another bombshell—his father's revelation that he's gay. (Fiction)

Honeycutt, Natalie. *Ask Me Something Easy,* Orchard/Richard Jackson, 1992.
Addie feels like an outsider as her older sister, Dinah, and their angry mother cling to each other following her parents' divorce. (Fiction)

Hoover, H. M. *Another Heaven, Another Earth,* Viking, 1981. •
Survivors of an unsuccessful attempt at colonization must choose between primitive life on a doomed planet or returning to a mechanized, crowded Earth. (Fiction)

————. *Dawn Palace: The Story of Medea,* Dutton, 1988.
Denied her inheritance of Dawn Palace, Medea marries Jason and helps him secure the Golden Fleece, only to endure the dissolution of their marriage and the murder of her children. (Fiction)

Hopkins, Lee Bennett. *Been to Yesterdays: Poems of Life,* Boyd Mills/Wordsong, 1996.
Hopkins' autobiographical poems capture his teenage feelings, experiences, and aspirations as he deals with his parents' divorce, his grandmother's death, and his hopes to become a writer. (Nonfiction)

Horan, James David. *New Vigilantes,* Crown, 1975.
Eight Vietnam veterans released from prison camp return to the United States to find justice a travesty. They decide to take the law into their own hands. (Fiction)

Horner, John R., and Gorman, James. *Digging Dinosaurs,* Workman, 1990.
The discovery of a baby dinosaur's bones during a six-year dig in Montana results in a revolutionary theory about cold-blooded creatures. (Nonfiction)

Horrigan, Kevin. *Right Kinds of Heroes: Coach Bob Shannon and the East St. Louis Flyers,* Algonquin, 1993.
Coach Bob Shannon of the East St. Louis Flyers isn't the easiest guy to play football for. But whoever said anything in East St. Louis was easy? (Nonfiction)

Horwitz, Elinor. *Madness, Magic, and Medicine: The Treatment and Mistreatment of the Mentally Ill,* Lippincott, 1977.
How mentally ill people have been treated from ancient times to the present is a bizarre, tragic, and inhumane chapter of history. (Nonfiction)

Hotchner, A. E. *Looking for Miracles: A Memoir about Loving,* Harper, 1975.
Results are hilarious and poignant when Aaron masquerades as an experienced camp counselor to get himself and his younger brother into a summer camp. (Fiction)

Hotze, Sollace. *Acquainted with the Night,* Clarion, 1993.
During a Maine island summer, seventeen-year-old Molly and her cousin Caleb, wounded in Vietnam, resist their romantic feelings for each other as they help a ghost find peace. (Fiction)

————. *Circle Unbroken,* Clarion, 1988.
Recaptured by her father after living with Sioux Indians for seven years, Rachel faces prejudice and needs great courage to find happiness. (Fiction)

Hough, John. *Peck of Salt: A Year in the Ghetto,* Little, Brown, 1970.
A very personal, moving story of a young white VISTA volunteer and his honorable failure to help black junior high school students in Detroit. (Nonfiction)

Houriet, Robert. *Getting Back Together,* Coward, 1971.
The rambling odyssey of one man who sets out to discover whether "the simple life" can be found in the more stable communes and communities throughout the country. For mature readers. (Nonfiction)

Houston, James. *Ghost Fox,* Harcourt, 1977. •
Kidnapped by the Abnaki Indians in colonial times, sixteen-year-old Sarah Wells gradually adopts the Abnaki way of life and must eventually choose between it and returning to the life from which she was taken. (Fiction)

————. *White Dawn,* Harcourt, 1971.
Based on a real incident in the 1890s, three lost white whalers are rescued by Eskimos and taken into their community where the lack of appreciation for and understanding of Eskimo tradition leads to tragedy. (Fiction)

Howard, Jane. *Please Touch: A Guided Tour of the Human Potential Movement,* McGraw-Hill, 1970.
A *Life* magazine writer subjects herself to many forms of encounter group and sensitivity-training programs before making this shrewd and delightfully witty assessment. (Nonfiction)

Howe, James. *The Watcher,* Simon & Schuster/Atheneum, 1998.
A lonely, troubled girl lives in an elaborate fantasy world. (Fiction)

Howker, Janni. *Badger on the Barge and Other Stories,* Greenwillow, 1985.
In each of five beautiful stories, a young person encounters an older stranger who helps to shed light on the problem each is posed. (Fiction)

————. *Isaac Campion,* Greenwillow, 1987.
The death of his older brother forces young Isaac to assume the entire burden of working

on his vicious father's horse farm in turn-of-the-century England. (Fiction)

Hudson, Jan. *Dawn Rider,* Putnam/Philomel, 1991.
Though she has hidden her early morning encounters with her Blackfoot tribe's first horse, sixteen-year-old Kit's riding experience proves vital during battle. (Fiction)

———. *Sweetgrass,* Philomel Books, 1990.
A fifteen-year-old Blackfoot girl of the 1830s must prove herself a capable woman before she can marry Eagle Sun. (Fiction)

Huffaker, Clair. *Cowboy and the Cossack,* Trident, 1973.
Confronted by nearly insurmountable odds—including a Tartar raid—fifteen American cowboys with a Cossack escort drive 500 cattle across several thousand miles of Russian wilderness in 1880. (Fiction)

Hughes, Langston. *The Block,* Viking, 1996.
Selections from Hughes' poetry match Bearden's rich six-panel collage "The Block," portraying a Harlem neighborhood. (Nonfiction)

Hughes, Monica. *Hunter in the Dark,* Atheneum, 1983.
In this rites-of-passage novel Mike, a fifteen-year-old leukemia patient, comes to terms with his illness during a solitary camping trip. (Fiction)

———. *Keeper of the Isis Light,* Atheneum, 1981.
Never having seen another human, Olwen does not know how different she is until Earth settlers come to Isis and she falls in love. (Fiction)

Human Rights in China. *Children of the Dragon: The Story of Tiananmen Square,* Macmillan/Collier, 1991.
Never before published photographs and words of student activists vividly recreate the 1989 Tiananmen Square massacre. (Nonfiction)

Hunter, Kristin. *Survivors,* Scribners, 1975.
Each is a survivor—Miss Lena, independent businesswoman, and B. J., a tough, appealing street kid—but they learn that they need each other. (Fiction)

Hunter, Mollie. *Cat, Herself,* Harper/C. Zolotow, 1986.
Cat finds ways to blend an old Scottish "on the road" lifestyle with her own needs. (Fiction)

Hurwin, Davida Wills. *A Time for Dancing,* Little, Brown, 1996.
Seventeen-year-old best friends Juliana and Samantha share a passion for dance, for life, and for each other—then Jules is diagnosed with cancer and must travel a path Sam cannot follow. (Fiction)

Huth, Angela. *Land Girls,* St. Martin's, 1997.
Three young city women find romance, true love, and danger in 1941 when they volunteer to help the war effort by working as farm laborers. (Fiction)

Huygen, Wil, and Poortvliet, Rien. *Gnomes,* Abrams, 1977.
Everything anyone ever wanted to know about gnomes, plus colorful illustrations identifying these unusual little creatures. (Nonfiction)

Ingold, Jeanette. *The Window,* Harcourt, 1997.
Blinded by the accident that took her mother's life, fifteen-year-old Mandy finds an unexpected trip back in time is the key to helping her cope. (Fiction)

Inouye, Daniel Ken, and Elliot, Lawrence. *Journey to Washington,* Prentice-Hall, 1967.
This exciting and inspiring autobiography is about the first Japanese-American to become a U.S. Senator. (Nonfiction)

Ipswitch, Elaine. *Scott Was Here,* Delacorte, 1979.
In a moving record of personal and family courage, Ipswitch tells the story of her son Scott, whose battle with Hodgkin's disease ended with his death at the age of fifteen. (Nonfiction)

Irwin, Hadley. *Abby, My Love,* Atheneum/Margaret K. McElderry, 1985. ◆
Chip loves Abby and can't understand why she keeps him at a distance, until she reveals that she has been sexually abused by her father. (Fiction)

———. *What about Grandma?* Atheneum/Margaret K. McElderry, 1982.
When Grandmother Wyn refuses to stay in a nursing home, sixteen-year-old Rhys and her mother spend the summer with her. It is a time of conflict, discovery, and Rhys's first love affair. (Fiction)

Isaacson, Philip M. *A Short Walk around the Pyramids and through the World of Art,* Knopf, 1994.
Unique examples of cars and radios, along with traditional art forms, beautifully and simply

---

■   Selected for "Still Alive: The Best of the Best, 1960–1974"

▲   Selected for "The Best of the Best Books: 1970–1983"

◆   Selected for "Nothin' but the Best: Best of the Best Books for Young Adults, 1966–1986"

●   Selected for "Here We Go Again: 25 Years of Best Books: Selections from 1967 to 1992"

introduce that intangible something that makes a work of art. (Nonfiction)

Ives, John. *Fear in a Handful of Dust,* Dutton, 1978.
Four kidnapped psychiatrists, one a woman, manage to survive the rigors and horrors of the desert after being left to die by a psychotic killer. (Fiction)

Jacobs, Anita. *Where Has Deedie Wooster Been All These Years?* Delacorte, 1981.
Because her English teacher has faith in her, Deedie blossoms, finds herself, and realizes that she no longer needs to beg for her mother's love. (Fiction)

Jacopetti, Alexandra. *Native Funk and Flash: An Emerging Folk Art,* Scrimshaw, 1974.
Beautiful color photos with brief text describe functional, unique lovingly hand-decorated objects: clothes, puzzles, furniture, and fine embroidery. (Nonfiction)

Jacot, Michael. *Last Butterfly,* Bobbs, 1974.
A half-Jewish clown is forced to entertain Jewish children at Terezin. When the International Red Cross team departs, children board carefully concealed cattle trains. Destination: Auschwitz. (Fiction)

Jacques, Brian. *Redwall,* Putman/Philomel, 1987.
With the help of animal allies, peace-loving mice defend their medieval abbey when it is beseiged by Cluny the Scourge and his fierce band of rats. (Fiction)

Jaffe, Rona. *Mazes and Monsters,* Delacorte, 1981.
Fantasy becomes terrifyingly real when four college students discover underground caverns near their campus and one of them confuses game strategy with reality. (Fiction)

James, J. Alison. *Sing for a Gentle Rain,* Atheneum, 1991.
Disturbing dreams pull James into the past where a lonely Native American girl and the timeless mystery of the Anasazi beckon. (Fiction)

James, P. D. *Unsuitable Job for a Woman,* Scribner, 1973.
When Cordelia Gray, slight but savvy, inherits a shabby detective agency after the suicide of her partner, her first case involves the apparently motiveless suicide of a Cambridge student. (Fiction)

Janeczko, Paul B. *Brickyard Summer,* Watts/ Orchard, 1990.
These poems set in a New England mill town evoke the feelings of growing up during the summer between eighth and ninth grades. (Nonfiction)

————. *Place My Words Are Looking For: What Poets Say about and through Their Work,* Bradbury, 1991.
Writers share their poems and give insights into their craft and life. (Nonfiction)

————. *Pocket Poems: Selected for a Journey,* Bradbury, 1985.
A pocket-size collection of 120 short modern poems by some 80 poets ranges from "Song against Broccoli" to "An Elegy." (Nonfiction)

————. *Stardust otel,* Orchard/Richard Jackson, 1994.
Fourteen-year-old Leary experiences loss and love in these poems that bring his friends, enemies, and acquaintances to life. (Nonfiction)

————, ed. *Don't Forget to Fly,* Bradbury, 1981.
A panorama of modern poems, by a variety of poets, span the range of human experience. (Nonfiction)

————. *Going Over to Your Place: Poems for Each Other,* Macmillan/Bradbury, 1987.
These contemporary poems tease the emotions of each of us. (Nonfiction)

————. *Looking for Your Name: A Collection of Contemporary Poems,* Orchard/Richard Jackson, 1994.
More than 100 poems representing the conflicts of contemporary life cover such topics as AIDS, war, gun control, and unemployment, and evoke anger, distrust, and many other emotions. (Nonfiction)

————. *Music of What Happens: Poems That Tell Stories,* Watts/Orchard/Richard Jackson, 1988.
Poems that are stories—and stories that are poems—tell of ghosts and lovers, triumph and tragedy. (Nonfiction)

————. *Poetspeak: In Their Work, about Their Work,* Bradbury, 1983.
Sixty-two living North American poets select and comment on their works for a teenage audience. (Nonfiction)

————. *Strings: A Gathering of Family Poems,* Bradbury, 1984.
More than seventy modern poets present a multifaceted view of families and their special relationships—husbands, wives, parents, children, etc.—in a 127-poem anthology. (Nonfiction)

Jenkins, Peter. *Walk across America,* Morrow, 1979.
The author begins his 1500-mile hike from New York to Louisiana with disdain for American lifestyles and ends it with a feeling of expectation and discovery. (Nonfiction)

Jenner, Bruce, and Finch, Philip. *Decathlon Challenge: Bruce Jenner's Story,* Prentice, 1977.
The 1976 American Olympic champion's story tells of his rigorous training and the many ups and downs he experienced before winning the decathlon gold medal. (Nonfiction)

Jiang, Ji-li. *Red Scarf Girl: A Memoir of the Cultural Revolution,* HarperCollins, 1998.
Ji-li Jiang's quiet, prosperous way of life is destroyed during the turmoil and tragedy of the Chinese Cultural Revolution. (Nonfiction)

Jimenez, Francisco. *The Circuit: Stories from the Life of a Migrant Child,* University of New Mexico, 1999.
Panchito dreams of living in a world without constant uprooting from migrant camps and schools, a world in which a compassionate teacher might help him learn and grow. (Fiction)

Johnson, Angela. *Heaven,* Simon & Schuster, 1999.
Young Marley's idyllic life in the small town of Heaven, Ohio, is suddenly disrupted when she discovers that her mother and father are not her real parents. (Fiction)

———. *Toning the Sweep,* Orchard/Richard Jackson, 1994.
Emmie and her mother have come to the desert to dismantle her dying grandmother's house, but the trip proves to be a healing process for these two strong women. (Fiction)

Johnson, Earvin "Magic." *What You Can Do to Avoid AIDS,* Times Books, 1993.
Facts, questions, answers, and interviews make up a thorough teen guide to AIDS. (Nonfiction)

Johnson, Lou Anne. *Making Waves: The Story of a Woman in This Man's Navy,* St. Martin's, 1987.
This bittersweet, raunchy, and eye-opening look at one woman's military experience in today's navy sprints from recruiting promises, through basic training, to a hitch overseas. (Nonfiction)

Johnson, Scott. *One of the Boys,* Atheneum, 1993.
Being part of the in-crowd is fun for Eric, until his new friend Marty's pranks become serious and criminal. (Fiction)

Johnston, Jennifer. *How Many Miles to Babylon? A Novel,* Doubleday, 1974.
A friendship between two young Englishmen from different social classes continues despite parental objection and leads to tragedy. (Fiction)

Jones, Adrienne. *Hawks of Chelney,* Harper, 1978.
Siri, a wild young outcast who takes refuge near the hawks that obsess him, incurs the wrath of superstitious villagers who fear his difference and blame the birds for their empty fishing nets. (Fiction)

Jones, Diana Wynne. *Archer's Goon,* Greenwillow, 1984.
A menacing, oversized Goon joins Howard's unusual family and refuses to leave until Howard's father has met the demands of his unrelenting master. (Fiction)

———. *Castle in the Air,* Greenwillow, 1992.
Abdullah is whisked away to a magic kingdom when he falls asleep on a magic carpet he has just bought, but is he really sleeping? (Fiction)

———. *Homeward Bounders,* Greenwillow, 1981.
When Jamie discovers a group of spectres warring with real people, he is condemned to wander the outer boundaries forever. (Fiction)

———. *Howl's Moving Castle,* Greenwillow, 1986. ●
When a witch turns seventeen-year-old Sophie into an old woman, Sophie goes to live with the feared wizard Howl in his castle and becomes embroiled in the zany events that lead to her happiness. (Fiction)

———. *Sudden Wild Magic,* Morrow, 1993.
The good witches of Earth band together to stop the magicians of Arth from stealing Earth's technology and creating disasters. (Fiction)

Jones, Douglas C. *Gone the Dreams and Dancing,* Holt, 1985.
Defeated but not beaten, the Comanche chief Kwahadi bargains with the whites to achieve a place for his people without betraying their past. (Fiction)

Jones, Maurice K. *Say It Loud! The Story of Rap Music,* Millbrook, 1995.
Full-color illustrations accompany the lively story of the history, personalities, and social

---

■   Selected for "Still Alive: The Best of the Best, 1960–1974"
▲   Selected for "The Best of the Best Books: 1970–1983"
◆   Selected for "Nothin' but the Best: Best of the Best Books for Young Adults, 1966–1986"
●   Selected for "Here We Go Again: 25 Years of Best Books: Selections from 1967 to 1992"

significance of rap—as well as the controversies that swirl around it. (Nonfiction)

Jordan, June. *His Own Where,* Crowell, 1971. ▲
Refusing to be trapped by the hopelessness of life in a black ghetto, sixteen-year-old Buddy Rivers escapes with his girl Angela to a deserted cemetery shed, in this short, honest, and poignant inner city love story for mature readers (Fiction)

——, ed. *Soulscript: Afro-American Poetry,* Doubleday, 1970.
The black experience seen through the prism of poetry—some poems are angry and bitter; others are eerie and enigmatic; some lash out reflexively; others brood philosophically. (Nonfiction)

Jordan, Robert. *Eye of the World,* St. Martin's, 1991.
Three teenagers take on a classic fantasy quest in this epic struggle between good and evil. (Fiction)

Jordan, Sherryl. *Winter of Fire,* Scholastic, 1994.
Elsha, saved from death on her sixteenth birthday when the Firelord chooses her as his Handmaiden, challenges centuries of social standards in her dark, frozen world. (Fiction)

——. *Wolf-Woman,* Houghton, 1995.
Sixteen-year-old Tanith must make a choice between the love of a young man and the call of the wolves who raised her until age three. (Fiction)

Kaplan, Helen Singer. *Making Sense of Sex: The New Facts about Sex and Love for Young People,* Simon & Schuster, 1979.
Addressing older teens, a leading sex therapist provides knowledgeable and detailed information, including some of the latest scientific findings, on human sexual functioning. (Nonfiction)

Katz, William Loren. *Breaking the Chains: African American Slave Resistance,* Atheneum, 1991.
The myth that black slaves wore their chains quietly is shattered by this account of how slaves actually fought for their freedom before, during, and after the Civil War. (Nonfiction)

Kavaler, Lucy. *Freezing Point: Cold as a Matter of Life and Death,* John Day, 1970.
Cold, once considered an enemy, is revealed as one of man's greatest allies when utilized in such areas as diet, medicine, and research to defer death. (Nonfiction)

Kaye, Geraldine. *Someone Else's Baby,* Hyperion, 1993.
Terry, seventeen, single, and pregnant, tells the truth in her journal as she fights to do what's right. (Fiction)

Kaysen, Susanna. *Girl, Interrupted,* Random/Turtle Bay, 1994.
A successful author who spent two of her adolescent years as a patient in a mental institution shares her harrowing experiences. (Nonfiction)

Kazimiroff, Theodore L. *Last Algonquin,* Walker, 1982. ◆
Joe Two Trees, an Algonquin Native American orphaned at age thirteen, first tries to make his way in the hostile white man's world, but finally returns to a traditional lifestyle. (Nonfiction)

Keane, John. *Sherlock Bones: Tracer of Missing Pets,* Lippincott, 1979.
Pet detective Keane describes his funny, sad, and suspenseful true adventures tracking down lost and stolen pets with his sidekick Paco, an old English sheep dog. (Nonfiction)

Keillor, Garrison, and Nilson, Jenny Lind. *The Sandy Bottom Orchestra,* Hyperion; dist. by Little, Brown, 1997.
Fourteen-year-old Rachel finds comfort in her violin while living with truly "strange" parents in a small town. (Fiction)

Kellogg, Marjorie. *Tell Me That You Love Me, Junie Moon,* Farrar, 1968. ▪
Junie Moon, an acid-scarred girl, Warren, a paraplegic, and Arthur, who is suffering from a progressive neurological disease, decide to leave the hospital and set up housekeeping together. (Fiction)

Kelly, Gary F. *Learning about Sex: The Contemporary Guide for Young Adults,* Barron's Educational Series, 1978.
This is a down-to-earth, nonjudgmental discussion of values, relationships, love, and sex. (Nonfiction)

Kelton, Elmer. *Cloudy in the West,* Tor/Forge; dist. by St. Martin's, 1998.
When twelve-year-old Joey flees his East Texas farm to escape the deadly intentions of his stepmother and her lover, he finds adventure and danger in the company of outlaws and his wastrel cousin. (Fiction)

Kennedy, William P. *Toy Soldiers,* St. Martin's, 1988.
When Arab terrorists take over an exclusive American boarding school in Rome, they face an implacable foe—high school student Billy Tepper, practical joker and computer whiz. (Fiction)

Kerner, Elizabeth. *Song in the Silence,* Tor/Forge; dist. by St. Martin's, 1998.
Vibrant young Lanen Kaelar is compelled to leave the farm on which she was raised to seek out the awe-inspiring dragons that she's dreamed of since childhood. (Fiction)

Kerr, M. E. *Deliver Us from Evie,*
    HarperCollins, 1995.
Parr has much to contend with—his small-town farm life, his emerging and raging hormones, and his older sister's lesbianism. (Fiction)

————. *Fell,* Harper, 1987.
Being paid $20,000 to impersonate another boy at a private school seems like child's play to John Fell, until he has to cope with the Sevens, a mysterious club that dominates the entire school. (Fiction)

————. *Gentlehands,* Harper, 1978. ◆ ●
Buddy's world is turned upside down when he falls in love and then, catastrophically, when he discovers that his refined and cultured grandfather is a notorious Nazi war criminal. (Fiction)

————. *I Stay near You,* Harper/Charlotte
    Zolotow, 1985.
Family members fall in love, cope with sudden death, and survive numerous separations in linked stories that follow three generations from the big-band forties to the hard-rock eighties. (Fiction)

————. *Is That You, Miss Blue?* Harper, 1975.
There are ups and downs in the lives of three teenage girls in a boarding school, where the unforgettable Miss Blue is "the best teacher" in spite of her unusual habits. (Fiction)

————. *Little Little,* Harper, 1981.
Teenage dwarfs Little Little La Belle and Sidney Cinnamon try to find romance in spite of a mother's matchmaking. (Fiction)

————. *Me Me Me Me Me: Not a Novel,*
    Harper/Charoltte Zolotow, 1983.
A series of autobiographical anecdotes from Kerr's youth relate to their use in her novels. (Nonfiction)

————. *Night Kites,* Harper, 1986. ◆
Seventeen-year-old Jim's relationships with his family and friends change when his older brother reveals he has AIDS. (Fiction)

Kilworth, Garry. *Foxes of Firstdark,*
    Doubleday, 1991.
Human encroachment makes survival in Trinity Woods a struggle for O-ha the she-fox, her mate, and her kits. (Fiction)

Kim, Richard. *Lost Names: Scenes from a
    Korean Boyhood,* Praeger, 1970.

A famous Korean writer tells what it was like to grow up during the oppressive Japanese regime of the 1930s and 1940s. (Nonfiction)

Kimble, Bo. *For You, Hank: The Story of Hank
    Gathers and Bo Kimble,* Delacorte, 1993.
Bo and Hank are inseparable friends and teammates who know that basketball is the road up, but Hank is in trouble—then dead, and all of Bo's memories lead to the same question—why? (Nonfiction)

Kincaid, Jamaica. *Annie John,* Farrar, 1985.
Growing up on the island of Antigua, Annie changes from happy child to defiant teenager in a fiercely painful separation from her strong, loving mother. (Fiction)

Kincaid, Nanci. *Crossing Blood,* Putnam,
    1993.
In the 1960s South, Lucy Conyers is fascinated by the people in the house across the way, and especially by Skippy, the handsome, clever son of their black maid—a fascination that is not only forbidden but dangerous. (Fiction)

Kindl, Patrice. *Owl in Love,* Houghton, 1995.
Girl by day, owl by night, fourteen-year-old Owl Tycho finds life is complicated—not only by a crush on her science teacher, but also by the presence of a deranged boy in the woods. (Fiction)

————. *The Woman in the Wall,* Houghton,
    1998.
Painfully and obsessively shy, Anna comes of age in a world of her own, which she builds within the walls of her family's Victorian house. (Fiction)

King, Coretta Scott. *My Life with Martin
    Luther King, Jr.,* Holt, 1969.
With dignity and emotion, Coretta Scott King tells her story of being black, of devotion to the movement, and of marriage to the man who said, "I have a dream." (Nonfiction)

King, Laurie R. *The Beekeeper's Apprentice;
    or, On the Segregation of the Queen,* St.
    Martin's, 1995.
Sherlock Holmes meets an intellectual equal, fifteen-year-old Mary Russell, who challenges him to investigate yet another case. (Fiction)

King, Stephen. *Firestarter,* Viking, 1980.
Eight-year-old Charlie can set things on fire just by looking at them, but will she use her awe-

---

- ■ Selected for "Still Alive: The Best of the Best, 1960–1974"
- ▲ Selected for "The Best of the Best Books: 1970–1983"
- ◆ Selected for "Nothin' but the Best: Best of the Best Books for Young Adults, 1966–1986"
- ● Selected for "Here We Go Again: 25 Years of Best Books: Selections from 1967 to 1992"

some power against The Shop, the secret government agency pursuing her and her father? (Fiction)

———. *Night Shift,* Doubleday, 1978. ◆
The author of *Carrie* serves up a horrifying collection of short stories packed with vampires, bogeymen, a cellar full of rats, and a fatal can of beer. (Fiction)

Kingsolver, Barbara. *Animal Dreams,* HarperCollins, 1992.
When Codi returns after fourteen years to the small Arizona town of her childhood, she finds a new career, a cause to fight for, and a man to love again. (Fiction)

———. *Bean Trees,* Harper, 1988.
Attempting to break away from her harsh life in Appalachia, Taylor Greer finds herself in a small Oklahoma town, with a new name, a new life, and strangest of all, a new Cherokee baby girl whom she names Turtle. (Fiction)

Kisor, Henry. *What's That Pig Outdoors? A Memoir of Deafness,* Hill & Wang, 1991.
The autobiography of a Chicago journalist who, though deaf, never lets it prevent him from doing what he wants. (Nonfiction)

Kittredge, Mary. *Teens with AIDS Speak Out,* Messner, 1993.
In the most important fight of their lives, teenagers confront past and current behaviors as they tell their AIDS stories. (Nonfiction)

Klass, David. *Danger Zone,* Scholastic, 1997.
The thrill of playing international basketball for the American high-school dream team becomes more than a series of games as Jim faces prejudice and politics. (Fiction)

———. *Wrestling with Honor,* Dutton/ Lodestar, 1990. ●
Ron Woods's anticipation of a championship wrestling season is complicated when he fails a drug test and refuses to take another. (Fiction)

Klass, Perri Elizabeth. *Not Entirely Benign Procedure: Four Years as a Medical Student,* Putman, 1987.
A young woman wittily describes her four years at Harvard Medical School. (Nonfiction)

Klass, Sheila Solomon. *Page Four,* Scribner, 1987.
When his father deserts the family, David channels his feelings of confused betrayal into his college application essay. (Fiction)

Klause, Annette Curtis. *Blood and Chocolate,* Delacorte, 1998.
Beautiful teenage werewolf Vivian falls in love with Aiden, a human—a meat-boy—and longs to share her secret with him. (Fiction)

———. *The Silver Kiss,* Delacorte, 1991. ●
Feeling alienated from everyone during her mother's terminal illness, Zoe comes under the spell of Simon, a vampire doomed to live until he avenges the death of his mother 300 years earlier. (Fiction)

Klein, Norma. *No More Saturday Nights,* Knopf, 1990.
Seventeen-year-old Tim's life is turned upside down when he decides to raise his baby alone while attending college. (Fiction)

Knowles, John. *Peace Breaks Out,* Holt, 1981.
Returning to teach at Devon School after World War II, Pete Hallam finds violence and tragedy among his students. (Fiction)

Knudson, R. R., and Swenson, May, eds. *American Sports Poems,* Watts/Orchard, 1988. ●
Representing a wide variety of sports, from skateboarding to baseball, this treasury of nearly 200 poems conveys the vigor of American sports and their heroes and heroines. (Nonfiction)

Koebner, Linda. *Zoo Book: The Evolution of Wildlife Conservation Centers,* Tor/Forge, 1995.
Complemented by handsome photographs, an inside in-depth look at the inner workings of a modern-day zoo examines the changing role of the zoo community as it reorients itself into a global conservation leader. (Nonfiction)

Koehn, Ilse. *Mischling, Second Degree: My Childhood in Nazi Germany,* Greenwillow, 1977. ◆
A young woman grows up in Nazi Germany, not knowing that she is part Jewish. (Nonfiction)

———. *Tilla,* Greenwillow, 1981.
Two young German survivors of World War II, Tilla and Rolf, flee to Berlin and slowly attempt to create a new life in the occupied, war-torn city. (Fiction)

Koertge, Ron. *The Arizona Kid,* Little, Brown/ Joy Street Books, 1988. ●
Working one summer at a racetrack, living with his gay uncle, and falling madly in love make wimpy, short, tenth-grader Billy Kennedy more self-confident and wiser in the ways of the world. (Fiction)

———. *Boy in the Moon,* Little, Brown/Joy Street, 1991.
Senior year changes everything for Nick, who copes with acne, love, and changing relationships while pondering the meaning of his essay "Who Am I?" (Fiction)

———. *Harmony Arms,* Little, Brown, 1993.
Gabriel struggles to survive the culture shock he suffers when he moves from small-town Bradleyville to Los Angeles. (Fiction)

————. *Tiger, Tiger Burning Bright,* Orchard/
Melanie Kroupa, 1995.
Afraid that his mother will send his beloved
but senile grandfather to a nursing home, Jesse
tries to cover for the old man when he insists
he has spotted tiger tracks in the nearby California hills. (Fiction)

————. *Where the Kissing Never Stops,*
Atlantic Monthly Press, 1986.
In a warmly humorous first-person narrative,
seventeen-year-old Walker deals with his father's death, his mother's new job as a stripper,
and his attraction to Rachel. (Fiction)

Kogan, Judith. *Nothing but the Best: The
Struggle for Perfection at the Juilliard
School,* Random, 1987.
A profile of the Juilliard School reveals the
ecstasy and disappointment of the exceptional
musicians, singers, and others who study there.
(Nonfiction)

Kohner, Hanna. *Hanna and Walter: A Love
Story,* Random, 1984.
Separated by the Nazi invasion of Czechoslo-
vakia, Walter Kohner goes to America and
Hanna Bloch to Holland. At the end of the war,
learning that Hanna is still alive after enduring
concentration camps and her husband's death,
Walter searches throughout Europe until they
are finally reunited. (Nonfiction)

Koller, Jackie French. *The Falcon,* Simon &
Schuster/Atheneum, 1999.
Seventeen-year-old Luke attempts death-defying
adventures while trying to hide the truth about
how he lost his eye. (Fiction)

————. *Primrose Way,* Harcourt, 1993.
In seventeenth-century America, sixteen-year-
old Rebekah Hall defies her missionary father's
beliefs and embraces the gentle ways of the
Pawtuckets—especially the wise and handsome
Mishannock. (Fiction)

Komunyakaa, Yusef. *Dien Cai Dau,* Wesleyan
University, 1988.
In these powerful poems, Komunyakaa remem-
bers the agony of the Vietnam War. (Nonfiction)

Konecky, Edith. *Allegra Maud Goldman,*
Harper, 1976.
A sensitive, funny, and at times sad story of a
precocious, strong-minded girl's struggle to find
her identity while growing up in Brooklyn during the 1930s. (Fiction)

Konigsburg, E. L. *Father's Arcane Daughter,*
Atheneum, 1976.
Overprotected children of wealthy parents get
a chance to grow up normally because of the efforts of their mysterious half sister. (Fiction)

Koontz, Dean R. *Watchers,* Putman, 1987.
Travis takes in a very special golden retriever
that is being stalked by The Outsider, a hid-
eous, evil monster. (Fiction)

Kopay, David, and Young, Perry. *David Kopay
Story: An Extraordinary Self-Revelation,*
Arbor House, 1977.
A pro football player candidly relates his agonizing journey in coming to terms with his
homosexuality and making public his sexual
preference. (Nonfiction)

Korman, Gordon A. *Losing Joe's Place,*
Scholastic, 1991.
Convinced his older brother Joe is the "cool-
est," Jason has been looking forward to spending an unchaperoned summer with two friends
in Joe's apartment, but he doesn't figure on his
brother's best friend, 300-pound Rootbeer,
moving in, too. (Fiction)

————. *Semester in the Life of a Garbage Bag,*
Scholastic, 1987.
Will Sean's sabotage of the school's solar power
plant thwart Raymond's hilarious schemes to
earn a trip to a Greek island? (Fiction)

————. *Son of Interflux,* Scholastic, 1986.
It's hilarious and improbable, this tale of high
school students who challenge Interflux, a major corporation. (Fiction)

Korschunow, Irina. *Night in Distant Motion,*
Godine, 1983.
Regine questions her loyalty to the Nazi party
after she meets Jan, a Polish prisoner considered
"sub-human." Only then does she begin to notice the injustice and horror, the muted rebellion and fear of the people around her. (Fiction)

Kotlowitz, Alex. *There Are No Children Here:
The Story of Two Boys Growing Up in the
Other America,* Doubleday, 1992. •
This searing portrait of life in Chicago's public
housing projects depicts the love and the terror
in the lives of two brothers. (Nonfiction)

Kovic, Ron. *Born on the Fourth of July,*
McGraw, 1976.
Beginning with the battle that leaves him para-
lyzed from the chest down, Kovic tells of his

---

struggle to reenter American society—a struggle which leads him to become a leading anti-war activist. (Nonfiction)

Kozol, Jonathon. *Amazing Grace: The Lives of Children and the Conscience of a Nation,* Crown, 1997.
Amid violence, AIDS, and terrible poverty, people keep hope alive in the South Bronx. (Nonfiction)

———. *Rachel and Her Children: Homeless Families in America,* Crown, 1988.
Kozol's look at families living on the streets challenges everyone who takes the word "home" for granted. (Nonfiction)

Krakauer, Jon. *Into Thin Air: A Personal Account of the Mt. Everest Disaster,* Villard, 1998.
Courage, cowardice, foolishness, and great adventure marked the 1996 rival expeditions' efforts to reach the summit of Everest when everything went terribly wrong. (Nonfiction)

———. *Into the Wild,* Villard, 1997.
Leaving a comfortable life behind for an adventurous one, Chris McCandless dies on a poorly planned hike in the Alaskan wilderness. (Nonfiction)

Kramer, Jerry. *Instant Replay; the Green Bay Diary of Jerry Kramer,* World, 1968.
In this day-by-day account, the physical wear and tear on the field and the business deals off it are equally important to this Green Bay Packers guard. (Nonfiction)

Krementz, Jill. *How It Feels to Be Adopted,* Knopf, 1983.
Kids from eight to sixteen share their feelings about being adopted. (Nonfiction)

———. *How It Feels to Fight for Your Life,* Little, Brown, 1990.
Fourteen courageous young people suffering from life-threatening illnesses talk about what it's like to live with constant pain. (Nonfiction)

———. *How It Feels When A Parent Dies,* Knopf, 1981.
Feeling lonely, frightened, and betrayed by death, eighteen young people talk candidly about the continuation of their lives after losing a parent. (Nonfiction)

Krentz, Harold. *To Race the Wind: An Autobiography,* Putnam, 1972. ▪
He is totally blind, but Harold and his parents determine that he will not be limited by his blindness. (Nonfiction)

Krisher, Trudy. *Kinship,* Delacorte, 1998.
Fifteen-year-old Pert longs for a permanently stable home, which she believes she will have if her absentee father returns. Then "Daddy" comes home. (Fiction)

———. *Spite Fences,* Delacorte, 1995.
It is the summer of 1960 in Kinship, Georgia, and living is not so easy for thirteen-year-old Maggie after the civil rights movement comes to town. (Fiction)

Kropp, Lloyd. *Greencastle,* Freundlich Books, 1987.
The difficulties faced by a bright, awkward high school student are captured in this haunting 1950s coming-of-age novel. (Fiction)

Kuklin, Susan. *After a Suicide: Young People Speak Up,* Putnam, 1995.
Friends and family members of suicide victims and survivors themselves share their experiences and feelings in this thought-provoking collection of essays. (Nonfiction)

———. *Fighting Back: What Some People Are Doing about AIDS,* Putnam, 1990.
A moving look—in words and inspired photographs—at a team of volunteers fighting the war against AIDS by offering practical and emotional support to patients. (Nonfiction)

———. *Reaching for Dreams: A Ballet from Rehearsal to Opening Night,* Lothrop, 1987.
Kuklin details the activities and emotions of the choreographer and dancers involved in Alvin Ailey's production of the ballet "Speeds." (Nonfiction)

———. *What Do I Do Now? Talking about Teenage Pregnancy,* Putnam, 1992.
"I can't believe how frightened I am," admits one young woman in this collection of honest interviews with pregnant teenagers, expectant fathers, and those who care for them. (Nonfiction)

Kullman, Harry. *Battle Horse,* Bradbury, 1981.
A modern-day joust, played in the magnificent style of Ivanhoe, goes astray when a young contender is compelled to beat a mysterious black knight. (Fiction)

Kunen, James Simon. *Strawberry Statement: Notes of a College Revolutionary,* Random, 1969.
An ex-varsity crew member at Columbia joins the 1968 confrontation over the university's indifference to war, racism, and poverty and records the struggle on the spot. (Nonfiction)

Kuper, Jack. *Child of the Holocaust,* Doubleday, 1968.
Jankel, a young Jewish boy, escapes Nazi persecution (in Poland) by posing as a Christian. When the war ends he begins a harrowing odyssey to find his family and his faith. (Nonfiction)

Kurtis, Bill. *Bill Kurtis on Assignment,* Rand McNally, 1984.
Danger, intrigue, power, and compassion are fact, not fiction, as CBS news-anchor Kurtis presents sensitive, on-the-scene investigative reports

of Agent Orange, Vietnam, the Iranian hostages, and the plight of Amerasian children. (Fiction)

Kuznetsov, Anatolli Petrovich. *Babi Yar,* Dial Press, 1967.
The German occupation of Kiev in 1941 is seen through the eyes of a Ukranian boy who witnesses Nazi barbarity and the mysterious disappearance of thousands of the city's Jews. (Fiction)

L'Engle, Madeleine. *Many Waters,* Farrar, 1987.
Intruding in their father's lab, twins Sandy and Dennys are flung across time to a desert where Noah's family lives among mythical creatures. (Fiction)

Lackey, Mercedes. *Arrows of the Queen,* NAL/DAW, 1987.
Discovered by a telepathic steed, Talia, a misfit in her society, is taken to be educated as herald to the queen. (Fiction)

————. *Bardic Voices: The Lark and the Wren,* Baen, 1993.
No risk is too daunting for fourteen-year-old Rune, daughter of a tavern wench, as she pursues her dream of joining the Bardic Guild. (Fiction)

Laird, Crista. *But Can the Phoenix Sing?* Greenwillow, 1996.
In a letter to his stepson, Misha Edelman describes the heroism and horrors he witnessed when, after losing his family to the Nazis, he becomes a fighter in the Polish Resistance during World War II. (Fiction)

Laird, Elizabeth. *Kiss the Dust,* Dutton, 1993.
It's Iraq, and Tara's family are Kurds. "He" has put out the word, and they must flee for their lives. (Fiction)

————. *Loving Ben,* Delacorte, 1990.
When Ann's hydrocephalic brother Ben is born, she finds herself overcome with ambivalent emotions—love, embarrassment, anger, and eventually acceptance. (Fiction)

Lamb, Wendy, ed. *Meeting the Winter Bike Rider and Other Prize Winning Plays,* Dell/Laurel-Leaf, 1986.
A wide range of topics and moods is explored by playwrights ages ten to eighteen in eight compelling works performed at the Young Playwrights Festival in New York. (Nonfiction)

Lane, Dakota. *Johnny Voodoo,* Delacorte, 1997.
Taken with her brother to rural south Louisiana by their father after their mother's death, fifteen-year-old Deidre searches for friendship, true love, and a place to belong. (Fiction)

Langone, John. *AIDS: The Facts,* Little, Brown, 1988.
By an experienced science writer, this comprehensive, understandable, and well-researched study presents a nonjudgmental overview of current knowledge about AIDS. (Nonfiction)

Lanker, Brian. *I Dream a World: Portraits of Black Women Who Changed America,* Stewart, Tabori & Chang, 1990.
Photographs and text highlight the strength of black women who have prevailed in the face of adversity and prejudice. (Nonfiction)

Lantz, Frances. *Someone to Love,* Avon, 1998.
In letters to her soon-to-be-adopted sibling, Sara explains how, defying her parents, she becomes friends with the birth mother, Iris, and ruins everything. (Fiction)

Larrick, Nancy, ed. *Crazy to Be Alive in Such a Strange World: Poems about People,* Evans, 1977.
Tinged with humor and irony, a collection of poems written by both well- and little-known poets about people of varied backgrounds and ages. (Nonfiction)

Larson, Gary. *Prehistory of The Far Side: A Tenth Anniversary Exhibit,* Andrews & McMeel, 1991.
In cartoons and words not for the "humorously squeamish," Larson describes his life as "The Far Side's" creator. (Nonfiction)

————. *There's a Hair in My Dirt: A Worm's Story,* HarperCollins, 1999.
Cartoonist Larson reminds us that though nature is pretty, it's just waiting to eat us. (Nonfiction)

Lasky, Kathryn. *Beyond the Burning Time,* Scholastic/Blue Sky, 1995.
In this shocking story, Mary Chase fights to save her mother from being executed as a witch in 1692 Salem. (Fiction)

————. *Beyond the Divide,* Macmillan, 1983.
Meribah runs away to join her father on a trek to California—and ends up surviving alone in the Sierra Nevada Mountains. (Fiction)

■ Selected for "Still Alive: The Best of the Best, 1960–1974"
▲ Selected for "The Best of the Best Books: 1970–1983"
◆ Selected for "Nothin' but the Best: Best of the Best Books for Young Adults, 1966–1986"
● Selected for "Here We Go Again: 25 Years of Best Books: Selections from 1967 to 1992"

———. *Pageant,* Macmillan/Four Winds, 1986.
Sarah's years at an exclusive high school are full of self-awareness, humor, and conflict with the teachers. (Fiction)

———. *Prank,* Macmillan, 1984.
While trying to determine her future plans, Birdie Flynn confronts her brother about his involvement in vandalizing a synagogue. (Fiction)

Lauber, Patricia. *Seeing Earth from Space,* Watts/Orchard, 1991.
Lauber's photo essay shows how scientists use various photographic methods to study the earth. (Nonfiction)

———. *Summer of Fire: Yellowstone, 1988,* Orchard, 1992.
In an account enhanced by stunning photographs, Lauber clearly describes the effects, both positive and negative, of the awesome fires that roared through our oldest national park in 1988. (Nonfiction)

Laure, Jason, and Laure, Ettagale. *South Africa: Coming of Age under Apartheid,* Farrar, 1980.
Eight young people talk about their lives and their aspirations in a country where color rules one's place in society. Photographs depict lifestyles unique to each. (Nonfiction)

LaVallee, David. *Event 1000,* Holt, 1971.
A nuclear-powered submarine is marooned in over 1200 feet of water, 160 miles from New York City, where for over a month the rescue team fights political and business interests to get an outmoded diving bell altered to rescue the trapped men below. (Fiction)

Lawick-Goodall, Jane Van. *In the Shadow of Man,* Houghton, 1971.
A young Englishwoman writes about the ten years she spent in Tanzania studying chimpanzees and describes with loving care each facet of their lives from birth to death. (Nonfiction)

Lawlor, Laurie. *Shadow Catcher: The Life and Works of Edward S. Curtis,* Walker, 1995.
Curtis' passion for documenting the lives of Native Americans through photographs and narrative claims thirty years of his life and nearly impoverishes him. (Nonfiction)

Lawrence, Iain. *The Wreckers,* Delacorte, 1999.
Eighteenth-century Cornwall provides an eerie backdrop for this heart-pounding mystery full of nautical adventure and with a fourteen-year-old hero. (Fiction)

Lawrence, Louise. *Calling B for Butterfly,* Harper, 1982.
Six young survivors of a destroyed starliner must depend on their own wits, a fragile radio link, and a mysterious alien presence. (Fiction)

———. *Children of the Dust,* Harper, 1985.
Three generations of the same family represent the two human factions—those who mutated due to exposure to the nuclear holocaust and those who were sheltered. (Fiction)

Lawson, Don. *United States in the Vietnam War,* Crowell, 1981.
Lawson traces U.S. involvement beginning with the use of advisors through the fall of Saigon and the final peace treaty. (Nonfiction)

Lawson, Donna. *Mother Nature's Beauty Cupboard: How to Make Beautiful, Money-Saving Natural Cosmetics and Other Beauty Preparations,* Crowell, 1973.
Strawberries and avocados are just two foods that you can turn into natural and inexpensive beauty aids that are fun to make. (Nonfiction)

Laxalt, Robert. *Dust Devils,* University of Nevada, 1999.
This is an Old West coming-of-age novella with bronc riding, horse rustling, Native American wisdom, and the desert landscape. (Fiction)

Le Flore, Ron, and Hawkins, Jim. *Breakout: From Prison to the Big Leagues,* Harper, 1978.
A former thief, drug addict, and ex-con recalls the people and events that led him from the prison baseball team to the Detroit Tigers and the All-Star game. (Nonfiction)

Le Guin, Ursula K. *Beginning Place,* Harper & Row, 1980.
Irena and Hugh each follow a hidden path to Tembreabrezi, a fantasy place, where they struggle to save their friends and make peace with the real world. (Fiction)

———. *Dispossessed,* Harper, 1974.
Shevek, the Dispossessed, a brilliant but politically naive scientist, attempts to establish interplanetary relations between two disparate societies, neither of which shares his utopian dream. (Fiction)

———. *Very Far Away from Anywhere Else,* Atheneum, 1976. ▲
In a brief and unique Le Guin story, Owen and Natalie, two gifted seventeen-year-olds, find friendship and love by sharing their dreams: one to be a scientist, the other, a musician. (Fiction)

Le Mieux, A. C. *The TV Guidance Counselor,* Morrow/Tambourine, 1994.
After his parents' bitter divorce, sixteen-year-old Michael becomes obsessed with photography but soon learns he can't hide his pain behind a camera. (Fiction)

Le Roy, Gen. *Cold Feet,* Harper, 1979.
Attempting to give her life new direction, Geneva draws away from family and school and becomes involved in a gambling ring . . . disguised as a boy! (Fiction)

Le Vert, John. *Flight of the Cassowary,*
Atlantic Monthly Press, 1986.
More and more obsessed with the animal char-
acteristics of people, sixteen-year-old Paul—
bright, normal, and athletic—comes to believe
that he can fly. (Fiction)

Leder, Jane M. *Dead Serious: A Book about*
Teenagers and Teenage Suicide,
Atheneum, 1987.
What to do and not to do for friends and par-
ents of those who are considering suicide is
discussed with sensitivity and good sense.
(Nonfiction)

Lee, Marie G. *Necessary Roughness,*
HarperCollins, 1998.
For Chan, it's football, and for his twin sister,
Young, it's her flute, as the two try to adapt to
small-town Minnesota life after moving from
L.A. Where does their Korean heritage fit in?
(Fiction)

Lee, Mildred. *Fog,* Seabury, 1972.
In October Luke Sawyer's life is going great; in
December everything in his comfortable world
starts to fall apart. (Fiction)

————. *People Therein,* Houghton/Clarion,
1980.
A turn-of-the-century love story set in southern
Appalachia joins together Lanthy, resigned to
life without marriage because she is crippled,
and Drew, a botanist who comes to the Great
Smoky Mountains from Boston to cure his fondness for alcohol. (Fiction)

Lee, Tanith. *Black Unicorn,* Atheneum, 1992.
Bored with her lonely life as the no-talent
daughter of a quirky sorceress, Tanaquil reconstructs a unicorn and, when it comes to life,
takes off for adventure. (Fiction)

————. *Red as Blood; or, Tales from the*
Sisters Grimmer, NAL/DAW, 1983.
These bizarre and chilling new twists to old
fairy tales are told by a master fantasy writer.
(Fiction)

Leekley, Sheryle, and Leekley, John.
Moments: The Pulitzer Prize Photographs,
Crown, 1978.
Dramatic, prize-winning photographs from 1942
to the 1970s illuminate small everyday human
happenings and make important historical
events come alive again. (Nonfiction)

Leffland, Ella. *Rumors of Peace,* Harper, 1979.
Growing up in California, a young girl finds the
anxieties of childhood and adolescence complicated by the turmoil of World War II. (Fiction)

Lehrman, Robert. *Juggling,* Harper, 1982.
In this touching novel, affluent high school student Howie Berger not only suffers the agonies
of first love but also is frustrated as he tries to
become an accepted member of an all-Jewish-
immigrant soccer team. (Fiction)

Leitner, Isabella. *Fragments of Isabella: A*
Memoir of Auschwitz, Crowell, 1978. ▲
The strength of the human spirit and the passionate will to survive the degradation and
death of Auschwitz are portrayed with searing
intensity through Leitner's fragmented memories. (Nonfiction)

Leslie, Robert. *Bears and I: Raising Three*
Cubs in the North Woods, Dutton, 1968.
While panning for gold in Canada the author is
"adopted" by three orphan bear cubs whom he
has to teach to find food, recognize danger, and
share his cabin. (Nonfiction)

Lester, Julius. *From Slave Ship to Freedom*
Road, Dial, 1999.
This stunning combination of art and prose
brings alive the effects of slavery on all hu-
manity. (Nonfiction)

————. *Othello,* Scholastic, 1996.
A powerful, accessible retelling of Shakespeare's
story of doomed love and jealousy, with an unusual twist, speaks to us across racial lines and
through the centuries. (Fiction)

————. *Search for the New Land,* Dial, 1969.
Combining autobiography, contemporary history,
and "found" poetry, a sensitive black militant
reveals the frustrations of his life, the sickness
in American society, and a revolutionary hope
for the future. (Nonfiction)

————. *This Strange New Feeling,* Dial, 1982.
Three black slave couples reach freedom by different paths, but all experience an emancipation
made richer by their dangerous struggle. (Fiction)

Levenkron, Steven. *Best Little Girl in the*
World, Contemporary Books, 1978. ▲
Obsessive dieting and bizarre rituals with food
are symptoms of Francesca's battle with anorexia nervosa, a disorder that afflicts one out of
every 300 teen-aged girls. (Fiction)

■   Selected for "Still Alive: The Best of the Best, 1960–1974"

▲   Selected for "The Best of the Best Books: 1970–1983"

◆   Selected for "Nothin' but the Best: Best of the Best Books for Young Adults, 1966–1986"

●   Selected for "Here We Go Again: 25 Years of Best Books: Selections from 1967 to 1992"

———. *The Luckiest Girl in the World,* Scribner, 1998.
Fifteen-year-old figure skater Katie Roskova inflicts pain on herself when she can't manage her feelings about her absent father, her overbearing mother, the pressures of her sport, and her school life. (Fiction)

Levin, Betty. *Brother Moose,* Greenwillow, 1991.
Survival takes on new meaning for orphans Louisa and Nell, as they trek through the Maine woods with an old Native American and his grandson. (Fiction)

Levin, Ira. *Boys from Brazil,* Random, 1976.
Nazis living in Brazil have an ingenious plot for establishing a Fourth Reich. (Fiction)

Levine, Ellen. *Freedom's Children: Young Civil Rights Activists Tell Their Own Stories,* Putnam, 1994.
Here is a thought-provoking collection of oral histories from thirty African Americans who were teenagers in the 1950s and 1960s and were involved in the desegregation effort and civil rights movement. (Nonfiction)

Levine, Gail Carson. *Ella Enchanted,* HarperCollins, 1998.
Imagine this: Cinderella's real problem isn't her cruel stepmother and stepsisters, it's just that she cannot refuse a direct command from anyone! (Fiction)

Levit, Rose. *Ellen: A Short Life Long Remembered,* Chronicle, 1974.
Told at fifteen that she has cancer, Ellen for two years finds the inner strength to live each day as fully as she can. (Nonfiction)

Levitin, Sonia. *Escape from Egypt,* Little, Brown, 1995.
Miracles, plagues, and love are only part of what two teens—Jesse, a Hebrew slave, and Jennat, a half-Egyptian, half-Syrian girl—confront in this retelling of the biblical story of the Exodus. (Fiction)

———. *Return,* Atheneum, 1987.
Desta, an Ethiopian Jew, and her family make a courageous and tragic journey across Ethiopia to Israel with the help of Operation Moses. (Fiction)

———. *Silver Days,* Atheneum, 1990.
Escaping from Nazi Germany, the Platts struggle to find a home in America and pursue their own dreams. (Fiction)

Levitt, Leonard. *African Season,* Simon & Schuster, 1967.
A swinging Peace Corps Volunteer in Tanganyika quickly became "broo," meaning brother, to the villagers. (Nonfiction)

Levoy, Myron. *Pictures of Adam,* Harper/ Charlotte Zolotow, 1986.
Though fourteen-year-old camera bug Lisa is drawn to class misfit Adam, she is dismayed when he claims to be an alien from the planet Vega-X. (Fiction)

———. *Shadow Like a Leopard,* Harper, 1981.
Ramon Santiago, a street punk and gifted poet, forms an unlikely friendship with an elderly artist, and each helps the other face his private fears. (Fiction)

Levy, Marilyn. *Run for Your Life,* Houghton, 1997.
A group of girls from a ghetto turn their lives around by running track. (Fiction)

Liang, Heng, and Shapiro, Judith. *Son of the Revolution,* Knopf, 1983.
Liang Heng recounts his growing up during the Chinese Cultural Revolution, which fractured his family and changed his life. (Nonfiction)

Lieberman, James E., and Peck, Ellen. *Sex & Birth Control: A Guide for the Young,* Crowell, 1973.
Mature, responsible sexual behavior is the cornerstone of a candid, comprehensive handbook offering facts about sex and sexual relationships. (Nonfiction)

Lindall, Edward. *Northward the Coast,* Morrow, 1966.
Having agreed to hide two political refugees, hard-boiled Lang Bowman takes them across the Australian wasteland with the police in pursuit. (Fiction)

Lipsyte, Robert. *Brave,* HarperCollins/C. Zolotow, 1992.
Sonny Bear, half-white and half-Moscondaga Indian, wants to be a boxer but has difficulty controlling his anger until he meets Alfred Brooks, a New York City cop and former contender. (Fiction)

———. *One Fat Summer,* Harper, 1977. ▲ ◆
Overweight Bobby Marks confronts the ridicule of friends and sheds his excess pounds, in a comical story of his last fat summer. (Fiction)

Lisle, Janet Taylor. *Sirens and Spies,* Bradbury, 1985.
Fourteen-year-old Elsie feels betrayed when she discovers that her beloved violin teacher, Miss Fitch, has a dark and painful secret she has been hiding since her girlhood in World War II France. (Fiction)

Littlefield, Bill. *Champions: Stories of Ten Remarkable Athletes,* Little, Brown, 1994.
The accomplishments and contributions of ten extraordinary athletes, from both genders and many cultural backgrounds, are explored through

moving essays and evocative full-color paintings. (Nonfiction)

Llewellyn, Chris. *Fragments from the Fire: The Triangle Shirtwaist Company Fire of March 25, 1911,* Viking, 1987.
This slim volume of poetry tells the story of the young women who died when fire destroyed the Triangle Shirtwaist Factory. (Nonfiction)

Llywelyn, Morgan. *Horse Goddess,* Houghton, 1982.
A young Celtic woman and a savage warrior journey throughout the ancient world pursued by a Druid priest, the horrible Shapechanger. (Fiction)

Lobel, Anita. *No Pretty Pictures: A Child of War,* Greenwillow, 1999.
A moving account of the award-winning illustrator's childhood in Nazi-occupied Poland, her imprisonment in a series of concentration camps, and her life after the war as a displaced person in Sweden. (Nonfiction)

Lockley, Ronald. *Seal Woman,* Bradbury, 1975.
Truth and fantasy blend in this haunting story of an Irish girl who becomes a princess of the seals and of the man she chooses as her prince. (Fiction)

Logan, Jane. *Very Nearest Room,* Scribner, 1973.
Fifteen-year-old Lee Kramer's life is bounded by family—a hard-working doctor father, boy-crazy younger sister, frail younger brother, and, especially, her dying mother. (Fiction)

London, Mel. *Getting into Film,* Ballantine, 1978.
An award-winning filmmaker shares the "inside dope" on career opportunities in all aspects of the film industry. (Nonfiction)

Lopes, Sal, ed. *Wall: Images and Offerings from the Vietnam Veterans Memorial,* Collins, 1988. •
Images of peace, war, and remembrance are evoked in this photo-essay about the healing force of the Vietnam Veterans Memorial. (Nonfiction)

Lopez, Barry. *Arctic Dreams: Imagination and Desire in a Northern Landscape,* Scribner, 1986.
This is an enchanting and challenging account of the animals, people, geology, and history of the Arctic. (Nonfiction)

Lopez, Steve. *Third and Indiana,* Viking, 1996.
Fourteen-year-old Gabriel runs away from home to protect his mother when he realizes that the boss of his drug-selling gang is crazy and murderous. (Fiction)

Lord, Bette Bao. *Legacies: A Chinese Mosaic,* Knopf, 1991.
These unique portraits of life in China during the past forty years form an affecting picture of events that led to Tiananmen Square. (Nonfiction)

Lord, Walter. *Incredible Victory,* Harper, 1967.
The crucial World War II Battle of Midway is stirringly re-created from both the American and Japanese points of view. (Nonfiction)

Lowenfels, Walter, ed. *Writing on the Wall: 108 American Poems of Protest,* Doubleday, 1969.
Martyrdom, inhumanity, war, and death confront the conscience of the reader in this anthology of protest poetry. (Nonfiction)

Lowry, Lois. *The Giver,* Houghton, 1994.
When he turns twelve, Jonas is given his life assignment from the committee of elders—to become the receiver of memories from far-past times—and discovers the horrible secret that his society has hidden for the "safety and happiness" of its citizens. (Fiction)

Lueders, Edward, and St. John, Primus, comps. *Zero Makes Me Hungry: A Collection of Poems for Today,* Lothrop, 1976.
Poems in a contemporary vein are excitingly presented with eye-catching modern graphics. (Nonfiction)

Lund, Doris Herold. *Eric,* Lippincott, 1975.
Told, at seventeen, that he has leukemia, Eric crowds his dreams for the future—college, sports, love—into the short time he has left. (Nonfiction)

Lydon, Michael. *Rock Folk: Portraits from the Rock 'n Roll Pantheon,* Dial, 1971.
These sketches bring to life the personality, lifestyle, and music of rock stars Chuck Berry, Carl Perkins, B. B. King, Smokey Robinson, Janis Joplin, The Grateful Dead, and The Rolling Stones. (Nonfiction)

Lynch, Chris. *Gypsy Davey,* HarperCollins, 1995.
Learning about love, life, and growing up, Davey challenges our perceptions of a mentally disabled teenager. (Fiction)

- ■ Selected for "Still Alive: The Best of the Best, 1960–1974"
- ▲ Selected for "The Best of the Best Books: 1970–1983"
- ◆ Selected for "Nothin' but the Best: Best of the Best Books for Young Adults, 1966–1986"
- ● Selected for "Here We Go Again: 25 Years of Best Books: Selections from 1967 to 1992"

———. *Iceman,* HarperCollins, 1995.
Eric plays hockey with a savage intensity, hoping that this only link to his father will improve their troubled relationship. (Fiction)

———. *Shadow Boxer,* HarperCollins, 1994.
Lynch writes about the love between two brothers, their dead father, and the sport that killed him. (Fiction)

———. *Slot Machine,* HarperCollins, 1996.
Elvin and his two best friends are sent to a summer camp for incoming freshmen at a Catholic boys' high school. Will short, round Elvin fit the slots the good fathers are trying to jam him into? (Fiction)

Lynd, Alice. *We Won't Go,* Beacon, 1968.
Told with utter sincerity, these are the personal accounts of Vietnam protesters. (Nonfiction)

Lynn, Elizabeth A. *Sardonyx Net,* Putman, 1982.
Star captain Dana Ikoro becomes Rhani Yago's slave, bodyguard, and lover, as well as her pilot, after he is convicted of smuggling dorazine. (Fiction)

Lyons, Mary E. *Letters from a Slave Girl: The Story of Harriet Jacobs,* Scribner, 1993.
Through letters to family and friends, Harriet Jacobs describes her life as a young slave girl in North Carolina and her daring escape to freedom. (Fiction)

———. *Sorrow's Kitchen: The Life and Folklore of Zora Neale Hurston,* Scribner, 1992.
A biography of Zora Neale Hurston who, wanting to preserve the cultural heritage of black Americans, achieves fame and triumph through her stories and plays, only to die poor and, until recently, almost forgotten. (Nonfiction)

Maas, Peter. *Rescuer,* Harper, 1967.
Charles Momsen utilizes his previously untried diving bell and succeeds in rescuing thirty-three men entombed in the sunken submarine *Squalus.* (Nonfiction)

———. *Serpico,* Viking, 1973. ■
Believing cops should be honest, New York policeman Frank Serpico attempts to get action from the top against corrupt fellow officers. (Nonfiction)

Macaulay, David. *Motel of the Mysteries,* Houghton, 1979.
"Plastic is forever" is an illustrated catalog of the wonderful things discovered by archaeologists in the year 4022, when they excavate the ruins of the Toot 'n' C'mon Motel. (Nonfiction)

———. *Way Things Work,* Houghton, 1990.
Little woolly mammoths help you learn everything you always wanted to know about machines and how they work. (Nonfiction)

MacCracken, Mary. *Circle of Children,* Lippincott, 1974. ▲
Involving herself in a school for emotionally disturbed children, Mary MacCracken learns that these children can be helped through the love, trust, and compassion of those who teach them. (Nonfiction)

———. *Lovey: A Very Special Child,* Lippincott, 1976.
A profoundly disturbed child, Hannah is trapped in the prison of her emotions until a gifted teacher helps her break free. (Nonfiction)

MacInnes, Helen. *Salzburg Connection,* Harcourt, 1968.
Tension mounts steadily as Bill Mathison, a young attorney sojourning in the Alps, finds himself facing a dangerous group of international agents. (Fiction)

Mackay, Donald A. *Building of Manhattan,* Harper, 1988.
Ever wonder how the Empire State Building was built, how the New York subway works, or what happened to the farmland on Manhattan Island? Mackay explains it all. (Nonfiction)

MacKinnon, Bernie. *Meantime,* Houghton, 1984. ◆
Told through the eyes of their son, this is the story of a middle-class black family living in a white suburb and facing the hostility of neighbors and schoolmates. (Fiction)

MacLachlan, Patricia. *Baby,* Delacorte, 1994.
Left on the doorstep—but only for temporary care—baby Sophie forces Larkin's family to deal with their own unresolved tragedy. (Fiction)

———. *Journey,* Delacorte, 1992.
Journey's grandparents find a way to restore his family to him after his mother abandons him and his sister. (Fiction)

MacLaine, Shirley. *You Can Get There from Here,* Norton, 1975.
Invited to visit the People's Republic of China, the author and a group of American women were not prepared for what they saw and learned. (Nonfiction)

MacLean, Alistair. *Circus,* Doubleday, 1975.
It takes a five-man circus act with a psychic tightrope artist to get in and out of an East European prison safely. (Fiction)

———. *When Eight Bells Toll,* Doubleday, 1966.
Philip Calvert, a ruthless agent for Britain's secret service, outwits a gang of modern pirates operating on the Irish Sea. (Fiction)

MacLean, John. *Mac,* Houghton, 1987.
Mac's world, which centers on sports, school, and girls, crumbles when he is molested by a

physician—and he tries to act as if it never happened. (Fiction)

MacLeish, Roderick. *First Book of Eppe: An American Romance,* Random, 1980.
Sherborne Eppe, a lovable bungler, reentering the world after seven years in an "insane asylum," encounters several opportunities to do good as he flees from his mother, searches for his father, and tries to find himself. (Fiction)

Macy, Sue. *A Whole New Ballgame: The Story of the All-American Girls Professional Baseball League,* Holt, 1994.
From 1943 to 1954, the U.S. had a professional women's baseball league that "packed 'em in" and inspires this noteworthy chapter of American sports history. (Nonfiction)

———. *Winning Ways: A Photohistory of American Women in Sports,* Holt, 1997.
Macy's social and photographic history treats women's sports in the United States—from the 1800s, when even bicycle riding was unacceptable, to the present. (Nonfiction)

Madaras, Lynda. *Lynda Madaras Talks to Teens about AIDS: An Essential Guide for Parents, Teachers, and Young People,* Newmarket, 1988.
The curious, worried, or scared will find information, help, and hope in this honest look at how AIDS affects teens today. (Nonfiction)

———, **and Madaras, Area.** *What's Happening to My Body? Book for Girls: A Growing Up Guide for Parents and Daughters,* Newmarket, 1983. ●
This illustrated guide discusses body images, body changes, menstruation, puberty in boys and sexuality, emphasizing the importance of liking and knowing one's own body. (Nonfiction)

Magorian, Michelle. *Back Home,* Harper/Charlotte Zolotow, 1984.
When Virginia (Rusty) Dickinson returns to England after being evacuated to America during World War II, she feels lonely and alienated until she and her mother grow toward mutual understanding and acceptance. (Fiction)

———. *Good Night, Mr. Tom,* Harper, 1982.
A badly battered and frightened young boy evacuated from London during World War II fills an empty void in the heart of a dour old man. (Fiction)

———. *Not a Swan,* HarperCollins/Laura Geringer, 1993.
Spending an unchaperoned summer in a seaside English town during World War II, three sisters discover their lives will never be the same. (Fiction)

Magubane, Peter. *Black Child,* Knopf, 1982.
The sad, harsh realities of life in South Africa are sensitively revealed in photographs of children's faces. (Nonfiction)

Maguire, Gregory. *I Feel Like the Morning Star,* Harper, 1990.
Pioneer Colony's three dissidents—Ella, Mort, and Sorb—plot to escape their underground post-nuclear holocaust community. (Fiction)

Mahy, Margaret. *Catalogue of the Universe,* Atheneum/Margaret K. McElderry, 1986.
Angela's search for the father she has never met leads to a surprising new relationship with her best friend, Tycho Potter. (Fiction)

———. *The Changeover: A Supernatural Romance,* Atheneum/Margaret K. McElderry, 1984. ●
With the help of an older boy who loves her, Laura "changes over" into a witch to fight the evil forces that are attacking her little brother. (Fiction)

———. *Memory,* Macmillan/Margaret K. McElderry, 1988.
After a wild, drunken night seeking the truth behind his confused memories of his sister's death, teenage Jonny meets Sophie, an old woman who has lost her memory but has retained her zest for life. (Fiction)

———. *Tricksters,* McMillan/Margaret K. McElderry, 1987.
Three strangers from nowhere are catalysts in the lives of Harry and her family when reality and fantasy merge to expose unexpected secrets. (Fiction)

Maiorano, Robert. *Worlds Apart: The Autobiography of a Dancer from Brooklyn,* Coward, 1980.
A soloist with the New York City Ballet recounts his first sixteen years by presenting the two contrasting worlds in which he grew up—the tough streets of Brooklyn and the demanding and exciting world of ballet. (Nonfiction)

- ■ Selected for "Still Alive: The Best of the Best, 1960–1974"
- ▲ Selected for "The Best of the Best Books: 1970–1983"
- ◆ Selected for "Nothin' but the Best: Best of the Best Books for Young Adults, 1966–1986"
- ● Selected for "Here We Go Again: 25 Years of Best Books: Selections from 1967 to 1992"

Manchester, William. *One Brief Shining Moment: Remembering Kennedy,* Little, Brown, 1984.
Twenty years after John F. Kennedy's assassination, friends, family, and associates offer sentimental, yet candid reminiscences in words and pictures. (Nonfiction)

Mandela, Winnie. *Part of My Soul Went with Him,* Norton, 1986.
Battered but unyielding, Winnie Mandela reveals brutal facts about apartheid through her personal account of life in South Africa. (Nonfiction)

Mann, Peggy, and Gizelle, Hersh. *Gizelle, Save the Children!* Everest, 1981.
Gizelle Hersh, inspired by her mother's parting words, attempts to save her three younger sisters and a brother from death in the Auschwitz concentration camp at the close of World War II. (Nonfiction)

Manry, Robert. *Tinkerbelle,* Harper, 1966.
A copy editor of the *Cleveland Plain Dealer* realizes a lifelong goal when he sails his 13½ foot sloop across the Atlantic alone. (Nonfiction)

Margolies, Marjorie, and Gruber, Ruth. *They Came to Stay,* Coward, 1976.
The heartwarming story of how a single woman adopted two daughters—one Korean and the other Vietnamese—and the problems they had until the three strangers became a family. (Nonfiction)

Marlette, Doug. *In Your Face: A Cartoonist at Work,* Houghton, 1993.
"Kudzu" creator and political cartoonist Doug Marlette describes—in words and art—his sometimes offbeat life. (Nonfiction)

Marrin, Albert. *Commander-in-Chief Abraham Lincoln and the Civil War,* Dutton, 1999.
Marrin vividly portrays Lincoln as a self-educated, inexperienced politician, who finds himself leading the North's armed forces through one of the greatest tragedies in U.S. history. (Nonfiction)

———. *Unconditional Surrender: U. S. Grant and the Civil War,* Atheneum, 1995.
In addition to pointing out the many ironies in Grant's life and his pivotal role in the Civil War, Marrin portrays a soldier's life, early medical services, and battle tactics. (Nonfiction)

———. *Virginia's General: Robert E. Lee and the Civil War,* Simon & Schuster/ Atheneum, 1996.
Marrin's spirited biography shows how Lee, though opposed to slavery and secession, felt compelled by his honor to take up arms for his home state of Virginia—and in doing so changed the course of history. (Nonfiction)

Marsden, John. *Letters from the Inside,* Houghton, 1995.
With each letter, teenage pen pals Tracey and Mandy share personal experiences, each fearing the future—then Tracey's letters come back stamped "Return to Sender." (Fiction)

———. *So Much to Tell You,* Little, Brown/Joy Street Books, 1990.
In her diary, Marina, a young Australian girl locked in a self-imposed silence, reveals her deepest feelings and the family problems that led to her muteness. (Fiction)

———. *Tomorrow, When the War Began,* Houghton, 1996.
When they return from a wilderness camping trip, Ellie and her friends are shocked to discover Australia has been invaded and soon find fighting and surviving have become their way of life. (Fiction)

Marsh, Dave. *Born to Run: The Bruce Springsteen Story,* Doubleday, 1979.
This illustrated biography of a rock star traces his beginnings in Asbury Park, N.J. to the top of the rock and roll charts. (Nonfiction)

Marshall, Kathryn. *In the Combat Zone: An Oral History of American Women in Vietnam, 1966–1975,* Little, Brown, 1987.
Dramatic, thoughtful, often tragic accounts by a few of the thousands of women who served in Vietnam and, years later, tell a story few people know about. (Nonfiction)

Martin, Valerie. *Mary Reilly,* Doubleday, 1991.
Intrigued by the mysterious Dr. Jekyll, housemaid Mary Reilly finds life taking a different twist as she learns more about his late-night prowling in Victorian England. (Fiction)

Marzollo, Jean. *Halfway down Paddy Lane,* Dial, 1981.
Kate experiences a drastic change in lifestyle when she is transported back in time to 1850 as the daughter of an Irish immigrant family that lives and works in a New England mill town. (Fiction)

Mason, Bobbie Ann. *In Country,* Harper, 1985. ◆
On a pilgrimage to the Vietnam War Memorial in Washington, D.C., Sam, a recent high school graduate, tries to understand the strange behavior of her uncle Emmett and the death of the father she never knew, both victims of the Vietnam War. (Fiction)

Mason, Robert C. *Chickenhawk,* Viking, 1983.
The account of an American helicopter pilot in Vietnam who recalls his military training, the horror of Vietnam combat, and the pain of coming home. (Fiction)

Mastoon, Adam. *The Shared Heart,* Morrow, 1999.
Thirty-nine young people pose for the camera and tell about their struggles, heartaches, fear, joys, and triumphs growing up gay. (Nonfiction)

Matas, Carol. *After the War,* Simon & Schuster, 1997.
Met with hatred and violence when she returns home from a concentration camp, Ruth joins with other Jews who are trying to make their way to Palestine. (Fiction)

Matcheck, Diane. T*he Sacrifice,* Farrar, 1999.
A fifteen-year-old Apsaalooka girl overcomes the objections of her family and her tribe as she tries to become a warrior, a hunter, and the "Great One" prophesied at the birth of her and her twin brother. (Fiction)

Mather, Melissa. *One Summer in Between,* Harper, 1967.
Harriet Brown, an African American college student working temporarily for a white family in Vermont, is shocked when she recognizes her own prejudice. (Fiction)

Mathis, Sharon Bell. *Listen for the Fig Tree,* Viking, 1974.
In spite of her blindness and an alcoholic mother, Muffin, with the help of a kind neighbor, celebrates Kwanza and is able to face the future. (Fiction)

———. *Teacup Full of Roses,* Viking, 1972.
Into the lives of a middle-class African American family reach the tragedies of drugs, demolished dreams, and sudden death. (Fiction)

Matsubara, Hisako. *Cranes at Dusk,* Doubleday/Dial, 1985.
Like her defeated country of Japan, ten-year-old Saya faces painful readjustments after World War II, as her mother, who can neither abandon tradition nor accept changes, attempts to turn Saya against her wise and progressive father. (Fiction)

Matthew, Christopher. *Long-Haired Boy,* Atheneum, 1980.
War, self-pity, endless skin grafts, and long hospitalizations face Hugh Fleming, a young British fighter pilot, as he learns about life and finds a purpose for living. (Fiction)

Maxwell, Robin. *Secret Diary of Anne Boleyn,* Arcade, 1998.
Elizabeth, England's monarch, receives her mother's secret diary and becomes acquainted with a mother she has never known. (Fiction)

Mayhar, Ardath. *Soul Singer of Tyrnos,* Atheneum, 1981.
Though only a novice at singing souls, Yeleeve becomes the singer chosen to help combat the great evil threatening to overpower the land. (Fiction)

Maynard, Joyce. *Looking Back: A Chronicle of Growing Up Old in the Sixties,* Doubleday, 1973.
Writing at age eighteen, the author takes a nostalgic look back at what it was like to grow up in middle-class, white America in the 1960s. (Nonfiction)

Mazer, Anne, ed. *Working Days: Short Stories about Teenagers at Work,* Persea; dist. by Braziller, 1998.
Fifteen short stories about teenagers finding their way in the world of work. (Fiction)

Mazer, Harry. *Girl of His Dreams,* Harper/Crowell, 1987.
Runner Willis Pierce has to reconcile his fantasy about the "girl of his dreams" with reality when he meets Sophie, a girl who makes the world a less lonely place. (Fiction)

———. *I Love You, Stupid!* Crowell, 1981.
Marcus Rosenbloom wants to love a girl but isn't sure he knows how—until he meets Wendy Barrett. (Fiction)

———. *Last Mission,* Delacorte, 1979. ▲ ◆
When fifteen-year-old Jack Raab lies his way into becoming a tail gunner during World War II, he has no idea of the terrifying experiences that await him. (Fiction)

———. *War on Villa Street: A Novel,* Delacorte, 1978.
Thirteen-year-old Willis, who has turned to running as an escape from an unhappy home, coaches a retarded boy in athletics, an experience that helps both gain self-respect. (Fiction)

———. *When the Phone Rang,* Scholastic, 1986.
When their parents are killed in an air crash, Billy, Lori, and their older college-age brother, Kevin, struggle against adults and among themselves to avoid separating the family. (Fiction)

■ Selected for "Still Alive: The Best of the Best, 1960–1974"
▲ Selected for "The Best of the Best Books: 1970–1983"
◆ Selected for "Nothin' but the Best: Best of the Best Books for Young Adults, 1966–1986"
● Selected for "Here We Go Again: 25 Years of Best Books: Selections from 1967 to 1992"

————. *Who Is Eddie Leonard?* Delacorte, 1994.

Orphaned by the death of his grandmother, fifteen-year-old Eddie convinces himself that he is the boy whose face is on a poster at the post office, but can he convince the Diaz family that he is their missing Jason? (Fiction)

————, **and Mazer, Norma Fox.** *Solid Gold Kid,* Delacorte, 1977. ●

When five teenagers accept a ride from strangers, they become the victims of a kidnap plot and experience six horror-filled days that change their lives. (Fiction)

Mazer, Norma Fox. *After the Rain,* Morrow, 1987.

Rachel tells the story of her growing understanding of her eighty-three-year-old grandfather, a cantankerous old man she finds hard to love and almost impossible to like. (Fiction)

————. *Dear Bill, Remember Me?* Delacorte, 1976.

Eight short stories, all featuring strong female characters, range from a sensitive portrayal of an eighteen-year-old dying from cancer to the tale of a turn-of-the-century immigrant girl who defies tradition by getting an education and not getting married. (Fiction)

————. *Downtown,* Morrow, 1984.

When his mother reappears after eight years, Pete Connors, son of antiwar activists who have been hiding, must reconcile his desire for normalcy with a realization of his parents' ideals and acts. (Fiction)

————. *Out of Control,* Morrow, 1994.

After Rollo joins his friends in assaulting the artistic loner Valerie, he begins to understand what it means to be violated. (Fiction)

————. *Silver, Morrow,* 1988. ●

When fourteen-year-old Sarabeth Silver transfers to a new school, she is thrilled to find herself a part of the in crowd, until she becomes privy to an awful secret. (Fiction)

————. *Someone to Love,* Delacorte, 1983.

When Nina and Mitch fall in love, it seems only natural for them to live together until Nina finishes college. (Fiction)

————. *Up in Seth's Room,* Delacorte, 1979. ▲

Though Finn's parents forbid her relationship with nineteen-year-old Seth, the two develop a real attachment that helps them understand more about themselves and each other. (Fiction)

————. *When She Was Good,* Scholastic Press/Arthur Levine, 1998.

Seventeen-year-old Em remembers what it was like living with her emotionally disturbed, abusive sister, Pamela. (Fiction)

McCaffrey, Anne. *Dragonsinger,* Atheneum, 1977. ●

With the help of Master-harper, Menolly and her fire lizards overcome the prejudice against a woman's becoming a harper on the planet Pern. (Fiction)

————. *Pegasus in Flight,* Ballantine/Del Rey, 1992.

In a future where the psychically talented are both exploited and shunned, quadriplegic Peter and slum-kid Tirla join forces to build a new space station and infiltrate a child-smuggling ring. (Fiction)

McCall, Nathan. *Makes Me Wanna Holler: A Young Black Man in America,* Random, 1995.

McCall remembers his journey from a working-class African American neighborhood to prison to a prestigious position on the *Washington Post.* (Nonfiction)

McCammon, Robert R. *Boy's Life,* Pocket Books, 1992.

Cory and his dad find a corpse handcuffed to the steering wheel of a sunken car and decide to search for the killer. (Fiction)

McCants, William D. *Much Ado about Prom Night,* Harcourt/Browndeer, 1996.

Honor student Becca Singleton, embroiled in a battle to save peer counseling from being shut down by the school board, worries about getting a date for the prom. (Fiction)

McCartney, Linda. *Linda's Pictures: A Collection of Photographs,* Knopf, 1977.

Large-size color photographs of the Beatles—especially McCartney and family—and other rock groups by Paul's photographer-wife provide a unique look at them. (Nonfiction)

McCaughrean, Geraldine. *The Pirate's Son,* Scholastic, 1999.

Imagine living your fantasy of sailing off to exotic Madagascar with pirates: fourteen-year-old Nathan Gull does just that but not always with the wished-for results. (Fiction)

McConnell, Joan. *Ballet as Body Language,* Harper, 1977.

A vivid and realistic introduction to the behind-the-scenes sweat and pain—as well as the onstage glamor—of ballet. (Nonfiction)

McCorkle, Jill. *Ferris Beach,* Algonquin, 1991.

Katie Burns is caught in the conflict between the conventional life of her family and the daring, romantic lives of her beautiful cousin Angela and her lively neighbor, Mo Rhodes. (Fiction)

McCoy, Kathy, and Wibbelsman, Charles. *The New Teenage Body Book,* Pocket Books, 1979. ▲ ●

Changes in the physical development of both girls and boys, nutrition, personal hygiene, and emotions are covered in this illustrated guide. (Nonfiction)

McCullough, Frances, ed. *Earth, Air, Fire and Water,* Harper/Charlotte Zolotow, 1990.
What is a poem? This revised edition of a memorable collection of poems by 125 poets from all over the world may change your definition of poetry in surprising and intriguing ways. (Fiction)

———. *Love Is Like the Lion's Tooth: An Anthology of Love Poems,* Harper, 1984.
Passion, not romance, is the theme of this diverse anthology of love poems from various times and places. (Nonfiction)

McDonald, Joyce. *Swallowing Stones,* Delacorte, 1998.
Depression, guilt, and fear plague Michael's dreams after a stray bullet from his rifle kills a man. (Fiction)

McFarlane, Milton C. *Cudjoe of Jamaica: Pioneer for Black Freedom in the New World,* Ridley Enslow, 1978.
This is a retelling of the story of General Cudjoe, who led the proud Maroons of Jamaica in their successful eighteenth-century fight against enslavement by the British. (Nonfiction)

McGuire, Paula. *It Won't Happen to Me: Teenagers Talk about Pregnancy,* Delacorte, 1983.
Interviews with fifteen young women who have faced unwanted pregnancies. (Nonfiction)

McIntyre, Vonda N. *Dreamsnake,* Houghton, 1978. ▲ ◆
Snake, a young healer in a dangerous post-Holocaust world, undertakes an arduous search for a replacement for Grass, the slain dreamsnake vital to her profession. (Fiction)

McKee, Tim, ed. *No More Strangers Now: Young Voices from a New South Africa,* DK Inc./Melanie Kroupa, 1999.
Twelve South African teenagers share their experiences of life under and since apartheid, as well as their hopes for the future of their country and themselves. (Nonfiction)

McKibben, Bill. *End of Nature,* Random, 1990.
McKibben explores and explains the environmental cataclysms and global climate changes facing planet Earth. (Nonfiction)

McKillip, Patricia A. *Fool's Run,* Warner, 1987.
Masked musician The Queen of Hearts and her band entertain in an orbiting prison and create an intergalactic emergency. (Fiction)

McKinley, Robin. *Beauty: A Retelling of the Story of Beauty and the Beast,* Harper, 1978. ▲ ◆ ●
Fantasy and romance are beautifully blended in an evocative, much-expanded version of the classic fairy tale. (Fiction)

———. *Blue Sword,* Greenwillow, 1982. ▲
Harry Crewe, bored with her dull and sheltered life, finds new magic, love, and her destiny as a woman warrior when kidnapped by a handsome king who has mysterious powers. (Fiction)

———. *Deerskin,* Berkley/Ace, 1994.
Charles Perrault's fairy tale "Donkeyskin," the story of a king who rapes his own daughter, is re-created here in the unforgettable adventure of Princess Lissar, whose faithful dog Ash helps her escape the obsessive love of her father. (Fiction)

———. *Hero and the Crown,* Greenwillow, 1985.
Struggling to become a dragon killer, Aerin almost dies subduing the Black Dragon—only to face the evil mage, Agsded. (Fiction)

———. *Outlaws of Sherwood,* Greenwillow, 1988.
In a retelling that transcends the centuries, Newbery medalist Robin McKinley gives readers a lively, romantic new version of Robin Hood and his merry band. (Fiction)

———. *Rose Daughter,* Greenwillow, 1998.
Beauty, who possesses the gift of growing roses, is compelled to stay at the Beast's castle and help him bring his magnificent garden, the heart of his magical kingdom, back to life. (Fiction)

McKissack, Patricia C., and McKissack, Fredrick L. *Rebels against Slavery: American Slave Revolts,* Scholastic, 1997.
Exciting profiles of heroic men and women tell accounts of those who rebelled against slavery in North America. (Nonfiction)

———, ———. *Red-Tail Angels: The Story of the Tuskegee Airmen of World War II,* Walker, 1996.
A fascinating, well-illustrated history of African American pilots tells of their integral role in World War II. (Nonfiction)

■ Selected for "Still Alive: The Best of the Best, 1960–1974"

▲ Selected for "The Best of the Best Books: 1970–1983"

◆ Selected for "Nothin' but the Best: Best of the Best Books for Young Adults, 1966–1986"

● Selected for "Here We Go Again: 25 Years of Best Books: Selections from 1967 to 1992"

———, ———. *Sojourner Truth: Ain't I a Woman?* Scholastic, 1993.
A slave for the first thirty years of her life, Sojourner Truth achieves freedom and becomes an eloquent orator for the abolition of slavery and the emancipation of women—in spite of never learning to read or write. (Nonfiction)

———, ———. *Young, Black, and Determined: A Biography of Lorraine Hansberry,* Holiday, 1999.
A lively biography of the young black playwright who achieved success and recognition for her contribution to the arts and her hard work as a civil rights activist. (Nonfiction)

McLaren, Clemence. *Inside the Walls of Troy,* Simon & Schuster/Atheneum, 1998.
The beautiful Helen and the prophetess Cassandra describe, from their respective viewpoints, the events that led to the great Trojan War. (Fiction)

Mead, Alice. *Adem's Cross,* Farrar, 1997.
Fourteen-year-old Adem endures the horrors of war in the former Yugoslavia until forced to flee for his life. (Fiction)

Meltzer, Milton. *Ain't Gonna Study War No More,* Harper, 1985.
A lively account of the individuals and groups that have protested against the wars in which the United States has been involved—people convinced that there are peaceful solutions to conflict. (Nonfiction)

———. *Benjamin Franklin: The New American,* Watts, 1990.
This biography is the life story of an American original—a self-made man of many interests and talents and one of the revolutionaries who bucked the establishment to found a new country. (Nonfiction)

———. *Columbus and the World around Him,* Watts, 1991.
Meltzer's "no holds barred" biography of Columbus details the explorer's voyages in search of Asia and describes the tragic impact of the Spaniards upon the native Americans. (Nonfiction)

———. *Never to Forget: The Jews of the Holocaust,* Harper, 1976. ▲
Based on diaries, letters, songs, and history books, this is a moving account of Jewish suffering in Nazi Germany before and during World War II. (Nonfiction)

———. *Rescue: The Story of How Gentiles Saved Jews in the Holocaust,* Harper, 1988.
In an account of individuals who risked their own lives to save thousands of others during the Holocaust, Meltzer shows the quiet but impressive courage of those who chose to stand firm in the face of monstrous evil. (Nonfiction)

———. *Voices from the Civil War: A Documentary History of the Great American Conflict,* Harper/Crowell, 1990.
Details and excerpts from letters, diaries, and other primary sources make the Civil War come alive through the voices of those who fought, died, and survived its ravages. (Nonfiction)

———, ed. *American Revolutionaries: A History in Their Own Words, 1750–1800,* Harper/Crowell, 1987.
Letters, journals, etc., provide the personal views of people living in a turbulent time. (Nonfiction)

Meriwether, Louise. *Daddy Was a Number Runner,* Prentice-Hall, 1970. ■ ●
Francie, a twelve-year-old black girl, faces the daily hazards of life in the Harlem of the 1930s. (Fiction)

Merrick, Monte. *Shelter,* Hyperion; dist. by Little, Brown, 1994.
Nelson, a teen saddled with the care of his three-year-old sister, inadvertently discovers what his life is missing when his friends con him into investigating the disappearance of a developmentally disabled man from the neighborhood. (Fiction)

Messing, Shep, and Hirshey, David. *Education of an American Soccer Player,* Dodd, 1978.
One of the North American Soccer League's great goalies, Messing relates anecdotes about his Bronx childhood, Harvard education, participation in the Munich Olympics, and career with the New York Cosmos. (Nonfiction)

Meyer, Carolyn. *C. C. Poindexter,* Atheneum, 1978.
In this zany story, C. C. (Cynthia Charlotte) Poindexter, who at age fifteen is 6'1" and still growing, tells how she coped with her own problems and with family conflicts during one chaotic summer. (Fiction)

———. *Center: From a Troubled Past to a New Life,* Atheneum/Margaret K. McElderry, 1979.
David, who smokes marijuana, pops pills, cuts school, and steals, is sent to the Center, where teenagers help each other. (Fiction)

———. *Denny's Tapes,* Macmillan/Margaret K. McElderry, 1987.
Rejected by his stepfather, Dennis goes across the country in search of his real father, detouring to visit both his grandmothers, from whom he learns about his biracial heritage. (Fiction)

———. *Drummers of Jericho,* Harcourt, 1996.
Jewish Panzit Trujillo challenges the traditions of her new community when she questions the high school marching band's use of a Christian symbol and hymns. (Fiction)

———. *Gideon's People,* Harcourt, 1997.
When Isaac, an Orthodox Jew, is injured and taken in by Gideon's Amish family, the two teenagers must learn about each other's culture. (Fiction)

———. *Jubilee Journey,* Harcourt/Gulliver, 1998.
Young biracial Emily is shocked out of her feelings of comfort as she discovers she needs to come to terms with her racial identity when she visits her African American family in Texas. (Fiction)

———. *Voices of South Africa: Growing Up in a Troubled Land,* Harcourt, 1987.
Meyer recounts her journey to South Africa in a moving record of life in that beautiful and violent country. (Nonfiction)

———. *Where the Broken Heart Still Beats: The Story of Cynthia Ann Parker,* Harcourt/Gulliver, 1993.
Discovered and forced to return to her own family in 1836, twenty-four years after her capture by Comanche Indians, Cynthia Ann Parker is tragically unable to adjust to life away from the tribe that she now claims as her own. (Fiction)

———. *White Lilacs,* Harcourt, 1994.
Rose Lee Jefferson, twelve, and her family have always lived in Freedom, the "Negro" community in Denton, Texas, until the white folks decide to turn Freedom into a municipal park. (Fiction)

Michaels, Barbara. *Ammie, Come Home,* Hawthorn, 1969.
A ghost that never quite materializes and the spirit of "Ammie" Campbell haunt an old Georgetown house, threatening the lives of its occupants. (Fiction)

———. *Be Buried in the Rain,* Atheneum, 1985.
Medical student Julie Newcomb rediscovers love as well as the terrors of her childhood when she goes to care for her sinister grandmother in a southern mansion that is—perhaps—haunted. (Fiction)

———. *Dark on the Other Side,* Dodd, 1971.
Writer Michael Collins does not believe in supernatural powers until he too sees the savage black dog that is driving Linda Randolph to the brink of insanity. (Fiction)

———. *Witch,* Dodd, 1973.
Ellen's beautiful house, rumored to be haunted by a witch and her cat, changes from a refuge to a prison as she tries to understand the strange and threatening events that crowd around her. (Fiction)

Michelson, Maureen R., ed. *Women and Work: Photographs and Personal Writings,* NewSage Press, 1987.
Handsome black-and-white photographs together with women's personal testimonies capture the depth and breadth of American working women. (Nonfiction)

Mickle, Shelley Fraser. *Queen of October,* Algonquin, 1990.
Sent to her grandparents while her parents contemplate divorce, Sally comes to terms with herself and her life in a story set in the 1950s. (Fiction)

Mikaelson, Ben. *Petey,* Hyperion; dist. by Little, Brown, 1999.
Born in 1905 and mistakenly diagnosed as an idiot, young Petey is sent to an insane asylum, where, sixty years later, his life is drastically changed by a teenage boy. (Fiction)

Miller, E. Ethelbert, ed. *In Search of Color Everywhere: A Collection of African-American Poetry,* Stewart, Tabori & Chang, 1996.
From spirituals to rap, these works by famous poets are a presentation to delight. (Nonfiction)

Miller, Frances A. *The Truth Trap,* Dutton/Unicorn, 1980. ●
Mathew McKendrick is fifteen and a nonconformist. When their parents are killed in an automobile accident, he and his nine-year-old deaf sister Kathie run away to Los Angeles where he finds himself unjustly accused of murder. (Fiction)

Miller, Jim Wayne. *Newfound,* Watts/Orchard, 1990.
Newfound Creek in Tennessee is home to teenager Robert Wells and his extended family in this haunting story of what it is really like to grow up in Appalachia. (Fiction)

Miller, Jonathan, and Pelham, David. *Facts of Life,* Viking, 1985.
Six three-dimensional, movable models illustrate the human reproductive system and fetal development from conception to birth. (Nonfiction)

■ Selected for "Still Alive: The Best of the Best, 1960–1974"

▲ Selected for "The Best of the Best Books: 1970–1983"

◆ Selected for "Nothin' but the Best: Best of the Best Books for Young Adults, 1966–1986"

● Selected for "Here We Go Again: 25 Years of Best Books: Selections from 1967 to 1992"

Mills, Judie. *John F. Kennedy,* Watts, 1988.
This biography reveals President John F. Kennedy's failures and faults as well as his moral courage and political successes. (Nonfiction)

Moeri, Louise. *Forty-third War,* Houghton, 1990.
Forced to join a Central American army, twelve-year-old Uno learns firsthand about soldiering and war. (Fiction)

Mohr, Nicholasa. *In Nueva York,* Dial, 1977.
Interrelated stories of love, friendship, and the struggle to survive show the tragic and comic sides of life in a Puerto Rican community on New York's Lower East Side. (Fiction)

Mojtabai, A. G. *400 Eels of Sigmund Freud,* Simon & Schuster, 1976.
Summer at a scientific community for gifted teenagers ends in tragedy for Isaiah, the rebel among them, who prefers music to science. (Fiction)

Moll, Richard. *Public Ivys: A Guide to America's Best Public Undergraduate Colleges and Universities,* Viking, 1986.
Assuming that some state-supported colleges offer programs equivalent to those of the higher-priced Ivy League, Moll's thoughtful evaluations of the "public ivys" are right on target. (Nonfiction)

Monk, Lorraine. *Photographs That Changed the World,* Doubleday, 1990.
Fifty-one memorable photographs, with short essays that explore their enduring meaning. (Nonfiction)

Montalbano, William D., and Hiaasen, Carl. *Death in China,* Atheneum, 1984.
Romance and murder lead a former Vietnam Special Forces officer on spectacular chases through thousands of clay soldiers who guard a Chinese emperor's tomb at Xi'an—where he finds clues to the mysterious death of his friend. (Fiction)

Montandon, Pat. *Intruders,* Coward, McCann, 1975.
A San Francisco television star becomes perplexed and terrified by the intrusion of unexplained violence into her glamorous hilltop home. (Nonfiction)

Montgomery, Sy. *Walking with the Great Apes: Jane Goodall, Dian Fossey, Birute Galdikas,* Houghton, 1992.
These are the fascinating stories of three intrepid women who leave civilization to study and share the lives of primates. (Nonfiction)

Moody, Anne. *Coming of Age in Mississippi: An Autobiography,* Dial, 1969. ■
This is what it's like to grow up poor and black in Mississippi; although flawed by the Southern racial system, Anne Moody refuses to be broken by it. (Nonfiction)

Moody, Raymond A., Jr. *Life after Life: The Investigation of Phenomenon—Survival of Bodily Health,* Stackpole, 1976.
What is it like to die? Here are speculations by Dr. Moody and reports on interviews with people who had clinically died but lived to relate their comforting near-death experiences. (Nonfiction)

Moore, Gilbert. *Special Rage,* Harper, 1971.
A black *Life* reporter assigned to the Huey Newton trial in 1968 writes convincingly of Oakland ghetto conditions, Newton's background, the Panthers, and the trial. (Nonfiction)

Moore, Martha. *Under the Mermaid Angel,* Delacorte, 1996.
Much to her mother's dismay, thirteen-year-old Jesse's new best friend is the thirty-year-old tattoo-sporting waitress who lives in the trailer next door, but helping Roxanne solve her problems helps Jesse get a grip on her own. (Fiction)

Mori, Kyoko. *One Bird,* Holt, 1996.
After she is abandoned by her mother, who is hurt by her husband's infidelities, fifteen-year-old Megumi struggles to find hope, love, and a sense of home. (Fiction)

———. *Shizuko's Daughter,* Holt, 1994.
In the years following her mother's suicide, Yuki develops an inner strength in coping with her distant father, her resentful stepmother, and her haunting, painful memories. (Fiction)

Morpurgo, Michael. *Waiting for Anya,* Viking, 1992.
In World War II France, young Jo helps Benjamin hide Jewish children from the Germans and conduct them over the mountains to safety in Spain. (Fiction)

———. *War of Jenkins' Ear,* Putnam/Philomel, 1996.
Convinced that Christopher is the Son of God, Toby watches as miracles unfold at his English boarding school (Fiction)

Morrison, Lillian, selections, *Rhythm Road: Poems to Move You,* Lothrop, 1988.
The essence of motion is captured in this collection of poetry by classic and contemporary writers. (Nonfiction)

Mowry, Jess. *Way Past Cool,* Farrar, 1993.
Struggling to survive the streets of Oakland, California, thirteen-year-old Gordon and his gang of "friends" join forces with a neighboring gang to run the local drug dealer off their turf but are hindered rather than helped by the police. (Fiction)

Murphy, Barbara Beasley, and Wolkoff, Judie. *Ace Hits the Big Time,* Delacorte, 1981. ●
A black eyepatch and a dragon-emblazoned jacket help transform Horace Hobart into "Ace"—gang member, movie star, and cool guy. (Fiction)

Murphy, Jim. *Boy's War: Confederate and Union Soldiers Talk about the Civil War,* Clarion, 1992.
Riveting photographs, diaries and painfully honest letters tell the little-known story of hundreds of thousands of boys who fought in the Civil War. (Nonfiction)

————. *Death Run,* Clarion, 1982.
Four high school boys try to evade the police after a malicious prank accidentally causes the death of a fellow student. (Fiction)

————. *The Great Fire,* Scholastic, 1996.
The terrible Chicago Fire of 1871 is seen from the viewpoints of eyewitnesses and illustrated with period drawings in Murphy's vivid look at the famous disaster. (Nonfiction)

————. *Long Road to Gettysburg,* Clarion, 1993.
The personal journals of two young soldiers, one from each side, illuminate the events leading up to this pivotal battle, the bloody fighting, and the aftermath. (Nonfiction)

Murphy, Pat. *City, Not Long After,* Doubleday/ Foundation, 1990.
Following a devastating plague, a teenage girl leads the surviving residents of San Francisco, all artists and dreamers, against an invasion by a cruel despot. (Fiction)

Murrow, Liza Ketchum. *Fire in the Heart,* Holiday, 1990.
Molly realizes that to reunite her family she must uncover the secret surrounding her mother's death. (Fiction)

Myers, Walter Dean. *Fallen Angels,* Scholastic, 1988.
Seventeen-year-old Richie Perry's stint in Vietnam brings home to him the agony and futility of war as he learns to kill and watches his comrades die. (Fiction)

————. *The Glory Field,* Scholastic, 1995.
From slavery to the present, the Lewis family clings to its piece of South Carolina land, despite adversity, discrimination, and family problems. (Fiction)

————. *Harlem,* Scholastic, 1998.
The sights and sounds of Harlem are vividly portrayed in this striking volume of colorful illustrations and melodious verse. (Nonfiction)

————. *Hoops,* Delacorte, 1981. ◆
Lonnie and the rest of his Harlem ghetto basketball team learn the fine art of playing and winning like pros from Cal, who once was one. (Fiction)

————. *Legend of Tarik,* Viking, 1981.
Having witnessed the annihilation of his West African family and tribesmen at the hands of El Muerte, young Tarik seeks justice after proving himself worthy. (Fiction)

————. *Malcolm X: By Any Means Necessary,* Scholastic, 1994.
This is a biography of a complex, intelligent man whose philosophy and beliefs still resonate today. (Nonfiction)

————. *Mouse Rap,* Harper, 1991.
Fourteen-year-old rapper Mouse, his ace Styx, and other friends search for money hidden by a 1930s gangland leader, finding friendship and romance along the way. (Fiction)

————. *Now Is Your Time! The African-American Struggle for Freedom,* HarperCollins, 1992.
Blending well-known facts, obscure incidents and his own family stories into a telling of African-American history, Myers brings the past to life. (Nonfiction)

————. *One More River to Cross: An African American Photograph Album,* Harcourt, 1997.
A celebration of the African American through carefully selected photographs of famous and unknown people and minimal text. (Nonfiction)

————. *Righteous Revenge of Artemis Bonner,* HarperCollins, 1993.
Wanting to recover his Uncle Ugly Ned's lost fortune for his widowed aunt, Artemis tracks evil Catfish Grimes through the Old West in a chase that turns into a wild, hilarious romp. (Fiction)

————. *Scorpions,* Harper, 1988. ●
Jamal's ability to be a good student and to live up to his father's expectations are challenged by his role as a gang leader. (Fiction)

————. *Slam,* Scholastic, 1997.
"Slam" Harris is a talented basketball player whose dreams of fame and fortune in the NBA can come true—if he can control his anger. (Fiction)

- ■   Selected for "Still Alive: The Best of the Best, 1960–1974"
- ▲   Selected for "The Best of the Best Books: 1970–1983"
- ◆   Selected for "Nothin' but the Best: Best of the Best Books for Young Adults, 1966–1986"
- ●   Selected for "Here We Go Again: 25 Years of Best Books: Selections from 1967 to 1992"

———. *Somewhere in the Darkness,* Scholastic, 1993.

Jimmy is shocked when an unexpected visitor turns out to be his father, who has been in prison for eight years and now wants Jimmy to drive with him to Chicago. (Fiction)

———. *Young Landlords,* Viking, 1979.

In an amusing story, Paul, his girlfriend Gloria, and their friends inadvertently become landlords of a slum apartment building inhabited by some unusual tenants. (Fiction)

Naar, Jon. *Design for a Livable Planet,* HarperCollins, 1991.

In an enviromental handbook for the nineties, Naar explains the causes and effects of pollution, offering practical solutions for individuals and groups. (Nonfiction)

Nabokov, Peter. *Native American Testimony: An Anthology of Indian and White Relations/First Encounter to Dispossession,* Crowell, 1978.

Authentic illustrations, photographs, and historical documents provide insight into Native American and white relationships through the nineteenth century. (Nonfiction)

Nader, Ralph. *Unsafe at Any Speed,* Grossman, 1966.

Nader exposes "the designed-in dangers of the American automobile." (Nonfiction)

Naidoo, Beverley. *Chain of Fire,* HarperCollins/Lippincott, 1991.

The South African government uses psychological abuse and physical brutality to force Naledi and others to relocate to a desolate township. (Fiction)

Namioka, Lensey. *Island of Ogres,* Harper, 1990.

An out-of-work samurai has to solve the mystery of an island's ogres before a political plot to free the deposed ruler is successful. (Fiction)

———. *Village of the Vampire Cat,* Delacorte, 1981.

Two young masterless samurai solve the mystery of the vampire cat that has been terrorizing the villagers. (Fiction)

Napoli, Donna Jo. *The Magic Circle,* Dutton, 1994.

When the Ugly One succumbs to the demons' trickery and is changed from good sorceress to evil witch, she flees to a remote forest, but her destiny lies in the arrival of two children, Hansel and Gretel. (Fiction)

———. *Sirena,* Scholastic, 1999.

With sexuality and innocence, the mermaid Sirena enchants her Greek sailor, only to find that passion may not bind the two together for eternity. (Fiction)

———. *Song of the Magdalene,* Scholastic, 1997.

Napoli tells a haunting story of Mary Magdalene's youth and the tragic romance that may have led to her biblical downfall. (Fiction)

———. *Stones in Water,* Dutton, 1998.

Abducted by Nazis from a movie house near his home in Venice, Roberto finds himself a slave laborer in German work camps, until he escapes in the frozen Ukraine and struggles to return home. (Fiction)

Naughton, Jim. *My Brother Stealing Second,* Harper, 1990.

Grief-stricken Bobby, coming to terms with his brother's death, is devastated to learn the truth about the fatal accident. (Fiction)

Naylor, Phyllis Reynolds. *Keeper,* Atheneum, 1986. ✦

His father's mental illness paralyzes the entire family, forcing Nick to make an agonizing decision. (Fiction)

———. *Outrageously Alice,* Simon & Schuster/Atheneum, 1998.

The irrepressible Alice, now in eighth grade, suffers an identity crisis that leads to outrageous experiments with her appearance and behavior. (Fiction)

———. *Send No Blessings,* Atheneum/Jean Karl, 1991.

A proposal from Harless Prather looks like the best escape from the cramped trailer sixteen-year-old Beth shares with her family, but she fears marriage will ultimately end her dreams of a better life. (Fiction)

———. *String of Chances,* Atheneum, 1982.

When she goes to spend the summer with her less religiously oriented cousin and her husband, sixteen-year-old Evie Hutchins is confronted with an unexpected tragedy that turns her life around. (Fiction)

———. *Unexpected Pleasures,* Putman, 1987.

A heartwarming romance between a thirty-two-year-old Tidewater, Maryland, bridge-worker and a sixteen-year-old girl fleeing a shiftless family. (Fiction)

———. *Year of the Gopher,* Atheneum, 1987.

Fed up with college-application writing and parental nagging, George Richards opts for a blue-collar job. (Fiction)

Naythons, Matthew. *Sarajevo: A Portrait of the Siege,* Warner, 1995.

Shocking, stark black-and-white photographs taken during the 1992–1993 war portray the suffering in Sarajevo, providing an unforgettable message about the horrors of war. (Nonfiction)

Nelson, Theresa. *And One for All*, Watts/ Orchard, 1990.
The time is 1967, and young men are struggling to make it to college to avoid the Vietnam War—except for Wing, whose decision affects his whole family. (Fiction)

———. *Beggar's Ride*, Orchard/Richard Jackson, 1993.
Fleeing an alcoholic mother and a sexually abusive stepfather, Clare joins a gang of young runaways in Atlantic City and earns to survive by depending on this new family. (Fiction)

———. *Earthshine*, Orchard/Richard Jackson, 1995.
Twelve-year-old Slim must face the truth that her beloved, irreplaceable father is dying from AIDS. (Fiction)

Newth, Mette. *Abduction*, Farrar, 1990.
An Inuit woman, kidnapped by brutal whalers, finds friendship and understanding from her Norwegian jailer, Christine. (Fiction)

———. *The Dark Light*, Farrar, 1999.
Tora must leave her village in nineteenth-century Norway when she contracts leprosy, and, at the hospital, where she endures the cruelty of a fellow patient, she struggles to learn to read the Bible so she can realize God's plan. (Fiction)

Newton, Suzanne. *I Will Call It Georgie's Blues*, Viking, 1983. ◆
In music, Neil has a secret escape from the dark tensions beneath his family's smooth public facade—but the strain pushes his little brother Georgie over the edge of sanity. (Fiction)

Nicholls, Peter. *Science in Science Fiction*, Knopf, 1983.
Presenting the scientific basis for many of the "what ifs?" raised in science fiction—from Jules Verne's submarines to extraterrestrials, Nicholls weaves fact and fiction into a fascinating account. (Nonfiction)

Nichols, Michael. *The Great Apes: Between Two Worlds*, National Geographic, 1995.
Descriptions of the lives of chimps, gorillas, and orangutans—so humanlike, yet disappearing because of us—are accompanied by stunning, full-color photographs that bring the reader into their worlds. (Nonfiction)

Nicholson, Joy. *Tribes of Palos Verdes*, St. Martin's, 1999.
Fourteen-year-old Medina Mason wants to surf away from her parents' bitter divorce, the pretty, tan girls who hate her, and her twin brother's slow self-destruction. (Fiction)

Nicol, Clive W. *White Shaman*, Little, Brown, 1979.
A young student undergoes a spiritual rebirth as he discovers a mystical kinship with the Inuit or Eskimo people of northern Canada. (Fiction)

Niven, Larry, and Pournelle, Jerry. *Mote in God's Eye*, Simon & Schuster, 1974.
Who will win out in man's first extragalactic contact with an alien civilization, totally different in life and culture but equal in technology, cunning, and suspicion? (Fiction)

Nix, Garth. *Sabriel*, HarperCollins, 1997.
Sabriel makes a desperate quest through the Gates of Death to free her necromancer father from the strengthening powers of the spirits of the dead. (Fiction)

———. *Shade's Children*, HarperCollins, 1998.
The few remaining human children must find and destroy the "Grand Projector" in order to release themselves from the mutant rulers of Earth. (Fiction)

Nolan, Han. *Dancing on the Edge*, Harcourt, 1998.
After her psychic grandmother tells her that her father has melted, Miracle McCloy, obsessed with finding him, sets out in search of self and the truth. (Fiction)

Nolen, William. *Making of a Surgeon*, Random, 1971.
An account of a young surgeon's training at New York's Bellevue Hospital is told with wit and honesty. (Nonfiction)

Nomberg-Prztyk, Sara. *Auschwitz: True Tales from a Grotesque Land*, University of North Carolina Press, 1985.
Forced to work for Dr. Josef Mengele as a teenage hospital attendant at Auschwitz during World War II, the author gives a firsthand account of the cruel medical experiments that left nearly 500,000 Jews dead. (Nonfiction)

■   Selected for "Still Alive: The Best of the Best, 1960–1974"
▲   Selected for "The Best of the Best Books: 1970–1983"
◆   Selected for "Nothin' but the Best: Best of the Best Books for Young Adults, 1966–1986"
●   Selected for "Here We Go Again: 25 Years of Best Books: Selections from 1967 to 1992"

Noonan, Michael. *McKenzie's Boots,* Watts/
Orchard, 1988.
Getting into the Australian army by lying about
his age, sixteen-year-old Rod McKenzie finds
himself alone, unarmed, and face-to-face with
the enemy in the person of soldier and butterfly collector, Hiroshi Ohara. (Fiction)

Norman, David, and Milner, Angela.
Dinosaur, Knopf, 1990.
Representative of the outstanding Eyewitness
series, this account traces the history of dinosaurs through photographs, other illustrations
and text. (Fiction)

North, James. *Freedom Rising,* Macmillan,
1985.
A young white journalist's 25,000-mile clan-
destine travels through southern Africa reveal
the daily reality of apartheid. (Nonfiction)

Nye, Naomi Shihab. *Habibi,* Simon &
Schuster, 1998.
Fourteen-year-old Palestinian American Liyana
Abboud must learn to fit into a new world and
understand the political conflicts when her fam-
ily moves from St. Louis to Jerusalem. (Fiction)

———, ed. *The Tree Is Older Than You Are: A
Bilingual Gathering of Poems and Stories
from Mexico with Paintings by Mexican
Artists,* Simon & Schuster, 1996.
Modern and ancient Mexican poetry, prose,
and paintings come vividly alive in this lavish
anthology. (Nonfiction)

———, **and Janeczko, Paul, eds.** *I Feel a Little
Jumpy around You,* Simon & Schuster,
1997.
In this anthology of thought-provoking poems,
male and female writers view life from a gen-
der perspective. (Nonfiction)

O'Brien, Robert C. *Report from Group 17,*
Atheneum, 1972.
A strange zoo in the Russian embassy, an ex-
Nazi biologist, and a missing twelve-year-old
girl—it is Fergus's job to find out how they all
fit together. (Fiction)

———. *Z for Zachariah,* Atheneum, 1975. ▲ ●
In a peaceful valley, two survivors of an atomic
holocaust are brought together—one a self-sufficient young girl, the other a killer bent on
killing again. (Fiction)

O'Brien, Tim. *If I Die in a Combat Zone, Box
Me Up and Ship Me Home,* Delacorte,
1973.
This introspective memoir of a foot soldier in
Vietnam is a perceptive statement on courage,
cowardice, and morality in war. (Nonfiction)

———. *Things They Carried,* Houghton, 1991.
In these candid short stories based on O'Brien's
Vietnam experiences, pictures, heartaches,

dreams and terror are among the things soldiers
in Vietnam carry. (Fiction)

O'Donohoe, Nick. *The Magic and the Healing,*
Berkley/Ace, 1995.
B. J. Vaughan and other veterinary students
participate in an internship that crosses beyond
science and enters the magical realm of mythical creatures. (Fiction)

Okimoto, Jean Davies. *Jason's Women,*
Atlantic Monthly Press, 1986.
Jason fights his "wimpy tendencies" by getting
a hot date through a newspaper ad and by work-
ing for a feisty old woman running for mayor.
(Fiction)

O'Leary, Brian. *Making of an Ex-Astronaut,*
Houghton, 1970.
A NASA "dropout" tells about his seven months
as an astronaut and why he was the first scientist to resign. (Nonfiction)

Olsen, Jack. *Black Is Best: The Riddle of
Cassius Clay,* Putnam, 1967.
A sportswriter describes the controversial career
of Cassius Clay and tells why the great fighter
believes that "black is best." (Nonfiction)

———. *Night of the Grizzlies,* Putnam, 1969.
On the night of August 12, 1967, grizzlies attack a campground in Glacier National Park—a
violent and inevitable clash between a vanishing species and the humans invading its territory. (Nonfiction)

Oneal, Zibby. *Formal Feeling,* Viking, 1982. ▲
A year after the death of her mother, Anne Cameron gradually comes to terms with their past
relationship while adjusting to a new life with
her stepmother. (Fiction)

———. *In Summer Light,* Viking Kestrel,
1985.
Reluctantly returning to her island home to re-
cuperate from mono, Kate hates the dominance
and power her famous artist father holds over
her, but her love for graduate art student Ian
Jackson helps her grow to understand her father and herself. (Fiction)

———. *Language of Goldfish,* Viking, 1980. ▲
Afraid of growing up, thirteen-year-old Carrie
Stokes suffers a mental breakdown when she
retreats to the happy childhood world where life
is uncomplicated and unthreatening. (Fiction)

Orlev, Uri. *Man from the Other Side,*
Houghton, 1992.
Knowing the way through the sewers, Marek
leads a Polish Jew, who wants to die among Jews,
back to the doomed Warsaw Ghetto. (Fiction)

Orr, Wendy. *Peeling the Onion,* Holiday, 1998.
Anna struggles to recover her health and her
life after a car accident shatters her body and
leaves her brain damaged. (Fiction)

Oughton, Jerrie. *The War in Georgia,* Houghton, 1998.
Orphaned Shanta Cola Morgan must reconcile her feelings of loss and confusion about not being part of a "real" family in a small southern town during World War II. (Fiction)

Ousseimi, Maria. *Caught in the Crossfire: Growing Up in a War Zone,* Walker, 1996.
Interviews and haunting photographs document the experiences of young people growing up in war-torn areas in Lebanon, Bosnia-Herzegovina, Mozambique, El Salvador, and Washington, D.C. (Nonfiction)

Page, Thomas. *Hephaestus Plague,* Putnam, 1974.
An eccentric entomologist, charged with finding a way to destroy flame-throwing roaches, develops an affinity for them and breeds them while others work to save the East Coast from the destructive insects. (Fiction)

Page, Tim. *Nam,* Knopf, 1983.
UPI photographer Tim Page utilizes the photo essay to demonstrate the reality and the horror found on the front lines of the Vietnam conflict. (Nonfiction)

Palmer, David R. *Emergence,* Bantam, 1985.
Heroic deeds become the daily routine for eleven-year-old Candy Smith-Foster who, as a member of a new human species, begins a trek with her pet macaw, Terry D., across an American landscape scarred by bionuclear war. (Fiction)

Palmer, Laura. *Shrapnel in the Heart: Letters and Remembrances from the Vietnam Memorial,* Random, 1987. •
Who can forget those who died in 'Nam? Not the buddies, sweethearts, families, and friends who leave remembrances at the Vietnam Memorial in Washington. (Nonfiction)

Panzer, Nora, ed. *Celebrate America: In Poetry and Art,* Hyperion, 1995.
Join in this celebration of the American way of life through this rich multicultural collection of poetry and art. (Nonfiction)

Parini, Jay. *Patch Boys,* Holt, 1986.
In a small Pennsylvania mining town in the 1920s, fifteen-year-old Sammy di Cantini learns about maturity and friendship and takes on responsibility when his brother is killed in a miners' protest. (Fiction)

Park, Ruth. *Playing Beatie Bow,* Atheneum, 1982.
When she is transported backward in time, Abigail must survive in nineteenth-century Australia while struggling to return home. (Fiction)

Parks, David. *G.I. Diary,* Harper, 1968.
A frank diary of a young African American draftee's service in the Army, during which he experiences a rough year in boot camp and a grim tour of Vietnam. (Nonfiction)

Parks, Gordon. *Born Black,* Lippincott, 1971.
The celebrated author-photographer interviews Malcolm X, Muhammed Ali, Eldridge Cleaver, and other black notables and concludes with the statement: "America is still a racist nation. It has not learned much from the turbulent decade just passed." (Nonfiction)

———. *Choice of Weapons,* Harper, 1966.
With love, dignity and hard work *Life*-photographer Gordon Parks wins his battle against the debasement of poverty and racial discrimination. (Nonfiction)

———. *Voices in the Mirror: An Autobiography,* Doubleday, 1991.
Breaking one racial barrier after another to rise above a life of bitter poverty, this celebrated black filmmaker, photographer, and renaissance man expands our views of life's possibilities. (Nonfiction)

Parks, Rosa, and Haskins, Jim. *Rosa Parks: My Story,* Dial, 1993.
Rosa Parks tells in her own words what it is like to defy the system and, in the process, become a symbol of freedom for African Americans. (Nonfiction)

Parnall, Peter. *Daywatchers,* Macmillan, 1985.
This is a beautifully illustrated, nontechnical narrative of Parnall's observations of and experiences with various birds of prey. (Nonfiction)

Pascal, Francine. *My First Love and Other Disasters,* Viking, 1979.
Fifteen-year-old Victoria humorously describes the summer of her first love, when she comes to realize that there's more to real affection than outward appearances. (Fiction)

- ■ Selected for "Still Alive: The Best of the Best, 1960–1974"
- ▲ Selected for "The Best of the Best Books: 1970–1983"
- ◆ Selected for "Nothin' but the Best: Best of the Best Books for Young Adults, 1966–1986"
- ● Selected for "Here We Go Again: 25 Years of Best Books: Selections from 1967 to 1992"

Paschen, Elise, and Neches, Neil, eds. *Poetry in Motion: One Hundred Poems from the Subways & Buses,* Norton, 1997.
A rich mix of short poems and excerpts of longer poems that are used on New York City's subways and buses. (Nonfiction)

Patent, Dorothy Hinshaw. *Quest for Artificial Intelligence,* Harcourt, 1986.
Patent examines the nature of intelligence and traces attempts to make machines duplicate such human behavior. (Nonfiction)

Paterson, Katherine. *Jacob Have I Loved,* Crowell, 1980. ●
While growing up among the "water people" on an island off the coast of eastern Maryland during the 1940s, Louise searches for her identity and fights the jealousy she feels toward her talented, fragile, and beautiful twin sister. (Fiction)

————. *Jip, His Story,* Dutton/Lodestar, 1997.
Unclaimed after falling off a wagon, Jip is sent to a poor farm, where he discovers, in 1855, that his life is in jeopardy because his past is unexpectedly uncovered. (Fiction)

————. *Lyddie,* Dutton/Lodestar, 1992.
Unable to pay off the debt on the family farm, feisty, single-minded Lyddie survives the dangers of the textile mills in 1840s Massachusetts, determined not to forfeit her dreams. (Fiction)

Paton Walsh, Jill. *Parcel of Patterns,* Farrar, Straus & Giroux, 1984.
Vividly and dramatically, Mall Percival writes in her journal of the tragic events that befell her and the other villagers of Eyam during the disastrous plague of the 1660s in England. (Fiction)

Patterson, Sarah. *Distant Summer,* Simon & Schuster, 1976.
Set in England during World War II, this is the story of seventeen-year-old Kate who is courted by two young fliers—a sensitive, serious Englishman and a happy-go-lucky American. (Fiction)

Paulsen, Gary. *Cookcamp,* Orchard/Richard Jackson, 1992.
What would cause a mother to pin a note to her five-year-old son's jacket, put him on a train, and send him far away to live in the north woods? (Fiction)

————. *Crossing,* Watts/Orchard/Richard Jackson, 1987.
An alcoholic army sergeant and a homeless Mexican orphan come together in an unlikely friendship. (Fiction)

————. *Dancing Carl,* Bradbury, 1983.
Carl comes to McKinley, Minnesota, in the winter, drunk and maybe crazy, but he soon holds the attention of the entire town with his power and strange dance. (Fiction)

————. *Dogsong,* Bradbury, 1985.
Fourteen-year-old Russell, an Eskimo boy, borrows a neighbor's sled and dog team for a 1,400-mile journey, encounters a mammoth from earlier times and a pregnant girl from the present, and discovers his own relationship to his Eskimo culture. (Fiction)

————. *Harris and Me: A Summer Remembered,* Harcourt, 1994.
The narrator and his cousin share adventures—often with both painful and hilarious results—in this short, action-packed story of one summer spent on a farm. (Fiction)

————. *Haymeadow,* Delacorte, 1993.
This survival story pits John, only fourteen, against 6,000 sheep, four dogs, two horses, and uncooperative Mother Nature. (Fiction)

————. *Island,* Watts/Orchard/Richard Jackson, 1988.
The island in the middle of Sucker Lake gives fifteen-year-old Wil Newton the opportunity to discover himself and the harmony of nature. (Fiction)

————. *Monument,* Delacorte, 1992.
Rocky, a mixed-race teen, has her life changed by the unusual artist who comes to her small town to design a war memorial. (Fiction)

————. *Nightjohn,* Delacorte, 1994.
Nightjohn, a free black man, returns to the South to secretly teach slaves to read, igniting a desire for learning in the heart of twelve-year-old Sarny. (Fiction)

————. *Puppies, Dogs, and Blue Northers: Reflections on Being Raised by a Pack of Sled Dogs,* Harcourt, 1997.
In an exciting narrative, experienced sled-dog racer Paulsen tells the story of his beloved dog Cookie and her pups. (Nonfiction)

————. *The Schernoff Discoveries,* Delacorte, 1998.
Everybody knows a Harold Schernoff—the nerd, the geek. In this laugh-out-loud tale, Harold and his buddy team up for everything—from scientifically retrieving golf balls to designing that first kiss. (Fiction)

————. *Soldier's Heart,* Delacorte, 1999.
After facing the reality of fighting in the Civil War, Charlie realizes that war is hell on earth—both mentally and physically. (Fiction)

————. *Tracker,* Bradbury, 1984.
The dramatic journey of an orphan, John, who, in tracking a deer through the Minnesota wilderness, comes to terms with his grandfather's approaching death. (Fiction)

———. *Voyage of the Frog,* Watts/Orchard, 1990.
Lost at sea without a radio, David fights for survival in his small sailboat during a fierce storm. (Fiction)

———. *Winter Room,* Watts/Orchard, 1990.
Seated around a cozy fire in "the winter room," Elton and his brother Wayne challenge the truth of Uncle David's almost mythological stories about death and survival during his earlier life in Norway. (Fiction)

———. *Winterdance: The Fine Madness of Running the Iditarod,* Harcourt, 1995.
Vividly bringing to life the Alaskan Iditarod, a dogsled race requiring intensive training, skill, endurance, and the ability to survive subzero temperatures, Paulsen highlights the dogs who made it possible for him to make it to the finish line. (Nonfiction)

———. *Woodsong,* Bradbury, 1991.
Through his dogsledding adventures in the Minnesota wilderness where there are wolves, deep snow, and minus-30-degree temperatures, the author comes to understand nature's ways and harrowing surprises. (Nonfiction)

Pausewang, Gudrun. *The Final Journey,* Viking, 1997.
Horrid images emerge in this story of the two days a young girl spends on a railway car on her way to a concentration camp. (Fiction)

Peck, Richard. *Are You in the House Alone?* Viking, 1976. ▲ ◆ ●
After receiving a series of threatening notes, Gail Osburne is raped by one of the richest and most popular boys in her school—but nobody believes her story. (Fiction)

———. *Close Enough to Touch,* Delacorte, 1981.
How do you recover from your girlfriend's sudden death? Matt's solution is Margaret, who helps change his pain into love. (Fiction)

———. *Father Figure: A Novel,* Viking, 1978. ▲
The security that Jim Atwater finds in his role as surrogate father to his eight-year-old brother is threatened when, after their mother's suicide, the boys are packed off to spend the summer with their father, who had long ago abandoned them. (Fiction)

———. *Ghosts I Have Been,* Viking, 1977. ▲ ◆
In a hilarious sequel to *The Ghost Belonged to Me,* Alexander Armsworth meets his match in Blossom Culp, whose wits and psychic powers save the day. (Fiction)

———. *The Last Safe Place on Earth,* Delacorte, 1996.
Todd, fifteen, thinks he's found the perfect girl in Laura, his little sister's baby-sitter—then he sees the effect that Laura's fundamentalist beliefs are having on his sister. (Fiction)

———. *A Long Way from Chicago,* Dial, 1999.
Grandma Dowdel creates more fun and surprises for Joe and Mary Alice during their summer visits to her small Illinois town. (Fiction)

———. *Princess Ashley,* Delacorte, 1987.
"New girl" Chelsea must decide what price she is willing to pay to win popular Ashley Packard's acceptance. (Fiction)

———. *Remembering the Good Times,* Delacorte, 1985.
Meeting at a time of change in their lives, Kate, Buck, and Trav develop a special friendship—but even their mutual caring can't keep the gap from widening or avert the tragedy of Trav's suicide. (Fiction)

———. *Representing Super Doll,* Viking, 1975.
Darlene Hoffmeister, beautiful but dumb Miss Hybrid Seed Corn, sets out on the Beauty Contest Road and runs into some unexpected traffic. (Fiction)

———. *Strays Like Us,* Dial, 1999.
Uprooted once again and dumped on her great-aunt, Molly learns that the world is full of strays and that all towns have secrets. (Fiction)

Peck, Robert Newton. *Day No Pigs Would Die,* Knopf, 1973. ■
Through his relationship with his hard-working father, twelve-year-old Rob learns to cope with the harshness of Shaker life and emerges a mature individual. (Fiction)

Pei, Lowry. *Family Resemblances,* Random, 1986.
Visiting her unconventional aunt, fifteen-year-old Karen becomes aware of the complexities of adult relationships and also experiences a love affair of her own. (Fiction)

Pele, do Nascimento, Edson A., and Fish, Robert. *My Life and the Beautiful Game: The Autobiography of Pele,* Doubleday, 1977.
An intimate and touching autobiography of the world's most famous soccer player on the eve

---

■ Selected for "Still Alive: The Best of the Best, 1960–1974"

▲ Selected for "The Best of the Best Books: 1970–1983"

◆ Selected for "Nothin' but the Best: Best of the Best Books for Young Adults, 1966–1986"

● Selected for "Here We Go Again: 25 Years of Best Books: Selections from 1967 to 1992"

of his retirement from "the beautiful game." (Nonfiction)

Penman, Sharon. *The Queen's Man,* Holt, 1998.
Young Justin de Quincey finds himself in a viper's nest of murderous nobles and false allies when the queen chooses him to discover the truth about her son, who's gone missing on his return from the Crusades. (Fiction)

Pennebaker, Ruth. *Don't Think Twice,* Holt, 1997.
Pregnant and living in a home for unwed mothers, seventeen-year-old Anne believes that once she puts her baby up for adoption, life will get back to normal. (Fiction)

Pershall, Mary K. *You Take the High Road,* Dial, 1991.
Samantha is delighted to have a new baby brother, but suddenly her life is torn apart when the baby is killed in a tragic accident. (Fiction)

Peters, Ellis. *Black Is the Colour of My True-Love's Heart,* Morrow, 1967.
A folk song festival in rural England goes awry when a thwarted romance erupts into violence and murder. (Fiction)

Peterson, P. J. *Nobody Else Can Walk It for You,* Delacorte, 1982.
Eighteen-year-old Laura desperately tries to lead a group of young backpackers to safety as they are pursued by three threatening motorcyclists through isolated mountainous country. (Fiction)

————. *Would You Settle for Improbable?* Delacorte, 1981.
Just released from juvenile hall, Arnold is befriended by a student teacher and some of his ninth-grade classmates, with unexpected results. (Fiction)

Petty, Richard. *King of the Road,* Macmillan, 1977.
An American race car driver and his family share their team spirit in a winning photographic documentary. (Nonfiction)

Pevsner, Stella. *How Could You Do It, Diana?* Clarion, 1990.
Bethany struggles to understand why her pretty, popular sister committed suicide. (Fiction)

Peyton, K. M. *Prove Yourself a Hero,* Collins, 1979.
After being released by kidnappers, sixteen-year-old Jonathan feels guilty for having acted like a coward and for having cost his family the ransom money. (Fiction)

Pfeffer, Susan Beth. *About David,* Delacorte, 1980.
When Lynn finds out that David, whom she has known since childhood, has murdered his adoptive parents and killed himself, she must confront new feelings about him before she can recover from this loss. (Fiction)

————. *Family of Strangers,* Bantam/Starfire, 1993.
Abby feels so alone and unloved that she attempts suicide. It takes a sympathetic therapist to help her recover from the damage done by her family of strangers. (Fiction)

————. *The Year without Michael,* Bantam, 1987. ●
The unexplained disappearance of a high school student throws his family into a state of uncertainty and agony. (Fiction)

Philbrick, Rodman. *Freak the Mighty,* Scholastic/Blue Sky, 1994.
Separately, hulking Max and tiny Freak are each missing something, but together they are the adventure-prone "Freak the Mighty." (Fiction)

Philip, Neil, ed. *In a Sacred Manner I Live: Native American Wisdom,* Clarion, 1998.
Prayers, poems, essays, and photographs portray the deep spirituality of Native American life in this visually handsome volume. (Nonfiction)

————. *War and the Pity of War,* Clarion, 1999.
Ranging from ancient Rome to modern-day Bosnia, this unforgettable collection of poems illustrates both the heroism and the horror of war. (Nonfiction)

Phipson, Joan. *Hit and Run,* Atheneum/ Margaret K. McElderry, 1985.
After stealing a Ferrari and running from an accident, sixteen-year-old Roland has to decide whether or not to abandon the injured constable who has followed him into the Australian bush. (Fiction)

Pierce, Meredith Ann. *The Darkangel,* Atlantic Monthly Press, 1982. ▲ ●
Although both fascinated and repelled by the vampyre, Aeriel tries to save her mistress and the other vampyre brides. (Fiction)

————. *Pearl of the Soul of the World,* Little, Brown/Joy Street, 1991.
In the conclusion of the Darkangel trilogy, Aeriel must carry the Pearl of the Soul of the World to the witch Irrylath, who seeks to destroy her. (Fiction)

————. *Woman Who Loved Reindeer,* Atlantic Monthly Press, 1985.
The daimon child that her sister-in-law brings Caribou to rear in the cold lands of the North grows into her unearthly companion and helps Caribou serve as the leader of her people. (Fiction)

Pierce, Ruth. *Single and Pregnant,* Beacon Press, 1971.
Here is a blunt, cautionary, never judgmental discussion by a social worker on the medical,

financial, and social problems facing the single, young, and pregnant. (Nonfiction)

Pierce, Tamora. *Emperor Mage,* Simon & Schuster/Atheneum, 1996.
Fifteen-year-old Daine uses her animal communication skills to help avert a war for her country. (Fiction)

Pinkwater, Jill. *Buffalo Brenda,* Macmillan, 1990.
The outrageous team of India Ink Teidlebaum and Brenda Tuna take on their high school and its cliques. (Fiction)

Plath, Sylvia. *The Bell Jar,* Harper, 1971. ■▲◆●
During a queer, sultry summer in New York, Esther Greenwood works as a junior editor on *Mademoiselle,* quarrels with her mother and boy friend, and is gradually aware of her descent into madness. (Fiction)

Platt, Kin. *Headman,* Morrow, 1975. ▲
Owen's desperate fight for survival through the streets of Los Angeles, in a "rehabilitative" youth camp, and as "headman" of a gang is told in swift, sharp, and realistic street language. (Fiction)

Plimpton, George. *Paper Lion,* Harper, 1966.
A writer-by-trade plays the part of a rookie quarterback with the Detroit Lions in order to write this entertaining inside view of pro football. (Nonfiction)

Plummer, Louise. *My Name is Sus5an Smith: The 5 is Silent,* Delacorte, 1992.
When Susan leaves her small town to study art in Boston, she loses her illusions of life and love but rediscovers herself and her independence. (Fiction)

Pohl, Frederik. *Man Plus,* Random, 1976.
To survive without mechanical help on the surface of Mars, Roger Torraway must become a biological monster and yet stay sane until he reaches his destination. (Fiction)

Pollack, Dale. *Skywalking: The Life and Times of George Lucas,* Harmony/Crown, 1983.
This is all about the man who created such spectacular movies as *Star Wars* and *Raiders of the Lost Ark.* (Nonfiction)

Popham, Melinda Worth. *Skywater,* Graywolf, 1991.
Brand X never intended to be a savior, and indeed most of his fellow coyotes never reach their destination. But their quest for the unpolluted water source Skywater leads to a deeper understanding of their desert world. (Fiction)

Porte, Barbara Ann. *Something Terrible Happened,* Orchard/Richard Jackson, 1995.
The happy and quiet life that Gillian has with her mother and grandmother begins to unravel when her mother is diagnosed with AIDS. (Fiction)

Porter, Tracey. *Treasures in the Dust,* HarperCollins/Joanna Cotler, 1999.
The friendship between Annie and Violet survives Dust Bowl Oklahoma through the letters they write after Violet's family leaves to look for work in California. (Fiction)

Portis, Charles. *True Grit: A Novel,* Simon & Schuster, 1968.
With her papa's pistol tied to her saddlehorn and a supersized ration of audacity, fourteen-year-old Mattie Ross sets out to avenge her father's murder. (Fiction)

Postman, Neil, and Weingartner, Charles. *Soft Revolution: A Student Handbook for Turning Schools Around,* Delacorte, 1971.
Here is a treatise on how students can change their schools without violence through innovative suggestions, persuasion, and gentle manipulation. (Nonfiction)

Potok, Chaim. *The Chosen,* Simon & Schuster, 1967. ■◆
Two Jewish boys growing to manhood in Brooklyn discover that differences can strengthen friendship and understanding. (Fiction)

————. *My Name Is Asher Lev,* Knopf, 1972.
Asher Lev is an ordinary Jewish boy from Brooklyn until his passion and genius for painting create a furor in the art world and alienate him from the parents he loves. (Fiction)

————. *Promise,* Knopf, 1969.
In this sequel to *The Chosen,* rabbinical student Reuven confronts his dogmatic teacher, and his friend Danny undertakes his first case as a clinical psychologist, one requiring a drastic, experimental treatment. (Fiction)

————. *Zebra and Other Stories,* Knopf, 1999.
In this collection of short stories, Zebra, Isabel, and other teens struggle to find themselves while confronting the rules and regulations of the adult world. (Fiction)

■ Selected for "Still Alive: The Best of the Best, 1960–1974"
▲ Selected for "The Best of the Best Books: 1970–1983"
◆ Selected for "Nothin' but the Best: Best of the Best Books for Young Adults, 1966–1986"
● Selected for "Here We Go Again: 25 Years of Best Books: Selections from 1967 to 1992"

Powell, Randy. *Dean Duffy,* Farrar, 1996.
At fifteen, Dean Duffy had it all and pitched for a world championship Little League team until he hit a slump. Now, at eighteen, he is trying to decide where to go with his life. (Fiction)

————. *Is Kissing a Girl Who Smokes Like Licking an Ashtray?* Farrar, Straus & Giroux, 1993.
Eighteen-year-old Biff looks fourteen, and he gets tongue-tied around girls, so he can't speak to Tommie, whom he's loved for two years. But, look out! He's about to meet Heidi, and his life will never be the same again. (Fiction)

Power, Susan. *Grass Dancer,* Putnam, 1995.
A multigenerational story about a Sioux family begins with the love of Ghost Horse and Red Dress and ends in the 1980s with Charlene Thunder, who falls in love with Harley Wind Soldier, a grass dancer. (Fiction)

Powers, John R. *Do Black Patent Leather Shoes Really Reflect Up?* Regnery, 1975.
Doing battle with an army of pimples, being a teenager, and spending four years in a South Side Chicago high school far exceed Eddie's worst fears. (Fiction)

————. *Unoriginal Sinner and the Ice-Cream God,* Contemporary Books, 1977.
The irreverently humorous adventures and misadventures of Tim Conroy, a Catholic teenager growing up on Chicago's South Side. (Fiction)

Powers, Thomas. *Diana: The Making of a Terrorist,* Houghton, 1971.
This is an examination of the tragic forces in the life of Weatherwoman Diana Oughton which lead her from a comfortable, wealthy home to a commitment to revolution and finally to her death in a "bomb factory" town house explosion in 1970. (Nonfiction)

Preston, Douglas, and Lincoln, Child. *Relic,* Tor/Forge; dist. by St. Martin's, 1996.
A PhD candidate knows something monstrous is living in the American Museum of Natural History but cannot convince the PR person to delay the opening of a new exhibit. The gruesome results will keep you up all night reading. (Fiction)

Preston, Richard. *Hot Zone,* Random, 1996.
Follow the terrifying history of the deadly Ebola virus and its journey from Zaire in Africa to Reston, Virginia. (Nonfiction)

Prince, Alison. *Turkey's Nest,* Morrow, 1980.
Eighteen-year-old Kate rejects the father of her unborn child for the security of her aunt's farm in Suffolk. There she comes to terms with herself and her future. (Fiction)

Pringle, Terry. *Fine Time to Leave Me,* Algonquin, 1990.
Chris and Lori experience ups and downs, joys and ordeals, as they discover the hard realities of marriage. (Fiction)

————. *Preacher's Boy,* Algonquin, 1988.
The community keeps an eagle eye on Michael's blossoming romance with Amy as her career and his first college year complicate his struggles for a better relationship with his father. (Fiction)

Prochnik, Leon. *Endings: Death, Glorious and Otherwise, As Faced by Ten Outstanding Figures of Our Time,* Crown, 1980.
Exploration of the lives and often unusual deaths of ten fascinating people, from Freud and Houdini to Isadora Duncan and Malcolm X. (Nonfiction)

Psihoyos, Louie, and Knoebber, John. *Hunting Dinosaurs,* Random, 1996.
With beautiful photographs and a zany sense of humor, Psihoyos and Knoebber impart the adventure of digging for fossils the world over. (Nonfiction)

Pullman, Philip. *Broken Bridge,* Knopf, 1993.
During her sixteenth summer, Ginny must come to terms with a brother she never knew she had, secrets her father won't share with her, and a tale of a long-ago kidnapping. (Fiction)

————. *The Golden Compass,* Knopf, 1997.
With the aid of friends, witches, and armored polar bears, twelve-year-old Lyra fights the evil that is stealing children and conducting horrible experiments on them. (Fiction)

————. *The Ruby in the Smoke,* Knopf, 1987. •
Sally, sixteen and an orphan, must find her way through a maze of nineteenth-century villains to claim her inheritance and her independence. (Fiction)

————. *Shadow in the North,* Knopf, 1988.
In an attempt to protect a client's investment, Sally Lockhart, a financial consultant in nineteenth-century London, comes up against an evil, rich industrialist who seeks to win her by any means. (Fiction)

————. *The Subtle Knife,* Knopf, 1998.
Will and Lyra are pulled into a parallel world, where they must fight the shadowy specters, as angels and witches aid them in their quest for the truth about dust. (Fiction)

————. *Tiger in the Well,* Knopf, 1991.
Did Sally Lockhart marry Arthur Parrish? Sally's certain that she didn't, but his legal evidence proves the contrary. What protection does Sally have against the evil forces that are threatening her? (Fiction)

Qualey, Marsha. *Come in from the Cold,*
Houghton, 1995.
Jeff and Maud, two seventeen-year-olds whose
families have suffered personal tragedies caused
by the Vietnam conflict, find comfort and love
when they meet during the 1969 antiwar movement. (Fiction)

————. *Revolutions of the Heart,* Houghton,
1994.
Seventeen-year-old Cory is caught between her
Native American boyfriend and her older broth-
er's prejudices, as native spearfishing in northern
Wisconsin tears their little town apart. (Fiction)

Quarles, Heather. *A Door Near Here,*
Delacorte, 1999.
Caring for her alcoholic mother and her three
younger siblings almost overwhelms fifteen-
year-old Katherine as she tries to keep her family's plight a secret from her father, her teachers,
her neighbors, and the authorities. (Fiction)

Ramati, Alexander. *And the Violins Stopped
Playing: A Story of the Gypsy Holocaust,*
Watts, 1986.
Based on a young survivor's account, this grip-
ping story tells of the Nazi massacre of the
Gypsies during World War II. (Nonfiction)

Randle, Kristen. *Only Alien on the Planet,*
Scholastic, 1996.
Moving to the East Coast, high school senior
Ginny becomes friends with a boy who never
speaks and uncovers his dark secret. (Fiction)

Rapp, Adam. *Missing the Piano,* Viking, 1995.
Initially thrilled when his younger sister wins
a role in the national tour of *Les Miserables,*
Mike Tegroff finds his enthusiasm waning when
he discovers that he is being sent to a military
academy while his mother and sister travel.
(Fiction)

Rappaport, Doreen. *American Women: Their
Lives in Their Words,* HarperCollins/
Crowell, 1992.
The vital and changing roles women have played
in American history from colonial times to the
present are vividly portrayed through their diaries, letters, and photos. (Nonfiction)

Rather, Dan, and Herskowitz, Mickey.
*Camera Never Blinks: Adventures of a TV
Journalist,* Morrow, 1977.
This controversial autobiography is by one of
the best known and most respected TV news-
casters. (Nonfiction)

Ray, Delia. *Nation Torn: The Story of How the
Civil War Began,* Dutton/Lodestar, 1991.
An accessible, well-illustrated account of pre-
Civil War events relates the way they lead to
the fateful firing on Fort Sumter. (Nonfiction)

Read, Piers Paul. *Alive: The Story of the
Andes Survivors,* Lippincott, 1974. ■
A compassionate account of sixteen young rugby
players who survive a plane crash in the Andes
and live for ten weeks on faith, finally choosing to use the bodies of their dead comrades for
sustenance. (Nonfiction)

Reader, Dennis J. *Coming Back Alive,*
Random, 1981.
Because Bridget's parents are dead and Dylan
is in conflict with his, the two seek refuge in the
rugged Trinity Mountains and in each other.
(Fiction)

Reaver, Chap. *Little Bit Dead,* Delacorte, 1993.
After Reece saves Shanti from being lynched,
information from a dance hall girl saves Reece
from the marshal and his posse. (Fiction)

Reed, Kit. *Ballad of T. Rantula,* Little, Brown,
1979.
Because his mother has left his father and his
best friend is committing suicide by not eating,
Futch hides in the monstrous alter ego of T.
Rantula. (Fiction)

Reese, Lyn. *I'm on My Way Running: Women
Speak on Coming of Age,* Avon, 1983.
Young women come of age in autobiography,
poetry, fiction, and anthropological accounts
from around the world. (Nonfiction)

Reidelbach, Maria. *Completely Mad: A
History of the Comic Book and Magazine,*
Little, Brown, 1993.
Mad magazine is funny and offensive. No won-
der teens love it and parents hate it! Read all
about it in this illustrated history. (Nonfiction)

Reiss, Kathryn. *Time Windows,* Harcourt, 1993.
Moving into a mysterious old house, Miranda
finds that she can see the horrifying things that
happened there in the past; but can she do anything now to change history? (Fiction)

Rendell, Ruth. *The Crocodile Bird,* Crown, 1994.
Liza has lived a completely sheltered life with
her obsessive mother on a remote English estate, but when her mother is arrested for murder, Liza is forced to flee, totally unprepared
for the real world. (Fiction)

■   Selected for "Still Alive: The Best of the Best, 1960–1974"

▲   Selected for "The Best of the Best Books: 1970–1983"

♦   Selected for "Nothin' but the Best: Best of the Best Books for Young Adults, 1966–1986"

●   Selected for "Here We Go Again: 25 Years of Best Books: Selections from 1967 to 1992"

———. *Heartstones,* Harper, 1987.
A victim of anorexia and bonded to her father, teenage Elvira leads her family to total destruction. (Fiction)

Renvoize, Jean. *Wild Thing,* Atlantic-Little, 1971.
Morag, a foster child, runs away to the isolated wilderness of the Scottish mountains, where she is happy for a time but soon realizes that no one can survive alone. (Fiction)

Reuter, Bjarne. *Boys from St. Petri,* Dutton, 1995.
When the Germans occupy Denmark during World War II, a group of teenage boys escalate their pranks to a series of increasingly dangerous resistance missions. (Fiction)

Reynolds, Marilyn. *Detour for Emmy,* Morning Glory, 1994.
Fifteen-year-old Emmy, an A student with college ambitions, must put her life on hold when she becomes pregnant and decides to keep her baby. (Fiction)

———. *Too Soon for Jeff,* Morning Glory, 1995.
Jeff's plans for the future, which include college, debate, and girls, but not his high-school girlfriend Christy, come crashing down when she has his baby. (Fiction)

Reynolds, Marjorie. *The Starlite Drive-In,* Morrow, 1998.
Thirteen-year-old Callie falls hard for the romantic drifter who disrupts the lives of her lonely mother and bitter father. (Fiction)

Rhodes, Richard. *Farm: A Year in the Life of an American Farmer,* Simon & Schuster, 1990.
Here's everything you didn't think you needed to know about the real life of a family earning its livelihood from the land. (Nonfiction)

Rice, Robert. *Last Pendragon,* Walker, 1993.
Sir Bedwyr disobeys Arthur's dying wish and hides the sword Caliburn instead of returning it to the lake, but when he returns to help Arthur's grandson fight the Saxons, the sword has disappeared. (Fiction)

Richards, Arlene Kramer, and Willis, Irene. *Under Eighteen and Pregnant: What to Do If You or Someone You Know Is,* Lothrop, 1983. ◆
This is information for teens on all aspects of pregnancy, including single parenting, adoption, abortion, marriage, and infant care. (Nonfiction)

Riddles, Libby. *Race across Alaska: The First Woman to Win the Iditarod Tells Her Story,* Stackpole Books, 1988.
A true tale recounts how Libby Riddles overcomes all odds to become the first woman to win the Iditarod. (Nonfiction)

Ridgway, John M., and Blyth, Chay. *Fighting Chance,* Lippincott, 1967.
Two young British paratroopers undertake a harrowing voyage across the Atlantic in a twenty-foot row boat. (Nonfiction)

Riley, Jocelyn. *Only My Mouth Is Smiling,* Morrow, 1982.
Merle desperately tries to hide her mother's mental illness from the whole world and especially from her own family. (Fiction)

Rinaldi, Ann. *Acquaintance with Darkness,* Harcourt/Gulliver, 1998.
After her mother's death, fourteen-year-old Emily Pigbrush must go to live with her uncle, a doctor she suspects is a grave robber. (Fiction)

———. *Break with Charity: A Story about the Salem Witch Trials,* Harcourt/Gulliver, 1993.
Susanna, fearful for the safety of her family, keeps silent about the motives of her friends who are accusing the Salem townspeople of witchcraft. (Fiction)

———. *Hang a Thousand Trees with Ribbons: The Story of Phillis Wheatley,* Harcourt/Gulliver, 1997.
Kidnapped in Senegal in 1761 and sold into slavery in America, Phillis Wheatley becomes educated and well-known for her poetry, only to face a struggle to fit into a white man's world. (Fiction)

———. *In My Father's House,* Scholastic, 1994.
During the Civil War, Oscie watches her Southern way of life disappear forever. (Fiction)

———. *Last Silk Dress,* Holiday, 1988.
As teenage Susan Chilmark champions the Confederate cause by collecting the last silk dresses in Richmond to build a hot air balloon, she examines her loyalty to family, friends, and country. (Fiction)

———. *Time Enough for Drums,* Holiday, 1986.
Fifteen-year-old Jemima, torn by her growing love for a supposed Tory sympathizer during the American Revolution, matures through her father's murder and her brothers' fight for independence. (Fiction)

———. *Wolf by the Ears,* Scholastic, 1992. ●
Harriet Hemings, rumored to be Thomas Jefferson's daughter, faces the choice of passing as white or remaining a slave in the sheltered but restricted life at Monticello. (Fiction)

Ritter, John H. *Choosing Up Sides,* Putnam/Philomel, 1999.
Luke's preacher father believes that left-handedness is a sign of the devil, and Luke's love of baseball, especially his left-handed pitching, leads to a family tragedy. (Fiction)

Ritter, Lawrence S. *Babe: A Life in Pictures,* Ticknor & Fields, 1988.
The life of Babe Ruth, the orphan who became the greatest legend in baseball history, is captured in this photobiography. (Nonfiction)

Rivers, Glenn, and Brooks, Bruce. *Those Who Love the Game: Glenn "Doc" Rivers on Life in the NBA,* Holt, 1995.
Doc Rivers tells it like it is—his life, his family, his teammates and coaches, and above all, how he lives and plays the game of basketball. (Nonfiction)

Roberson, Jennifer. *Lady of the Forest: A Novel of Sherwood,* Zebra, 1994.
Maid Marian is the lady in this romantic retelling of the Robin Hood legend. (Fiction)

Robertson, Dougal. *Survive the Savage Sea,* Praeger, 1973. ■ ▲
Having survived the wreck of their boat by killer whales, the Robertson family and a friend face an incredible thirty-eight-day battle for life in a secondhand raft, 1,000 miles from land. (Nonfiction)

Robertson, James I. *Civil War! America Becomes One Nation,* Knopf, 1993.
A vivid portrayal of the Civil War shows the way it was on both the battlefield and the home front. (Nonfiction)

Robeson, Susan. *Whole World in His Hands: A Pictorial Biography of Paul Robeson,* Citadel, 1982. ◆
A memoir of a brilliant, talented and controversial black singer is lovingly told in words and pictures by his granddaughter. (Nonfiction)

Robinson, Spider. *Callahan's Crosstime Saloon,* Ridley Enslow, 1977.
The misfits of earth and elsewhere who belly up to Callahan's bar have lived some of the wildest and funniest stories in the galaxies. (Fiction)

Rochman, Hazel, ed. *Somehow Tenderness Survives: Stories of Southern Africa,* Harper, 1988.
Ten short stories and autobiographical sketches by both whites and blacks from southern Africa reveal how it is to grow up under apartheid. (Fiction)

——, **and McCampbell, Darlene Z., eds.** *Bearing Witness: Stories of the Holocaust,* Orchard/Melanie Kroupa, 1996.

Twenty-four selections confront the Holocaust with intensity and realism, wrestling art and meaning from the unspeakable. (Nonfiction)

——, ——. *Leaving Home,* HarperCollins, 1998.
Leaving whatever one considers "home" can cause many emotions, as experienced in this collection of short stories, poems, and essays. (Fiction)

——, ——. *Who Do You Think You Are? Stories of Friends and Enemies,* Little, Brown/Joy Street, 1994.
These sixteen thought-provoking stories and autobiographical excerpts tell about friends and enemies. (Fiction)

Rodowsky, Colby. *Hannah in Between,* Farrar, 1995.
Hannah is caught between childhood and adult responsibilities as she desperately tries to keep her mother's alcoholism a secret. (Fiction)

——. *Julie's Daughter,* Farrar, 1985.
Slug meets the mother who deserted her when she was a baby and finally learns to accept the past. (Fiction)

Rogasky, Barbara. *Smoke and Ashes: The Story of the Holocaust,* Holiday, 1988. ●
Photographs and a graphic text trace the annihilation of the Jews before and during World War II. (Nonfiction)

Rose, Louise Blecher. *Launching of Barbara Fabrikant,* McKay, 1974.
A witty, empathetic, and earthy first-person story about the freshman college year of the overweight daughter of a rabbi. (Fiction)

Ross, Stewart. *Shakespeare and Macbeth: The Story behind the Play,* Viking, 1995.
Both Shakespeare's England and the exciting story behind the bard's most bloody play are illuminated in Ross's vivid account. (Nonfiction)

Rosten, Leo. *Most Private Intrigue,* Atheneum, 1967.
A sophisticated and intriguing novel in which former espionage agent Peter Galton attempts to bring three important scientists out of Russia. (Fiction)

Rostkowski, Margaret I. *After the Dancing Days,* Harper, 1986.
Thirteen-year-old Annie befriends hideously disfigured Andrew, a World War I veteran. (Fiction)

■   Selected for "Still Alive: The Best of the Best, 1960–1974"

▲   Selected for "The Best of the Best Books: 1970–1983"

◆   Selected for "Nothin' but the Best: Best of the Best Books for Young Adults, 1966–1986"

●   Selected for "Here We Go Again: 25 Years of Best Books: Selections from 1967 to 1992"

Rothenberg, Mira. *Children with Emerald Eyes: Histories of Extraordinary Boys and Girls,* Dial, 1977.
Heartrending case histories of autistic and schizophrenic children are told by a psychologist who works closely with them. (Nonfiction)

Rottman, S. L. *Hero,* Peachtree Publishing Ltd., 1999.
Sean, an angry fifteen-year-old from an abusive home, learns that he can take control of his own life while doing community service on a farm owned by an old man. (Fiction)

Roueche, Berton. *Feral,* Harper, 1975.
What happens to a fictional, rural Long Island community when stray cats turn wild and terrorize the town's residents? (Fiction)

Rowling, J. K. *Harry Potter and the Sorcerer's Stone,* Scholastic/Arthur Levine, 1999.
With only a lightning-bolt scar on his forehead as a clue to his true identity, Harry Potter, by a twist of fate, leaves his unloving foster family for a life of wizardry and celebrity. (Fiction)

Roybal, Laura. *Billy,* Houghton, 1995.
A confused sixteen-year-old, who had been kidnapped at age ten, must decide whether he is Billy Melendez, a New Mexico cowboy from a rural community, or Will Campbell, a middle-class midwesterner. (Fiction)

Ruby, Lois. *Arriving at a Place You've Never Left,* Dial, 1977.
Seven moving short stories deal with such personal crises as coping with a mother's nervous breakdown; being seventeen, pregnant, and unmarried; and facing anti-Semitism. (Fiction)

———. *Miriam's Well,* Scholastic, 1994.
When Miriam is diagnosed with bone cancer, her life hangs in the balance while advocates of her religion, which prohibits medical treatment, battle doctors and lawyers. (Fiction)

Ruskin, Cindy. *Quilt: Stories from the Names Project,* Pocket Books, 1988.
The lovers, friends, and relatives of the thousands who have died from AIDS express their love and loss in handcrafted 3-by-6-foot panels sewn into an enormous memorial quilt. (Nonfiction)

Russell, Bill, and McSweeney, William. *Go Up for Glory,* Coward-McCann, 1966.
The Boston Celtics' superstar recounts the highlights of his career and gives his opinions on subjects ranging from coaches to civil rights in an outspoken autobiography. (Nonfiction)

Ryan, Cheli Duran, ed. *Yellow Canary Whose Eye Is So Black,* Macmillan, 1978.
A rich bilingual collection of poems by more than forty poets reflects the variegated tapestry of life in Latin America. (Nonfiction)

Ryan, Cornelius. *Last Battle,* Simon & Schuster, 1966.
This is an exciting day-by-day chronicle, based on eye-witness accounts, of the twenty-one days prior to the fall of Berlin in 1945. (Nonfiction)

Ryan, Joan. *Little Girls in Pretty Boxes: The Making and Breaking of Elite Gymnasts and Figure Skaters,* Doubleday, 1996.
You'll never look at Olympic champion gymnasts and figure skaters in the same way after reading this startling exposé of how young female athletes suffer physically and psychologically for their gold. (Nonfiction)

Ryden, Hope. *God's Dog,* Coward, 1975.
A naturalist's two-year field study of coyotes results in a compassionate plea for changes in our attitudes toward these misunderstood creatures. (Nonfiction)

Ryerson, Eric. *When Your Parent Drinks Too Much: A Book for Teenagers,* Facts on File, 1985.
In addition to letting young adults know they are not alone, Ryerson provides hope: "You can't control your parent's drinking, but you can make changes that will make your life better." (Nonfiction)

Rylant, Cynthia. *Couple of Kooks and Other Stories about Love,* Watts/Orchard, 1991.
Many faces of love are found in these short stories—from love for an unborn child to romantic love and love that can never be reciprocated. (Fiction)

———. *Fine White Dust,* Bradbury, 1986.
When the traveling preacher comes to town, Peter's religious beliefs find a focus—but is running away with the preacher the answer to Peter's needs? (Fiction)

———. *Kindness,* Watts/Orchard/Richard Jackson, 1988.
Chip must cope with many conflicting emotions when his mother reveals that she is pregnant and refuses to name the father. (Fiction)

———. *Missing May,* Orchard/Richard Jackson, 1993.
After the death of her beloved Aunt May, Summer is afraid that she will also lose her Uncle Ob to his grief, but a quirky boy and the remembrance of May's extraordinary love help them to heal and to reaffirm life. (Fiction)

———. *Soda Jerk,* Watts/Orchard/Richard Jackson, 1991.
In poetic observations, a young drugstore soda jerk in a small Virginia town comments on the people and activity around him. (Fiction)

———. *Something Permanent,* Harcourt, 1995.
Rylant reinterprets Walker Evans' well-known Depression-era photographs in poetry that is as

unforgettable as that extraordinary time in history. (Nonfiction)

Sachar, Louis. *Holes,* Farrar/Frances Foster, 1999.
Stanley Yelnats is sentenced to Camp Green Lake, where he finds a treasure and puts an end to a long-running curse on his family. (Fiction)

Sachs, Marilyn. *Fat Girl,* Dutton, 1984.
Jeff Lyons is obsessed with creating a new person out of an unhappy fat girl, but loses control of the situation when the girl begins to think for herself. (Fiction)

Sagan, Carl. *Cosmos,* Random House, 1980.
Based on the PBS series, this chronicle of the life of our galactic backyard includes history, science, astronomy, and philosophy in a format that can be enjoyed in bits and pieces or from cover to cover. (Nonfiction)

Salassi, Otto R. *Jimmy D., Sidewinder, and Me,* Greenwillow, 1987.
In jail, fifteen-year-old Dumas Monk is writing—on the judge's orders—the story of how he became a pool hustler and a murderer. (Fiction)

Saleh, Dennis. *Rock Art: The Golden Age of Record Album Covers,* Ballantine, 1978.
Printed in full color from original negatives, this is a lavish collection of the best rock album covers from the preceding decade. (Nonfiction)

Salisbury, Graham. *Blue Skin of the Sea,* Delacorte, 1993.
In a series of eleven stories, Sonny Mendoza faces fear, love, and challenges as he comes of age in a small Hawaiian fishing village. (Fiction)

———. *Jungle Dogs,* Delacorte, 1999.
While growing up in Hawaii, James "Boy" Regis learns some tough lessons about courage and respect when he faces his darkest fears. (Fiction)

———. *Under the Blood-Red Sun,* Delacorte, 1995.
Tomi, a Japanese American teen living in Hawaii, must become the man of his family when his father and grandfather are interned after the bombing of Pearl Harbor. (Fiction)

Sallis, Susan. *Only Love,* Harper & Row, 1980.
The adversity of a wheelchair existence does not overwhelm Fran, and the knowledge that she is dying leads her to live each day to the fullest with humor, adventure, and love. Fran's love

affair with Lucas, another wheelchair occupant at Thornton Hall, is full of surprises. (Fiction)

Salzman, Mark. *Iron and Silk,* Random, 1987. ●
A young Yale graduate describes his two years in China teaching English to medical students, perfecting his Chinese, and studying martial arts with a master. (Nonfiction)

———. *Lost in Place: Growing Up Absurd in Suburbia,* Random, 1997.
Growing up in the Connecticut suburbs is not easy for a wanna-be kung fu expert and wandering Zen monk. (Nonfiction)

Samson, Joan. *The Auctioneer,* Simon & Schuster, 1976.
What begins as a harmless Saturday pastime turns sinister when the auctioneering stranger in town becomes its most influential and evil citizen. (Fiction)

Samuels, Gertrude. *Run, Shelley, Run!* Crowell, 1974. ■ ▲
Runaway Shelley, a victim of family neglect and juvenile injustice, finally gets the help she needs through the concern of a sympathetic judge and the intercession of a kind neighbor. (Fiction)

Sanders, Dori. *Clover,* Algonquin, 1991.
When her father is killed in an automobile accident in rural South Carolina, ten-year-old Clover is left to be reared by her white stepmother within the black community. (Fiction)

Sanders, Scott R. *Bad Man Ballad,* Bradbury, 1986.
In the early 1800s, two unlikely partners, a backwoods boy and a Philadelphia lawyer, go in search of a frontier "bigfoot" who has been accused of murder. (Fiction)

Sanderson, Ivan. *Uninvited Visitors: A Biologist Looks at UFO's,* Cowles, 1968.
Using exacting scientific methodology, the author delves deep into such problems as what could UFOs be, where do they come from, when did they start coming, and what would they want from us? (Nonfiction)

Sandler, Martin. *Story of American Photography: An Illustrated History for Young People,* Little, Brown, 1979.
From daguerreotypes to Polaroids, this illustrated history tells the story of the men and women who shaped the course of a major art and industry. (Nonfiction)

■   Selected for "Still Alive: The Best of the Best, 1960–1974"

▲   Selected for "The Best of the Best Books: 1970–1983"

◆   Selected for "Nothin' but the Best: Best of the Best Books for Young Adults, 1966–1986"

●   Selected for "Here We Go Again: 25 Years of Best Books: Selections from 1967 to 1992"

Santiago, Danny. *Famous All over Town,* Simon & Schuster, 1983.
Chato, a young Mexican American growing up in a Los Angeles barrio, has an IQ of 135 but gets bad grades in school because his first loyalty is to his family and gang. (Fiction)

Santoli, Al. *Everything We Had: An Oral History of the Vietnam War As Told by Thirty-three American Soldiers Who Fought It,* Random, 1981. ▲
Thirty-three veterans of the Vietnam War recount its impact on their lives one decade later. (Nonfiction)

Sargent, Pamela. *Earthseed,* Harper, 1983.
Ship has created and raised a generation of Earth children as it carries them through space toward a new planet where they must survive alone without Ship's care. (Fiction)

————, ed. *Women of Wonder: Science Fiction Stories by Women about Women,* Vintage, 1975.
These exceptional stories show that science fiction is no longer a field completely reserved for men. (Fiction)

Saul, John. *Creature,* Bantam, 1990.
Seemingly perfect Silverdale hides a horrible secret brought to light only when the coach's boys begin turning into monsters—both on and off the football field. (Fiction)

Savage, Candace. *Cowgirls,* Ten Speed, 1997.
From real life to reel life, this photo history tells the story of sharpshooting women who settled the American West and rode the rodeo circuit from Wyoming to Madison Square Garden. (Nonfiction)

Savage, Georgia. *House Tibet,* Graywolf, 1992.
After she is raped by her father, Vicky and her autistic younger brother run away, learn survival skills from street kids in an Australian beach town, and are befriended by some unusual people. (Fiction)

Say, Allen. *Ink-Keeper's Apprentice,* Harper, 1979.
Living on his own in post-World War II Tokyo, thirteen-year-old Kiyoi begins a new life when he becomes an apprentice to a famous cartoonist. (Fiction)

Scaduto, Anthony. *Bob Dylan,* Grosset, 1972.
What makes Dylan tick—from his early days in Hibbing, Minnesota, to his current silent stance, is told in this story of the complicated man. (Nonfiction)

Schaap, Richard. *Turned On: The Friede-Crenshaw Case,* NAL, 1967.
At nineteen Celeste Crenshaw is dead of an overdose of drugs and her wealthy, socially prominent boyfriend is on his way to prison. (Nonfiction)

Schami, Rafik. *Hand Full of Stars,* Dutton, 1991.
A young teenage boy in modern Damascus faces career choices, political ferment, and romance. (Fiction)

Schell, Jonathan. *Fate of Earth,* Knopf, 1982.
The possibility of human extinction from nuclear disaster is discussed in this frightening, and important, book. (Nonfiction)

Schiff, Ken. *Passing Go,* Dodd, 1972.
A curious blend of the real and surreal, this is an eighteen-year-old boy's day-by-day account of four bleak months in a mental hospital. (Fiction)

Schirer, Eric W., and Allman, William F. *Newton at the Bat: The Science in Sports,* Scribner, 1984.
From Schirer's sports column in *Science 84* magazine, these essays survey the part that physics, physiology, and aerodynamics play in baseball, Frisbee, skiing, sailing, and many other sports. (Nonfiction)

Schmidt, Gary D. *The Sin Eater,* Dutton/Lodestar, 1997.
When Cole hears stories of the mysterious "Sin Eater," he sets out to solve the mystery, making many self-discoveries along the way. (Fiction)

Scholl, Hans, and Scholl, Sophie. *At the Heart of the White Rose: Letters and Diaries of Hans and Sophie Scholl,* Harper, 1988.
The personal writings of a brother and sister beheaded by the Nazis for their opposition to the Hitler terror are poignant and passionate. (Nonfiction)

Schulke, Flip. *Martin Luther King, Jr.: A Documentary . . . Montgomery to Memphis,* Norton, 1976. ▲
Striking pictures and text graphically recapitulate the entire Civil Rights movement through the story of Dr. King's struggle to fulfill his dream. (Nonfiction)

Schulman, Audrey. *The Cage,* Algonquin, 1995.
When she is chosen to join an expedition to photograph polar bears from behind the thin bars of a tiny metal cage, Beryl's courage is tested to the limit. (Fiction)

Schulz, Charles. *Peanuts Treasury,* Holt, 1968. ■
Lucy, the natural-born fussbudget turned amateur psychiatrist, Charlie Brown, much maligned but dedicated manager of the world's most defeated baseball team, and Snoopy, the only dog in existence with a split personality, devise their own inimitable philosophies to cope with life's adversities. (Fiction)

Schwarz-Bart, Andre. *Woman Named Solitude,* Atheneum, 1973.
Understated and suffused with imagery and irony, this is the tale of a beautiful mulatto slave girl who is eventually driven into a zombie-like state of madness. (Fiction)

Schwarzenegger, Arnold, and Hall, Douglas Kent. *Arnold: The Education of a Bodybuilder,* Simon & Schuster, 1977.
The six-time winner of the Mr. Olympia title and star of *Pumping Iron* recounts his life and presents a program for successful body building. (Nonfiction)

Scieszka, Jon. *Math Curse,* Viking, 1996.
Math can be a real curse when you begin to think of everything as a math problem. (Fiction)

———. *Stinky Cheese Man and Other Fairly Stupid Tales,* Viking, 1993.
This is a wickedly hysterical parody of childhood stories, complete with wild illustrations and a "surgeon general's warning." (Fiction)

Scoppettone, Sandra. *Happy Endings Are All Alike,* Harper, 1978.
Traditional values are questioned and love is tested when Jaret is raped by a disturbed boy and everyone learns of her lesbian relationship with Peggy. (Fiction)

———. *Trying Hard to Hear You,* Harper, 1974. ■ ▲ ●
Sixteen-year-old Camilla recalls the tumultuous summer of 1973 when her best friend, Jeff, and Phil, the boy she has a crush on, fall in love with each other. (Fiction)

Scortia, Thomas N., and Robinson, Frank G. *Prometheus Crisis,* Doubleday, 1975.
Did human error, sabotage, or carelessness cause the final breaking point at the nuclear power station Prometheus? (Fiction)

Searls, Hank. *Sounding,* Random, 1982.
As the old sperm whale seeks his former pod, a disabled Russian submarine teeters on a reef; perhaps the ancient cetacean hope that man can communicate will come true. (Fiction)

Sebestyen, Ouida. *Far from Home,* Atlantic/ Little, Brown, 1980.
After the death of his mother, fourteen-year-old Salty follows the words in a note his mother left him to find a home for himself and his elderly grandmother, and begins to learn about love and family. (Fiction)

———. *IOU's,* Atlantic Monthly Press, 1982.
Stowe Garrett is torn between the loyalty and love he feels for his mother and his longing to break free and experiment with life. (Fiction)

———. *Words by Heart,* Atlantic/Little, 1979.
Lena learns what it means to be black in a white world, but, helped by her brave father, she also learns how to be a real person. (Fiction)

Seed, Suzanne. *Fine Trades,* Follett, 1979.
In photographs and words, ten craftspersons explain their trades—ranging from violin making to bookbinding—and tell of the personal satisfaction they get from their work. (Nonfiction)

Segal, Erich. *Love Story,* Harper, 1970. ◆
Oliver Barrett IV, a rich, cocky Harvard senior, and Jennie Cavilleri, a poor and serious Radcliffe music type, discover they are made for each other in this funny but touching love story. (Fiction)

Senn, Steve. *Circle in the Sea,* Atheneum, 1981.
After wearing a special ring, Robin dreams that she is the dolphin Breee. In fact, her mind actually inhabits the body of Breee, who is involved in the fight against those who are destroying the seas with pollution. (Fiction)

Severin, Tim. *Sinbad Voyage,* Putnam, 1983.
In a hand-sewn boat, Severin follows the trading routes, attributed to Sinbad, to China by way of the Indian Ocean. (Nonfiction)

———. *Ulysses Voyage: Sea Search for the Odyssey,* Dutton, 1988.
Severin tells how he and a crew of scholars and adventurers sailed the Mediterranean in a Bronze Age-style galley in an attempt to follow the path of Ulysses and identify sites made famous by Homer. (Nonfiction)

Shannon, George. *Unlived Affections,* Harper/Charoltte Zolotow, 1990.
Discovering a box of old letters, Willie learns the truth about his parents' relationship. (Fiction)

Sharpe, Roger C. *Pinball!* Dutton, 1977.
For players and lovers of the pinball machine— here's a vicarious experience enlivened by full-page color photos of the real thing. (Nonfiction)

Shaw, Arnold. *World of Soul: Black America's Contribution to the Pop Music Scene,* Cowles, 1970.
The brothers and sisters of soul—Otis Redding, James Brown, and Aretha Franklin—are all here in this full story of blues and R & B. (Nonfiction)

■ Selected for "Still Alive: The Best of the Best, 1960–1974"

▲ Selected for "The Best of the Best Books: 1970–1983"

◆ Selected for "Nothin' but the Best: Best of the Best Books for Young Adults, 1966–1986"

● Selected for "Here We Go Again: 25 Years of Best Books: Selections from 1967 to 1992"

Sheehan, Carolyn, and Sheehan, Edmund.
Magnifi-Cat, Doubleday, 1972.
When a cat appears at the gates of heaven with an extraordinary halo, the whole computerized admissions process grinds to a halt. (Fiction)

Sheehan, Susan. *Ten Vietnamese,* Knopf, 1967.
Revealing interviews with men and women represent a cross section of the Vietnamese people, including the Viet Cong. (Nonfiction)

Sheldon, Mary. *Perhaps I'll Dream of Darkness,* Random, 1981.
Effie is dead now, and her sister Susan, through her diary, asks why. The answer lies with David Angel, the self-destructive rock star whom Effie idolized. (Fiction)

Sherman, D. R. *Brothers of the Sea,* Little, Brown, 1966.
This simple and moving tale is about a fisherman's son whose friendship with a dolphin leads to tragedy. (Fiction)

————. *Lion's Paw,* Doubleday, 1975.
An obsessed white hunter, a young Bushman, and a crippled lion confront one another in the conflict for survival. (Fiction)

Sherman, Josepha. *Child of Faerie, Child of Earth,* Walker, 1993.
Percinet, the son of the queen of Faerie, is in love with a mortal girl, but can she accept his love and the presence of magic in her life? (Fiction)

Shevelev, Raphael, and Schomer, Karine.
Liberating the Ghosts: Photographs and Text from the March of the Living, Lenswork, 1997.
Photographs and memories from the March of the Living, the 1994 journey of Holocaust survivors and 5,000 teenagers from forty countries. (Nonfiction)

Shihab Nye, Naomi, ed. *The Space between Our Footsteps: Poems and Paintings from the Middle East,* Simon & Schuster, 1999.
Heartfelt poems from the Middle East are paired with equally beautiful art reproductions in a collection that captures the imagination. (Nonfiction)

Shilts, Randy. *And the Band Played On: Politics, People, and the AIDS Epidemic,* St. Martin's, 1987. •
The shocking story of the failure of the U.S. government, the medical establishment, and the American people themselves to face the devastating modern AIDS plague is both tragic and frightening. (Nonfiction)

Shoup, Barbara. *Stranded in Harmony,* Hyperion; dist. by Little, Brown, 1998.
How can Lucas, a high-school senior, loosen the grip of his parents, his girlfriend, and his best friend, all of whom want him to live up to their expectations? (Fiction)

————. *Wish You Were Here,* Hyperion; dist. by Little, Brown, 1995.
Jax experiences life's highs and lows during his senior year when he falls in love and also has to deal with his father's near-fatal accident and his best friend's running away. (Fiction)

Shreve, Susan. *Masquerade,* Knopf, 1980.
After their father is arrested for embezzlement and their mother has a nervous breakdown, the Walker family—especially seventeen-year-old Rebecca—must learn to cope with the disturbing truth and begin to sort out their lives. (Fiction)

Shusterman, Neal. *The Dark Side of Nowhere,* Little, Brown, 1998.
Feeling trapped and bored in his normal, peaceful hometown, Jason slowly learns that he and most of the townspeople are aliens. (Fiction)

————. *What Daddy Did,* Little, Brown, 1992.
After the murder of his mother, Preston must find a way to face, and even forgive, his father—the man who killed her. (Fiction)

Sieruta, Peter D. *Heartbeats and Other Stories,* Harper, 1990.
Depicting joy and pain, love and sorrow, family conflicts and relationships, these nine short stories feature teenagers dealing with life's problems and issues. (Fiction)

Silverberg, Robert. *Lord Valentine's Castle,* Harper, 1980. ◆
Joining a troupe of itinerant jugglers, young Valentine gathers a motley, many-specied party of supporters and journeys across the continent of Majipoor to regain his rightful throne. (Fiction)

Silvey, Anita, ed. *Help Wanted: Short Stories about Young People Working,* Little, Brown, 1999.
This diverse collection of stories by Michael Dorris, Ray Bradbury, Vivien Alcock, and nine others shows just how momentous a first job can be. (Fiction)

Simak, Clifford D. *Enchanted Pilgrimage,* Putnam, 1975.
This is a strange, enchanting, allegorical journey in a world where elves, gnomes, and goblins are as normal as bacon and eggs. (Fiction)

————. *Werewolf Principle,* Putnam, 1967.
Strange adventure follows when Andrew Blake is found frozen in a space capsule and is brought back to earth after 200 years. (Fiction)

Simon, Neil. *Brighton Beach Memoirs,* Random, 1984.
Sex and baseball are the primary preoccupations of fifteen-year-old Eugene, in this play about lower middle-class Jewish family life in New York City during the Depression. (Nonfiction)

———. *Lost in Yonkers*, Random, 1993.
Two young brothers rely on their sense of humor when they are sent to live with their fearsome, irascible grandmother during World War II. (Nonfiction)

Simon, Nissa. *Don't Worry, You're Normal: Teenager's Guide to Self Health*, Crowell, 1982.
This brief but thorough guide answers many questions about physical and psychological changes occurring during the teen years. (Nonfiction)

Sinclair, April. *Coffee Will Make You Black*, Hyperion; dist. by Little, Brown, 1995.
Stevie, a young African American girl growing up in the late 1950s, struggles—humorously—to make sense of the adult world she is entering. (Fiction)

Singer, Marilyn. *Course of True Love Never Did Run Smooth*, Harper, 1983.
While acting the role of love-sick Helena in a high-school production of *A Midsummer Night's Dream*, Becky is infatuated with the handsome lead, until she discovers that she loves her long-time friend Nemi. (Fiction)

Skurzynski, Gloria. *Manwolf*, Houghton/Clarion, 1981.
Adam's heritage as the son of a masked knight and a serf in medieval Poland results in some unearthly tendencies and the need to turn to Kasia, the witch, for survival and true identity. (Fiction)

———. *Tempering*, Clarion/Ticknor & Fields, 1983.
Karl faces a decision to stay in school or go to work in a Pennsylvania steel mill, in the early twentieth century. (Fiction)

———. *Virtual War*, Simon & Schuster, 1998.
In this quick read, genetically engineered soldiers prepare for a virtual war. Even in cyberspace, adolescents rebel and there are FLKs (funny-looking kids). (Fiction)

Sleator, William. *Boy Who Reversed Himself*, Dutton, 1987.
How strange is Omar? Laura's question is answered when her high school friend takes her into the fourth dimension. (Fiction)

———. *Duplicate*, Dutton, 1988.
When David needs to be in two places at once, he duplicates himself with a machine he picked up on the beach—and finds his life in danger. (Fiction)

———. *House of Stairs*, Dutton, 1974. ■ ▲ ◆
Five sixteen-year-old orphans find themselves alone in an experimental nightmare where stairs and landings stretch as far as the eye can see and a weird red light trains them to dance for their food. (Fiction)

———. *Interstellar Pig*, Dutton, 1984. ◆ ●
Barney's strange new neighbors invite him to play a bizarre board game called Interstellar Pig, which actually spans the universe and can destroy worlds. (Fiction)

———. *Oddballs*, Dutton, 1994.
Growing up as part of an unusual family isn't so bad when everyone is an oddball. (Fiction)

———. *Singularity*, Dutton, 1985.
Rivalry between sixteen-year-old twins Barry and Harry Krasner intensifies after their discovery of a foreboding playhouse leads them to the gateway of a universe that accelerates time's passage 3,600-fold and may unleash a monster. (Fiction)

———. *Strange Attractors*, Dutton, 1991.
With a time travel phaser in his pocket and no memory of how it got there, Max must determine where it belongs without sending himself into oblivion. (Fiction)

Slepian, Jan. *Night of the Bozos*, Dutton, 1983.
George, a teenaged electronic musician, and his young uncle see their lives change when they meet a strange carnival girl and the Bozo, the clown who dares passersby to knock him into a tub of water. (Fiction)

Slesar, Henry. *Thing at the Door*, Random, 1974.
Haunted by memories of her mother's suicide when she was a child, Gail Gunnison at twenty-six is driven to the edge of suicide by strange events. (Fiction)

Smith, Dennis. *Report from Engine Co. 82*, Saturday Review Press, 1972.
On crowded, angry city streets, firemen respond when no one else does—to fire alarms, heart attacks, childbirth, and mob violence. (Nonfiction)

Smith, K. *Skeeter*, Houghton, 1990.
Hoping to enhance their hunting skills, two boys stumble on the best hunting terrain while tres-

---

- ■ Selected for "Still Alive: The Best of the Best, 1960–1974"
- ▲ Selected for "The Best of the Best Books: 1970–1983"
- ◆ Selected for "Nothin' but the Best: Best of the Best Books for Young Adults, 1966–1986"
- ● Selected for "Here We Go Again: 25 Years of Best Books: Selections from 1967 to 1992"

passing on the property of an ornery black man. (Fiction)

Smith, Martin Cruz. *Nightwing,* Norton, 1978.
A young Hopi Indian searches desperately for the cave of the vampire bats that have swarmed into the Southwest, bringing the threat of bubonic plague. (Fiction)

Smith, Mary-Anne Tirone. *Book of Phoebe,* Doubleday, 1985.
In a novel that is at once hilarious and moving, Yale senior Phoebe goes to Paris to have her illegitimate baby, finds a man who loves her, and tells him a bizarre story from her adolescence—the time she and a friend held Grant's tomb hostage. (Fiction)

———. *Lament for a Silver-eyed Woman,* Morrow, 1987.
After a carefree stint as Peace Corps volunteers in Cameroon, Mattie's and Jo's friendship is destroyed by Jo's life-threatening involvement with tragic victims of the Mideast conflict. (Fiction)

Smith, Robert Kimmel. *Jane's House,* Morrow, 1983.
When Paul Klein remarries after his wife's sudden death, Hilary, sixteen, and Bobby, ten, reluctantly accept bright, independent, businesswoman Ruth. (Fiction)

Smith, Rukshana. *Sumitra's Story,* Coward, 1983.
Sumitra, an East Indian girl, is torn between her traditional home, loving but repressive, and English society, which offers freedom as well as prejudice. (Fiction)

Smith, W. Eugene, and Smith, Aileen M. *Minamata,* Holt, 1975.
Using their cameras, the Smiths have recorded the horrors of industrial pollution that has killed or disabled more than 800 people in a Japanese town. (Nonfiction)

Smith, Wayne. *Thor,* St. Martin's/Thomas Dunne, 1994.
It isn't easy being the German shepherd Thor when the family needs protection from a visitor—who happens to be a werewolf. (Fiction)

Snyder, Zilpha Keatley. *Fabulous Creature,* Atheneum, 1981.
James Fielding almost causes the death of a magnificent stag he has gentled. (Fiction)

———. *Libby on Wednesday,* Delacorte, 1991.
Membership in the small class of Future Writers of America helps previously home-educated Libby overcome the shock of entering eighth grade in public school. (Fiction)

Sorrentino, Joseph. *Up from Never,* Prentice-Hall, 1971.
The son of a street sweeper, Joe Sorrentino tells of his youth in Brooklyn in the 1940s and of his journey from street punk to Harvard graduate. (Nonfiction)

Soto, Gary. *Baseball in April and Other Stories,* Harcourt, 1991.
These short stories reflect the funny and touching side of growing up Latino in Fresno, California, including one about Gilbert, who decides to emulate a character in a popular movie by finding a karate teacher and becoming an expert. (Fiction)

———. *Buried Onions,* Harcourt, 1998.
Mexican American Eddie tries desperately to escape his violence-infested life in Fresno, California. (Fiction)

Southerland, Ellease. *Let the Lion Eat Straw,* Scribner, 1979.
Choosing marriage over a musical career that promises escape from the poverty she has always known, Abeba Williams fights to achieve a decent life for her husband and children. (Fiction)

Southgate, Martha. *Another Way to Dance,* Delacorte, 1997.
Being selected for the School of American Ballet is a dream come true for African American Vicki—until she encounters racism and disappointment in meeting her dancing idol. (Fiction)

Southhall, Ivan. *Long Night Watch,* Farrar, 1984.
During World War II a young sentry fails in his duty, and causes the death of all but a few of the religious refugees on an isolated island in the South Pacific. (Fiction)

Speare, Elizabeth George. *Sign of the Beaver,* Houghton, 1983.
A proud, resourceful Native American boy deigns to help Matt survive the raw Maine wilderness winter when he is left alone to guard the newly built cabin. (Fiction)

Spiegelman, Art. *Maus: A Survivor's Tale,* Pantheon, 1986. •
In a comic book of revolutionary graphic design, a cartoonist juxtaposes his frustration with his father's insensitivity today and his father's desperate struggle to stay alive forty years earlier during the Holocaust. (Nonfiction)

———. *Maus: A Survivor's Tale II: And Here My Troubles Began,* Pantheon, 1992.
This graphic novel, the sequel to *Maus,* recreates Vladek and Anja's agonizing struggles to survive in the concentration camp. (Fiction)

Spielman, Ed. *Mighty Atom: The Life and Times of Joseph L. Greenstein,* Viking, 1980.
This biography relates the story of the amazing Yosselle (Joe) Greenstein, born in 1893 in a Jewish ghetto in Poland, an asthmatic and sickly

child, who trains himself to become the world's strongest man. (Nonfiction)

Spinelli, Jerry. *Crash,* Knopf, 1997.
Self-centered John "Crash" Coogan has always had everything go his way, but after years of teasing Penn, Crash must choose between right and wrong. (Fiction)

————. *Knots in My Yo-Yo String: The Autobiography of a Kid,* Knopf, 1999.
A popular author relates this rollicking account of his first sixteen years—before he even liked to read. (Nonfiction)

————. *Maniac Magee,* Little, Brown, 1991.
"Maniac, Maniac he's so cool." The orphan Jeffrey Lionel Magee blitzes into the town of Two Mills and changes it forever. (Fiction)

————. *There's a Girl in My Hammerlock,* Simon & Schuster, 1992.
Whoever heard of a girl on a wrestling team? She might get hurt; besides, it's embarrassing and dumb! (Fiction)

Springer, Nancy. *I Am Mordred: A Tale from Camelot,* Putnam/Philomel, 1999.
Mordred struggles to escape a fate that will lead him to kill his own father. (Fiction)

————. *Toughing It,* Harcourt/Browndeer, 1995.
After witnessing his older brother's senseless murder, sixteen-year-old Tuff leaves home in shocked anger, determined to find the killer—but finds a father instead. (Fiction)

Staples, Suzanne Fisher. *Dangerous Skies,* Farrar/Frances Foster, 1997.
In the back creeks of Chesapeake Bay, Buck discovers a dead body, and nothing is ever the same when his best friend, Tunes, becomes the primary murder suspect. (Fiction)

————. *Haveli,* Knopf, 1994.
A young woman struggles against the strictures of her rigid culture to find freedom for herself and her small daughter in modern-day Pakistan. (Fiction)

————. *Shabanu: Daughter of the Wind,* Knopf, 1990.
Torn between allegiance to her family and her growing independence and strength, Shabanu tells the story of her life as a member of a nomadic tribe in the Pakistani desert. (Fiction)

Steffan, Joseph. *Honor Bound: A Gay American Fights for the Right to Serve His Country,* Villard, 1993.
Revealing he is gay two weeks before his Annapolis graduation, all-American boy Joe Steffan is discharged and begins to fight for the right to serve his country. (Nonfiction)

Steger, Will, and Bowermaster, Jon. *Over the Top of the World: Explorer Will Steger's Trek across the Arctic,* Scholastic, 1998.
The account of Steger's breathtaking 1995 Arctic adventure includes dazzling photos and details of human and canine party members. (Nonfiction)

Steinem, Gloria. *Outrageous Acts and Everyday Rebellions,* Holt, 1983.
The founder and editor of *MS.* magazine writes about her life and work and discusses politics, pornography, and literature from a feminist point of view. (Nonfiction)

Sterling, Dorothy, ed. *We Are Your Sisters: Black Women in the Nineteenth Century,* Norton, 1984.
This documents the history of African American women in the nineteenth-century, based on transcripts of interviews with former slaves, memoirs, letters, and other primary sources. (Nonfiction)

Stevenson, Florence. *Curse of the Concullens,* World, 1971.
Beautiful, eighteen-year-old Lucinda Ayers longs to be a governess, but she gets more than she bargained for when she obtains a position with an eccentric Irish family that comes complete with a castle, ghosts, and werewolves. (Fiction)

Stevermer, Carolyn. *River Rats,* Harcourt/Jane Yolen, 1993.
Tomcat and his teenage friends try to survive after a nuclear holocaust by taking over a Mississippi riverboat, but their lives are endangered when killers come after the boat. (Fiction)

Stewart, Fred. *Mephisto Waltz,* Coward-McCann, 1969.
A dead, diabolical genius inhabits the body of Myles Clarkson, concert pianist; only Myles's wife suspects what has happened but she has no proof. (Fiction)

■   Selected for "Still Alive: The Best of the Best, 1960–1974"
▲   Selected for "The Best of the Best Books: 1970–1983"
◆   Selected for "Nothin' but the Best: Best of the Best Books for Young Adults, 1966–1986"
●   Selected for "Here We Go Again: 25 Years of Best Books: Selections from 1967 to 1992"

Stewart, Mary. *Crystal Cave,* Morrow, 1970. ▲
Merlin, the base-born son of royalty in fifth-century Britain, uses magic to outwit his enemies until he sets the stage for the birth of Arthur, the future king. (Fiction)

——. *Hollow Hills,* Morrow, 1973.
In this sequel to *The Crystal Cave,* Merlin conceals and grooms the child Arthur until the time of his coronation. (Fiction)

Stoehr, Shelley. *Crosses,* Delacorte, 1993.
Nancy loves cutting herself; the bloody designs and scars are "cool." Then there are always alcohol and other drugs—all thanks to Katie, the best teacher at school. (Fiction)

Stoll, Cliff. *The Cuckoo's Egg: Tracking a Spy through the Maze of Computer Espionage,* Doubleday, 1991. ◆
A young astrophysicist turns detective as he embarks on the trail of an elusive computer hacker who has managed to break into top-secret government and military data banks. (Nonfiction)

Stolz, Mary. *Cezanne Pinto,* Knopf, 1995.
As an old man, Cezanne relives his experiences as a slave, a stable hand in Canada, and a Texas cowboy during the late 1800s. (Fiction)

Stone, Bruce. *Half Nelson, Full Nelson,* Harper, 1985.
Nelson Gato tells how he faked the kidnapping of his little sister and her friend in an effort to bring about a reconciliation between his wrestler father and his mother, who could no longer stand life in a tacky Florida trailer park. (Fiction)

Strasser, Todd. *Friends till the End,* Delacorte, 1981. ◆
David thinks he has problems—with soccer, his girlfriend, parents, and college plans—until he meets Howie, the new guy in school, who has leukemia. (Fiction)

——. *Rock 'n' Roll Nights,* Delacorte, 1982.
Determined to make it to the top in rock music, Gary Specter plays lead guitar and sings with his group almost every night. (Fiction)

Strauss, Gwen. *Trail of Stones,* Knopf, 1991.
These dark and dramatic retellings of fairy tales in poetic monologues are accompanied by equally stark drawings. (Fiction)

Strieber, Whitley. *Wolf of Shadows,* Knopf, 1985. ●
In their attempt to survive after a nuclear war, a woman and her daughter join and learn from a wolf pack led by Wolf of Shadows. (Fiction)

Styron, William. *Confessions of Nat Turner,* Random House, 1967.
While awaiting execution, the instigator of the 1831 slave rebellion in Virginia reconstructs the agonizing events that led to insurrection and murder. (Fiction)

Sullivan, Charles, ed. *Children of Promise: African-American Literature and Art for Young People,* Abrams, 1992. ●
A choice sampling of art and literature conveys the image of African Americans over the past 200 years. (Nonfiction)

——. *Imaginary Animals,* Abrams, 1998.
Meet talking cats, purple cows, "long-legety" beasties, wicked dragons, and other fantastic creatures in this beautifully illustrated book of incredible poetry. (Nonfiction)

Sullivan, Jack, ed. *Penguin Encyclopedia of Horror and the Supernatural,* Viking, 1986.
Surpassing the typical reference book, this collection of articles leads the reader from Stephen King to *The Birds* to Prokofiev. (Nonfiction)

Sullivan, Tom, and Gill, Derek L. T. *If You Could See What I Hear,* Harper, 1975.
Tom Sullivan refuses to let blindness interfere with school or sports, his marriage, his career, or his life. (Nonfiction)

Summers, Ian, ed. *Tomorrow and Beyond: Masterpieces of Science Fiction Art,* Workman, 1979.
A magical mystery tour through the imaginative images used to illustrate speculative fiction is surprising and fascinating. (Nonfiction)

Sussman, Alan N. *Rights of Young People: The Basic ACLU Guide to a Young Person's Rights,* Avon, 1977.
This legal bible for those less than age eighteen states what the law allows and what it prohibits, emphasizing differences in state laws and offering advice on legal defense. (Nonfiction)

Sutcliff, Rosemary. *Black Ships before Troy: The Story of the Illiad,* Delacorte, 1994.
Helen of Troy is stolen from her husband by her lover Paris—and the Trojan War begins! (Nonfiction)

——. *Road to Camlann: The Death of King Arthur,* Dutton, 1983.
King Arthur strives to preserve the Round Table as Mordred plots against him and gossip about Lancelot and Guinivere intensifies. (Fiction)

Sutton, Roger. *Hearing Us Out: Voices from the Gay and Lesbian Community,* Little, Brown, 1995.
Documenting a wide range of experience, fifteen gay and lesbian individuals narrate their joys and struggles to be who they are. (Nonfiction)

Swanson, Walter S. J. *Deepwood,* Little, Brown, 1981.
A young man's desire for sexual fulfillment and personal freedom challenges his moral values

and his devoted relationship to an older woman. (Fiction)

Swarthout, Glendon. *Bless the Beasts and Children*, Doubleday, 1970. ■ ▲ ◆ ●
Five misfits in an Arizona boys' camp sneak out on a daring escapade to save a herd of buffaloes from bloodthirsty gun-toting tourists. (Fiction)

Sweeney, Joyce. *Center Line*, Delacorte, 1984.
Fearing for their safety, five teenage brothers steal their abusive, alcoholic father's car and run away from home. (Fiction)

———. *Shadow*, Delacorte, 1995.
Shadow died a year earlier, but Sarah still senses her beloved cat's presence, which is fortunate because she has started dreaming about blood, violence, and broken glass, and needs all the help she can get. (Fiction)

———. *The Spirit Window*, Delacorte, 1999.
Miranda must convince her father that love—be it for family or for wild creatures—is more important than money, when she tries to save her grandmother's bird sanctuary. (Fiction)

———. *The Tiger Orchard*, Delacorte, 1994.
Zach comes face-to-face with his dreams when he discovers that his father, who his mother claimed was dead, is alive and then decides to meet him. (Fiction)

Switzer, Ellen. *How Democracy Failed*, Atheneum, 1975.
Personal reminiscences of Germany under Hitler from people who were then only teenagers make plain how he came to power. (Nonfiction)

Szabo, Joseph. *Almost Grown*, Crown/ Harmony, 1978.
Provocative photographs and telling poems written by teenagers themselves express the concerns and feelings, the highs and the lows, of kids who are "almost grown." (Nonfiction)

Szulc, Tad. *Bombs of Palomares*, Viking, 1967.
Four H-bombs lost over Spain in 1966 create potentially explosive social and political situations. (Nonfiction)

Talbert, Marc. *Dead Birds Singing*, Little, Brown, 1985.
Left alone because of a tragic accident, Matt must face the reality of losing the last of his family—his mother and sister—and cope with his feelings for the drunken driver who killed them. (Fiction)

Tamar, Erika. *Fair Game*, Harcourt, 1994.
Cara, a mentally challenged teen, claims she was sexually assaulted by a group of athletes from her school, but the boys swear she was a willing participant. (Fiction)

Tan, Amy. *The Joy Luck Club*, Putman, 1990. ●
Chinese American daughters find conflict, love, and connection with their mothers, who are haunted by their early lives in China. (Fiction)

Tang, Hsi-yang. *Living Treasures: An Odyssey through China's Extraordinary Nature Reserves*, Bantam, 1988.
A beautifully photographed description of China's wildlife and landscapes is testament to its stunning natural reserves. (Nonfiction)

Tapert, Annette, ed. *Lines of Battle: Letters from U.S. Servicemen, 1941–45*, Times Books, 1987.
Letters from the battle lines of World War II convey a sense of adventure, loneliness, and tragedy. (Nonfiction)

Tate, Sonsyrea. *Little X: Growing Up in the Nation of Islam*, Harper, 1998.
Sonsyrea, who was raised in a Nation of Islam family, honestly describes life in the strict religious community (Nonfiction)

Taylor, Clark. *House That Crack Built*, Chronicle, 1993.
Following the same pattern as the children's nursery rhyme, this bleak picture book shows the strung-out addicts, the crack lord's mansion, and the hungry baby of a crack addict. (Fiction)

Taylor, David. *Zoo Vet: Adventures of a Wild Animal Doctor*, Lippincott, 1977.
An authority on treating wild animals describes unusual cases from his veterinary practice around the world. (Nonfiction)

Taylor, Gordon. *Biological Time Bomb*, World, 1968.
The biological revolution is at hand and in the offing are memory-erasing drugs, choice of sex in offspring, reconstructed organisms, and the indefinite postponement of death. (Nonfiction)

Taylor, Mildred D. *Let the Circle Be Unbroken*, Dial, 1981.
In this sequel to *Roll of Thunder, Hear My Cry*, the Logan family survives the Depression, a murder trial, and the jailing of a son. (Fiction)

- ■   Selected for "Still Alive: The Best of the Best, 1960–1974"
- ▲   Selected for "The Best of the Best Books: 1970–1983"
- ◆   Selected for "Nothin' but the Best: Best of the Best Books for Young Adults, 1966–1986"
- ●   Selected for "Here We Go Again: 25 Years of Best Books: Selections from 1967 to 1992"

———. *Road to Memphis,* Dial, 1991.
On the eve of World War II, Cassie Logan is finishing high school and dreaming of college when a violent racial incident forces her to help a good friend escape to the north. (Fiction)

Taylor, Theodore. *The Bomb,* Harcourt, 1996.
Teenage Sorry will do anything to stop the Americans from using his island home for nuclear testing. (Fiction)

———. *Sniper,* Harcourt, 1990.
A gunman begins killing the big cats the week Ben, fifteen, is left in charge of the family's animal preserve. (Fiction)

———. *Timothy of the Cay,* Harcourt, 1994.
In alternating chapters, this compelling prequel-sequel to *The Cay* outlines the lives of Timothy Gumbs before he meets twelve-year-old Philip on the cay and of Philip immediately after his rescue from the cay. (Fiction)

———. *Weirdo,* Harcourt, 1993.
Disfigured in a plane crash and called Weirdo by the locals, Chip seeks refuge in the swamp with his recovering alcoholic artist father. There he befriends Samantha, and the two teens find themselves threatened by murderous bear poachers. (Fiction)

Teague, Robert. *Letters to a Black Boy,* Walker, 1968.
A former college football star (now a New York television newscaster) voices the frustrations of being considered a black man rather than an individual. (Nonfiction)

Teitz, Joyce. *What's a Nice Girl Like You Doing in a Place Like This?* Coward, 1972.
Women talk candidly about their careers and ambitions, their challenges and dreams. (Nonfiction)

Telander, Rick. *Heaven Is a Playground,* St. Martin's, 1977.
The inspirational story of the dreams, hopes, and frustrations of talented African American urban youths whose love of basketball is their lifeline to the future. (Nonfiction)

Temple, Frances. *Grab Hands and Run,* Orchard/Richard Jackson, 1994.
When his father, a political revolutionary in El Salvador, "disappears" one day, Felipe's mother is forced to "grab hands and run" with the children on a dangerous journey north to Canada. (Fiction)

———. *The Ramsay Scallop,* Orchard/Richard Jackson, 1995.
Betrothed, though they barely know each other, fourteen-year-old Elenor and eighteen-year-old Thomas are sent by their castle priest on a pilgrimage from their English village through France to Spain in 1299. (Fiction)

Tepper, Sheri S. *Beauty,* Doubleday, 1992.
In this modern retelling of the fairy tale, Beauty avoids the sleeping spell and trips through time into different worlds, searching for beauty and love. (Fiction)

Terkel, Studs. *American Dreams: Lost and Found,* Pantheon, 1980.
Sharing their innermost hopes and dreams through interviews with Studs Terkel is a cross section of Americans ranging from celebrities such as Joan Crawford, Bill Veeck, and Coleman Young to steelworker Ed Sadlowski and sixteen-year-old Linda Haas. (Nonfiction)

———. *"Good War": An Oral History of World War Two,* Pantheon, 1984.
This vibrant Second World War oral history offers wonderfully readable tales that are alive, spontaneous, and personal as Americans from all walks of life recall their involvement and participation. (Nonfiction)

Terris, Susan. *Nell's Quilt,* Farrar, 1987.
Not knowing how to resist her parents' plans for her marriage, Nell stitches her lost dreams of college and independence into a quilt—all the while literally wasting away. (Fiction)

Terry, Douglas. *Last Texas Hero,* Doubleday, 1982.
A humorous, bawdy, and explicit look at life as a college freshman and all-American football hero, told in the inspiring words of Homer Jones. (Fiction)

Terry, Wallace. *Bloods: An Oral History of the Vietnam War by Black Veterans,* Random, 1984.
From their own perspectives, twenty black soldiers give graphically detailed accounts of the Vietnam War and its emotional aftereffects on themselves, their families, and their friends. (Nonfiction)

Testa, Maria. *Dancing Pink Flamingos and Other Stories,* Lerner, 1996.
In these ten urban short stories, teens of various ethnicities strive to find hope in a world of crime and violence. (Fiction)

Tevis, Walter. *Queen's Gambit,* Random, 1983.
In the orphanage where she lives Beth learns the game of chess, beginning an obsession that takes her all the way to the top. (Fiction)

Thesman, Jean. *The Ornament Tree,* Houghton, 1997.
Moving in with two progressive aunts who own a Seattle boardinghouse, Bonnie must seek her identity against the tumultuous backdrop of labor riots, women's suffrage, and the temperance movement. (Fiction)

———. *Rain Catchers,* Houghton, 1992.
Abandoned by her mother and growing up in a household of women, Grayling, at fourteen,

must deal with love, death, and her relationship with her mother. (Fiction)

———. *When the Road Ends,* Houghton, 1993. Can four abandoned strangers—a twelve-year-old, a teenager, a silent child and a brain-injured woman—come together as a loving family? (Fiction)

Thomas, Jane Resh. *Behind the Mask: The Life of Queen Elizabeth I,* Clarion, 1999. This spirited, authentic picture of Elizabeth I is a historical account of a woman who overcomes vast odds to become one of the most important and influential people in history. (Nonfiction)

Thomas, Joyce Carol. *Marked by Fire,* Avon/ Flare, 1982. When tragedy strikes Abby, her proud black rural Oklahoma community gathers around to protect and save her from all harm. (Fiction)

Thomas, Kurt, and Hannon, Kent. *Kurt Thomas and Gymnastics,* Simon & Schuster, 1980. This portrayal of Kurt Thomas's life provides an insight into the world of men's gymnastics— the training, dedication, and lifestyle necessary to reach the level of Olympic competition. (Nonfiction)

Thomas, Lewis. *Youngest Science: Notes of a Medicine Watcher,* Viking, 1983. These autobiographical musings by the author of *Lives of a Cell* appeal because of their "celebration and a warning about the nature of man and the future of life on our planet." (Nonfiction)

Thomas, Rob. *Doing Time: Notes from the Undergrad,* Simon & Schuster, 1998. Ten high school students doing mandatory community service in order to graduate give ten different voices and viewpoints to the enterprise. (Fiction)

———. *Rats Saw God,* Simon & Schuster, 1997. "Troubled teen" Steve York reflects on his life and his relationship with his famous father. (Fiction)

Thomas, Velma Maia. *Lest We Forget: The Passage from Africa to Slavery and Emancipation,* Crown, 1999. Artifacts from the black Holocaust exhibit are used to create a three-dimensional interactive history of slavery in America. (Nonfiction)

Thompson, Estelle. *Hunter in the Dark,* Walker, 1979. The only witness to the kidnapping of a child who is later murdered, blind teacher Philip Blair determines to find the criminal. (Fiction)

Thompson, Jean. *House of Tomorrow,* Harper, 1967. ■ In a home for unwed mothers, Jean overcomes despair and faces many decisions about her future and that of her unborn child. (Nonfiction)

Thompson, Joyce. *Conscience Place,* Doubleday, 1984. The Place, an idyllic, protected secret settlement for the mutant offspring of nuclear-energy workers, has come to the attention of scientists who want to use its inhabitants for experimentation. (Fiction)

Thompson, Julian. *Band of Angels,* Scholastic, 1986. Unaware that government agents are pursuing them with the intent to kill, five teenagers camp in the wilderness to plan a crusade against nuclear war. (Fiction)

Thornton, Yvonne S., and Coudert, Jo. *Ditchdigger's Daughters: A Black Family's Astonishing Success Story,* Birch Land, 1996. Dr. Yvonne Thornton tells the story of her 1950s upbringing by her father, a poor African American man, who raises five daughters to succeed in a world that prefers them invisible. (Nonfiction)

Tiburzi, Bonnie. *Takeoff! The Story of America's First Woman Pilot for a Major Airline,* Crown, 1984. In this autobiography, the first woman pilot for a major U.S. airline shares her love of flying and tells of her challenging and often frustrating climb to success. (Nonfiction)

Tidyman, Ernest. *Dummy,* Little, Brown, 1974. What defense does an illiterate deaf-mute African American have against a murder charge? His deaf lawyer must contend not only with his client's inability to communicate but also with an unfeeling court system and circumstantial evidence. (Nonfiction)

Tillage, Leon Walter. *Leon's Story,* Farrar, 1998. Tillage tells the story of his life as the son of a southern sharecropper, killed by the KKK, and

---

■ Selected for "Still Alive: The Best of the Best, 1960–1974"

▲ Selected for "The Best of the Best Books: 1970–1983"

◆ Selected for "Nothin' but the Best: Best of the Best Books for Young Adults, 1966–1986"

● Selected for "Here We Go Again: 25 Years of Best Books: Selections from 1967 to 1992"

of the changes brought about by the Civil Rights movement. (Nonfiction)

Torchia, Joseph. *Kryptonite Kid,* Holt, 1979.
Jerry's letters to his hero, Superman, reveal his sinking into insanity and his discovery of who Superman really is. (Fiction)

Townsend, John. *Good Night, Prof. Dear,* Lippincott, 1971.
Seventeen-year-old Graham Hollis, unhappy with himself and his home life, runs off with Lynn, a waitress, and finds her a surprising but beautiful person. (Fiction)

Townsend, Sue. *Adrian Mole Diaries,* Grove Press, 1986.
In cryptically funny entries, teenager Adrian worries incessantly about his problems—acne, his parents' separation, sexual urges, and much more. (Fiction)

Trevor, Elleston. *Theta Syndrome,* Doubleday, 1977.
"For God's sake help me" is the desperate telepathic cry of a young woman deep in a coma prolonged by her fear of another attempt on her life. (Fiction)

Trudeau, G. B. *Doonesbury Chronicles,* Holt, 1975.
No one can feel the pulse of the world like Garry Trudeau, whose satirical look at the 1960s and early 1970s is a real delight. (Nonfiction)

————. *Doonesbury's Greatest Hits,* Holt, 1978.
Washington politics, student activists, talking to plants, and relations between the U.S. and China are among the popular cartoonist's current targets. (Nonfiction)

Trull, Patti. *On with My Life,* Putnam, 1983.
A courageous young cancer victim at fifteen, Patti Trull loses her leg despite numerous treatments and surgery but finds hope as an occupational therapist for other young victims. (Nonfiction)

Turner, Ann Marshall. *A Lion's Hunger: Poems of First Love,* Marshall Cavendish, 1999.
Turner's series of poems expresses the emotions of a young girl falling in and out of love for the first time. (Nonfiction)

Turner, Megan Whalen. *The Thief,* Greenwillow, 1997.
Gen prides himself on being a master thief and is delighted to be rescued from prison under the condition that he steal a precious item from a long-lost temple. (Fiction)

Turney, David C. *Why Are They Weeping? South Africans under Apartheid,* Stewart, Tabori & Chang, 1990.
One hundred color photographs vividly show the brutal conflict in a troubled and beautiful land. (Nonfiction)

Tyler, Anne. *Slipping-Down Life,* Knopf, 1970.
The story of fat, plain Evie Decker's romance and marriage to a rock singer and their slipping-down life together. (Fiction)

Uchida, Yoshiko. *Invisible Thread,* Messner, 1993.
The author describes growing up in Berkeley as a second-generation Japanese American and her family's humiliating experience in Utah internment camps during World War II. (Nonfiction)

Uhlman, Fred. *Reunion,* Farrar, 1977.
Thirty years later, the Jewish narrator recalls his doomed friendship with the son of a nobleman in Nazi Germany. A poignant and provocative novella. (Fiction)

Ure, Jean. *Plague,* Harcourt/Jane Yolen, 1993.
Returning to London from a wilderness camping trip, Fran finds her family and friends dead from a plague that has engulfed the city. (Fiction)

————. *See You Thursday,* Delacorte, 1983.
Marianne, a sixteen-year-old British schoolgirl, helps her family's boarder, Abe, a twenty-four-year-old blind music teacher, achieve independence as their friendship grows into love. (Fiction)

Van Devanter, Lynda, and Morgan, Christopher. *Home before Morning: The Story of an Army Nurse in Vietnam,* Beaufort, 1983. ◆
Lt. Lynda Van Devanter recounts her experiences as an army surgical nurse in Vietnam and the stress after coming home. (Nonfiction)

Van de Velde, Vivian. *Companions of the Night,* Harcourt/Jane Yolen, 1996.
Is Ethan really just an innocent college student kidnapped by vampire-hunting crazies? Sixteen-year-old Kerry, who saves him and loves him, finds that the allure of the vampire is alive and well. (Fiction)

Van Leeuwen, Jean. *Seems Like This Road Goes on Forever,* Dial, 1979.
Guided by an empathetic psychologist, the seventeen-year-old daughter of a fundamentalist minister learns to separate her needs from the expectations of her remote, domineering parents. (Fiction)

Van Raven, Pieter. *Great Man's Secret,* Scribner, 1990.
Jerry, a fourteen-year-old student reporter, is sent to interview reclusive writer Paul Bernard and discovers not only Bernard's secret, but also those hidden within himself and others. (Fiction)

————. *Pickle and Price,* Scribner, 1991.
Pickle, the son of a white prison farm supervisor, and Price, a newly released African American convict Pickle has befriended, travel across America. (Fiction)

Vare, Ethlie Ann. *Mothers of Invention: From the Bra to the Bomb: Forgotten Women and Their Unforgettable Ideas,* Morrow, 1988.
Vare presents and praises the often ignored accomplishments of women in areas that include nuclear physics and the invention of the cotton gin. (Nonfiction)

Verhoeven, Rian, and Van Der Rol, Ruud. *Anne Frank: Beyond the Diary: A Photographic Remembrance,* Viking, 1994.
The combination of family photos, biographical sketches of Anne Frank and others in the "secret annex," with brief essays identifying stages of the Holocaust lets readers begin to know the real Anne. (Nonfiction)

Vick, Helen Hughes. *Walker of Time,* Harbinger, 1994.
Walker, a fifteen-year-old Hopi, is thrust abruptly back in time to the last days of the ancient, cliff-dwelling Sinagua people, where he finds enmity, friendship, and family. (Fiction)

Vinge, Joan D. *Psion,* Delacorte, 1982. ◆
In the year 2417, a poor orphan, taken from the slums to participate in a dangerous experiment, soon finds that his extraordinary telepathic powers endanger his life. (Fiction)

Voigt, Cynthia. *Izzy, Willy-Nilly,* Atheneum, 1986. ◆ ●
Who are your real friends? Izzy struggles to rethink her friendships after losing a leg in a car crash. (Fiction)

————. *On Fortune's Wheel,* Atheneum, 1991.
Fourteen-year-old Birle's impulsive attempt to stop a stranger from stealing a boat leads to romance and adventure with a young runaway lord. (Fiction)

————. *Runner,* Atheneum, 1985. ◆
Bullet, a seventeen-year-old cross country runner, finds that compromise is sometimes necessary if an athlete is going to be the best. (Fiction)

————. *Solitary Blue,* Atheneum, 1983. ◆
Jeff Green's mother leaves home when he is only seven, and when she shows up in his life again Jeff learns some hard lessons about loving and caring. (Fiction)

————. *Sons from Afar,* Atheneum, 1987.
Dicey's brothers, on the brink of growing up, search for the father who deserted them as infants—and find unforeseen truths. (Fiction)

————. *Tell Me If the Lovers Are Losers,* Atheneum, 1982.
Three college roomates—each very different, but gifted—clash and come together as they learn values from one another. (Fiction)

————. *When She Hollers,* Scholastic, 1995.
Tish takes a knife and her destiny in hand on the day she decides to stop her father from sexually abusing her. (Fiction)

Volavkova, Hana, ed. *I Never Saw Another Butterfly: Children's Drawings and Poems from Terezin Concentration Camp, 1942–1944,* Schocken, 1994.
Through the agony and hope expressed in the poems and drawings of the children of Terezin, the reader sees the sheer hell experienced by the 15,000 children under age fifteen who passed through the Terezin Concentration Camp between 1942 and 1945. (Nonfiction)

Von Canon, Claudia. *Inheritance,* Houghton, 1983.
A young medical student faces the horrors of the Inquisition in sixteenth-century Spain. (Fiction)

Vonnegut, Kurt. *Jailbird,* Delacorte/Seymour Lawrence, 1979.
Harvard, the New Deal, the Holocaust, World War II, Watergate, two prison terms, and a giant conglomerate—Walter Starbuck, who tries to live by the Sermon on the Mount, experiences them all. Shall the meek inherit the earth? Perhaps on a short-term basis. (Fiction)

Vonnegut, Mark. *Eden Express,* Praeger, 1975.
Kurt Vonnegut's son reflects on his life in the counterculture and his battle with schizophrenia. (Nonfiction)

Wagenheim, Kal. *Clemente!* Praeger, 1973.
The tragic death of Roberto Clemente, well known as a great baseball player, reveals the depths of his commitment and his concern for others. (Nonfiction)

Wagoner, David. *Road to Many a Wonder,* Farrar, 1974.
Setting out with his wheelbarrow to seek his fortune in western gold fields, Ike Bender marries a high-spirited young woman, and together they travel roads which do indeed lead to many a wonder. (Fiction)

- ■ Selected for "Still Alive: The Best of the Best, 1960–1974"
- ▲ Selected for "The Best of the Best Books: 1970–1983"
- ◆ Selected for "Nothin' but the Best: Best of the Best Books for Young Adults, 1966–1986"
- ● Selected for "Here We Go Again: 25 Years of Best Books: Selections from 1967 to 1992"

Wain, John. *Free Zone Starts Here,* Delacorte, 1984.
After his younger sister is killed in a plane crash, seventeen-year-old Paul Waterford flies to Lisbon for a memorial service and finally gives up his escapist private world after a disturbing night in Lisbon makes him aware of his own imperfections. (Fiction)

Walker, Alice. *In Search of Our Mothers' Gardens: Womanist Prose,* Harcourt, 1984. ◆
Thirty-five essays examine Walker's development as a human being, writer, and woman. (Nonfiction)

Walker, Kate. *Peter,* Houghton, 1994.
Outwardly, fifteen-year-old Peter lives by the rough-playing, rough-talking rules of his dirt-bike crowd, but inside he questions this male image as well as his own sexuality. (Fiction)

Walker, Margaret. *Jubilee,* Houghton, 1966.
Life at the time of the Civil War as experienced by Vyry, daughter of a slave and the white plantation owner. (Fiction)

Wallace, Duncan R. *Mountebank,* Houghton, 1972.
Lee, who wants to be a writer, is drawn to Nonno, the prankster, as they enter prep school together. (Fiction)

Wallace, Rich. *Wrestling Sturbridge,* Knopf/Borzoi, 1997.
Living in Sturbridge, Pennsylvania, where wrestling is king, high-school senior Benny must compete against his best friend for a spot on the team. (Fiction)

Wallin, Luke. *Redneck Poacher's Son,* Bradbury, 1981.
The son of a redneck poacher in an Alabama swamp, Jesse hates—perhaps enough to kill—his father, whom he blames for his mother's death. (Fiction)

Walsh, John, and Gannon, Robert. *Time Is Short and the Water Rises,* Dutton, 1967.
"Operation Gwamba: The story of the rescue of 10,000 animals from certain death in a South American rain forest" is the subtitle. (Nonfiction)

Walsh, M. M. B. *Four-colored Hoop,* Putnam, 1976.
Surviving the cruelty of the reservation, Mildred Shoot-Eagle becomes a feared mystic and medicine woman and revenges herself on the white man. (Fiction)

Walter, Virginia. *Making Up Megaboy,* DK Inc./Richard Jackson, 1999.
Why would a quiet kid who likes to draw kill a man after school one day? (Fiction)

Watkins, Yoko Kawashima. *My Brother, My Sister, and I,* Bradbury, 1995.
After escaping war-torn Korea in 1947, Yoko and her brother and sister return to face harsh prejudice in Japan, struggling for survival after their mother's death as they await the return of their missing father. (Fiction)

Watson, James. *Double Helix: A Personal Account of the Discovery of the Structure of DNA,* Atheneum, 1968.
A young scientist gives an inside view of how he and a colleague pursuing fame and the Nobel Prize manage to discover the structure of DNA, the molecule of heredity. (Nonfiction)

Watson, Larry. *Montana 1948,* Milkweed, 1994.
The summer he is twelve David watches as his family and small town are shattered by scandal and tragedy. (Fiction)

Watson, Lyall. *Dreams of Dragons: Riddles of Natural History,* Morrow, 1987.
Random numbers, movement of water, chance, and the pulse of the earth are among the subjects of essays that extol the magic and wonder of science and the world. (Nonfiction)

Weaver, Will. *Farm Team,* HarperCollins, 1996.
Billy is left in charge of the family farm when his dad is sent to prison, and so begins the "farm team," a ragtag group of local baseball players who try to whip the town team in the big game. (Fiction)

———. *Hard Ball,* HarperCollins, 1999.
When Billy and King's rivalry extends beyond the baseball field to a fight over a girl, a coach comes up with an unusual solution. (Fiction)

———. *Striking Out,* HarperCollins, 1994.
Five years after his brother's death, Billy discovers baseball can be an escape from his grim farm life. (Fiction)

Webb, Sheyann, and Nelson, Rachel West. *Selma, Lord, Selma: Girlhood Memories of the Civil-Rights Days,* University of Alabama Press, 1980. ◆
In this recollection of the events of 1965 in Selma, Alabama, Sheyann, eight, and Rachel, nine, face nightsticks, dogs, and mounted police, alongside Dr. Martin Luther King Jr. and the other adults who fight to achieve the right to vote. (Fiction)

Weiss, Ann E. *Who's to Know? Information, the Media and Public Awareness,* Houghton, 1991.
Putting the public's right to know in historical perspective, Weiss illustrates how business, advertising, special interest groups, politics, and

the media shape and manipulate the news and information Americans receive. (Nonfiction)

Wells, Evelyn. *I Am Thinking of Kelda,* Doubleday, 1974.
Kelda's story moves from New York sweat shops to a pioneer farm in Kansas and finally to California, where she is captivated by a new entertainment called "movies." (Fiction)

Wells, Rosemary. *Through the Hidden Door,* Dial, 1987.
A bullied prep school student discovers his inner strengths as he helps the school misfit excavate a mysterious ruin. (Fiction)

———. *When No One Was Looking,* Dial, 1980.
Fourteen-year-old Kathy thrives on pressure to become a tennis star until the death, possibly murder, of a competitor forces her to question her ambition and her future. (Fiction)

Welter, John. *I Want to Buy a Vowel,* Algonquin, 1997.
Guatemalan Alfredo learns what limited English he knows from TV commercials and *Wheel of Fortune* as he searches for the American dream. (Fiction)

Werlin, Nancy. *The Killer's Cousin,* Delacorte, 1999.
After David is acquitted of murder and moves in with his aunt and uncle, he finds his new home to be less safe and secure than he'd hoped. (Fiction)

Wersba, Barbara. *Carnival in My Mind,* Harper/Charlotte Zolotow, 1982.
Harvey Beaumont is fourteen, five feet tall, and in love for the first time—with a twenty-year-old, six-foot tall, would-be actress. (Fiction)

———. *Country of the Heart,* Atheneum, 1975.
A brief, poignant romance between a dying older woman who is a famous poet and a young man who aspires to be a writer. (Fiction)

———. *Run Softly, Go Fast,* Atheneum, 1970. ▲ ◆ ●
This is the story, written in diary form, of nineteen-year-old David Marks and his attempt to reconcile his love-hate relationship with his father. (Fiction)

———. *Tunes for a Small Harmonica,* Harper, 1976.
Sixteen-year-old J. F. McAllister, a constant source of worry to everyone, masters the har-

monica and then uses her talents to help her poetry teacher, with whom she is in love. (Fiction)

———. *Whistle Me Home,* Holt, 1998.
Tomboy Noli and TJ are friends and almost a couple, and Noli is totally shocked when she discovers that he is gay. (Fiction)

West, Jessamyn. *Massacre at Fall Creek,* Harcourt, 1975.
Seventeen-year-old Hannah Cape is only one of the people affected by the first trial (in 1824) of white men accused of murdering Native Americans. (Fiction)

Westall, Robert. *Devil on the Road,* Greenwillow, 1979.
In a time fantasy set in present day England, John Webster travels from a barn with strange symbols and an unusual cat to a trial 300 years in the past, where he fights to save a young woman sentenced to die for being a witch. (Fiction)

———. *Futuretrack 5,* Greenwillow, 1984.
This is the story of Henry Kitson, one of a small group responsible for keeping the highly computerized, manipulative, twenty-first-century British society functioning, and Keri, the London bike-riding champion of Futuretrack 5. (Fiction)

———. *Gulf,* Scholastic, 1997.
During the Gulf War, Tom grapples with his sense of guilt when his brother is possessed by the spirit of an Iraqi solder and committed to a mental institution. (Fiction)

———. *Kingdom by the Sea,* Farrar, 1992.
It's 1942, and Harry has just become a war orphan. Will he and the stray dog he takes up with be able to survive on their own? (Fiction)

———. *Stormsearch,* Farrar, 1993.
Tim's summer vacation turns into a quest when an antique model ship, washed up on the beach after a terrible storm, brings with it secrets of love and death. (Fiction)

———. *Wind Eye,* Greenwillow, 1978.
The members of a professor's family are transported, via an old boat said to have belonged to St. Cuthbert, back into medieval times—where the not altogether friendly monk touches each of their lives. (Fiction)

———. *Yaxley's Cat,* Scholastic, 1993.
Renting the wrong vacation cottage proves to be an almost fatal mistake for a mother and two teen-

---

■ Selected for "Still Alive: The Best of the Best, 1960–1974"

▲ Selected for "The Best of the Best Books: 1970–1983"

◆ Selected for "Nothin' but the Best: Best of the Best Books for Young Adults, 1966–1986"

● Selected for "Here We Go Again: 25 Years of Best Books: Selections from 1967 to 1992"

agers, especially after a stray cat moves in and starts digging around in the garden. (Fiction)

Wetherby, Terry, ed. *Conversations: Working Women Talk about Doing a "Man's Job,"* Les Femmes, 1978.
Twenty-two women talk about their experiences in such traditionally male-dominated jobs as welder, carpenter, butcher, grain elevator operator, and chairperson of the board. (Nonfiction)

Wharton, William. *Birdy,* Knopf, 1979.
In a V.A. hospital, Birdy is prompted by his friend Al to review his bird-obsessed youth, and discovers freedom without flight. (Fiction)

————. *Midnight Clear,* Knopf, 1982.
A group of unseasoned teenage soldiers standing guard in an old chalet in the Ardennes Forest in December 1944 experience first hand the irony and tragedy of war when they desperately try to set up peaceful communications with a similar group of Germans. (Fiction)

Whipple, Dorothy. *Is the Grass Greener?: Answers to Questions about Drugs,* Luce, 1971.
In question and answer form, a physician reports with total objectivity on the facts about drugs of all kinds, the laws, the uses, and the ways to confront the problem. (Nonfiction)

White, Ellen Emerson. *Long Live the Queen,* Scholastic, 1990.
Abducted by terrorists, Megan, the President's daughter, realizes her survival is completely up to her. (Fiction)

————. *The Road Home,* Scholastic, 1996.
Lt. Rebecca Phillips, who served as a combat nurse in Vietnam, comes to terms with what she experienced there as she tries to readjust to life in the U.S. (Fiction)

White, Robb. *Deathwatch,* Doubleday, 1972. ■ ▲ ◆ ●
Ben's hunting expedition for bighorn sheep becomes a deathwatch in the desert—with hope of survival forty-five miles away! (Fiction)

White, Ruth. *Belle Prater's Boy,* Farrar, 1997.
What really happened to the parents of twelve-year-old Gypsy and her cousin Woodrow? (Fiction)

————. *Weeping Willow,* Farrar, 1993.
Life in idyllic 1950s Virginia is difficult for Tiny Lambert as she struggles to emerge whole from her stepfather's brutal attention. (Fiction)

White, Ryan, and Cunningham, Ann Marie. *Ryan White: My Own Story,* Dial, 1992.
Teenager Ryan White not only fights AIDS but also prejudice and his own fears in a personal account about the medical disaster facing all of us. (Nonfiction)

Whitney, Phyllis. *Hunter's Green,* Doubleday, 1968.
Returning to Athmore for a reconciliation with her husband, Eve North finds herself the pawn in a deadly game of chess with the black rook out to destroy her. (Fiction)

Wibberley, Leonard. *Mouse on Wall Street,* Morrow, 1969.
Gloriana, ruler of Grand Fenwick, conqueror of the United States, sender of the first rocket to the moon, now is possessed by a "Midas touch" which almost wrecks the simple economy of her country. (Fiction)

Wieler, Diana. *Bad Boy,* Delacorte, 1993.
AJ and Tulley have been best friends both on and off the ice for years, but AJ's discovery of Tulley's secret threatens their friendship and AJ's control over his own violence. (Fiction)

Wiesenthal, Simon. *Murderers among Us,* McGraw-Hill, 1967.
A survivor of the concentration camps searches out and brings to justice Adolf Eichmann, the Gestapo officer, Karl Silberbauer, who arrested Anne Frank, and some 900 other Nazi murderers. (Nonfiction)

Wilcox, Fred A. *Waiting for an Army to Die: The Tragedy of Agent Orange,* Random, 1983.
Based on interviews with Vietnam veterans and on government documents, this comprehensive look at the effects of the defoliant Agent Orange also points to the callous disregard for its victims. (Nonfiction)

Wilford, John Noble. *Riddle of the Dinosaur,* Knopf, 1986.
The science editor of the *New York Times* has produced a humorous and readable history of paleontology, including surprising new discoveries that have revolutionized dinosaur theory. (Nonfiction)

Wilhelm, Kate. *Where Late the Sweet Birds Sang,* Harper, 1976.
When humankind is faced with annihilation by the sterilizing effects of pollution and plague, cloning becomes the only hope of man's continued existence—or is it? (Fiction)

Wilkinson, Brenda. *Ludell and Willie,* Harper, 1977. ▲
Two high school seniors from a poor, black Georgia community fall in love but are separated because of family tragedy. (Fiction)

Wilkomirski, Benjamin. *Fragments: Memories of a Childhood, 1939–1948,* Schocken; dist. by Pantheon, 1997.
Found wandering near Auschwitz at the end of the war, a small boy has no language or knowledge of who he is. Here, he shares his fragmented memories of surviving as a toddler. (Nonfiction)

Willard, Nancy. *Things Invisible to See,* Knopf, 1985.

Mystical visions, romance, and the struggle of making choices are intertwined in the story of twins, Ben and Willie, and Clare Bishop after Ben's stray ball paralyzes Clare. (Fiction)

Willeford, Charles. *I Was Looking for a Street,* Countryman, 1988.

A writer's memoir of his survival from age eight when he was orphaned to his life on the road as a teenager during the Great Depression. (Nonfiction)

Willey, Margaret. *Bigger Book of Lydia,* Harper, 1983.

Lydia Bitte is small and unhappy and her rock-musician boyfriend calls her "Littlebit." She acquires a new perspective when she meets Michelle, who has anorexia. (Fiction)

———. *Finding David Dolores,* Harper, 1986.

"Oh God, I whispered. At last I've found someone." Thirteen-year-old Arly experiences the intensity of a first crush when she secretly follows handsome, older David Dolores. (Fiction)

———. *Saving Lenny,* Bantam/Starfire, 1991.

When Jesse falls in love with handsome, mysterious Lenny, she willingly gives up everything for him—family, friends, and college. (Fiction)

Williams, Carol Lynch. *The True Colors of Caitlynne Jackson,* Delacorte, 1998.

Caitlynne and her sister, forced to fend for themselves when their mother storms out and never returns, take off on their bikes to search for a grandmother they barely know. (Fiction)

Williams, Juan. *Eyes on the Prize: America's Civil Rights Years, 1954–1965,* Viking, 1987.

A history of the dramatic events of the years between the Supreme Court's ruling against segregated schools in 1954 and the approval of the Voting Rights Act of 1965. (Nonfiction)

Williams, Martin. *Where's the Melody?* Pantheon, 1966.

Listeners are introduced to jazz using record notes. (Nonfiction)

Williams, Michael. *Crocodile Burning,* Dutton/Lodestar, 1993.

Joining the cast of a play about apartheid headed for the New York stage, Seraki leaves his native Soweto, where life under white rule has become unbearable. (Fiction)

Williams, Ted, and Underwood, John. *My Turn at Bat: The Story of My Life,* Simon & Schuster, 1969.

One of baseball's greatest hitters, Ted Williams, explains himself and his controversial career with honesty and frankness. (Nonfiction)

Williams-Garcia, Rita. *Fast Talk on a Slow Track,* Dutton/Lodestar, 1992.

Denzel Watson has always been a star; now he faces his first taste of failure the summer before his freshman year at Princeton. (Fiction)

———. *Like Sisters on the Homefront,* Dutton/Lodestar, 1996.

When Gayle, a streetwise mother at fourteen, becomes pregnant again, she is sent south to stay with relatives. (Fiction)

Willis, Connie. *To Say Nothing of the Dog; or, How We Found the Bishop's Bird Stump at Last,* Bantam, 1999.

When time-traveling historian Ned Henry rescues a cat in Victorian England, the twenty-first century begins to unravel. (Fiction)

Wilson, Budge. *Leaving,* Putnam/Philomel, 1993.

Nine stories about growing up female reveal the roller coaster of teenage emotions. (Fiction)

Wilson, David Henry. *Coachman Rat,* Carroll & Graf, 1990.

When the clock tolls midnight, the rat the fairy godmother had turned into a coachman accidentally remains human in all but physical form; will he be as inhumane as the people he encounters? (Fiction)

Wilson, Diane Lee. *I Rode a Horse of Milk White Jade,* Orchard, 1999.

Through sheer determination, crippled Oyuna rides her magical horse in search of the great Kublai Khan. (Fiction)

Wilson, F. Paul. *Dydeetown World,* Baen, 1990.

Private detective Sigmundo Dreyer takes on the underworld and corporate crime when he helps a client in this futuristic hard-boiled detective saga. (Fiction)

Wilson, Robert Charles. *Gypsies,* Doubleday/Foundation, 1990.

Fifteen-year-old Michael suddenly realizes his mom shares his unusual psychic ability, and now they must flee for their lives. (Fiction)

- ■ Selected for "Still Alive: The Best of the Best, 1960–1974"
- ▲ Selected for "The Best of the Best Books: 1970–1983"
- ◆ Selected for "Nothin' but the Best: Best of the Best Books for Young Adults, 1966–1986"
- ● Selected for "Here We Go Again: 25 Years of Best Books: Selections from 1967 to 1992"

———. *Mysterium,* Bantam/Spectra, 1995.
Following an explosion at a secret government installation, the town of Two Rivers wakes up in a parallel dimension, where the church rules and teens are hanged for rebelling. (Fiction)

Windsor, Patricia. *Summer Before,* Harper, 1973.
Alexandra fights her way back to reality with the help of her parents and a psychiatrist, after the death of her special friend Bradley. (Fiction)

Winthrop, Elizabeth. *Knock, Knock, Who's There?* Holiday, 1979.
While Sam and Michael try to cope with their father's death, they discover that their mother has a problem even more devastating to their lives. (Fiction)

Winton, Tim. *Lockie Leonard, Human Torpedo,* Little, Brown/Joy Street Books, 1993.
Lockie gets thrown out of class his first day at his new high school—a good start, he decides. Things look even better when the prettiest girl in school takes an interest in him. (Fiction)

Wirths, Claudine G., and Bowman-Kruhm, Mary. *I Hate School: How to Hang In and When to Drop Out,* Harper, 1986.
This self-help manual for potential dropouts offers usable, nonpreachy suggestions for improving academic performance and coping with problems. (Nonfiction)

Wisler, G. Clifton. *Red Cap,* Dutton/Lodestar, 1992.
Starvation, disease and despair destroy the lives of Union soldiers at Andersonville. How can Ransom, a thirteen-year-old prisoner of war, expect to survive? (Fiction)

Wittlinger, Ellen. *Lombardo's Law,* Houghton, 1994.
When fifteen-year-old Justine finally finds a boy who loves the same things she does, such as foreign films, she fights her feelings for him because he is only thirteen (Fiction)

Wolf, David. *Foul! The Connie Hawkins Story,* Holt, 1972.
Slum beginnings and a college basketball scandal do not keep Connie Hawkins from becoming a superstar with the Phoenix Suns. (Nonfiction)

Wolf, Sylvia. *Focus: Five Women Photographers,* Albert Whitman, 1995.
Wolf views the creative process from very different perspectives through crisp, well-selected photographs by Julia Margaret Cameron, Margaret Bourke-White, Flor Garduno, Sandy Skoglund, and Lorna Simpson. (Nonfiction)

Wolfe, Tom. *The Right Stuff,* Farrar, 1980.
Wolfe provides a fascinating and often irreverant history of manned space flight from the late 1940s exploits of Chuck Yeager to the NASA missions of John Glenn, Alan Shepard, and Gus Grissom—who all had the "right stuff." (Fiction)

Wolff, Tobias. *This Boy's Life: A Memoir,* Atlantic Monthly Press, 1990.
A witty, wrenching autobiography of Wolff's coming-of-age with a loving mother and a cruel stepfather. (Nonfiction)

Wolff, Virginia Euwer. *Make Lemonade,* Holt, 1994.
High-school student LaVaughn, determined to earn money for college, baby-sits for Jolly, an unwed teenage mother of two, and matures in the process. (Fiction)

———. *Mozart Season,* Holt, 1992.
Allegra Shapiro plays Mozart on her violin with the same intensity that she plays softball; her decision to enter a music competition turns her twelfth summer into the "Mozart season." (Fiction)

———. *Probably Still Nick Swansen,* Holt, 1988. •
Slow but proud special education student Nick Swansen must deal with the pain of rejection and the lingering guilt over his sister's death. (Fiction)

Wood, Bari. *Killing Gift: A Novel,* Putnam, 1975.
Does Jennifer Gilbert really have the psychic power to kill? (Fiction)

Woodson, Jacqueline. *From the Notebooks of Melanin Sun,* Scholastic/Blue Sky, 1996.
Melanin Sun finds being a teenager is hard enough without learning that his mother's new boyfriend is a woman. (Fiction)

———. *I Hadn't Meant to Tell You This,* Delacorte, 1995.
Marie and Lena become friends despite race and class differences, but can their friendship protect Lena from the terrifying secret she is forced to keep? (Fiction)

———. *If You Come Softly,* Putnam, 1999.
Jeremiah, who is white, and Ellie, who is African American, feel an immediate connection and then must cope with the reactions to their relationship by the people around them. (Fiction)

———. *Maizon at Blue Hill,* Delacorte, 1993.
After winning a scholarship to a mostly white boarding school, Maizon is forced to confront issues of racism, friendship, and fitting in. (Fiction)

Woolley, Persia. *Child of the Northern Spring,* Poseidon, 1987.
The first book in an Arthurian trilogy views life through the eyes of lively fifteen-year-old Guinevere. (Fiction)

———. *Queen of the Summer Stars,* Poseidon, 1991.
Young Queen Guinevere is torn between loyalty to her king and love for his closest com-

panion, Lancelot, in this sequel to *Child of the Northern Spring.* (Fiction)

Wrede, Patricia C. *Dealing with Dragons,* Harcourt/Jane Yolen, 1991. ●
Unconventional Cimorene, fed up with her dull life as a princess, runs away to join the dragons in this fun book that turns fairy tales upside down. (Fiction)

———. *Searching for Dragons,* Harcourt/Jane Yolen, 1993.
Princess Cimorene and Mendabar, king of the Enchanted Forest, triumph over wizards to rescue Kazul, the king of the dragons. (Fiction)

Wyden, Peter. *Day One: Before Hiroshima and After,* Simon & Schuster, 1985.
The author not only chronicles the making of the atomic bomb and its first use, but also follows the aftermath to the present day. (Nonfiction)

Wyss, Thelma Hatch. *Here at the Scenic-Vu Motel,* Harper, 1988. ●
Living too far away to be bused to the local high school, a coed group of teens room at a motel, with seventeen-year-old Jake in charge—but by no means ready for such awesome responsibilities. (Fiction)

Yeager, Chuck, and Janos, Leo. *Yeager: An Autobiography,* Bantam, 1985.
Air Force general Chuck Yeager, World War II ace and first man to break the sound barrier, candidly shares the drama of his life and career. (Nonfiction)

Yee, Paul. *Breakaway,* Douglas & McIntyre/ Groundwood; dist. by Publishers Group West, 1998.
Eighteen-year-old Kwok Wong desperately wants to play soccer and attend the university— it's his way out of his Chinese family's traditions and their dirt-poor farm. (Fiction)

Yep, Laurence, ed. *American Dragons: Twenty-five Asian American Voices,* HarperCollins, 1994.
Growing up can be agonizing and traumatic, yet filled with hope and love, as these short stories, poems, and excerpts from plays poignantly demonstrate. (Nonfiction)

Yolen, Jane. *Briar Rose,* Tor, 1993.
Grandmother Gemma always told the story of Briar Rose, and after she dies, her granddaugh-

ter discovers that Gemma was a real-life Sleeping Beauty—a Holocaust survivor. (Fiction)

———. *Dragon's Blood,* Delacorte, 1982.
In an original and engrossing fantasy, Jakkin's freedom is ensured when the dragon he steals and secretly trains wins its first fight. (Fiction)

———. *Gift of Sarah Barker,* Viking, 1981.
Vivacious Sarah and stalwart Abel create havoc in a quiet, modest Shaker community when they fall in love. (Fiction)

———. *Heart's Blood,* Delacorte, 1984.
Jakkin wants only to possess and train his own red dragon—until his love for Akki leads him into the maze of Austarian politics. (Fiction)

———, **and Coville, Bruce.** *Armageddon Summer,* Harcourt, 1999.
In alternating chapters, Marina and Jed tell how they witnessed a cult's preparation for the end of the world. (Fiction)

———, **and Greenberg, Martin H., eds.** *Vampires: A Collection of Original Stories,* HarperCollins, 1992. ●
Meet the vampire of your dreams—in the mall, in a neighbor's garden, or haunting the streets at night. (Fiction)

Young, Al. *Snakes,* Holt, 1970.
MC, a young ghetto musician, makes the stormy journey through adolescence with the help of his grandmother, a hit record, and his friends. (Fiction)

Young, Jean. *Woodstock Craftsman's Manual,* Praeger, 1972.
This how-to book covers everything from beads to batik. (Nonfiction)

———. *Woodstock Craftsman's Manual 2,* Praeger, 1973.
In this second how-to volume, such crafts as needle-point, applique, quilting, songwriting, and woodblock printing are covered along with how to make stained glass, bronze jewelry, sandals, and videotapes. (Nonfiction)

Zambreno, Mary Frances. *Plague of Sorcerers,* Harcourt/Jane Yolen, 1993.
A magic plague is infecting the wizards in the land. Only sixteen-year-old Jermyn can break the spell, with the help of his most unusual familiar—an overprotective skunk. (Fiction)

■ Selected for "Still Alive: The Best of the Best, 1960–1974"

▲ Selected for "The Best of the Best Books: 1970–1983"

◆ Selected for "Nothin' but the Best: Best of the Best Books for Young Adults, 1966–1986"

● Selected for "Here We Go Again: 25 Years of Best Books: Selections from 1967 to 1992"

Zassenhaus, Hiltgunt. *Walls: Resisting the Third Reich—One Woman's Story,* Beacon, 1974.
Refusing to be intimidated by the Nazi regime in Germany, Hiltgunt uses her knowledge of the Scandinavian language to help, at some risk to herself, the Scandinavian prisoners in Germany. (Nonfiction)

Zelazny, Roger. *Doorways in the Sand,* Harper, 1976.
Interstellar espionage is magical and fantastic with two zany alien agents, disguised as a wombat and a kangaroo, and an acrophobic earthman hero. (Fiction)

Zerman, Melvyn Bernard. *Taking on the Press: Constitutional Rights in Conflict,* Harper/Crowell, 1986.
The Black Panthers, Vietnam, and nuclear secrets are only some of the legal issues explained in Zerman's lively, entertaining book. (Nonfiction)

Zindel, Paul. *Begonia for Miss Applebaum,* Harper, 1990.
Henry and Zelda use a cash card to help their offbeat favorite teacher and her homeless friends. (Fiction)

————. *Confessions of a Teenage Baboon,* Harper, 1977.
Sixteen-year-old Chris Boyd gains self-confidence and control over his life after a tragic encounter with a thirty-year-old misfit who befriends lonely teenagers. (Fiction)

————. *Effects of Gamma Rays on Man-in-the-Moon-Marigolds,* Harper, 1971. ▲ ◆
An alcoholic mother stifles the lives of her two teenage daughters, one who is bordering on madness and the other who is a sensitive, loving person, in this prize-winning drama. (Fiction)

————. *Pardon Me, You're Stepping on My Eyeball!* Harper, 1976.
Marsh Mellow, an offbeat teenager with an alcoholic mother and a missing father, begins to accept himself when Edna, a new acquaintance, decides to shed her aloofness and help him. (Fiction)

————. *Pigman and Me,* HarperCollins/Charlotte Zolotow, 1993.
Zindel recounts his bizarre adventures growing up on Staten Island, when his neighbor's father becomes his personal "pigman" and teaches him to cope with his rootless family. (Nonfiction)

————. *Pigman's Legacy,* Harper, 1980.
John and Lorraine befriend an old man who is hiding from the IRS in the Pigman's house, and through the hilarious and poignant experiences they share with him, they discover the legacy of love which the Pigman left them. (Fiction)

Zolotow, Charlotte, ed. *Early Sorrow: Ten Stories of Youth,* Harper, 1986.
Themes range from the end of a special relationship to the loss of a special possession, from the death of a loved one to a loss of self, in these stories about the first sorrows of youth. (Fiction)

The Books by Year

1966 SELECTIONS

Abel, Elie   *Missile Crisis*
Asimov, Isaac   *Fantastic Voyage*
Bach, Richard   *Biplane*
Barker, S. Omar   *Little World Apart*
Boyd, Malcolm   *Are You Running with Me, Jesus?*
Brooks, Earle, and Brooks, Rhoda   *Barrios of Manta*
Capps, Benjamin   *Woman of the People*
Clifford, Francis   *Naked Runner*
Dufresne, Frank   *My Way Was North*
Durrell, Gerald   *Two in the Bush*
Friel, Brian   *Philadelphia, Here I Come!*
Fuller, John G.   *Incident at Exeter*
Gallery, Daniel   *Stand By-y-y to Start Engines*
Gilman, Dorothy   *Unexpected Mrs. Pollifax*
Hallet, Jean-Pierre   *Congo Kitabu*
Hollinger, Carol   *Mai Pen Rai Means Never Mind*
Lindall, Edward   *Northward the Coast*
MacLean, Alistair   *When Eight Bells Toll*
Manry, Robert   *Tinkerbelle*
Nader, Ralph   *Unsafe at Any Speed*
Parks, Gordon   *Choice of Weapons*
Plimpton, George   *Paper Lion*
Russell, Bill, and McSweeney, William   *Go Up for Glory*
Ryan, Cornelius   *Last Battle*
Sherman, D. R.   *Brothers of the Sea*
Walker, Margaret   *Jubilee*
Williams, Martin   *Where's the Melody?*

1967 SELECTIONS

Amosov, Nikolai   *Open Heart*
Armstrong, Charlotte   *Gift Shop*
Bagley, Desmond   *Landslide*
Ball, John Dudley   *Cool Cottontail*
Cole, Ernest, and Flaherty, Thomas   *House of Bondage*
Conot, Robert   *Rivers of Blood, Years of Darkness*
Hardy, William Marion   *U.S.S. Mudskipper: The Submarine That Wrecked a Train*
Hartog, Jan De   *Captain*
Head, Ann   *Mr. and Mrs. Bo Jo Jones*
Inouye, Daniel Ken, and Elliot, Lawrence   *Journey to Washington*
Kuznetsov, Anatolli Petrovich   *Babi Yar*
Levitt, Leonard   *African Season*
Lord, Walter   *Incredible Victory*
Maas, Peter   *Rescuer*
Mather, Melissa   *One Summer in Between*
Olsen, Jack   *Black Is Best: The Riddle of Cassius Clay*
Peters, Ellis   *Black Is the Colour of My True-Love's Heart*
Potok, Chaim   *The Chosen*
Ridgway, John M., and Blyth, Chay   *Fighting Chance*
Rosten, Leo   *Most Private Intrigue*
Schaap, Richard   *Turned On: The Friede-Crenshaw Case*
Sheehan, Susan   *Ten Vietnamese*
Simak, Clifford D.   *Werewolf Principle*
Styron, William   *Confessions of Nat Turner*

Szulc, Tad   *Bombs of Palomares*
Thompson, Jean   *House of Tomorrow*
Walsh, John, and Gannon, Robert   *Time Is Short and the Water Rises*
Wiesenthal, Simon   *Murderers among Us*

1968 SELECTIONS

Bagley, Desmond   *Vivero Letter*
Bradford, Richard   *Red Sky at Morning*
Braithwaite, Edward   *Paid Servant*
Cleaver, Eldridge   *Soul on Ice*
Collins, Larry, and Lapierre, Dominique   *Or I'll Dress You in Mourning*
Courlander, Harold   *African, a Novel*
David, Jay, ed.   *Growing Up Black*
Davies, Hunter   *Beatles: The Authorized Biography*
Durrell, Gerald   *Rosy Is My Relative*
Kellogg, Marjorie   *Tell Me That You Love Me, Junie Moon*
Kramer, Jerry   *Instant Replay; the Green Bay Diary of Jerry Kramer*
Kuper, Jack   *Child of the Holocaust*
Leslie, Robert   *Bears and I: Raising Three Cubs in the North Woods*
Lynd, Alice   *We Won't Go*
MacInnes, Helen   *Salzburg Connection*
Parks, David   *G.I. Diary*
Portis, Charles   *True Grit: A Novel*
Sanderson, Ivan   *Uninvited Visitors: A Biologist Looks at UFO's*
Schulz, Charles   *Peanuts Treasury*
Taylor, Gordon   *Biological Time Bomb*
Teague, Robert   *Letters to a Black Boy*
Watson, James   *Double Helix: A Personal Account of the Discovery of the Structure of DNA*
Whitney, Phyllis   *Hunter's Green*

1969 SELECTIONS

Ball, John Dudley   *Johnny Get Your Gun*
Bradbury, Ray   *I Sing the Body Electric!*
Brown, Turner Jr.   *Black Is*
Cohn, Nik   *Rock from the Beginning*
Crichton, Michael   *Andromeda Strain*
Decker, Sunny   *Empty Spoon*
Durrell, Gerald   *Birds, Beasts, and Relatives*
Ferris, Louanne   *I'm Done Crying*
Gaines, William, ed., and Feldstein, Albert, ed.   *Ridiculously Expensive MAD*
Granatelli, Anthony   *They Call Me Mister 500*
Hay, Jacob, and Keshishian, John M.   *Autopsy for a Cosmonaut*
King, Coretta Scott   *My Life with Martin Luther King, Jr.*
Kunen, James Simon   *Strawberry Statement: Notes of a College Revolutionary*
Lester, Julius   *Search for the New Land*

Lowenfels, Walter, ed.   *Writing on the Wall: 108 American Poems of Protest*
Michaels, Barbara   *Ammie, Come Home*
Moody, Anne   *Coming of Age in Mississippi: An Autobiography*
Olsen, Jack   *Night of the Grizzlies*
Potok, Chaim   *Promise*
Stewart, Fred   *Mephisto Waltz*
Wibberley, Leonard   *Mouse on Wall Street*
Williams, Ted, and Underwood, John   *My Turn at Bat: The Story of My Life*

1970 SELECTIONS

Angelou, Maya   *I Know Why the Caged Bird Sings*
Birmingham, John   *Our Time Is Now: Notes from the High School Underground*
Blum, Ralph   *Simultaneous Man*
Bouton, Jim   *Ball Four: My Life and Hard Times Throwing the Knuckleball in the Big Leagues*
Brenner, Joseph H., and Coles, Robert M.D., et al.   *Drugs and Youth: Medical, Psychiatric and Legal Facts*
Chisholm, Shirley   *Unbought and Unbossed*
Cousteau, Jacques-Yves, and Cousteau, Philippe   *Shark: Splendid Savage of the Sea*
Dorman, Michael   *Under Twenty-one: A Young People's Guide to Legal Rights*
Dowdey, Landon, comp.   *Journey to Freedom: A Casebook with Music*
Dribben, Judith   *Girl Called Judith Strick*
Eisen, Jonathan, ed.   *Altamont: Death of Innocence in the Woodstock Nation*
Fall, Thomas   *Ordeal of Running Standing*
Finney, Jack   *Time and Again*
Gaylin, Willard M.D.   *In the Service of Their Country: War Resistors in Prison*
Goro, Herb   *Block*
Greenberg, Joanne   *In This Sign*
Gregory, Susan   *Hey, White Girl!*
Hammer, Richard   *One Morning in the War: The Tragedy at Son My*
Hedgepeth, William, and Stock, Dennis   *Alternative: Communal Life in New America*
Hillerman, Tony   *Blessing Way*
Hough, John   *Peck of Salt: A Year in the Ghetto*
Howard, Jane   *Please Touch: A Guided Tour of the Human Potential Movement*
Jordan, June, ed.   *Soulscript: Afro-American Poetry*
Kavaler, Lucy   *Freezing Point: Cold as a Matter of Life and Death*
Kim, Richard   *Lost Names: Scenes from a Korean Boyhood*
Meriwether, Louise   *Daddy Was a Number Runner*

O'Leary, Brian   *Making of an Ex-Astronaut*
Segal, Erich   *Love Story*
Shaw, Arnold   *World of Soul: Black America's Contribution to the Pop Music Scene*
Stewart, Mary   *Crystal Cave*
Swarthout, Glendon   *Bless the Beasts and Children*
Tyler, Anne   *Slipping-Down Life*
Wersba, Barbara   *Run Softly, Go Fast*
Young, Al   *Snakes*

1971 SELECTIONS

Anonymous   *Go Ask Alice*
Balducci, Caroyln   *Is There a Life after Graduation, Henry Birnbaum?*
Barjavel, Rene   *Ice People*
Brand, Stewart   *Last Whole Earth Catalog*
Brown, Dee   *Bury My Heart at Wounded Knee: An Indian History of the American West*
Campbell, Hope   *No More Trains to Tottenville*
Cousteau, Jacques-Yves, and Diole, Philippe   *Life and Death in a Coral Sea*
Gaines, Ernest J.   *The Autobiography of Miss Jane Pittman*
Goulart, Ron   *What's Become of Screwloose? and Other Inquiries*
Guffy, Ossie, and Ledner, Caryl   *Ossie: The Autobiography of a Black Woman*
Henderson, Zenna   *Holding Wonder*
Heyerdahl, Thor   *Ra Expeditions*
Hinton, S. E.   *That Was Then, This Is Now*
Houriet, Robert   *Getting Back Together*
Houston, James   *White Dawn*
Jordan, June   *His Own Where*
LaVallee, David   *Event 1000*
Lawick-Goodall, Jane Van   *In the Shadow of Man*
Lydon, Michael   *Rock Folk: Portraits from the Rock 'n Roll Pantheon*
Michaels, Barbara   *Dark on the Other Side*
Moore, Gilbert   *Special Rage*
Nolen, William   *Making of a Surgeon*
Parks, Gordon   *Born Black*
Pierce, Ruth   *Single and Pregnant*
Plath, Sylvia   *The Bell Jar*
Postman, Neil, and Weingartner, Charles   *Soft Revolution: A Student Handbook for Turning Schools Around*
Powers, Thomas   *Diana: The Making of a Terrorist*
Renvoize, Jean   *Wild Thing*
Sorrentino, Joseph   *Up from Never*
Stevenson, Florence   *Curse of the Concullens*
Townsend, John   *Good Night, Prof. Dear*
Whipple, Dorothy   *Is the Grass Greener?: Answers to Questions about Drugs*
Zindel, Paul   *Effects of Gamma Rays on Man-in-the-Moon-Marigolds*

1972 SELECTIONS

Allen, Terry, ed.   *Whispering Wind; Poetry by Young American Indians*
Blue, Vida, and Libby, Bill   *Vida: His Own Story*
Blum, Ralph   *Old Glory and the Real-Time Freaks*
Carlson, Dale   *Mountain of Truth*
Conrat, Maisie, and Conrat, Richard   *Executive Order 9066: The Internment of 110,000 Japanese Americans*
Crichton, Michael   *Terminal Man*
Del Rey, Lester   *Pstalemate*
Durham, Marilyn   *The Man Who Loved Cat Dancing*
Elfman, Blossom   *Girls of Huntington House*
Fair, Ronald   *We Can't Breathe*
Fast, Howard   *Hessian*
Friedman, Philip   *Rage*
Giovanni, Nikki   *Gemini*
Graham, Robin Lee, and Gill, Derek L. T.   *Dove*
Hall, Lynn   *Sticks and Stones*
Herbert, Frank   *Soul Catcher*
Holland, Isabelle   *Man without a Face*
Krentz, Harold   *To Race the Wind: An Autobiography*
Lee, Mildred   *Fog*
Mathis, Sharon Bell   *Teacup Full of Roses*
O'Brien, Robert C.   *Report from Group 17*
Potok, Chaim   *My Name Is Asher Lev*
Scaduto, Anthony   *Bob Dylan*
Schiff, Ken   *Passing Go*
Sheehan, Carolyn, and Sheehan, Edmund   *Magnifi-Cat*
Smith, Dennis   *Report from Engine Co. 82*
Teitz, Joyce   *What's a Nice Girl Like You Doing in a Place Like This?*
Wallace, Duncan R.   *Mountebank*
White, Robb   *Deathwatch*
Wolf, David   *Foul! The Connie Hawkins Story*
Young, Jean   *Woodstock Craftsman's Manual*

1973 SELECTIONS

Aldridge, James   *Sporting Proposition*
Bickham, Jack M.   *Katie, Kelly and Heck*
Carlson, Dale   *Girls Are Equal Too: The Women's Movement for Teenagers*
Carrighar, Sally   *Home to the Wilderness*
Castaneda, Carlos   *Journey to Ixtlan: The Lessons of Don Juan*
Childress, Alice   *Hero Ain't Nothin but a Sandwich*
Clarke, Arthur C.   *Rendezvous with Rama*
Cooper, Henry S. F., Jr.   *Thirteen: The Flight That Failed*
Freemantle, Brian   *Good-bye to an Old Friend*

Friedman, Myra   *Buried Alive: The Biography of Janis Joplin*
Giovanni, Nikki   *My House: Poems*
Glasser, Ronald J.   *Ward 402*
Gray, Martin, and Gallo, Max   *For Those I Loved*
Greenburger, Ingrid   *Private Treason: A German Memoir*
Guy, Rosa   *The Friends*
Habenstreit, Barbara   *To My Brother Who Did a Crime . . . : Former Prisoners Tell Their Stories in Their Own Words*
Harris, Marilyn   *Hatter Fox*
Hillerman, Tony   *Dance Hall of the Dead*
Huffaker, Clair   *Cowboy and the Cossack*
James, P. D.   *Unsuitable Job for a Woman*
Lawson, Donna   *Mother Nature's Beauty Cupboard: How to Make Beautiful, Money-Saving Natural Cosmetics and Other Beauty Preparations*
Lieberman, James E., and Peck, Ellen   *Sex & Birth Control: A Guide for the Young*
Logan, Jane   *Very Nearest Room*
Maas, Peter   *Serpico*
Maynard, Joyce   *Looking Back: A Chronicle of Growing Up Old in the Sixties*
Michaels, Barbara   *Witch*
O'Brien, Tim   *If I Die in a Combat Zone, Box Me Up and Ship Me Home*
Peck, Robert Newton   *Day No Pigs Would Die*
Robertson, Dougal   *Survive the Savage Sea*
Schwarz-Bart, Andre   *Woman Named Solitude*
Stewart, Mary   *Hollow Hills*
Wagenheim, Kal   *Clemente!*
Windsor, Patricia   *Summer Before*
Young, Jean   *Woodstock Craftsman's Manual 2*

1974 SELECTIONS

Adams, Richard   *Watership Down*
Angelou, Maya   *Gather Together in My Name*
Baldwin, James   *If Beale Street Could Talk*
Benchley, Nathaniel   *Bright Candles: A Novel of the Danish Resistance*
Blum, Ralph, and Blum, Judy   *Beyond Earth: Man's Contact with UFO's*
Cherry, Mike   *On High Steel: The Education of an Ironworker*
Cormier, Robert   *The Chocolate War: A Novel*
Craven, Margaret   *I Heard the Owl Call My Name*
Demas, Vida   *First Person, Singular*
Fields, Jeff   *Cry of Angels*
Frazier, Walt, and Berkow, Ira   *Rockin' Steady: A Guide to Basketball and Cool*
Greenfield, Josh, and Mazursky, Paul   *Harry & Tonto*
Hamilton, Virginia   *M. C. Higgins, the Great*
Herriot, James   *All Things Bright and Beautiful*

Herzog, Arthur   *Swarm*
Holman, Felice   *Slake's Limbo*
Jacopetti, Alexandra   *Native Funk and Flash: An Emerging Folk Art*
Jacot, Michael   *Last Butterfly*
Johnston, Jennifer   *How Many Miles to Babylon? A Novel*
Le Guin, Ursula K.   *Dispossessed*
Levit, Rose   *Ellen: A Short Life Long Remembered*
MacCracken, Mary   *Circle of Children*
Mathis, Sharon Bell   *Listen for the Fig Tree*
Niven, Larry, and Pournelle, Jerry   *Mote in God's Eye*
Page, Thomas   *Hephaestus Plague*
Read, Piers Paul   *Alive: The Story of the Andes Survivors*
Rose, Louise Blecher   *Launching of Barbara Fabrikant*
Samuels, Gertrude   *Run, Shelley, Run!*
Scoppettone, Sandra   *Trying Hard to Hear You*
Sleator, William   *House of Stairs*
Slesar, Henry   *Thing at the Door*
Tidyman, Ernest   *Dummy*
Wagoner, David   *Road to Many a Wonder*
Wells, Evelyn   *I Am Thinking of Kelda*
Zassenhaus, Hiltgunt   *Walls: Resisting the Third Reich—One Woman's Story*

1975 SELECTIONS

Ali, Muhammad, and Durham, Richard   *Greatest: My Own Story*
Beck, Calvin   *Heroes of the Horrors*
Bell, David, M.D.   *Time to Be Born*
Bleier, Rocky, and O'Neill, Terry   *Fighting Back*
Cavagnaro, David, and Cavagnaro, Maggie   *Almost Home: A Life-style*
Coleman, Lonnie   *Orphan Jim*
Davis, Mildred   *Tell Them What's Her Name Called*
Dixon, Paige   *May I Cross Your Golden River?*
Ellison, Harlan   *Deathbird Stories: A Pantheon of Modern Gods*
Ferazani, Larry   *Rescue Squad*
Gilman, Dorothy   *Clairvoyant Countess*
Giovanni, Nikki   *Women and the Men*
Higgins, Jack   *Eagle Has Landed*
Hinton, S. E.   *Rumblefish*
Holland, Isabelle   *Of Love and Death and Other Journeys*
Horan, James David   *New Vigilantes*
Hotchner, A. E.   *Looking for Miracles: A Memoir about Loving*
Hunter, Kristin   *Survivors*
Kerr, M. E.   *Is That You, Miss Blue?*
Lockley, Ronald   *Seal Woman*
Lund, Doris Herold   *Eric*

MacLaine, Shirley   *You Can Get There from Here*
MacLean, Alistair   *Circus*
Montandon, Pat   *Intruders*
O'Brien, Robert C.   *Z for Zachariah*
Peck, Richard   *Representing Super Doll*
Platt, Kin   *Headman*
Powers, John R.   *Do Black Patent Leather Shoes Really Reflect Up?*
Roueche, Berton   *Feral*
Ryden, Hope   *God's Dog*
Sargent, Pamela, ed.   *Women of Wonder: Science Fiction Stories by Women about Women*
Scortia, Thomas N., and Robinson, Frank G.   *Prometheus Crisis*
Sherman, D. R.   *Lion's Paw*
Simak, Clifford D.   *Enchanted Pilgrimage*
Smith, W. Eugene, and Smith, Aileen M.   *Minamata*
Sullivan, Tom, and Gill, Derek L.T.   *If You Could See What I Hear*
Switzer, Ellen   *How Democracy Failed*
Trudeau, G. B.   *Doonesbury Chronicles*
Vonnegut, Mark   *Eden Express*
Wersba, Barbara   *Country of the Heart*
West, Jessamyn   *Massacre at Fall Creek*
Wood, Bari   *Killing Gift: A Novel*

1976 SELECTIONS

Angelou, Maya   *Swingin' & Singin' & Gettin' Merry Like Christmas*
Archer, Jeffrey   *Not a Penny More, Not a Penny Less*
Boston Women's Health Book Collective   *Our Bodies, Ourselves: A Book by and for Women*
Bova, Ben   *Multiple Man: A Novel of Suspense*
Bradley, William Warren   *Life on the Run*
Bridgers, Sue Ellen   *Home before Dark*
Claire, Keith   *Otherwise Girl*
Clarke, Arthur C.   *Imperial Earth*
Conford, Ellen   *Alfred G. Graebner Memorial High School Handbook of Rules and Regulations: A Novel*
Derby, Pat, and Beagle, Peter   *Lady and Her Tiger*
Eagan, Andrea Boroff   *Why Am I So Miserable If These Are the Best Years of My Life? A Survival Guide for the Young Woman*
Fuller, John G.   *Ghost of Flight 401*
Gordon, Sol, and Conant, Roger   *You! The Teenage Survival Book*
Guest, Judith   *Ordinary People*
Guy, Rosa   *Ruby*
Haley, Alex   *Roots*
Hobbs, Anne, and Specht, Robert   *Tisha: The Story of a Young Teacher in the Alaskan Wilderness*

Konecky, Edith   *Allegra Maud Goldman*
Konigsburg, E. L.   *Father's Arcane Daughter*
Kovic, Ron   *Born on the Fourth of July*
Le Guin, Ursula K.   *Very Far Away from Anywhere Else*
Levin, Ira   *Boys from Brazil*
Lueders, Edward, and St. John, Primus, comps.   *Zero Makes Me Hungry: A Collection of Poems for Today*
MacCracken, Mary   *Lovey: A Very Special Child*
Margolies, Marjorie, and Gruber, Ruth   *They Came to Stay*
Mazer, Norma Fox   *Dear Bill, Remember Me?*
Meltzer, Milton   *Never to Forget: The Jews of the Holocaust*
Mojtabai, A. G.   *400 Eels of Sigmund Freud*
Moody, Raymond A., Jr.   *Life after Life: The Investigation of Phenomenon—Survival of Bodily Health*
Patterson, Sarah   *Distant Summer*
Peck, Richard   *Are You in the House Alone?*
Pohl, Frederik   *Man Plus*
Samson, Joan   *Auctioneer*
Schulke, Flip   *Martin Luther King, Jr.: A Documentary . . . Montgomery to Memphis*
Walsh, M. M. B.   *Four-colored Hoop*
Wersba, Barbara   *Tunes for a Small Harmonica*
Wilhelm, Kate   *Where Late the Sweet Birds Sang*
Zelazny, Roger   *Doorways in the Sand*
Zindel, Paul   *Pardon Me, You're Stepping on My Eyeball!*

1977 SELECTIONS

Rolling Stone Illustrated History of Rock and Roll, 1950–1980
Anson, Jay   *Amityville Horror*
Atwood, Ann   *Haiku-Vision: In Poetry and Photography*
Banks, Lynne Reid   *Dark Quartet: The Story of the Brontës*
Begley, Kathleen   *Deadline*
Brancato, Robin F.   *Winning*
Bredes, Don   *Hard Feelings*
Brooks, Terry   *Sword of Shannara*
Cook, Robin   *Coma*
Cormier, Robert   *I Am the Cheese*
Dolan, Edward F.   *How to Leave Home—and Make Everybody Like It*
Elfman, Blossom   *House for Jonnie O.*
Garani, Gary, and Schulman, Paul   *Fantastic Television*
Garfield, Brian   *Recoil*
Gedge, Pauline   *Child of the Morning*
Hall, Elizabeth   *Possible Impossibilities: A Look at Parapsychology*
Hayes, Billy, and Hoffer, William   *Midnight Express*

Heyman, Anita   *Exit from Home*

Highwater, Jamake   *Anpao: An American Indian Odyssey*

Horwitz, Elinor   *Madness, Magic, and Medicine: The Treatment and Mistreatment of the Mentally Ill*

Houston, James   *Ghost Fox*

Huygen, Wil, and Poortvliet, Rien   *Gnomes*

Jenner, Bruce, and Finch, Philip   *Decathlon Challenge: Bruce Jenner's Story*

Koehn, Ilse   *Mischling, Second Degree: My Childhood in Nazi Germany*

Kopay, David, and Young, Perry   *David Kopay Story: An Extraordinary Self-Revelation*

Larrick, Nancy, ed.   *Crazy to Be Alive in Such a Strange World: Poems about People*

Lipsyte, Robert   *One Fat Summer*

Mazer, Harry, and Mazer, Norma Fox   *Solid Gold Kid*

McCaffrey, Anne   *Dragonsinger*

McCartney, Linda   *Linda's Pictures: A Collection of Photographs*

McConnell, Joan   *Ballet as Body Language*

Mohr, Nicholasa   *In Nueva York*

Peck, Richard   *Ghosts I Have Been*

Pele, do Nascimento, Edson A., and Fish, Robert   *My Life and the Beautiful Game: The Autobiography of Pele*

Petty, Richard   *King of the Road*

Powers, John R.   *Unoriginal Sinner and the Ice-Cream God*

Rather, Dan, and Herskowitz, Mickey   *Camera Never Blinks: Adventures of a TV Journalist*

Robinson, Spider   *Callahan's Crosstime Saloon*

Rothenberg, Mira   *Children with Emerald Eyes: Histories of Extraordinary Boys and Girls*

Ruby, Lois   *Arriving at a Place You've Never Left*

Schwarzenegger, Arnold, and Hall, Douglas Kent   *Arnold: The Education of a Bodybuilder*

Sharpe, Roger C.   *Pinball!*

Sussman, Alan N.   *Rights of Young People: The Basic ACLU Guide to a Young Person's Rights*

Taylor, David   *Zoo Vet: Adventures of a Wild Animal Doctor*

Telander, Rick   *Heaven Is a Playground*

Trevor, Elleston   *Theta Syndrome*

Uhlman, Fred   *Reunion*

Wilkinson, Brenda   *Ludell and Willie*

Zindel, Paul   *Confessions of a Teenage Baboon*

1978 SELECTIONS

Adoff, Arnold, ed.   *Celebrations: A New Anthology of Black American Poetry*

Arrick, Fran   *Steffie Can't Come Out to Play*

Ash, Brian, ed.   *Visual Encyclopedia of Science Fiction*

Blankfort, Michael   *Take the A Train*

Burnford, Sheila   *Bel Ria*

Campbell, Wright R.   *Where Pigeons Go to Die*

Curtis, Edward S.   *Girl Who Married a Ghost, and Other Tales from the North American Indian*

De Larrabeiti, Michael   *Borribles*

Duncan, Lois   *Killing Mr. Griffin*

Elder, Lauren, and Streshinsky, Shirley   *And I Alone Survived*

Francke, Linda Bird   *Ambivalence of Abortion*

Fuller, John G.   *Poison That Fell from the Sky*

Glass, Frankcina   *Marvin & Tige*

Guy, Rosa   *Edith Jackson*

Hamilton, Eleanor   *Sex with Love: A Guide for Young People*

Hautzig, Deborah   *Hey, Dollface*

Hayes, Kent, and Lazzarino, Alex   *Broken Promise*

Holliday, Laurel, ed.   *Heart Songs: The Intimate Diaries of Young Girls*

Ives, John   *Fear in a Handful of Dust*

Jones, Adrienne   *Hawks of Chelney*

Kelly, Gary F.   *Learning about Sex: The Contemporary Guide for Young Adults*

Kerr, M. E.   *Gentlehands*

King, Stephen   *Night Shift*

Leekley, Sheryle, and Leekley, John   *Moments: The Pulitzer Prize Photographs*

LeFlore, Ron, and Hawkins, Jim   *Breakout: From Prison to the Big Leagues*

Leitner, Isabella   *Fragments of Isabella: A Memoir of Auschwitz*

Levenkron, Steven   *Best Little Girl in the World*

London, Mel   *Getting into Film*

Mazer, Harry   *War on Villa Street: A Novel*

McFarlane, Milton C.   *Cudjoe of Jamaica: Pioneer for Black Freedom in the New World*

McIntyre, Vonda N.   *Dreamsnake*

McKinley, Robin   *Beauty: A Retelling of the Story of Beauty and the Beast*

Messing, Shep, and Hirshey, David   *Education of an American Soccer Player*

Meyer, Carolyn   *C. C. Poindexter*

Nabokov, Peter   *Native American Testimony: An Anthology of Indian and White Relations/First Encounter to Dispossession*

Peck, Richard   *Father Figure: A Novel*

Ryan, Cheli Duran, ed.   *Yellow Canary Whose Eye Is So Black*

Saleh, Dennis   *Rock Art: The Golden Age of Record Album Covers*

Scoppettone, Sandra   *Happy Endings Are All Alike*

Smith, Martin Cruz　*Nightwing*
Szabo, Joseph　*Almost Grown*
Trudeau, G. B.　*Doonesbury's Greatest Hits*
Westall, Robert　*Wind Eye*
Wetherby, Terry, ed.　*Conversations: Working Women Talk about Doing a "Man's Job"*

1979 SELECTIONS

Bachman, Richard　*Long Walk*
Bridgers, Sue Ellen　*All Together Now*
Comfort, Alex, and Comfort, Jane　*Facts of Love: Living, Loving and Growing Up*
Cormier, Robert　*After the First Death*
Craig, John　*Chappie and Me: An Autobiographical Novel*
Culin, Charlotte　*Cages of Glass, Flowers of Time*
Davis, Terry　*Vision Quest*
Dickinson, Peter, and Anderson, Wayne　*Flight of Dragons*
Dickinson, Peter　*Tulku*
Forman, James D.　*Ballad for Hogskin Hill*
Girion, Barbara　*Tangle of Roots*
Guy, Rosa　*Disappearance*
Hanckel, Frances, and Cunningham, John　*Way of Love, A Way of Life: A Young Person's Introduction to What It Means to Be Gay*
Hartman, David, and Asbell, Bernard　*White Coat, White Cane*
Helms, Tom　*Against All Odds*
Hinton, S. E.　*Tex*
Ipswitch, Elaine　*Scott Was Here*
Jenkins, Peter　*Walk across America*
Kaplan, Helen Singer　*Making Sense of Sex: The New Facts about Sex and Love for Young People*
Keane, John　*Sherlock Bones: Tracer of Missing Pets*
Leffland, Ella　*Rumors of Peace*
LeRoy, Gen　*Cold Feet*
Macaulay, David　*Motel of the Mysteries*
Marsh, Dave　*Born to Run: The Bruce Springsteen Story*
Mazer, Harry　*Last Mission*
Mazer, Norma Fox　*Up in Seth's Room*
McCoy, Kathy, and Wibbelsman, Charles　*The New Teenage Body Book*
Meyer, Carolyn　*Center: From a Troubled Past to a New Life*
Myers, Walter Dean　*Young Landlords*
Nicol, Clive W.　*White Shaman*
Pascal, Francine　*My First Love and Other Disasters*
Peyton, K. M.　*Prove Yourself a Hero*
Reed, Kit　*Ballad of T. Rantula*
Sandler, Martin　*Story of American Photography: An Illustrated History for Young People*
Say, Allen　*Ink-Keeper's Apprentice*
Sebestyen, Ouida　*Words by Heart*

Seed, Suzanne　*Fine Trades*
Southerland, Ellease　*Let the Lion Eat Straw*
Summers, Ian, ed.　*Tomorrow and Beyond: Masterpieces of Science Fiction Art*
Thompson, Estelle　*Hunter in the Dark*
Torchia, Joseph　*Kryptonite Kid*
Van Leeuwen, Jean　*Seems Like This Road Goes on Forever*
Vonnegut, Kurt　*Jailbird*
Westall, Robert　*Devil on the Road*
Wharton, William　*Birdy*
Winthrop, Elizabeth　*Knock, Knock, Who's There?*

1980 SELECTIONS

Adams, Douglas　*The Hitchhiker's Guide to the Galaxy*
Auel, Jean　*Clan of the Cave Bear*
Bach, Alice　*Waiting for Johnny Miracle*
Barlow, Wayne Douglas, and Summers, Ian　*Barlow's Guide to Extraterrestrials*
Bode, Janet　*Kids Having Kids: The Unwed Teenage Parent*
Bogle, Donald　*Brown Sugar: Eighty Years of America's Black Female Superstars*
Boissard, Janice　*Matter of Feeling*
Bradshaw, Gillian　*Hawk of May*
Brancato, Robin F.　*Come Alive at 505*
Brown, Dee　*Creek Mary's Blood*
Brown, Michael　*Laying Waste: The Poisoning of America by Toxic Chemicals*
Butterworth, W. E.　*Leroy and the Old Man*
Calvert, Patricia　*Snow Bird*
Cohen, Barbara　*Unicorns in the Rain*
Curtis, Patricia　*Animal Rights: The Stories of People Who Defend the Rights of Animals*
De Veaux, Alexis　*Don't Explain: A Song of Billie Holiday*
Due, Linnea A.　*High and Outside*
Garfield, Brian　*Paladin*
Hall, Lynn　*Leaving*
Haugaard, Erik Christian　*Chase Me, Catch Nobody!*
Hayden, Torey L.　*One Child*
Hogan, William　*Quartzsite Trip*
King, Stephen　*Firestarter*
Laure, Jason, and Laure, Ettagale　*South Africa: Coming of Age under Apartheid*
Le Guin, Ursula K.　*Beginning Place*
Lee, Mildred　*People Therein*
MacLeish, Roderick　*First Book of Eppe: An American Romance*
Maiorano, Robert　*Worlds Apart: The Autobiography of a Dancer from Brooklyn*
Matthew, Christopher　*Long-Haired Boy*
Miller, Frances A.　*The Truth Trap*
Oneal, Zibby　*Language of Goldfish*
Paterson, Katherine　*Jacob Have I Loved*
Pfeffer, Susan Beth　*About David*
Prince, Alison　*Turkey's Nest*

Prochnik, Leon   *Endings: Death, Glorious and Otherwise, As Faced by Ten Outstanding Figures of Our Time*
Sagan, Carl   *Cosmos*
Sallis, Susan   *Only Love*
Sebestyen, Ouida   *Far from Home*
Shreve, Susan   *Masquerade*
Silverberg, Robert   *Lord Valentine's Castle*
Spielman, Ed   *Mighty Atom: The Life and Times of Joseph L. Greenstein*
Terkel, Studs   *American Dreams: Lost and Found*
Thomas, Kurt, and Hannon, Kent   *Kurt Thomas and Gymnastics*
Webb, Sheyann, and Nelson, Rachel West   *Selma, Lord, Selma: Girlhood Memories of the Civil-Rights Days*
Wells, Rosemary   *When No One Was Looking*
Wolfe, Tom   *The Right Stuff*
Zindel, Paul   *Pigman's Legacy*

1981 SELECTIONS

Alexander, Lloyd   *Westmark*
Bauer, Steven   *Satyrday: A Fable*
Bell, Ruth   *Changing Bodies, Changing Lives: A Book for Teens on Sex and Relationships*
Blume, Judy   *Tiger Eyes*
Booher, Dianna Daniels   *Rape: What Would You Do If . . . ?*
Bridgers, Sue Ellen   *Notes for Another Life*
Bykov, Vasil   *Pack of Wolves*
Chester, Deborah   *Sign of the Owl*
Childress, Alice   *Rainbow Jordan*
Dolan, Edward F.   *Adolf Hitler: A Portrait in Tyranny*
Duncan, Lois   *Stranger with My Face*
Eckert, Allan   *Song of the Wild*
Grace, Fran   *Branigan's Dog*
Guy, David   *Football Dreams*
Hentoff, Nat   *Does This School Have Capital Punishment?*
Herring, Robert   *Hub*
Hoover, H. M.   *Another Heaven, Another Earth*
Hughes, Monica   *Keeper of the Isis Light*
Jacobs, Anita   *Where Has Deedie Wooster Been All These Years?*
Jaffe, Rona   *Mazes and Monsters*
Janeczko, Paul B., ed.   *Don't Forget to Fly*
Jones, Diana Wynne   *Homeward Bounders*
Kerr, M. E.   *Little Little*
Knowles, John   *Peace Breaks Out*
Koehn, Ilse   *Tilla*
Krementz, Jill   *How It Feels When a Parent Dies*
Kullman, Harry   *Battle Horse*
Lawson, Don   *United States in the Vietnam War*
Levoy, Myron   *Shadow Like a Leopard*
Mann, Peggy, and Gizelle, Hersh   *Gizelle, Save the Children!*

Marzollo, Jean   *Halfway down Paddy Lane*
Mayhar, Ardath   *Soul Singer of Tyrnos*
Mazer, Harry   *I Love You, Stupid!*
Murphy, Barbara Beasley, and Wolkoff, Judie   *Ace Hits the Big Time*
Myers, Walter Dean   *Hoops*
———   *Legend of Tarik*
Namioka, Lensey   *Village of the Vampire Cat*
Peck, Richard   *Close Enough to Touch*
Peterson, P. J.   *Would You Settle for Improbable?*
Reader, Dennis J.   *Coming Back Alive*
Santoli, Al   *Everything We Had: An Oral History of the Vietnam War as Told by Thirty-three American Soldiers Who Fought It*
Senn, Steve   *Circle in the Sea*
Sheldon, Mary   *Perhaps I'll Dream of Darkness*
Skurzynski, Gloria   *Manwolf*
Snyder, Zilpha Keatley   *Fabulous Creature*
Strasser, Todd   *Friends till the End*
Swanson, Walter S. J.   *Deepwood*
Taylor, Mildred D.   *Let the Circle Be Unbroken*
Wallin, Luke   *Redneck Poacher's Son*
Yolen, Jane   *Gift of Sarah Barker*

1982 SELECTIONS

Alexander, Lloyd   *Kestrel*
Banks, Lynne Reid   *Writing on the Wall*
Bradley, Marion Zimmer   *Hawkmistress!*
Brancato, Robin F.   *Sweet Bells Jangled out of Tune*
Butterworth, Emma Macalik   *As the Waltz Was Ending*
Clapp, Patricia   *Witches' Children: A Story of Salem*
Cohen, Barbara, and Lovejoy, Bahija   *Seven Daughters and Seven Sons*
Davis, Daniel S.   *Behind Barbed Wire: Imprisonment of Japanese Americans during World War II*
Dragonwagon, Crescent, and Zindel, Paul   *To Take a Dare*
Duncan, Lois   *Chapters: My Growth as a Writer*
Epstein, Sam, and Epstein, Beryl   *Kids in Court: The ACLU Defends Their Rights*
Ford, Richard   *Quest for the Faradawn*
Garden, Nancy   *Annie on My Mind*
Girion, Barbara   *Handful of Stars*
Glenn, Mel   *Class Dismissed! High School Poems*
Goldston, Robert   *Sinister Touches: The Secret War against Hitler*
Hamilton, Virginia   *Sweet Whispers, Brother Rush*
Hellman, Peter, and Meier, Lili   *Auschwitz Album: A Book Based upon an Album*

Discovered by Concentration Camp Survivor, Lili Meier

Irwin, Hadley   *What about Grandma?*
Kazimiroff, Theodore L.   *Last Algonquin*
Lawrence, Louise   *Calling B for Butterfly*
Lehrman, Robert   *Juggling*
Lester, Julius   *This Strange New Feeling*
Llywelyn, Morgan   *Horse Goddess*
Lynn, Elizabeth A.   *Sardonyx Net*
Magorian, Michelle   *Good Night, Mr. Tom*
Magubane, Peter   *Black Child*
McKinley, Robin   *Blue Sword*
Murphy, Jim   *Death Run*
Naylor, Phyllis Reynolds   *String of Chances*
Oneal, Zibby   *Formal Feeling*
Park, Ruth   *Playing Beatie Bow*
Peterson, P. J.   *Nobody Else Can Walk It for You*
Pierce, Meredith Ann   *The Darkangel*
Riley, Jocelyn   *Only My Mouth Is Smiling*
Robeson, Susan   *Whole World in His Hands: A Pictorial Biography of Paul Robeson*
Schell, Jonathan   *Fate of Earth*
Searls, Hank   *Sounding*
Sebestyen, Ouida   *IOU's*
Simon, Nissa   *Don't Worry, You're Normal: Teenager's Guide to Self Health*
Strasser, Todd   *Rock 'n' Roll Nights*
Terry, Douglas   *Last Texas Hero*
Thomas, Joyce Carol   *Marked by Fire*
Vinge, Joan D.   *Psion*
Voigt, Cynthia   *Tell Me If the Lovers Are Losers*
Wersba, Barbara   *Carnival in My Mind*
Wharton, William   *Midnight Clear*
Yolen, Jane   *Dragon's Blood*

1983 SELECTIONS

Adler, C. S.   *Shell Lady's Daughter*
Arrick, Fran   *God's Radar*
Asimov, Isaac et al., eds.   *Creations: The Quest for Origins in Story and Science*
Bell, Clare   *Ratha's Creature*
Boulle, Pierre   *Whale of the Victoria Cross*
Briggs, Raymond   *When the Wind Blows*
Chambers, Aidan   *Dance on My Grave*
Cormier, Robert   *Bumblebee Flies Anyway*
Crutcher, Chris   *Running Loose*
Faber, Doris   *Love and Rivalry: Three Exceptional Pairs of Sisters*
Ferry, Charles   *Raspberry One*
Fretz, Sada   *Going Vegetarian: A Guide for Teen-agers*
Gaan, Margaret   *Little Sister*
Gaines, Ernest J.   *Gathering of Old Men*
Geras, Adele   *Voyage*
Golden, Frederic   *Trembling Earth: Probing and Predicting Quakes*
Goldman, Peter, and Fuller, Tony   *Charlie Company: What Vietnam Did to Us*

Gordon, Suzanne   *Off Balance: The Real World of Ballet*
Greenberg, Joanne   *Far Side of Victory*
Hamilton, Virginia   *Magical Adventures of Pretty Pearl*
Hayden, Torey L.   *Murphy's Boy*
Heidish, Marcy   *Secret Annie Oakley*
Holman, Felice   *Wild Children*
Hughes, Monica   *Hunter in the Dark*
Janeczko, Paul B., ed.   *Poetspeak: In Their Work, about Their Work*
Kerr, M. E.   *Me Me Me Me Me: Not a Novel*
Korschunow, Irina   *Night in Distant Motion*
Krementz, Jill   *How It Feels to Be Adopted*
Lasky, Kathryn   *Beyond the Divide*
Lee, Tanith   *Red as Blood; or, Tales from the Sisters Grimmer*
Liang, Heng, and Shapiro, Judith   *Son of the Revolution*
Madaras, Lynda, and Madaras, Area   *What's Happening to My Body? Book for Girls: A Growing Up Guide for Parents and Daughters*
Mason, Robert C.   *Chickenhawk*
Mazer, Norma Fox   *Someone to Love*
McGuire, Paula   *It Won't Happen to Me: Teenagers Talk about Pregnancy*
Newton, Suzanne   *I Will Call It Georgie's Blues*
Nicholls, Peter   *Science in Science Fiction*
Page, Tim   *Nam*
Paulsen, Gary   *Dancing Carl*
Pollack, Dale   *Skywalking: The Life and Times of George Lucas*
Reese, Lyn   *I'm on My Way Running: Women Speak on Coming of Age*
Richards, Arlene Kramer, and Willis, Irene   *Under Eighteen and Pregnant: What to Do If You or Someone You Know Is*
Santiago, Danny   *Famous All over Town*
Sargent, Pamela   *Earthseed*
Severin, Tim   *Sinbad Voyage*
Singer, Marilyn   *Course of True Love Never Did Run Smooth*
Skurzynski, Gloria   *Tempering*
Slepian, Jan   *Night of the Bozos*
Smith, Robert Kimmel   *Jane's House*
Smith, Rukshana   *Sumitra's Story*
Speare, Elizabeth George   *Sign of the Beaver*
Steinem, Gloria   *Outrageous Acts and Everyday Rebellions*
Sutcliff, Rosemary   *Road to Camlann: The Death of King Arthur*
Tevis, Walter   *Queen's Gambit*
Thomas, Lewis   *Youngest Science: Notes of a Medicine Watcher*
Trull, Patti   *On with My Life*
Ure, Jean   *See You Thursday*
Van Devanter, Lynda, and Morgan, Christopher   *Home before Morning: The Story of an Army Nurse in Vietnam*

Voigt, Cynthia   *Solitary Blue*
Von Canon, Claudia   *Inheritance*
Wilcox, Fred A.   *Waiting for an Army to Die: The Tragedy of Agent Orange*
Willey, Margaret   *Bigger Book of Lydia*

1984 SELECTIONS

Abercrombie, Barbara   *Run for Your Life*
Alexander, Lloyd   *Beggar Queen*
Anthony, Piers   *On a Pale Horse*
Ashabranner, Brent   *To Live in Two Worlds: American Indian Youth Today*
Avi   *The Fighting Ground*
Bond, Nancy   *Place to Come Back To*
Bunting, Eve   *If I Asked You, Would You Stay?*
Burch, Jennings Michael   *They Cage the Animals at Night*
Carter, Alden R.   *Growing Season*
Conover, Ted   *Rolling Nowhere*
Crichton, Michael   *Electronic Life: How to Think about Computers*
Dear, William   *Dungeon Master: The Disappearance of James Dallas Egbert III*
Durkin, Barbara Wernecke   *Oh, You Dundalk Girls, Can't You Dance the Polka?*
Durrell, Gerald, and Durrell, Lee   *Amateur Naturalist*
Fox, Paula   *One-Eyed Cat*
Gale, Jay   *Young Man's Guide to Sex*
Gallo, Donald R., ed.   *Sixteen: Short Stories by Outstanding Writers for Young Adults*
Godden, Rumer   *Thursday's Children*
Greenberg, Jan   *No Dragons to Slay*
Hall, Lynn   *Uphill All the Way*
Hamilton, Virginia   *Little Love*
Harris, Rosemary   *Zed*
Highwater, Jamake   *Legend Days*
Hirshey, Gerri   *Nowhere to Run: The Story of Soul Music*
Janeczko, Paul B., ed.   *Strings: A Gathering of Family Poems*
Jones, Diana Wynne   *Archer's Goon*
Kohner, Hanna   *Hanna and Walter: A Love Story*
Kurtis, Bill   *Bill Kurtis on Assignment*
Lasky, Kathryn   *Prank*
MacKinnon, Bernie   *Meantime*
Magorian, Michelle   *Back Home*
Mahy, Margaret   *The Changeover: A Supernatural Romance*
Manchester, William   *One Brief Shining Moment: Remembering Kennedy*
Mazer, Norma Fox   *Downtown*
McCullough, Frances, ed.   *Love Is Like the Lion's Tooth: An Anthology of Love Poems*
Montalbano, William D., and Hiaasen, Carl   *Death in China*
Paton Walsh, Jill   *Parcel of Patterns*
Paulsen, Gary   *Tracker*

Sachs, Marilyn   *Fat Girl*
Schirer, Eric W., and Allman, William F.   *Newton at the Bat: The Science in Sports*
Simon, Neil   *Brighton Beach Memoirs*
Sleator, William   *Interstellar Pig*
Southhall, Ivan   *Long Night Watch*
Sterling, Dorothy, ed.   *We Are Your Sisters: Black Women in the Nineteenth Century*
Sweeney, Joyce   *Center Line*
Terkel, Studs   *"Good War": An Oral History of World War Two*
Terry, Wallace   *Bloods: An Oral History of the Vietnam War by Black Veterans*
Thompson, Joyce   *Conscience Place*
Tiburzi, Bonnie   *Takeoff! The Story of America's First Woman Pilot for a Major Airline*
Wain, John   *Free Zone Starts Here*
Walker, Alice   *In Search of Our Mothers' Gardens: Womanist Prose*
Westall, Robert   *Futuretrack 5*
Yolen, Jane   *Heart's Blood*

1985 SELECTIONS

Angell, Judie   *One-way to Ansonia*
Ballard, J. G.   *Empire of the Sun*
Bridgers, Sue Ellen   *Sara Will*
Brin, David   *The Postman*
Brooks, Bruce   *The Moves Make the Man*
Burchard, Sue   *Statue of Liberty: Birth to Rebirth*
Burns, Olive Ann   *Cold Sassy Tree*
Card, Orson Scott   *Ender's Game*
Carter, Alden R.   *Wart, Son of Toad*
Conrad, Pamela   *Prairie Songs*
Couper, Heather, and Pelham, David   *Universe*
Cross, Gillian   *On the Edge*
Dahl, Roald   *Boy: Tales of Childhood*
Dickson, Margaret   *Maddy's Song*
Edelman, Bernard   *Dear America: Letters Home from Vietnam*
Edmonds, Walter D.   *South African Quirt*
Ferris, Timothy   *Spaceshots: The Beauty of Nature beyond Earth*
Foster, Rory C.   *Dr. Wildlife: A Northwoods Veterinarian*
Gallagher, Hugh Gregory   *FDR's Splendid Deception*
Greenbaum, Dorothy, and Laiken, Deidre S.   *Lovestrong*
Halberstam, David   *Amateurs*
Hall, Lynn   *Just One Friend*
Hermes, Patricia   *Solitary Secret*
Highwater, Jamake   *Ceremony of Innocence*
Howker, Janni   *Badger on the Barge and Other Stories*
Irwin, Hadley   *Abby, My Love*
Janeczko, Paul B.   *Pocket Poems: Selected for a Journey*

Jones, Douglas C.   *Gone the Dreams and Dancing*

Kerr, M. E.   *I Stay near You*

Kincaid, Jamaica   *Annie John*

Lawrence, Louise   *Children of the Dust*

Lisle, Janet Taylor   *Sirens and Spies*

Mason, Bobbie Ann   *In Country*

Matsubara, Hisako   *Cranes at Dusk*

McKinley, Robin   *Hero and the Crown*

Meltzer, Milton   *Ain't Gonna Study War No More*

Michaels, Barbara   *Be Buried in the Rain*

Miller, Jonathan, and Pelham, David   *Facts of Life*

Nomberg-Prztyk, Sara   *Auschwitz: True Tales from a Grotesque Land*

North, James   *Freedom Rising*

Oneal, Zibby   *In Summer Light*

Palmer, David R.   *Emergence*

Parnall, Peter   *Daywatchers*

Paulsen, Gary   *Dogsong*

Peck, Richard   *Remembering the Good Times*

Phipson, Joan   *Hit and Run*

Pierce, Meredith Ann   *Woman Who Loved Reindeer*

Rodowsky, Colby   *Julie's Daughter*

Ryerson, Eric   *When Your Parent Drinks Too Much: A Book for Teenagers*

Sleator, William   *Singularity*

Smith, Mary-Anne Tirone   *Book of Phoebe*

Stone, Bruce   *Half Nelson, Full Nelson*

Strieber, Whitley   *Wolf of Shadows*

Talbert, Marc   *Dead Birds Singing*

Voigt, Cynthia   *Runner*

Willard, Nancy   *Things Invisible to See*

Wyden, Peter   *Day One: Before Hiroshima and After*

Yeager, Chuck, and Janos, Leo   *Yeager: An Autobiography*

1986 SELECTIONS

Angelou, Maya   *All God's Children Need Traveling Shoes*

Appel, Allen   *Time after Time*

Archer, Jules   *Incredible Sixties: The Stormy Years That Changed America*

Arnosky, Jim   *Flies in the Water, Fish in the Air: A Personal Introduction to Fly Fishing*

Atwood, Margaret   *Handmaid's Tale*

Avi   *Wolf Rider*

Bess, Clayton   *Tracks*

Blume, Judy   *Letters to Judy: What Your Kids Wish They Could Tell You*

Bodanis, David   *Secret House: 24 Hours in the Strange and Unexpected World in Which We Spend Our Nights and Days*

Branscum, Robbie   *Girl*

Brooks, Bruce   *Midnight Hour Encores*

Brooks, Terry   *Magic Kingdom for Sale—Sold!*

Callahan, Steven   *Adrift: Seventy-Six Days Lost at Sea*

Calvert, Patricia   *Yesterday's Daughter*

Caras, Roger   *Mara Simba: The African Lion*

Card, Orson Scott   *Speaker for the Dead*

Cohen, Susan, and Cohen, Daniel   *Six-pack and a Fake I.D.*

Collier, James Lincoln   *When the Stars Begin to Fall*

Cooney, Caroline B.   *Don't Blame the Music*

Crutcher, Chris   *Stotan!*

Dahl, Roald   *Going Solo*

Dana, Barbara   *Necessary Parties*

Dann, Patty   *Mermaids*

Derby, Pat   *Visiting Miss Pierce*

Fante, John   *1933 Was a Bad Year*

Fine, Judylaine   *Afraid to Ask: A Book for Families to Share about Cancer*

Finnegan, William   *Crossing the Line: A Year in the Land of Apartheid*

Gingher, Marianne   *Bobby Rex's Greatest Hit*

Greenberg, Joanne   *Simple Gifts*

Greene, Constance C.   *Love Letters of J. Timothy Owen*

Grunwald, Lisa   *Summer*

Guy, David   *Second Brother*

Hall, Lynn   *Solitary*

Hambly, Barbara   *Dragonsbane*

Hill, Susan   *Woman in Black*

Hunter, Mollie   *Cat, Herself*

Jones, Diana Wynne   *Howl's Moving Castle*

Kerr, M. E.   *Night Kites*

Koertge, Ron   *Where the Kissing Never Stops*

Korman, Gordon A.   *Son of Interflux*

Lamb, Wendy, ed.   *Meeting the Winter Bike Rider and Other Prize Winning Plays*

Lasky, Kathryn   *Pageant*

LeVert, John   *Flight of the Cassowary*

Levoy, Myron   *Pictures of Adam*

Lopez, Barry   *Arctic Dreams: Imagination and Desire in a Northern Landscape*

Mahy, Margaret   *Catalogue of the Universe*

Mandela, Winnie   *Part of My Soul Went with Him*

Mazer, Harry   *When the Phone Rang*

Moll, Richard   *Public Ivys: A Guide to America's Best Public Undergraduate Colleges and Universities*

Naylor, Phyllis Reynolds   *Keeper*

Okimoto, Jean Davies   *Jason's Women*

Parini, Jay   *Patch Boys*

Patent, Dorothy Hinshaw   *Quest for Artificial Intelligence*

Pei, Lowry   *Family Resemblances*

Ramati, Alexander   *And the Violins Stopped Playing: A Story of the Gypsy Holocaust*

Rinaldi, Ann   *Time Enough for Drums*

Rostkowski, Margaret I.   *After the Dancing Days*

Rylant, Cynthia   *Fine White Dust*

Sanders, Scott R.   *Bad Man Ballad*
Spiegelman, Art   *Maus: A Survivor's Tale*
Sullivan, Jack, ed.   *Penguin Encyclopedia of Horror and the Supernatural*
Thompson, Julian   *Band of Angels*
Townsend, Sue   *Adrian Mole Diaries*
Voigt, Cynthia   *Izzy, Willy-Nilly*
Wilford, John Noble   *Riddle of the Dinosaur*
Willey, Margaret   *Finding David Dolores*
Wirths, Claudine G., and Bowman-Kruhm, Mary   *I Hate School: How to Hang In and When to Drop Out*
Zerman, Melvyn Bernard   *Taking on the Press: Constitutional Rights in Conflict*
Zolotow, Charlotte, ed.   *Early Sorrow: Ten Stories of Youth*

1987 SELECTIONS

Allen, Maury   *Jackie Robinson: A Life Remembered*
Anson, Robert Sam   *Best Intentions: The Education and Killing of Edmund Perry*
Bacon, Katherine Jay   *Shadow and Light*
Benedict, Helen   *Safe, Strong, and Streetwise*
Bosse, Malcolm   *Captives of Time*
Bradshaw, Gillian   *Beacon at Alexandria*
Bridgers, Sue Ellen   *Permanent Connections*
Bull, Emma   *War for the Oaks*
Card, Orson Scott   *Seventh Son*
Carter, Alden R.   *Sheila's Dying*
Carter, Peter   *Bury the Dead*
Cole, Brock   *The Goats*
Collins, Max Allan   *Dark City*
Conrad, Pamela   *What I Did for Roman*
Cross, Gillian   *Chartbreaker*
Crutcher, Chris   *Crazy Horse Electric Game*
Cullen, Brian   *What Niall Saw*
Davis, Jenny   *Good-bye and Keep Cold*
Dolmetsch, Paul, and Mauricette, Gail, eds.   *Teens Talk about Alcohol and Alcoholism*
Dorris, Michael   *Yellow Raft in Blue Water*
Einstein, Charles, ed.   *Fireside Book of Baseball,* 4th ed.
Feinstein, John   *Season on the Brink: A Year with Bob Knight and the Indiana Hoosiers*
Ferris, Jean   *Invincible Summer*
Fink, Ida   *Scrap of Time: And Other Stories*
Freedman, Russell   *Indian Chiefs*
Gallo, Donald R., ed.   *Visions: Nineteen Short Stories by Outstanding Writers for Young Adults*
Gibbons, Kaye   *Ellen Foster*
Gies, Miep, and Gold, Alison Leslie   *Anne Frank Remembered: The Story of Miep Gies, Who Helped to Hide the Frank Family*
Gordon, Ruth, ed.   *Under All Silences: Shades of Love: An Anthology of Poems*
Gordon, Sheila   *Waiting for the Rain*
Hamlin, Liz   *I Remember Valentine*

Haskins, James   *Black Music in America: A History through Its People*
Hearne, Betsy   *Love Lines: Poetry in Person*
Hentoff, Nat   *American Heroes: In and out of School*
Howker, Janni   *Isaac Campion*
Jacques, Brian   *Redwall*
Janeczko, Paul B., ed.   *Going Over to Your Place: Poems for Each Other*
Johnson, Lou Anne   *Making Waves: The Story of a Woman in This Man's Navy*
Kerr, M. E.   *Fell*
Klass, Perri Elizabeth   *Not Entirely Benign Procedure: Four Years as a Medical Student*
Klass, Sheila Solomon   *Page Four*
Kogan, Judith   *Nothing but the Best: The Struggle for Perfection at the Juilliard School*
Koontz, Dean R.   *Watchers*
Korman, Gordon A.   *Semester in the Life of a Garbage Bag*
Kropp, Lloyd   *Greencastle*
Kuklin, Susan   *Reaching for Dreams: A Ballet from Rehearsal to Opening Night*
L'Engle, Madeleine   *Many Waters*
Lackey, Mercedes   *Arrows of the Queen*
Leder, Jane M.   *Dead Serious: A Book about Teenagers and Teenage Suicide*
Levitin, Sonia   *Return*
Llewellyn, Chris   *Fragments from the Fire: The Triangle Shirtwaist Company Fire of March 25, 1911*
MacLean, John   *Mac*
Mahy, Margaret   *Tricksters*
Marshall, Kathryn   *In the Combat Zone: An Oral History of American Women in Vietnam, 1966–1975*
Mazer, Harry   *Girl of His Dreams*
Mazer, Norma Fox   *After the Rain*
McKillip, Patricia A.   *Fool's Run*
Meltzer, Milton, ed.   *American Revolutionaries: A History in Their Own Words, 1750–1800*
Meyer, Carolyn   *Denny's Tapes*
———   *Voices of South Africa: Growing Up in a Troubled Land*
Michelson, Maureen R., ed.   *Women and Work: Photographs and Personal Writings*
Naylor, Phyllis Reynolds   *Unexpected Pleasures*
———   *Year of the Gopher*
Palmer, Laura   *Shrapnel in the Heart: Letters and Remembrances from the Vietnam Memorial*
Paulsen, Gary   *Crossing*
Peck, Richard   *Princess Ashley*
Pfeffer, Susan Beth   *The Year without Michael*
Pullman, Philip   *The Ruby in the Smoke*

Rendell, Ruth   *Heartstones*
Salassi, Otto R.   *Jimmy D., Sidewinder, and Me*
Salzman, Mark   *Iron and Silk*
Shilts, Randy   *And the Band Played On: Politics, People, and the AIDS Epidemic*
Sleator, William   *Boy Who Reversed Himself*
Smith, Mary-Anne Tirone   *Lament for a Silver-eyed Woman*
Tapert, Annette, ed.   *Lines of Battle: Letters from U.S. Servicemen, 1941–45*
Terris, Susan   *Nell's Quilt*
Voigt, Cynthia   *Sons from Afar*
Watson, Lyall   *Dreams of Dragons: Riddles of Natural History*
Wells, Rosemary   *Through the Hidden Door*
Williams, Juan   *Eyes on the Prize: America's Civil Rights Years, 1954–1965*
Woolley, Persia   *Child of the Northern Spring*

1988 SELECTIONS

Ashabranner, Brent   *Always to Remember: The Vietnam Veterans Memorial*
Bova, Ben   *Welcome to Moonbase*
Brown, Rita Mae   *Starting from Scratch: A Different Kind of Writers' Manual*
Cable, Mary   *Blizzard of '88*
Cagin, Seth   *We Are Not Afraid: The Story of Goodman, Schwerner, and Chaney and the Civil Rights Campaign for Mississippi*
Cleary, Beverly   *Girl from Yamhill: A Memoir*
Coman, Carolyn   *Body and Soul: Ten American Women*
Cormier, Robert   *Fade*
Deaver, Julie Reece   *Say Goodnight, Gracie*
Edgerton, Clyde   *Floatplane Notebooks*
Feldbaum, Carl B., and Bee, Ronald J.   *Looking the Tiger in the Eye: Confronting the Nuclear Threat*
Flanigan, Sara   *Alice*
Fleischman, Paul   *Joyful Noise: Poems for Two Voices*
Freedman, Russell   *Lincoln: A Photobiography*
Gelman, Rita Golden   *Inside Nicaragua: Young People's Dreams and Fears*
Giddings, Robert   *War Poets*
Gordon, Jacquie   *Give Me One Wish*
Greenberg, Joanne   *Of Such Small Differences*
Greene, Marilyn, and Provost, Gary   *Finder: The Story of a Private Investigator*
Hailey, Kendall   *Day I Became an Autodidact: And the Advice, Adventures, and Acrimonies That Befell Me Thereafter*
Haing, Ngor, and Warner, Roger   *Cambodian Odyssey*
Hambly, Barbara   *Those Who Hunt the Night*
Hamilton, Virginia   *Anthony Burns: The Defeat and Triumph of a Fugitive Slave*
———   *In the Beginnning: Creation Stories from Around the World*

Haskins, James, and Benson, Kathleen   *60's Reader*
Hillerman, Tony   *Thief of Time*
Hinton, S. E.   *Taming the Star Runner*
Hoffman, Alice   *At Risk*
Hoover, H. M.   *Dawn Palace: The Story of Medea*
Hotze, Sollace   *Circle Unbroken*
Janeczko, Paul B., ed.   *Music of What Happens: Poems That Tell Stories*
Kennedy, William P.   *Toy Soldiers*
Kingsolver, Barbara   *Bean Trees*
Knudson, R. R., and Swenson, May, eds.   *American Sports Poems*
Koertge, Ron   *The Arizona Kid*
Komunyakaa, Yusef   *Dien Cai Dau*
Kozol, Jonathon   *Rachel and Her Children: Homeless Families in America*
Langone, John   *AIDS: The Facts*
Lopes, Sal, ed.   *Wall: Images and Offerings from the Vietnam Veterans Memorial*
Mackay, Donald A.   *Building of Manhattan*
Madaras, Lynda   *Lynda Madaras Talks to Teens about AIDS: An Essential Guide for Parents, Teachers, and Young People*
Mahy, Margaret   *Memory*
Mazer, Norma Fox   *Silver*
McKinley, Robin   *Outlaws of Sherwood*
Meltzer, Milton   *Rescue: The Story of How Gentiles Saved Jews in the Holocaust*
Mills, Judie   *John F. Kennedy*
Morrison, Lillian, Selections.   *Rhythm Road: Poems to Move You*
Myers, Walter Dean   *Fallen Angels*
———   *Scorpions*
Noonan, Michael   *McKenzie's Boots*
Paulsen, Gary   *Island*
Pringle, Terry   *Preacher's Boy*
Pullman, Philip   *Shadow in the North*
Riddles, Libby   *Race across Alaska: The First Woman to Win the Iditarod Tells Her Story*
Rinaldi, Ann   *Last Silk Dress*
Ritter, Lawrence S.   *Babe: A Life in Pictures*
Rochman, Hazel, ed.   *Somehow Tenderness Survives: Stories of Southern Africa*
Rogasky, Barbara   *Smoke and Ashes: The Story of the Holocaust*
Ruskin, Cindy   *Quilt: Stories from the Names Project*
Rylant, Cynthia   *Kindness*
Scholl, Hans, and Scholl, Sophie   *At the Heart of the White Rose: Letters and Diaries of Hans and Sophie Scholl*
Severin, Tim   *Ulysses Voyage: Sea Search for the Odyssey*
Sleator, William   *Duplicate*
Tang, Hsi-yang   *Living Treasures: An Odyssey through China's Extraordinary Nature Reserves*

Vare, Ethlie Ann   *Mothers of Invention: From the Bra to the Bomb: Forgotten Women and Their Unforgettable Ideas*

Willeford, Charles   *I Was Looking for a Street*

Wolff, Virginia Euwer   *Probably Still Nick Swansen*

Wyss, Thelma Hatch   *Here at the Scenic-Vu Motel*

1990 SELECTIONS

Amos, James   *Memorial: A Novel of the Vietnam War*

Anderson, Joan   *American Family Farm*

Andronik, Catherine M.   *Quest for a King: Searching for the Real King Arthur*

Armor, John, and Wright, Peter   *Manzanar*

Banfield, Susan   *Rights of Man, The Reign of Terror: The Story of the French Revolution*

Block, Francesca Lia   *Weetzie Bat*

Bode, Janet   *New Kids on the Block: Oral Histories of Immigrant Teens*

Brooks, Bruce   *No Kidding*

———   *On the Wing*

Busselle, Rebecca   *Bathing Ugly*

Carson, Jo   *Stories I Ain't Told Nobody Yet: Selections from the People Pieces*

Carter, Alden R.   *Up Country*

Childress, Mark   *V for Victor*

Cohen, Susan, and Cohen, Daniel   *When Someone You Know Is Gay*

Cole, Brock   *Celine*

Conrad, Pamela   *My Daniel*

Conway, Jill Ker   *Road from Coorain*

Crew, Linda   *Children of the River*

Crutcher, Chris   *Chinese Handcuffs*

Davis, Lindsey   *Silver Pigs*

Deuker, Carl   *On the Devil's Court*

Dickinson, Peter   *Eva*

Duder, Tessa   *In Lane Three, Alex Archer*

Duncan, Lois   *Don't Look behind You*

Grant, Cynthia D.   *Phoenix Rising; or, How to Survive Your Life*

Green, Connie Jordan   *War at Home*

Hayslip, Le Ly, and Wurts, Jay   *When Heaven and Earth Changed Places: A Vietnamese Woman's Journal from War to Peace*

Helprin, Mark   *Swan Lake*

Hobbs, Will   *Bearstone*

Hodges, Margaret   *Making a Difference: The Story of an American Family*

Homes, A. M.   *Jack*

Horner, John R., and Gorman, James   *Digging Dinosaurs*

Hudson, Jan   *Sweetgrass*

Janeczko, Paul B.   *Brickyard Summer*

Klass, David   *Wrestling with Honor*

Klein, Norma   *No More Saturday Nights*

Krementz, Jill   *How It Feels to Fight for Your Life*

Kuklin, Susan   *Fighting Back: What Some People Are Doing about AIDS*

Laird, Elizabeth   *Loving Ben*

Lanker, Brian   *I Dream a World: Portraits of Black Women Who Changed America*

Levitin, Sonia   *Silver Days*

Macaulay, David   *Way Things Work*

Maguire, Gregory   *I Feel Like the Morning Star*

Marsden, John   *So Much to Tell You*

McCullough, Frances, ed.   *Earth, Air, Fire and Water*

McKibben, Bill   *End of Nature*

Meltzer, Milton   *Benjamin Franklin: The New American*

———   *Voices from the Civil War: A Documentary History of the Great American Conflict*

Mickle, Shelley Fraser   *Queen of October*

Miller, Jim Wayne   *Newfound*

Moeri, Louise   *Forty-third War*

Monk, Lorraine   *Photographs That Changed the World*

Murphy, Pat   *City, Not Long After*

Murrow, Liza Ketchum   *Fire in the Heart*

Namioka, Lensey   *Island of Ogres*

Naughton, Jim   *My Brother Stealing Second*

Nelson, Theresa   *And One for All*

Newth, Mette   *Abduction*

Norman, David, and Milner, Angela   *Dinosaur*

Paulsen, Gary   *Voyage of the Frog*

———   *Winter Room*

Pevsner, Stella   *How Could You Do It, Diana?*

Pinkwater, Jill   *Buffalo Brenda*

Pringle, Terry   *Fine Time to Leave Me*

Rhodes, Richard   *Farm: A Year in the Life of an American Farmer*

Saul, John   *Creature*

Shannon, George   *Unlived Affections*

Sieruta, Peter D.   *Heartbeats and Other Stories*

Smith, K.   *Skeeter*

Staples, Suzanne Fisher   *Shabanu: Daughter of the Wind*

Tan, Amy   *The Joy Luck Club*

Taylor, Theodore   *Sniper*

Turney, David C.   *Why Are They Weeping? South Africans under Apartheid*

Van Raven, Pieter   *Great Man's Secret*

White, Ellen Emerson   *Long Live the Queen*

Wilson, David Henry   *Coachman Rat*

Wilson, F. Paul   *Dydeetown World*

Wilson, Robert Charles   *Gypsies*

Wolff, Tobias   *This Boy's Life: A Memoir*

Zindel, Paul   *Begonia for Miss Applebaum*

1991 SELECTIONS

Abdul-Jabbar, Kareem, and McCarthy, Mignon   *Kareem*

Agard, John, comp.   *Life Doesn't Frighten Me at All*

Anderson, Scott   *Distant Fires*

Ansa, Tina McElroy   *Baby of the Family*

Appel, Allen   *Till the End of Time*

Avi   *True Confessions of Charlotte Doyle*

Baldwin, J., ed.   *Whole Earth Ecolog: The Best of Environmental Tools and Ideas*

Bell, Clare   *Ratha and Thistle-chaser*

Bennett, James   *I Can Hear the Mourning Dove*

Blake, Jeanne   *Risky Times: How to Be AIDS-Smart and Stay Healthy*

Bode, Janet   *Voices of Rape*

Brooks, Polly Schoyer   *Beyond the Myth: The Story of Joan of Arc*

Cannon, A. E.   *Shadow Brothers*

Carter, Peter   *Borderlands*

Caseley, Judith   *Kisses*

Chestnut, J. L.   *Black in Selma: The Uncommon Life of J. L. Chestnut, Jr.*

Chetwin, Grace   *Collidescope*

Clarke, J.   *The Heroic Life of Al Capsella*

Clements, Bruce   *Tom Loves Anna Loves Tom*

Crispin, A. C.   *Starbridge*

Cushman, Kathleen, and Miller, Montana   *Circus Dreams*

Doherty, Berlie   *White Peak Farm*

Donofrio, Beverly   *Riding in Cars with Boys*

Embury, Barbara   *Dream Is Alive: A Flight of Discovery Aboard the Space Shuttle*

Ferris, Jean   *Across the Grain*

Freedman, Russell   *Franklin Delano Roosevelt*

Freedman, Samuel G.   *Small Victories: The Real World of a Teacher, Her Students and Their High School*

Friedman, Ina R.   *Other Victims: First-Person Stories of Non-Jews Persecuted by the Nazis*

Fuer, Elizabeth   *Paper Doll*

Gallo, Donald R., ed.   *Speaking for Ourselves: Autobiographical Sketches by Notable Authors of Books for Young Adults*

Gilmore, Kate   *Enter Three Witches*

Hall, Barbara   *Dixie Storms*

Hamanaka, Sheila   *Journey*

Hamilton, Virginia   *Cousins*

Harrison, Sue   *Mother Earth Father Sky*

Haskins, James   *Black Dance in America*

Hendry, Frances Mary   *Quest for a Maid*

Ho, Minfong   *Rice without Rain*

Hudson, Jan   *Dawn Rider*

Human Rights in China   *Children of the Dragon: The Story of Tiananmen Square*

James, J. Alison   *Sing for a Gentle Rain*

Janeczko, Paul B.   *Place My Words Are Looking For: What Poets Say about and through Their Work*

Jordan, Robert   *Eye of the World*

Katz, William Loren   *Breaking the Chains: African American Slave Resistance*

Kilworth, Garry   *Foxes of Firstdark*

Kisor, Henry   *What's That Pig Outdoors? A Memoir of Deafness*

Klause, Annette Curtis   *The Silver Kiss*

Koertge, Ron   *Boy in the Moon*

Korman, Gordon A.   *Losing Joe's Place*

Larson, Gary   *Prehistory of The Far Side: A Tenth Anniversary Exhibit*

Lauber, Patricia   *Seeing Earth from Space*

Levin, Betty   *Brother Moose*

Lord, Bette Bao   *Legacies: A Chinese Mosaic*

Martin, Valerie   *Mary Reilly*

McCorkle, Jill   *Ferris Beach*

Meltzer, Milton   *Columbus and the World around Him*

Myers, Walter Dean   *Mouse Rap*

Naar, Jon   *Design for a Livable Planet*

Naidoo, Beverley   *Chain of Fire*

Naylor, Phyllis Reynolds   *Send No Blessings*

O'Brien, Tim   *Things They Carried*

Parks, Gordon   *Voices in the Mirror: An Autobiography*

Paulsen, Gary   *Woodsong*

Pershall, Mary K.   *You Take the High Road*

Pierce, Meredith Ann   *Pearl of the Soul of the World*

Popham, Melinda Worth   *Skywater*

Pullman, Philip   *Tiger in the Well*

Ray, Delia   *Nation Torn: The Story of How the Civil War Began*

Rylant, Cynthia   *Couple of Kooks and Other Stories about Love*

———   *Soda Jerk*

Sanders, Dori   *Clover*

Schami, Rafik   *Hand Full of Stars*

Sleator, William   *Strange Attractors*

Snyder, Zilpha Keatley   *Libby on Wednesday*

Soto, Gary   *Baseball in April and Other Stories*

Spinelli, Jerry   *Maniac Magee*

Stoll, Cliff   *The Cuckoo's Egg: Tracking a Spy through the Maze of Computer Espionage*

Strauss, Gwen   *Trail of Stones*

Taylor, Mildred D.   *Road to Memphis*

Van Raven, Pieter   *Pickle and Price*

Voigt, Cynthia   *On Fortune's Wheel*

Weiss, Ann E.   *Who's to Know? Information, the Media and Public Awareness*

Willey, Margaret   *Saving Lenny*

Woolley, Persia   *Queen of the Summer Stars*

Wrede, Patricia C.   *Dealing with Dragons*

1992 SELECTIONS

Aaron, Henry, and Wheeler, Lonnie   *I Had a Hammer*

Adams, Douglas, and Carwardine, Mark   *Last Chance to See*

Anastos, Phillip   *Illegal: Seeking the American Dream*

Arter, Jim   *Gruel and Unusual Punishment*

Avi   *Nothing but the Truth*

Bing, Leon   *Do or Die*

Bode, Janet   *Beating the Odds: Stories of Unexpected Achievers*

Brooks, Bruce   *Predator!*

Buss, Fran Leeper, and Cubias, Daisy   *Journey of the Sparrows*

Cannon, A. E.   *Amazing Gracie*

Cary, Lorene   *Black Ice*

Choi, Sook Nyul   *Year of Impossible Goodbyes*

Cooper, J. California   *Family*

Corman, Avery   *Prized Possessions*

Cormier, Robert   *We All Fall Down*

Counter, S. Allen   *North Pole Legacy: Black, White and Eskimo*

Crichton, Michael   *Jurassic Park*

Crutcher, Chris   *Athletic Shorts: Six Short Stories*

Davis, Jenny   *Checking on the Moon*

Durham, Michael S.   *Powerful Days: The Civil Rights Photography of Charles Moore*

Fleischman, Paul   *Borning Room*

Fluek, Toby Knobel   *Memories of My Life in a Polish Village, 1930–1949*

Fox, Paula   *Monkey Island*

Freedman, Russell   *Wright Brothers: How They Invented the Airplane*

Fussell, Samuel Wilson   *Muscle: Confessions of an Unlikely Bodybuilder*

Gaiman, Neil, and Pratchett, Terry   *Good Omens: The Nice and Accurate Prophecies of Agnes Nutter, Witch*

Glenn, Mel   *My Friend's Got This Problem, Mr. Candler*

Hall, Lynn   *Flying Changes*

Hathorn, Libby   *Thunderwith*

Hayden, Torey L.   *Ghost Girl: The True Story of a Child Who Refused to Talk*

Hayes, Daniel   *Trouble with Lemons*

Henry, Sue   *Murder on the Iditarod Trail*

Higa, Tomiko   *Girl with the White Flag: An Inspiring Tale of Love and Courage in War Time*

Hobbs, Will   *Downriver*

Honeycutt, Natalie   *Ask Me Something Easy*

Jones, Diana Wynne   *Castle in the Air*

Kingsolver, Barbara   *Animal Dreams*

Kotlowitz, Alex   *There Are No Children Here: The Story of Two Boys Growing Up in the Other America*

Kuklin, Susan   *What Do I Do Now? Talking about Teenage Pregnancy*

Lauber, Patricia   *Summer of Fire: Yellowstone, 1988*

Lee, Tanith   *Black Unicorn*

Lipsyte, Robert   *Brave*

Lyons, Mary E.   *Sorrow's Kitchen: The Life and Folklore of Zora Neale Hurston*

MacLachlan, Patricia   *Journey*

McCaffrey, Anne   *Pegasus in Flight*

McCammon, Robert R.   *Boy's Life*

Montgomery, Sy   *Walking with the Great Apes: Jane Goodall, Dian Fossey, Birute Galdikas*

Morpurgo, Michael   *Waiting for Anya*

Murphy, Jim   *Boy's War: Confederate and Union Soldiers Talk about the Civil War*

Myers, Walter Dean   *Now Is Your Time! The African-American Struggle for Freedom*

Orlev, Uri   *Man from the Other Side*

Paterson, Katherine   *Lyddie*

Paulsen, Gary   *Cookcamp*

——— *Monument*

Plummer, Louise   *My Name Is Sus5an Smith: The 5 is Silent*

Rappaport, Doreen   *American Women: Their Lives in Their Words*

Rinaldi, Ann   *Wolf by the Ears*

Savage, Georgia   *House Tibet*

Shusterman, Neal   *What Daddy Did*

Spiegelman, Art   *Maus: A Survivor's Tale II: And Here My Troubles Began*

Spinelli, Jerry   *There's a Girl in My Hammerlock*

Sullivan, Charles, ed.   *Children of Promise: African-American Literature and Art for Young People*

Tepper, Sheri S.   *Beauty*

Thesman, Jean   *Rain Catchers*

Westall, Robert   *Kingdom by the Sea*

White, Ryan, and Cunningham, Ann Marie   *Ryan White: My Own Story*

Williams-Garcia, Rita   *Fast Talk on a Slow Track*

Wisler, G. Clifton   *Red Cap*

Wolff, Virginia Euwer   *Mozart Season*

Yolen, Jane, and Greenberg, Martin H., eds.   *Vampires: A Collection of Original Stories*

1993 SELECTIONS

Armstrong, Jennifer   *Steal Away*

Arrick, Fran   *What You Don't Know Can Kill You*

Avi   *Blue Heron*

Beattie, Owen, and Geiger, John   *Buried in Ice: The Mystery of a Lost Arctic Expedition*

Berry, James   *Ajeemah and His Son*

Block, Francesca Lia   *Cherokee Bat and the Goat Guys*

Bonner, Cindy   *Lily*

Brooks, Bruce   *What Hearts*

Brooks, Martha   *Two Moons in August*

Bunting, Eve   *Jumping the Nail*

Campbell, Eric   *Place of Lions*

Caseley, Judith   *My Father, the Nutcase*

Cooney, Caroline B.   *Flight #116 Is Down*

Cooper, Louise   *Sleep of Stone*

Cormier, Robert   *Tunes for Bears to Dance To*

Craig, Kit   *Gone*

Currie, Elliott   *Dope and Trouble: Portraits of Delinquent Youth*

Davis, Terry   *If Rock and Roll Were a Machine*

Dickinson, Peter   *AK*

Doherty, Berlie   *Dear Nobody*

Duncan, Lois   *Who Killed My Daughter? The True Story of a Mother's Search for Her Daughter's Murderer*

Edelman, Marian Wright   *Measure of Our Success: A Letter to My Children and Yours*

Ferry, Charles   *Binge*

Ford, Michael Thomas   *100 Questions and Answers about AIDS: A Guide for Young People*

Forman, James D.   *Becca's Story*

Freedman, Russell   *Indian Winter*

Garland, Sherry   *Song of the Buffalo Boy*

Gould, Steven   *Jumper*

Gravelle, Karen, and Peterson, Leslie   *Teenage Fathers*

Gregory, Kristiana   *Earthquake at Dawn*

Grisham, John   *Pelican Brief*

Gurney, James   *Dinotopia: A Land Apart from Time*

Guy, Rosa   *Music of Summer*

Hall, Barbara   *Fool's Hill*

Haskins, James   *One More River to Cross: The Stories of Twelve Black Americans*

Hesse, Karen   *Letters from Rifka*

Hobbs, Will   *Big Wander*

Hoffman, Alice   *Turtle Moon*

Horrigan, Kevin   *Right Kinds of Heroes: Coach Bob Shannon and the East St. Louis Flyers.*

Hotze, Sollace   *Acquainted with the Night*

Johnson, Earvin "Magic"   *What You Can Do to Avoid AIDS*

Johnson, Scott   *One of the Boys*

Jones, Diana Wynne   *Sudden Wild Magic*

Kaye, Geraldine   *Someone Else's Baby*

Kimble, Bo   *For You, Hank: The Story of Hank Gathers and Bo Kimble*

Kincaid, Nanci   *Crossing Blood*

Kittredge, Mary   *Teens with AIDS Speak Out*

Koertge, Ron   *Harmony Arms*

Koller, Jackie French   *Primrose Way*

Lackey, Mercedes   *Bardic Voices: The Lark and the Wren*

Laird, Elizabeth   *Kiss the Dust*

Lyons, Mary E.   *Letters from a Slave Girl: The Story of Harriet Jacobs*

Magorian, Michelle   *Not a Swan*

Marlette, Doug   *In Your Face: A Cartoonist at Work*

McKissack, Patricia C., and McKissack, Fredrick   *Sojourner Truth: Ain't I a Woman?*

Meyer, Carolyn   *Where the Broken Heart Still Beats: The Story of Cynthia Ann Parker*

Mowry, Jess   *Way Past Cool*

Murphy, Jim   *Long Road to Gettysburg*

Myers, Walter Dean   *Righteous Revenge of Artemis Bonner*

———   *Somewhere in the Darkness*

Nelson, Theresa   *Beggar's Ride*

Parks, Rosa, and Haskins, Jim   *Rosa Parks: My Story*

Paulsen, Gary   *Haymeadow*

Pfeffer, Susan Beth   *Family of Strangers*

Powell, Randy   *Is Kissing a Girl Who Smokes Like Licking an Ashtray?*

Pullman, Philip   *Broken Bridge*

Reaver, Chap   *Little Bit Dead*

Reidelbach, Maria   *Completely Mad: A History of the Comic Book and Magazine*

Reiss, Kathryn   *Time Windows*

Rice, Robert   *Last Pendragon*

Rinaldi, Ann   *Break with Charity: A Story about the Salem Witch Trials*

Robertson, James I.   *Civil War! America Becomes One Nation*

Rylant, Cynthia   *Missing May*

Salisbury, Graham   *Blue Skin of the Sea*

Scieszka, Jon   *Stinky Cheese Man and Other Fairly Stupid Tales*

Sherman, Josepha   *Child of Faerie, Child of Earth*

Simon, Neil   *Lost in Yonkers*

Steffan, Joseph   *Honor Bound: A Gay American Fights for the Right to Serve His Country*

Stevermer, Carolyn   *River Rats*

Stoehr, Shelley   *Crosses*

Taylor, Clark   *House That Crack Built*

Taylor, Theodore   *Weirdo*

Thesman, Jean   *When the Road Ends*

Uchida, Yoshiko   *Invisible Thread*

Ure, Jean   *Plague*

Westall, Robert   *Stormsearch*

———   *Yaxley's Cat*

White, Ruth   *Weeping Willow*

Wieler, Diana   *Bad Boy*

Williams, Michael   *Crocodile Burning*

Wilson, Budge   *Leaving*

Winton, Tim   *Lockie Leonard, Human Torpedo*

Woodson, Jacqueline   *Maizon at Blue Hill*

Wrede, Patricia C.   *Searching for Dragons*

Yolen, Jane   *Briar Rose*

Zambreno, Mary Frances   *Plague of Sorcerers*

Zindel, Paul   *Pigman and Me*

1994 SELECTIONS

Alcock, Vivien   *Singer to the Sea God*

Anderson, Rachel   *Bus People*

Ashe, Arthur   *Days of Grace*

Atkin, S. Beth   *Voices from the Fields: Children of Migrant Farmworkers Tell Their Stories*

Berg, Elizabeth   *Durable Goods*

Block, Francesca Lia   *Missing Angel Juan*

Blume, Judy   *Here's to You Rachel Robinson*

Brandenburg, Jim   *To the Top of the World: Adventures with Arctic Wolves*

Bruchac, Joseph   *Dawn Land*

Conly, Jane Leslie   *Crazy Lady!*

Cooney, Caroline B.   *Whatever Happened to Janie?*

Crutcher, Chris   *Staying Fat for Sarah Byrnes*

Delany, Sarah, and Delany, A. Elizabeth   *Having Our Say: The Delany Sisters' First 100 Years*

Deuker, Carl   *Heart of a Champion*

Dickinson, Peter   *Bone from a Dry Sea*

Drucker, Olga Levy   *Kindertransport*

Esquivel, Laura   *Like Water for Chocolate*

Feelings, Tom   *Soul Looks Back in Wonder*

Fleischman, Paul   *Bull Run*

Freedman, Russell   *Eleanor Roosevelt: A Life of Discovery*

Gaines, Ernest J.   *A Lesson before Dying*

Garland, Sherry   *Shadow of the Dragon*

Gee, Maurice   *The Champion*

Gibbons, Kaye   *Charms for an Easy Life*

Grant, Cynthia D.   *Shadow Man*

——   *Uncle Vampire*

Hahn, Mary Downing   *The Wind Blows Backward*

Haynes, David   *Right by My Side*

Hobbs, Will   *Beardance*

Hodge, Merle   *For the Life of Laetitia*

Isaacson, Philip M.   *A Short Walk around the Pyramids and through the World of Art*

Janeczko, Paul B.   *Stardust otel*

——, ed.   *Looking for Your Name: A Collection of Contemporary Poems*

Johnson, Angela   *Toning the Sweep*

Jordan, Sherryl   *Winter of Fire*

Kaysen, Susanna   *Girl, Interrupted*

Le Mieux, A. C.   *The TV Guidance Counselor*

Levine, Ellen   *Freedom's Children: Young Civil Rights Activists Tell Their Own Stories*

Littlefield, Bill   *Champions: Stories of Ten Remarkable Athletes*

Lowry, Lois   *The Giver*

Lynch, Chris   *Shadow Boxer*

MacLachlan, Patricia   *Baby*

Macy, Sue   *A Whole New Ballgame: The Story of the All-American Girls Professional Baseball League*

Mazer, Harry   *Who Is Eddie Leonard?*

Mazer, Norma Fox   *Out of Control*

McKinley, Robin   *Deerskin*

Merrick, Monte   *Shelter*

Meyer, Carolyn   *White Lilacs*

Mori, Kyoko   *Shizuko's Daughter*

Myers, Walter Dean   *Malcolm X: By Any Means Necessary*

Napoli, Donna Jo   *The Magic Circle*

Paulsen, Gary   *Harris and Me: A Summer Remembered*

——   *Nightjohn*

Philbrick, Rodman   *Freak the Mighty*

Qualey, Marsha   *Revolutions of the Heart*

Rendell, Ruth   *The Crocodile Bird*

Reynolds, Marilyn   *Detour for Emmy*

Rinaldi, Ann   *In My Father's House*

Roberson, Jennifer   *Lady of the Forest: A Novel of Sherwood*

Rochman, Hazel, and McCampbell, Darlene Z., eds.   *Who Do You Think You Are? Stories of Friends and Enemies*

Ruby, Lois   *Miriam's Well*

Sleator, William   *Oddballs*

Smith, Wayne   *Thor*

Staples, Suzanne Fisher   *Haveli*

Sutcliff, Rosemary   *Black Ships before Troy: The Story of the Illiad*

Sweeney, Joyce   *The Tiger Orchard*

Tamar, Erika   *Fair Game*

Taylor, Theodore   *Timothy of the Cay*

Temple, Frances   *Grab Hands and Run*

Verhoeven, Rian, and Van Der Rol, Ruud   *Anne Frank: Beyond the Diary: A Photographic Remembrance*

Vick, Helen Hughes   *Walker of Time*

Volavkova, Hana, ed.   *I Never Saw Another Butterfly: Children's Drawings and Poems from Terezin Concentration Camp, 1942–1944*

Walker, Kate   *Peter*

Watson, Larry   *Montana 1948*

Weaver, Will   *Striking Out*

Wittlinger, Ellen   *Lombardo's Law*

Wolff, Virginia Euwer   *Make Lemonade*

Yep, Laurence, ed.   *American Dragons: Twenty-five Asian American Voices*

1995 SELECTIONS

Alvarez, Julia   *In the Time of the Butterflies*

Bachrach, Susan D.   *Tell Them We Remember: The Story of the Holocaust*

Bauer, Marion Dane, ed.   *Am I Blue? Coming Out from the Silence*

Beake, Lesley   *Song of Be*

Bennett, James   *Dakota Dream*

Bode, Janet, and Mack, Stan   *Heartbreak and Roses: Real-life Stories of Troubled Love*

Bonner, Cindy   *Looking after Lily*

Bosse, Malcolm   *The Examination*

Brooks, Martha   *Traveling on into the Light and Other Stories*

Brown, Mary   *Pigs Don't Fly*

Bull, Emma   *Finder: A Novel of the Borderlands*

Butler, Octavia E.   *Parable of the Sower*

Carlson, Lori M., ed.   *Cool Salsa: Bilingual Poems on Growing Up Latino in the United States*

Cooney, Caroline B.   *Driver's Ed*
Coville, Bruce   *Oddly Enough*
Cushman, Karen   *Catherine, Called Birdy*
Farmer, Nancy   *The Ear, the Eye, and the Arm*
Fletcher, Susan   *Flight of the Dragon Kyn*
Freedman, Russell   *Kids at Work: Lewis Hine and the Crusade against Child Labor*
French, Albert   *Billy*
Hambly, Barbara   *Stranger at the Wedding*
Hayes, Daniel   *No Effect*
Hesse, Karen   *Phoenix Rising*
Hite, Sid   *It's Nothing to a Mountain*
Jones, Maurice K.   *Say It Loud! The Story of Rap Music*
Jordan, Sherryl   *Wolf-Woman*
Kerr, M. E.   *Deliver Us from Evie*
Kindl, Patrice   *Owl in Love*
King, Laurie R.   *The Beekeeper's Apprentice; or, On the Segregation of the Queen*
Koebner, Linda   *Zoo Book: The Evolution of Wildlife Conservation Centers*
Koertge, Ron   *Tiger, Tiger Burning Bright*
Krisher, Trudy   *Spite Fences*
Kuklin, Susan   *After a Suicide: Young People Speak Up*
Lasky, Kathryn   *Beyond the Burning Time*
Lawlor, Laurie   *Shadow Catcher: The Life and Works of Edward S. Curtis*
Levitin, Sonia   *Escape from Egypt*
Lynch, Chris   *Gypsy Davey*
———   *Iceman*
Marrin, Albert   *Unconditional Surrender: U. S. Grant and the Civil War*
Marsden, John   *Letters from the Inside*
McCall, Nathan   *Makes Me Wanna Holler: A Young Black Man in America*
Myers, Walter Dean   *The Glory Field*
Naythons, Matthew   *Sarajevo: A Portrait of the Siege*
Nelson, Theresa   *Earthshine*
Nichols, Michael   *The Great Apes: Between Two Worlds*
O'Donohoe, Nick   *The Magic and the Healing*
Panzer, Nora, ed.   *Celebrate America: In Poetry and Art*
Paulsen, Gary   *Winterdance: The Fine Madness of Running the Iditarod*
Porte, Barbara Ann   *Something Terrible Happened*
Power, Susan   *Grass Dancer*
Qualey, Marsha   *Come in from the Cold*
Rapp, Adam   *Missing the Piano*
Reuter, Bjarne   *Boys from St. Petri*
Reynolds, Marilyn   *Too Soon for Jeff*
Rivers, Glenn, and Brooks, Bruce   *Those Who Love the Game: Glenn "Doc" Rivers on Life in the NBA*
Rodowsky, Colby   *Hannah in Between*

Ross, Stewart   *Shakespeare and Macbeth: The Story behind the Play*
Roybal, Laura   *Billy*
Rylant, Cynthia   *Something Permanent*
Salisbury, Graham   *Under the Blood-Red Sun*
Schulman, Audrey   *The Cage*
Shoup, Barbara   *Wish You Were Here*
Sinclair, April   *Coffee Will Make You Black*
Springer, Nancy   *Toughing It*
Stolz, Mary   *Cezanne Pinto*
Sutton, Roger   *Hearing Us Out: Voices from the Gay and Lesbian Community*
Sweeney, Joyce   *Shadow*
Temple, Frances   *The Ramsay Scallop*
Voigt, Cynthia   *When She Hollers*
Watkins, Yoko Kawashima   *My Brother, My Sister, and I*
Wilson, Robert Charles   *Mysterium*
Wolf, Sylvia   *Focus: Five Women Photographers*
Woodson, Jacqueline   *I Hadn't Meant to Tell You This*

1996 SELECTIONS

Adoff, Arnold   *Slow Dance Heart Break Blues*
Alder, Elizabeth   *King's Shadow*
Ayer, Eleanor, et al.   *Parallel Journeys*
Banks, Russell   *Rule of the Bone*
Bauer, Joan   *Thwonk*
Begay, Shonto   *Navajo: Voices and Visions across the Mesa*
Bennet, James   *Squared Circle*
Blais, Madeleine   *In These Girls, Hope Is a Muscle*
Block, Francesca Lia   *Baby Be-Bop*
Boas, Jacob   *We Are Witnesses: The Diaries of Five Teenagers Who Died in the Holocaust*
Bober, Natalie   *Abigail Adams: Witness to a Revolution*
Brandenburg, Jim   *An American Safari: Adventures on the North American Prairie*
Carlson, Lori M., ed.   *American Eyes: New Asian-American Short Stories for Young Adults*
Carter, Alden R.   *Between a Rock and a Hard Place*
Childers, Thomas   *Wings of Morning: The Story of the Last American Bomber Shot Down over Germany in World War II*
Christiansen, C. B.   *I See the Moon*
Clute, John   *Science Fiction: The Illustrated Encyclopedia*
Cofer, Judith Ortiz   *An Island Like You*
Colman, Penny   *Rosie the Riveter*
Cormier, Robert   *In the Middle of the Night*
Crutcher, Chris   *Ironman*
Curtis, Christopher Paul   *The Watsons Go to Birmingham—1963*

Cushman, Karen   *The Midwife's Apprentice*
D'Aguiar, Fred   *The Longest Memory*
Denenberg, Barry   *Voices from Vietnam*
Dijk, Lutz Van   *Damned Strong Love: A True Story of Willi G. and Stefan K.*
Draper, Sharon M.   *Tears of a Tiger*
Feelings, Tom   *The Middle Passage: White Ships/Black Cargo*
Feintuch, David   *Midshipman's Hope*
Ford, Michael Thomas   *Voices of AIDS*
Frank, Anne   *Diary of a Young Girl: The Definitive Edition*
Fraustino, Lisa R.   *Ash*
Fremon, Celeste   *Father Greg & the Homeboys*
Frey, Darcy   *The Last Shot: City Streets, Basketball Dreams*
Galloway, Priscilla   *Truly Grim Tales*
Garland, Sherry   *Indio*
Giblin, James Cross   *When Plague Strikes: The Black Death, Smallpox, AIDS*
Goldman, E. M.   *Getting Lincoln's Goat*
Gordon, Ruth, ed.   *Pierced by a Ray of Sun*
Grant, Cynthia D.   *Mary Wolf*
Greenberg, Jan, and Jordan, Sandra   *American Eye: Eleven Artists of the Twentieth Century*
Hamilton, Virginia   *Her Stories: African American Folktales, Fairy Tales, and True Tales*
Hobbs, Valerie   *How Far Would You Have Gotten If I Hadn't Called You Back?*
Hockenberry, John   *Moving Violations*
Hopkins, Lee Bennett   *Been to Yesterdays: Poems of Life*
Hughes, Langston   *The Block*
Hurwin, Davida Wills   *A Time for Dancing*
Laird, Crista   *But Can the Phoenix Sing?*
Lester, Julius   *Othello*
Lopez, Steve   *Third and Indiana*
Lynch, Chris   *Slot Machine*
Marrin, Albert   *Virginia's General: Robert E. Lee and the Civil War*
Marsden, John   *Tomorrow, When the War Began*
McCants, William D.   *Much Ado about Prom Night*
McKissack, Patricia C., and McKissack, Fredrick   *Red-Tail Angels: The Story of the Tuskegee Airmen of World War II*
Meyer, Carolyn   *Drummers of Jericho*
Miller, E. Ethelbert, ed.   *In Search of Color Everywhere: A Collection of African-American Poetry*
Moore, Martha   *Under the Mermaid Angel*
Mori, Kyoko   *One Bird*
Morpurgo, Michael   *War of Jenkins' Ear*
Murphy, Jim   *The Great Fire*
Nye, Naomi Shihab, ed.   *Tree Is Older Than You Are: A Bilingual Gathering of Poems*

and Stories from Mexico with Paintings by Mexican Artists
Ousseimi, Maria   *Caught in the Crossfire: Growing Up in a War Zone*
Peck, Richard   *The Last Safe Place on Earth*
Pierce, Tamora   *Emperor Mage*
Powell, Randy   *Dean Duffy*
Preston, Douglas, and Lincoln, Child   *Relic*
Preston, Richard   *Hot Zone*
Psihoyos, Louie, and Knoebber, John   *Hunting Dinosaurs*
Randle, Kristen   *Only Alien on the Planet*
Rochman, Hazel, and McCampbell, Darlene Z., eds.   *Bearing Witness: Stories of the Holocaust*
Ryan, Joan   *Little Girls in Pretty Boxes: The Making and Breaking of Elite Gymnasts and Figure Skaters*
Scieszka, Jon   *Math Curse*
Taylor, Theodore   *The Bomb*
Testa, Maria   *Dancing Pink Flamingos and Other Stories*
Thornton, Yvonne S., and Coudert, Jo   *Ditchdigger's Daughters: A Black Family's Astonishing Success Story*
Vande Velde, Vivian   *Companions of the Night*
Weaver, Will   *Farm Team*
White, Ellen E.   *The Road Home*
Williams-Garcia, Rita   *Like Sisters on the Homefront*
Woodson, Jacqueline   *From the Notebooks of Melanin Sun*

1997 SELECTIONS

Atkin, S. Beth   *Voices from the Streets: Young Former Gang Members Tell Their Stories*
Avi   *Beyond the Western Sea, Book One: The Escape from Home*
Barron, T. A.   *The Lost Years of Merlin*
Berry, Liz   *The China Garden*
Blum, Joshua, and Pellington, Mark, eds., et al.   *The United States of Poetry*
Bode, Janet, and Mack, Stan   *Hard Time: A Real Life Look at Juvenile Crime and Violence*
Card, Orson Scott   *Pastwatch: The Redemption of Christopher Columbus*
Cart, Michael   *My Father's Scar*
Chambers, Veronica   *Mama's Girl*
Coles, William E.   *Another Kind of Monday*
Conly, Jane Leslie   *Trout Summer*
Cooney, Caroline B.   *The Voice on the Radio*
Dash, Joan   *We Shall Not Be Moved: The Woman's Factory Strike of 1909*
De Vries, Anke   *Bruises*
Denenberg, Barry   *An American Hero: The True Story of Charles A. Lindbergh*
Dessen, Sarah   *That Summer*

Farmer, Nancy   *A Girl Named Disaster*
Fleischman, Paul   *Dateline: Troy*
Fleischman, Sid   *The Abracadabra Kid: A Writer's Life*
Freedman, Russell   *The Life and Death of Crazy Horse*
Freeman, Suzanne   *The Cuckoo's Child*
Gilstrap, John   *Nathan's Run*
Glenn, Mel   *Who Killed Mr. Chippendale? A Mystery in Poems*
Gould, Steven   *Wildside*
Haddix, Margaret Peterson   *Don't You Dare Read This, Mrs. Dunphrey*
——   *Running Out of Time*
Hanauer, Cathi   *My Sister's Bones*
Hautman, Pete   *Mr. Was*
Hesse, Karen   *The Music of Dolphins*
Hobbs, Will   *Far North*
Huth, Angela   *Land Girls*
Ingold, Jeanette   *The Window*
Keillor, Garrison, and Nilson, Jenny Lind   *The Sandy Bottom Orchestra*
Klass, David   *Danger Zone*
Kozol, Jonathon   *Amazing Grace: The Lives of Children and the Conscience of a Nation*
Krakauer, Jon   *Into the Wild*
Lane, Dakota   *Johnny Voodoo*
Levy, Marilyn   *Run for Your Life*
Macy, Sue   *Winning Ways: A Photohistory of American Women in Sports*
Matas, Carol   *After the War*
McKissack, Patricia C., and McKissack, Fredrick L.   *Rebels against Slavery: American Slave Revolts*
Mead, Alice   *Adem's Cross*
Meyer, Carolyn   *Gideon's People*
Myers, Walter Dean   *One More River to Cross: An African American Photograph Album*
——   *Slam*
Napoli, Donna Jo   *Song of the Magdalene*
Nix, Garth   *Sabriel*
Nye, Naomi Shihab, and Janeczko, Paul, eds.   *I Feel a Little Jumpy around You*
Paschen, Elise, and Neches, Neil, eds.   *Poetry in Motion: One Hundred Poems from the Subways & Buses*
Paterson, Katherine   *Jip, His Story*
Paulsen, Gary   *Puppies, Dogs, and Blue Northers: Reflections on Being Raised by a Pack of Sled Dogs*
Pausewang, Gudrun   *The Final Journey*
Pennebaker, Ruth   *Don't Think Twice*
Pullman, Philip   *The Golden Compass*
Rinaldi, Ann   *Hang a Thousand Trees with Ribbons: The Story of Phillis Wheatley*
Salzman, Mark   *Lost in Place: Growing Up Absurd in Suburbia*
Savage, Candace   *Cowgirls*
Schmidt, Gary D.   *The Sin Eater*

Shevelev, Raphael, and Schomer, Karine   *Liberating the Ghosts: Photographs and Text from the March of the Living*
Southgate, Martha   *Another Way to Dance*
Spinelli, Jerry   *Crash*
Staples, Suzanne Fisher   *Dangerous Skies*
Thesman, Jean   *The Ornament Tree*
Thomas, Rob   *Rats Saw God*
Turner, Megan Whalen   *The Thief*
Wallace, Rich   *Wrestling Sturbridge*
Welter, John   *I Want to Buy a Vowel*
Westall, Robert   *Gulf*
White, Ruth   *Belle Prater's Boy*
Wilkomirski, Binjamin   *Fragments: Memories of a Childhood, 1939–1948*

1998 SELECTIONS

Alexander, Lloyd   *The Iron Ring*
Appelt, Kathi   *Just People and Other Poems for Young Readers & Paper/Pen/Poem: A Young Writer's Way to Begin*
Bartoletti, Susan Campbell   *Growing Up in Coal Country*
Berg, Elizabeth   *Joy School*
Bernstein, Sara Tuvel   *The Seamstress*
Bitton-Jackson, Livia   *I Have Lived a Thousand Years*
Bloor, Edward   *Tangerine*
Brooks, Martha   *Bone Dance*
Buck, Rinker   *Flight of Passage*
Carroll, Joyce Armstrong, and Wilson, Edward E.   *Poetry after Lunch: Poems to Read Aloud*
Carter, Alden R.   *Bull Catcher*
Chadwick, Douglas, and Sartore, Joel   *The Company We Keep: America's Endangered Species*
Chang, Pang-Mei Natasha   *Bound Feet & Western Dress*
Cook, Karin   *What Girls Learn*
Cooney, Caroline B.   *What Child Is This? A Christmas Story*
Corbett, Sara   *Venus to the Hoop*
Cormier, Robert   *Tenderness*
Creech, Sharon   *Chasing Redbird*
De Lint, Charles   *Trader*
Del Calzo, Nick, et al.   *The Triumphant Spirit: Portraits & Stories of Holocaust Survivors . . . Their Messages of Hope & Compassion*
Deuker, Carl   *Painting the Black*
Dorris, Michael   *The Window*
Draper, Sharon M.   *Forged by Fire*
Dyer, Daniel   *Jack London: A Biography*
Elders, Joycelyn, and Chanoff, David   *Joycelyn Elders, M.D.: From Sharecropper's Daughter to Surgeon General of the United States of America*
Fleischman, Paul   *Seedfolks*
Fogle, Bruce   *Encyclopedia of the Cat*

Fradin, Dennis B.   *Planet Hunters*

Gallo, Donald R., ed.   *No Easy Answers: Short Stories about Teenagers Making Tough Choices*

Giblin, James Cross   *Charles A. Lindbergh: A Human Hero*

Glenn, Mel   *Jump Ball: A Basketball Season in Poems*

———   *The Taking of Room 114*

Greenfield, Susan, ed.   *The Human Mind Explained: An Owner's Guide to the Mysteries of the Mind*

Griffin, Adele   *Sons of Liberty*

Haddix, Margaret Peterson   *Leaving Fishers*

Hayes, Daniel   *Flyers*

Hesse, Karen   *Out of the Dust*

Hogan, James P.   *Bug Park*

Howe, James   *The Watcher*

Jiang, Ji-li   *Red Scarf Girl: A Memoir of the Cultural Revolution*

Kelton, Elmer   *Cloudy in the West*

Kerner, Elizabeth   *Song in the Silence*

Kindl, Patrice   *The Woman in the Wall*

Klause, Annette Curtis   *Blood and Chocolate*

Krakauer, Jon   *Into Thin Air: A Personal Account of the Mt. Everest Disaster*

Krisher, Trudy   *Kinship*

Lantz, Frances   *Someone to Love*

Lee, Marie G.   *Necessary Roughness*

Levenkron, Steven   *The Luckiest Girl in the World*

Levine, Gail Carson   *Ella Enchanted*

Maxwell, Robin   *Secret Diary of Anne Boleyn*

Mazer, Anne, ed.   *Working Days: Short Stories about Teenagers at Work*

Mazer, Norma Fox   *When She Was Good*

McDonald, Joyce   *Swallowing Stones*

McKinley, Robin   *Rose Daughter*

McLaren, Clemence   *Inside the Walls of Troy*

Meyer, Carolyn   *Jubilee Journey*

Myers, Walter Dean   *Harlem*

Napoli, Donna Jo   *Stones in Water*

Naylor, Phyllis Reynolds   *Outrageously Alice*

Nix, Garth   *Shade's Children*

Nolan, Han   *Dancing on the Edge*

Nye, Naomi Shihab   *Habibi*

Orr, Wendy   *Peeling the Onion*

Oughton, Jerrie   *The War in Georgia*

Paulsen, Gary   *The Schernoff Discoveries*

Penman, Sharon   *The Queen's Man*

Philip, Neil, ed.   *In a Sacred Manner I Live: Native American Wisdom*

Pullman, Philip   *The Subtle Knife*

Reynolds, Marjorie   *The Starlite Drive-In*

Rinaldi, Ann   *Acquaintance with Darkness*

Rochman, Hazel, and McCampbell, Darlene Z., eds.   *Leaving Home*

Shoup, Barbara   *Stranded in Harmony*

Shusterman, Neal   *The Dark Side of Nowhere*

Skurzynski, Gloria   *Virtual War*

Soto, Gary   *Buried Onions*

Steger, Will, and Bowermaster, Jon   *Over the Top of the World: Explorer Will Steger's Trek across the Arctic*

Sullivan, Charles, ed.   *Imaginary Animals*

Tate, Sonsyrea   *Little X: Growing Up in the Nation of Islam*

Thomas, Rob   *Doing Time: Notes from the Undergrad*

Tillage, Leon Walter   *Leon's Story*

Wersba, Barbara   *Whistle Me Home*

Williams, Carol Lynch   *The True Colors of Caitlynne Jackson*

Yee, Paul   *Breakaway*

1999 SELECTIONS

Abelove, Joan   *Go and Come Back*

Alabisco, Vincent, et al., eds.   *Flash! The Associated Press Covers the World*

Arnoldi, Katherine   *The Amazing True Story of a Teenage Single Mom*

Bauer, Joan   *Rules of the Road*

Bennett, Cherie   *Life in the Fat Lane*

Blackwood, Gary L.   *The Shakespeare Stealer*

Bolden, Tonya   *Thirty-three Things Every Girl Should Know: Stories, Songs, Poems and Smart Talk by Thirty-three Extraordinary Women*

Burgess, Melvin   *Smack*

Clinton, Catherine, ed.   *I, Too, Sing America: Three Centuries of African American Poetry*

Colman, Penny   *Corpses, Coffins, and Crypts: A History of Burial*

Cormier, Robert   *Heroes*

Dessen, Sarah   *Someone Like You*

Farrell, Jeanette   *Invisible Enemies: Stories of Infectious Disease*

Ferris, Jean   *Love among the Walnuts*

Flake, Sharon G.   *The Skin I'm In*

Fleischman, Paul   *Whirligig*

Fletcher, Susan   *Shadow Spinner*

Freedman, Russell   *Martha Graham: A Dancer's Life*

Griffin, Adele   *The Other Shepards*

Haddix, Margaret   *Among the Hidden*

Hardman, Ric Lynden   *Sunshine Rider: The First Vegetarian Western*

Helfer, Ralph   *Modoc: The Story of the Greatest Elephant That Ever Lived*

Hesser, Terry Spencer   *Kissing Doorknobs*

Hill, Ernest   *A Life for a Life*

Hobbs, Will   *The Maze*

Holt, Kimberly Willis   *My Louisiana Sky*

Jimenez, Francisco   *The Circuit: Stories from the Life of a Migrant Child*

Johnson, Angela   *Heaven*

Koller, Jackie French   *The Falcon*

Larson, Gary   *There's a Hair in My Dirt: A Worm's Story*

Lawrence, Iain   *The Wreckers*

Laxalt, Robert   *Dust Devils*

Lester, Julius   *From Slave Ship to Freedom Road*

Lobel, Anita   *No Pretty Pictures: A Child of War*

Marrin, Albert   *Commander-in-Chief Abraham Lincoln and the Civil War*

Mastoon, Adam   *The Shared Heart*

Matcheck, Diane   *The Sacrifice*

McCaughrean, Geraldine   *The Pirate's Son*

McKee, Tim, ed.   *No More Strangers Now: Young Voices from a New South Africa*

McKissack, Patricia C., and McKissack, Fredrick L.   *Young, Black, and Determined: A Biography of Lorraine Hansberry*

Mikaelson, Ben   *Petey*

Napoli, Donna Jo   *Sirena*

Newth, Mette   *The Dark Light*

Nicholson, Joy   *Tribes of Palos Verdes*

Paulsen, Gary   *Soldier's Heart*

Peck, Richard   *A Long Way from Chicago*
——— *Strays Like Us*

Philip, Neil, ed.   *War and the Pity of War*

Porter, Tracey   *Treasures in the Dust*

Potok, Chaim   *Zebra and Other Stories*

Quarles, Heather   *A Door Near Here*

Ritter, John H.   *Choosing Up Sides*

Rottman, S. L.   *Hero*

Rowling, J. K.   *Harry Potter and the Sorcerer's Stone*

Sachar, Louis   *Holes*

Salisbury, Graham   *Jungle Dogs*

Shihab Nye, Naomi, ed.   *The Space between Our Footsteps: Poems and Paintings from the Middle East*

Silvey, Anita, ed.   *Help Wanted: Short Stories about Young People Working*

Spinelli, Jerry   *Knots in My Yo-Yo String: The Autobiography of a Kid*

Springer, Nancy   *I Am Mordred: A Tale from Camelot*

Sweeney, Joyce   *The Spirit Window*

Thomas, Jane Resh   *Behind the Mask: The Life of Queen Elizabeth I*

Thomas, Velma Maia   *Lest We Forget: The Passage from Africa to Slavery and Emancipation*

Turner, Ann Marshall   *A Lion's Hunger: Poems of First Love*

Walter, Virginia   *Making Up Megaboy*

Weaver, Will   *Hard Ball*

Werlin, Nancy   *The Killer's Cousin*

Willis, Connie   *To Say Nothing of the Dog; or, How We Found the Bishop's Bird Stump at Last*

Wilson, Diane Lee   *I Rode a Horse of Milk White Jade*

Woodson, Jacqueline   *If You Come Softly*

Yolen, Jane, and Coville, Bruce   *Armageddon Summer*

The Best of the Best
by Preconference

STILL ALIVE

Selections from 1960 to 1974

Adams, Richard *Watership Down*

Adamson, Joy *Born Free*

Angelou, Maya *Gather Together in My Name*
—— *I Know Why the Caged Bird Sings*

Anonymous *Go Ask Alice*

Asimov, Isaac *Fantastic Voyage*

Baldwin, James *If Beale Street Could Talk*

Borland, Hal *When the Legend Dies*

Boston Women's Health Book Collective *Our Bodies, Ourselves: A Book by and for Women*

Braithwaite, E. R. *To Sir, with Love*

Brautigan, Richard *Trout Fishing in America*

Brown, Claude *Manchild in the Promised Land*

Burnford, Sheila *Incredible Journey*

Carson, Rachel *Silent Spring*

Castaneda, Carlos *Journey to Ixtlan: The Lessons of Don Juan*

Childress, Alice *Hero Ain't Nothin but a Sandwich*

Clarke, Arthur C. *2001: A Space Odyssey*

Cleaver, Eldridge *Soul on Ice*

Cormier, Robert *Chocolate War: A Novel*

Craven, Margaret *I Heard the Owl Call My Name*

Crichton, Michael *Andromeda Strain*

Dunning, Stephen, ed. *Reflections on a Gift of Watermelon Pickle*

Elfman, Blossom *Girls of Huntington House*

Fast, Howard *April Morning*

Frazier, Walt, and Berkow, Ira *Rockin' Steady: A Guide to Basketball and Cool*

Friedman, Myra *Buried Alive: The Biography of Janis Joplin*

Gaines, Ernest J. *The Autobiography of Miss Jane Pittman*

Gaines, William, ed., and Feldstein, Albert, ed. *Ridiculously Expensive MAD*

Graham, Robin Lee, and Gill, Derek L.T. *Dove*

Green, Hannah *I Never Promised You a Rose Garden*

Griffin, John *Black Like Me*

Guy, Rosa *The Friends*

Hall, Lynn *Sticks and Stones*

Harris, Marilyn *Hatter Fox*

Head, Ann *Mr. and Mrs. Bo Jo Jones*

Heinlein, Robert *Stranger in a Strange Land*

Heller, Joseph *Catch-22*

Herbert, Frank *Dune*

Herriot, James *All Creatures Great and Small*

Herzog, Arthur *Swarm*

Hinton, S. E. *The Outsiders*
—— *That Was Then, This Is Now*

Jackson, Shirley *We Have Always Lived in the Castle*

Kellogg, Marjorie *Tell Me That You Love Me, Junie Moon*

Kesey, Ken *One Flew Over the Cuckoo's Nest*

Keyes, Daniel *Flowers for Algernon*

Knowles, John *Separate Peace*

Krentz, Harold *To Race the Wind: An Autobiography*

Lee, Harper *To Kill a Mockingbird*

Maas, Peter *Serpico*

Meriwether, Louise   *Daddy Was a Number Runner*

Moody, Anne   *Coming of Age in Mississippi: An Autobiography*

Neufeld, John   *Lisa Bright and Dark*

Peck, Robert Newton   *Day No Pigs Would Die*

Plath, Sylvia   *The Bell Jar*

Potok, Chaim   *The Chosen*

Read, Piers Paul   *Alive: The Story of the Andes Survivors*

Robertson, Dougal   *Survive the Savage Sea*

Samuels, Gertrude   *Run, Shelley, Run!*

Schulz, Charles   *Peanuts Treasury*

Scoppettone, Sandra   *Trying Hard to Hear You*

Sleator, William   *House of Stairs*

Solzhenitsyn, Alexander   *One Day in the Life of Ivan Denisovich*

Swarthout, Glendon   *Bless the Beasts and Children*

Thompson, Jean   *House of Tomorrow*

Vonnegut, Kurt, Jr.   *Slaughterhouse Five; or, The Children's Crusade*

Westheimer, David   *My Sweet Charlie*

——   *Von Ryan's Express*

White, Robb   *Deathwatch*

Wigginton, Eliot   *Foxfire Book*

X, Malcolm, and Haley, Alex   *Autobiography of Malcolm X*

Zindel, Paul   *The Pigman*

THE BEST OF THE BEST BOOKS

Selections from 1970 to 1983

Adams, Richard   *Watership Down*

Alexander, Lloyd   *Westmark*

Ali, Muhammad, and Durham, Richard   *Greatest: My Own Story*

Angelou, Maya   *I Know Why the Caged Bird Sings*

Anonymous   *Go Ask Alice*

Arrick, Fran   *Tunnel Vision*

Auel, Jean   *Clan of the Cave Bear*

Baldwin, James   *If Beale Street Could Talk*

Bell, Ruth   *Changing Bodies, Changing Lives: A Book for Teens on Sex and Relationships*

Bethancourt, T. Ernesto   *Tune in Yesterday*

Bleier, Rocky, and O'Neill, Terry   *Fighting Back*

Blume, Judy   *Forever*

Boston Women's Health Book Collective   *Our Bodies, Ourselves: A Book by and for Women*

Brancato, Robin F.   *Winning*

Bridgers, Sue Ellen   *Notes for Another Life*

Brown, Dee   *Bury My Heart at Wounded Knee: An Indian History of the American West*

Childress, Alice   *Hero Ain't Nothin but a Sandwich*

Christopher, John   *Empty World*

Conroy, Pat   *Great Santini*

Cormier, Robert   *After the First Death*

——   *Chocolate War: A Novel*

——   *I Am the Cheese*

Due, Linnea A.   *High and Outside*

Duncan, Lois   *Killing Mr. Griffin*

——   *Stranger with My Face*

Elder, Lauren, and Streshinsky, Shirley   *And I Alone Survived*

Elfman, Blossom   *Girls of Huntington House*

Garden, Nancy   *Annie on My Mind*

Glenn, Mel   *Class Dismissed! High School Poems*

Greenberg, Joanne   *In This Sign*

Greene, Bette   *Summer of My German Soldier*

Guest, Judith   *Ordinary People*

Guy, Rosa   *Edith Jackson*

——   *The Friends*

Hamilton, Virginia   *Sweet Whispers, Brother Rush*

Harris, Marilyn   *Hatter Fox*

Hayden, Torey L.   *One Child*

Hinton, S. E.   *Tex*

Hogan, William   *Quartzsite Trip*

Holland, Isabelle   *Man without a Face*

Holman, Felice   *Slake's Limbo*

Johnston, Norma   *Keeping Days*

Jordan, June   *His Own Where*

Kerr, M. E.   *Dinky Hocker Shoots Smack*

King, Stephen   *Carrie*

Le Guin, Ursula K.   *Farthest Shore*

——   *Tombs of Atuan*

——   *Very Far Away from Anywhere Else*

Leitner, Isabella   *Fragments of Isabella: A Memoir of Auschwitz*

Levenkron, Steven   *Best Little Girl in the World*

Lipsyte, Robert   *One Fat Summer*

MacCracken, Mary   *Circle of Children*

MacDougall, Ruth   *Cheerleader*

Mazer, Harry   *Last Mission*

Mazer, Norma Fox   *Up in Seth's Room*

McCaffrey, Anne   *Dragonsong*

McCoy, Kathy, and Wibbelsman, Charles   *The New Teenage Body Book*

McIntyre, Vonda N.   *Dreamsnake*

McKinley, Robin   *Beauty: A Retelling of the Story of Beauty and the Beast*

——   *Blue Sword*

Meltzer, Milton   *Never to Forget: The Jews of the Holocaust*

Niven, Larry   *Ringworld*

O'Brien, Robert C.   *Z for Zachariah*

Oneal, Zibby   *Formal Feeling*

——   *Language of Goldfish*

Peck, Richard   *Are You in the House Alone?*

——   *Father Figure: A Novel*

——   *Ghosts I Have Been*

Pierce, Meredith Ann   *The Darkangel*
Plath, Sylvia   *The Bell Jar*
Platt, Kin   *Headman*
Powers, John R.   *Last Catholic in America: A Fictionalized Memoir*
Robertson, Dougal   *Survive the Savage Sea*
Samuels, Gertrude   *Run, Shelley, Run!*
Santoli, Al   *Everything We Had: An Oral History of the Vietnam War As Told by Thirty-three American Soldiers Who Fought It*
Schulke, Flip   *Martin Luther King, Jr.: A Documentary . . . Montgomery to Memphis*
Scoppettone, Sandra   *Trying Hard to Hear You*
Sleator, William   *House of Stairs*
Stewart, Mary   *Crystal Cave*
Swarthout, Glendon   *Bless the Beasts and Children*
Taylor, Mildred D.   *Roll of Thunder, Hear My Cry*
Wersba, Barbara   *Run Softly, Go Fast*
White, Robb   *Deathwatch*
Wilkinson, Brenda   *Ludell and Willie*
Zindel, Paul   *Effects of Gamma Rays on Man-in-the-Moon-Marigolds*

NOTHIN' BUT THE BEST

Selections from 1966 to 1986

Rolling Stone Illustrated History of Rock and Roll, 1950–1980
Adams, Douglas   *The Hitchhiker's Guide to the Galaxy*
Angelou, Maya   *I Know Why the Caged Bird Sings*
Bell, Ruth   *Changing Bodies, Changing Lives: A Book for Teens on Sex and Relationships*
Blume, Judy   *Forever*
Brancato, Robin F.   *Winning*
Bridgers, Sue Ellen   *All Together Now*
Briggs, Raymond   *When the Wind Blows*
Callahan, Steven   *Adrift: Seventy-Six Days Lost at Sea*
Card, Orson Scott   *Ender's Game*
Childress, Alice   *Hero Ain't Nothin but a Sandwich*
——— *Rainbow Jordan*
Clark, Mary Higgins   *Where Are the Children?*
Cormier, Robert   *After the First Death*
——— *Chocolate War: A Novel*
Crutcher, Chris   *Running Loose*
——— *Stotan!*
Duncan, Lois   *Killing Mr. Griffin*
Edelman, Bernard   *Dear America: Letters Home from Vietnam*
Fox, Paula   *One-Eyed Cat*
Gallo, Donald R., ed.   *Sixteen: Short Stories by Outstanding Writers for Young Adults*

Garden, Nancy   *Annie on My Mind*
Garfield, Brian   *Paladin*
Greenberg, Joanne   *In This Sign*
Guest, Judith   *Ordinary People*
Guy, Rosa   *Disappearance*
——— *The Friends*
Head, Ann   *Mr. and Mrs. Bo Jo Jones*
Hinton, S. E.   *The Outsiders*
——— *Tex*
——— *That Was Then, This Is Now*
Hogan, William   *Quartzsite Trip*
Holland, Isabelle   *Man without a Face*
Holman, Felice   *Slake's Limbo*
Irwin, Hadley   *Abby, My Love*
Kazimiroff, Theodore L.   *Last Algonquin*
Kerr, M. E.   *Gentlehands*
——— *Night Kites*
Keyes, Daniel   *Flowers for Algernon*
King, Stephen   *Night Shift*
Koehn, Ilse   *Mischling, Second Degree: My Childhood in Nazi Germany*
Lipsyte, Robert   *One Fat Summer*
MacKinnon, Bernie   *Meantime*
Mason, Bobbie Ann   *In Country*
Mazer, Harry   *Last Mission*
McCaffrey, Anne   *Dragonsong*
McIntyre, Vonda N.   *Dreamsnake*
McKinley, Robin   *Beauty: A Retelling of the Story of Beauty and the Beast*
Myers, Walter Dean   *Hoops*
Naylor, Phyllis Reynolds   *Keeper*
Newton, Suzanne   *I Will Call It Georgie's Blues*
Peck, Richard   *Are You in the House Alone?*
——— *Ghosts I Have Been*
Plath, Sylvia   *The Bell Jar*
Potok, Chaim   *The Chosen*
Richards, Arlene Kramer, and Willis, Irene   *Under Eighteen and Pregnant: What to Do If You or Someone You Know Is*
Robeson, Susan   *Whole World in His Hands: A Pictorial Biography of Paul Robeson*
Segal, Erich   *Love Story*
Silverberg, Robert   *Lord Valentine's Castle*
Sleator, William   *House of Stairs*
——— *Interstellar Pig*
Strasser, Todd   *Friends till the End*
Swarthout, Glendon   *Bless the Beasts and Children*
Van Devanter, Lynda, and Morgan, Christopher   *Home before Morning: The Story of an Army Nurse in Vietnam*
Vinge, Joan D.   *Psion*
Voigt, Cynthia   *Homecoming*
——— *Izzy, Willy-Nilly*
——— *Runner*
——— *Solitary Blue*
Walker, Alice   *In Search of Our Mothers' Gardens: Womanist Prose*

Webb, Sheyann, and Nelson, Rachel West
    *Selma, Lord, Selma: Girlhood Memories of
    the Civil-Rights Days*
Wersba, Barbara   *Run Softly, Go Fast*
White, Robb   *Deathwatch*
Zindel, Paul   *Effects of Gamma Rays on
    Man-in-the-Moon-Marigolds*
———   *The Pigman*

HERE WE GO AGAIN . . .
25 YEARS OF BEST BOOKS
Selections from 1967 to 1992

Adams, Douglas   *The Hitchhiker's Guide to
    the Galaxy*
Angelou, Maya   *I Know Why the Caged Bird
    Sings*
Anonymous   *Go Ask Alice*
Anthony, Piers   *On a Pale Horse*
Avi   *Nothing but the Truth*
Baldwin, James   *If Beale Street Could Talk*
Barlow, Wayne Douglas, and Summers, Ian
    Barlow's Guide to Extraterrestrials
Block, Francesca Lia   *Weetzie Bat*
Blume, Judy   *Forever*
Boston Women's Health Book Collective   *Our
    Bodies, Ourselves: A Book by and for Women*
Bridgers, Sue Ellen   *Permanent Connections*
Brooks, Bruce   *The Moves Make the Man*
Cannon, A. E.   *Amazing Gracie*
Card, Orson Scott   *Ender's Game*
Carter, Alden R.   *Up Country*
Childress, Alice   *Rainbow Jordan*
Cole, Brock   *The Goats*
Corman, Avery   *Prized Possessions*
Cormier, Robert   *We All Fall Down*
Crew, Linda   *Children of the River*
Crutcher, Chris   *Athletic Shorts: Six Short
    Stories*
———   *Stotan!*
Dahl, Roald   *Boy: Tales of Childhood*
Davis, Jenny   *Sex Education*
Davis, Terry   *Vision Quest*
Deuker, Carl   *On the Devil's Court*
Dickinson, Peter   *Eva*
Duncan, Lois   *Killing Mr. Griffin*
Fox, Paula   *One-Eyed Cat*
Gaines, Ernest J.   *The Autobiography of Miss
    Jane Pittman*
Gallo, Donald R., ed.   *Sixteen: Short Stories
    by Outstanding Writers for Young Adults*
Garden, Nancy   *Annie on My Mind*
Gies, Miep, and Gold, Alison Leslie   *Anne
    Frank Remembered: The Story of Miep
    Gies, Who Helped to Hide the Frank
    Family*
Goldman, Peter, and Fuller, Tony   *Charlie
    Company: What Vietnam Did to Us*
Grant, Cynthia D.   *Phoenix Rising; or, How to
    Survive Your Life*

Greenberg, Joanne   *Of Such Small
    Differences*
Guest, Judith   *Ordinary People*
Guy, Rosa   *The Friends*
Hayden, Torey L.   *Ghost Girl: The True Story
    of a Child Who Refused to Talk*
Hentoff, Nat   *American Heroes: In and out of
    School*
Hinton, S. E.   *The Outsiders*
Hobbs, Will   *Downriver*
Holman, Felice   *Slake's Limbo*
Hoover, H. M.   *Another Heaven, Another
    Earth*
Houston, James   *Ghost Fox*
Jacques, Brian   *Redwall*
Jones, Diana Wynne   *Howl's Moving Castle*
Kerr, M. E.   *Gentlehands*
King, Stephen   *Carrie*
Klass, David   *Wrestling with Honor*
Klause, Annette Curtis   *The Silver Kiss*
Knudson, R. R., and Swenson, May, eds.
    American Sports Poems
Koertge, Ron   *The Arizona Kid*
Kotlowitz, Alex   *There Are No Children
    Here: The Story of Two Boys Growing Up
    in the Other America*
Lee, Gus   *China Boy*
Levoy, Myron   *Alan and Naomi*
Lipsyte, Robert   *The Contender*
Lopes, Sal, ed.   *Wall: Images and Offerings
    from the Vietnam Veterans Memorial*
Madaras, Lynda, and Madaras, Area   *What's
    Happening to My Body? Book for Boys: A
    Growing Up Guide for Parents and Sons*
———   *What's Happening to My Body? Book
    for Girls: A Growing Up Guide for Parents
    and Daughters*
Mahy, Margaret   *The Changeover: A
    Supernatural Romance*
Mazer, Harry, and Mazer, Norma Fox   *Solid
    Gold Kid*
Mazer, Norma Fox   *Silver*
McCaffrey, Anne   *Dragonsinger*
McCoy, Kathy, and Wibbelsman, Charles
    The New Teenage Body Book
McKinley, Robin   *Beauty: A Retelling of the
    Story of Beauty and the Beast*
Meriwether, Louise   *Daddy Was a Number
    Runner*
Miller, Frances A.   *The Truth Trap*
Murphy, Barbara Beasley, and Wolkoff, Judie
    Ace Hits the Big Time
Myers, Walter Dean   *Scorpions*
O'Brien, Robert C.   *Z for Zachariah*
Palmer, Laura   *Shrapnel in the Heart: Letters
    and Remembrances from the Vietnam
    Memorial*
Paterson, Katherine   *Jacob Have I Loved*
Paulsen, Gary   *Hatchet*
Peck, Richard   *Are You in the House Alone?*

Pfeffer, Susan Beth   *The Year without Michael*

Pierce, Meredith Ann   *The Darkangel*

Plath, Sylvia   *The Bell Jar*

Pullman, Philip   *The Ruby in the Smoke*

Rinaldi, Ann   *Wolf by the Ears*

Rogasky, Barbara   *Smoke and Ashes: The Story of the Holocaust*

Salzman, Mark   *Iron and Silk*

Scoppettone, Sandra   *Trying Hard to Hear You*

Shilts, Randy   *And the Band Played On: Politics, People, and the AIDS Epidemic*

Sleator, William   *Interstellar Pig*

Spiegelman, Art   *Maus: A Survivor's Tale*

Stoll, Cliff   *The Cuckoo's Egg: Tracking a Spy through the Maze of Computer Espionage*

Strieber, Whitley   *Wolf of Shadows*

Sullivan, Charles, ed.   *Children of Promise: African-American Literature and Art for Young People*

Swarthout, Glendon   *Bless the Beasts and Children*

Tan, Amy   *The Joy Luck Club*

Voigt, Cynthia   *Izzy, Willy-Nilly*

Walker, Alice   *The Color Purple*

Wersba, Barbara   *Run Softly, Go Fast*

Westall, Robert   *Blitzcat*

White, Robb   *Deathwatch*

Wolff, Virginia Euwer   *Probably Still Nick Swansen*

Wrede, Patricia C.   *Dealing with Dragons*

Wyss, Thelma Hatch   *Here at the Scenic-Vu Motel*

Yolen, Jane, and Greenberg, Martin H., eds.   *Vampires: A Collection of Original Stories*

Zindel, Paul   *The Pigman*

APPENDIX
BBYA Policies and Procedures

**YOUNG ADULT LIBRARY SERVICES ASSOCIATION
BEST BOOKS FOR YOUNG ADULTS
POLICIES AND PROCEDURES**

Charge

To select from the year's publications, significant adult and young adult books; to annotate the selected titles.

Purpose of the List

The list presents books published in the past 16 months that are recommended reading for young adults (12 to 18).

It is a general list of fiction and nonfiction titles selected for their proven or potential appeal to the personal reading tastes of the young adult.

Such titles should incorporate acceptable literary quality and effectiveness of presentation. Standard selection criteria consonant with the Library Bill of Rights shall be applied.

Librarianship focuses on individuals, in all their diversity, and that focus is a fundamental value of the Young Adult Library Services Association and its members. Diversity is, thus, honored in the Association and in the collections and services that libraries provide to young adults.

Fiction should have characterization and dialog believable within the context of the novel or story.

Nonfiction should have an appealing format and a readable text. Although the list attempts to present a variety of reading tastes and levels, no effort will be made to balance the list according to subject or area of interest.

Target Audience

The list is prepared for the use of young adults themselves and annotations will be written to attract the YA reader.

Eligibility Time Frame

The Committee will consider and vote on books published within their assigned calendar year, January 1 to December 31, in addition to those published between September 1 and December 31 of the previous year. Only committee members may nominate titles published the last four months (September–December) of the previous year.

Nominations may be accepted from the field and Committee up to November 1 of that calendar year.

Field nominations require a second from a BBYA committee member. Nominations must be submitted on the official form, which is available on the YALSA web site at www.ala.org/YALSA or from the YALSA office or the current Chair.

The Chair informs the Committee of field nominations and waits 60 days for a second from a committee member before adding a title to the list of nominations. If no committee member seconds the field nomination, the title is dropped from consideration.

Nominations from publishers for their own titles are not eligible for the list.

Discussing the List

After observer comments, the Chair will provide each book's nominator with the first opportunity to address that title if he/she so desires.

Committee Members

Members are appointed by the Vice-President/President-Elect of YALSA for a one-year term renewable for a two-year consecutive term. Members are expected to attend all Committee meetings and read widely from books eligible for nomination. Reappointment is not automatic, but instead is based upon participation.

Members will be appointed on a staggered basis so that the ideal committee will have five new members appointed each year. Each term begins at the conclusion of one Midwinter and ends at the conclusion of Midwinter at the end of the term. Members who have served two consecutive terms may not be reappointed to the Committee for five years from the conclusion of their last term.

If someone resigns, the current President of the Association appoints a new person to fill that particular term.

There are 15 personal committee members. The Editor of the "Books for Youth" section of *Booklist* is a non-voting member of the committee and serves as an advisor.

Chair

The Chair is appointed by the Vice-President/President-Elect for a one-year term; and, as such, has the right to vote, to validate titles (by a vote) for consideration on the list, and to enter into discussion of titles. It should be understood, however, that the primary responsibility of the Chair is facilitator of the Committee's charge, including all business matters. The Chair should only discuss a title after other committee members have had an opportunity to speak so as not to unduly influence the decision.

An administrative assistant will be appointed in consultation with the Committee Chair by the Vice-President/President-Elect of YALSA. The administrative assistant will assist the Chair in duties which may include the following: maintaining the nominations database, tabulating votes, and other such duties assigned by the Chair. The administrative assistant is a non-voting member of the Committee.

Voting Procedures

Final selections are made at the Midwinter Meeting during an intensive series of meetings. After comments from observers and discussion by committee members, a vote is taken to determine if a title should be included on the final list.

A book must receive a minimum of nine "yes" votes to be placed on the final list regardless of the number of the 15-member committee present and voting. Only members attending the Midwinter Meeting will be allowed to vote. Members can only vote on books they have read. If a committee member must leave before the final vote, that member must give a signed ballot to the Chair who will designate a voting proxy for the absent member. The final vote will be counted by the Advisor and the Administrative Assistant.

After the final discussion and selection, titles are then annotated by the Committee. These annotations are completed at the last meeting of the Committee.

Availability of Lists for General Distribution

The list of nominations will be updated monthly. The cumulative list will be available electronically on YALSA-BK on a monthly basis. The final list of nominations will be available after November 1.

The final list of selected titles will be available, as a press release, from the ALA Public Information Office the morning following the Committee's last meeting. The press release will be posted on YALSA-L. The list is also available from Fax-on-Demand, 1-800-545-2433 press 8, and the YALSA web site at www.ala.org/YALSA. The list will also appear in a spring issue of *Booklist* and the ALA publication *ALA's Guide to Best Reading.*

Comments from Observers

All Committee meetings will be open to ALA members and persons with guest badges. Persons with guest badges may speak if recognized by the chair.

Guidelines for observers are:

1. Before the Committee discusses each suggested title, an opportunity will be given to observers to make short comments about the books (2–4 minutes per title), but the Chair reserves the right to cut short the discussion if necessary.
2. Publisher's representatives are requested to refrain from participating in discussion or asking for comments about their own books.

Approved by YALSA Board, July 1991. Revised by YALSA Board, June 1994.

---

c:\wpwin\handbook\bb-viii.7\8-99

INDEX